The Historical Method of Herodotus

Herodotus was the first writer in the West to conceive the value of creating a record of the recent past. He found a way to co-ordinate the often conflicting data of history, ethnology, and culture. *The Historical Method of Herodotus* explores the intellectual habits and the literary principles of this pioneer writer of prose. Donald Lateiner argues, against the perception that Herodotus' work seems amorphous and ill organized, that the *Histories* contain their own definition of historical significance. He examines patterns of presentation and literary structure in narratives, speeches, and direct communications to the reader, in short, the conventions and rhetoric of history as Herodotus created it. This rhetoric includes the use of recurring themes, the relation of speech to reported actions, indications of doubt, stylistic idiosyncrasies, frequent reference to nonverbal behaviours, and strategies of opening and ending. Lateiner shows how Herodotus sometimes suppresses information on principle and sometimes compels the reader to choose among contending versions of events. His inventories of Herodotus' methods allow the reader to focus on typical practice, not misleading exception. In his analysis of the structuring concepts of the *Histories*, Lateiner scrutinizes Herodotean time and chronology. He considers the historian's admiration for ethnic freedom and autonomy, the rule of law, and the positive values of conflict. Despite these apparent biases, he argues, the text's intellectual and moral preferences present a generally cool and detached account from which an authorial personality rarely emerges.

The Historical Method of Herodotus illuminates the idiosyncrasies and ambitious nature of a major text in classics and the Western tradition and touches on aspects of historiography, ancient history, rhetoric, and the history of ideas.

DONALD LATEINER is Professor of Humanities and Classics at Ohio Wesleyan University, where he also teaches ancient history.

PHOENIX

Journal of the Classical Association of Canada
Revue de la Société canadienne des études classiques
Supplementary Volume XXIII
Tome supplémentaire XXIII

DONALD LATEINER

The Historical Method
of Herodotus

UNIVERSITY OF TORONTO PRESS
Toronto Buffalo London

© University of Toronto Press 1989
Toronto Buffalo London
Printed in Canada
ISBN 0-8020-5793-4

Printed on acid-free paper

Canadian Cataloguing in Publication Data

Lateiner, Donald
The historical method of Herodotus

(Phoenix. Supplementary volume; 23 = Phoenix.
Tome supplémentaire, ISSN 0079-1784; 23)
Bibliography: p.
Includes index.
ISBN 0-8020-5793-4

1. Herodotus – History. 2. Historiography.
I. Title. II. Series: Phoenix. Supplementary
volume (Toronto, Ont.); 23.

D56.52.H45L38 1989   938'.0072024   C89-094684-1

CONTENTS

vii Contents

PREFACE

To record the debts incurred in the making of this book gives me real pleasure. I owe the most to two friends unstinting of their time and thought, the historiographers Carolyn Dewald and Daniel Tompkins. They have obtained obscure materials for me for a decade. Their criticisms improved nearly every page. Professor Dewald transformed the organization of this book, and we await impatiently her promised study of Herodotus. The editor of *Phoenix* at the University of Toronto, Malcolm B. Wallace, also contributed generously – by pointed marginalia, by a myriad of specific comments, and by searching general questions. To the limited extent that this essay meets the standards of an exacting discipline, he is to be thanked.

My Stanford mentor and academic conscience, A.E. Raubitschek, as always, made helpful and caustic suggestions. Several colleagues read the typescript at various stages and improved the book's English, logic, organization, and substance. For their generous encouragement, time, and learned advice – too often not followed, perhaps – I thank A. John Graham, Martin Ostwald, Rosaria Munson, and Eliot Wirshbo (once my teachers, students, and colleagues at the University of Pennsylvania), and my first Greek teacher, James Redfield at the University of Chicago. John Graham sustained my spirit in difficult times; so did Jennifer Roberts, by her wit and warmth. Anonymous readers also improved the manuscript. I heeded their always friendly but sometimes cryptic advice to the best of my ability. My copy-editor at the University of Toronto Press, William Barker, has saved the reader many times from the author's original lack of clarity and deserves his thanks for making the result read more soundly. None of these scholars and friends is to blame for what is wrong with this essay, but they deserve more credit than may be apparent for what is right.

Earlier versions of chapters 7 and 8 appeared in *Quaderni di Storia,* volumes 20 and 22. I thank the editor, Luciano Canfora, for permission to use this material in revised form. An earlier version of chapter 6 was delivered at Stanford University and was published in *The Greek Historians. Papers Presented to A.E. Raubitschek.* I thank that event's organizer and guiding spirit, Michael Jameson, for permission to publish a revision of that study.

This book has been published with the help of a grant from the Canadian Federation for the Humanities, using funds provided by the Social Sciences and Humanities Research Council of Canada. I warmly thank these generous patrons of ancient studies.

I am also grateful to Ohio Wesleyan University for employing the hardy typists of several revisions, Shirley Kellert, Wilma Holland, and Eleanor Kroninger, and for helping me to remunerate Terry Stockdale and Carol Doubikan for entering text in electronic form. Computer technology was a blessing and a complication in this book's production. Ruth Baurle taught me how to index electronically. No financially supported release from duties or honorific fellowship expedited the writing and revising of this book, but the cheerful help and perhaps misplaced confidence of my wife, Marianne Gabel, kept the process bearable, even when I despaired of ever seeing the end.

I learned, as Dr Samuel Johnson did, in completing a task both vexatious and exhilarating, that often 'one enquiry only gave occasion to another, that book referred to book, that to search was not always to find, and to find was not always to be informed.' I have reduced polemic to the unavoidable instances and relegated most of it to footnotes. This result was the more easily achieved because many topics considered were not the immediate concern of previous commentators and other students of the *Histories.* All literary and historical scholars, however, depend on their predecessors and I have frequently acknowledged specific debts in the notes. The work of others stimulated my effort to apprehend fairly an underestimated pioneer in the history of Western thought and literature.

I hope that any who read Herodotus in his original, unique Greek, or in English, or in another tongue, will gain here some better estimation of his various methods of investigating the evanescent past and of crafting a prose memorial of remarkable choices and achievements, barbarian and Hellenic. May those who cannot yet enjoy his original text be encouraged to study this delicate but incisive instrument of historical understanding.

Delaware, Ohio
8 April 1988

DIS MANIBVS SACRVM
ALFRED LATEINER
PATRIS

ABBREVIATIONS

FGrHist	Felix Jacoby *Die Fragmente der griechischen Historiker* (Leiden 1923–)
Roberts	W. Rhys Roberts *Dionysius of Halicarnassus: The Three Literary Letters* (Cambridge 1901)
Sp	L. Spengel *Rhetores Graeci* (Leipzig 1856)
U-R	H. Usener and L. Radermacher *Dionysii Halicarnassei Opera Quae Extant* Vol 5 (Stuttgart 1899)
Vors	Hermann Diels and Walther Kranz *Die Fragmente der Vorsokratiker* (Berlin 1951–2^6)

The Historical Method of Herodotus

INTRODUCTION

The Nature of the Investigation

This book is about the present form of Herodotus' *Histories* and the intellectual habits of the author. A reconstruction of Herodotus' thought can come only from looking at his actual literary product. What categories of things did he choose to write about and why? What principles organize the telling of his stories, and why those particular ones? What patterns of literary structure enabled him to be the first prose author to create order and meaning from the confusion and partiality of memory and from the tangible memorials of past events? Herodotus broke new ground for literature and knew it, as his proem and insistence on the newness of his materials indicate (eg, 3.103; 6.55).[1] Later preconceptions of what history is, or ought to be or once was, may illuminate Herodotus' peculiarities, but should not conceal his sophisticated techniques for telling a story and getting at the truth.

The present study does not intend to exhaust the richness of Herodotus' conception and literary texture, but it does support a central thesis: the *Histories* have a conscious method, purpose, and literary construction. The argument for intellectual and artistic control is cumulative. These chapters approach Herodotus' strange machine by analysing recurring stylistic peculiarities, philosophical prejudices, argumentative habits, research techniques, and shaping concepts. Too often unique passages in Herodotus have been misunderstood as typical of the author's varied methods. In order to grasp his pioneering literary and historiographical achievement, this study concentrates on the settled *habits* of the text.

An innovative writer in an innovative century, Herodotus made sense of a congeries of myth, poetry, monuments, and oral narratives suffused with parochial and ethnic prejudices. Now for the first time these were made to contribute to an intellectual enterprise, historical analysis. This study will show the reader how the machine works, how Herodotus argues and connects his seemingly unrelated incidents, customs, geography, and stories, distant and recent. If the historian treats problems of evidence, organization, and significance in a consistent and meaningful fashion, then we can form legitimate hypotheses regarding the method, purpose, and thinking processes of the author prior to the final redaction.

Two schools of Herodotean criticism dominate the debates over the origins, development, leading ideas, and final form of the *Histories*: the 'analytic' and the 'unitarian' (the terms are borrowed from Homeric criticism). I shall not here review the many contributions that each approach has made, but the briefest summary of their critiques will be helpful. The 'analysts' of the late nineteenth and early twentieth centuries produced a developmental hypothesis: they have determined the existence of separate narratives or λόγοι, of unfulfilled promises, and they indicate the likelihood of shifting interests over the presumed years of composition and editing, the surprisingly varied lengths of the so-called 'digressions,' the absence of a clear and dominant central theme. The 'unitarians' of the last two generations, however, have shifted attention to the continuity of themes in all parts of the *Histories*, the distribution throughout the work of formal and narrational patterns, the persistence of political and moral values in all parts of the work, a common set of historiographical impulses, and the allegedly successful subordination of the many parts to the whole.

I do not believe that either approach has answered, or can answer, all the interesting questions that this great text poses, but my inquiries have proceeded on the only secure basis: the extant text. This book therefore studies what we have in order to see how and how well it conveys its intellectual and affective messages. For this reason my book often shares the 'unitarian' literary approach and method, but questions of historiographical method and principle often return us to 'analytic' or 'separatist' historical issues, fissures that require the critic to examine discrepancies of apparent method and actual substance.

I assume a unity in this ancient text, an admittedly imperfect unity, but one that deserves elucidation. I examine the *Histories* as they are; I do not reconstruct the hypothetical intellectual development of the author from tourist, merchant, or captain into an historian, although I do consider how his inquiries led to writing the *Histories*. From a literary point of view, it may be naive to trace the development of a man's mind from a single book. Jacoby and von Fritz worked from this assumption – and their results show a top-heavy complex of hypotheses resting on uncontrollable and often unstated assumptions.[2] 'Analysts' often argue that the development of

historiography should be equated with the personal maturation of Herodotus, by which true history was freed from the crippling shackles of
ethnography.[3] No one has established, however, agreed-upon stages of
development in the author's growth, and even the 'analysts' themselves
cannot agree on something so basic as whether the composition of books 7
through 9 preceded or followed the writing of books 1 through 5.[4]

The virtue of the analytic or 'genetic' approach, when compared to the
'unitarian,' consists in the necessary questions that it poses about the
Hellenic world in which Herodotus grew up and lived. The text we have is
unlikely to be what Herodotus first conceived, whether or not we can
discover anything about earlier stages. The fiercest 'unitarian'[5] can see
ideological and literary differences between the oriental and the Greek
sections of the *Histories*. 'Unitarians' are embarrassed by the absence of a
central theme that all can acknowledge. This school believes that Herodotean
historie embraces all the breadth of reported information as fitting into a
comprehensive view of the human condition. A variant contends that the
Great Event, the Persian Wars, produced intellectual and political ferment in
Hellas which Herodotus distilled into historiography. The shattering event,
not the pre-existing genres of ethnography, chronography, mythography,
and geography, produced a new idea in literature and thought.[6] It is hard for
'unitarians' to avoid the intentionalist fallacy, in which the received text is
unconsciously equated with the product intended from first to last, perfect
even in its blemishes: Herodotus never nods.

I endorse Ch. Fornara's observation: the two approaches 'are not
incompatible with each other since they serve different ends.'[7] 'Analysts'
better explain how a Greek came to write history, why he reported so much
about the river and customs of Egypt, and why he shaped each *logos* in its
particular form and at its particular length. Alert to real inconsistencies in
different sections, they produce information which can be subjected to
literary and historical criticism. The 'unitarians' explain more adequately
the masterful final text: the pervasive intellectual concerns of the author and
the literary skills which shaped his narrative techniques. The unity, it may
be, is one not of conception or theme, but of purpose, or even more vaguely,
of attitude, an historically motivated but personally detached stance.
Modern historians tend to gravitate towards the 'analysts'' camp,[8] philolo-
gists to the 'unitarians',[9] depending on their interests either in the
subject-matter or in the author's literary methods.

This work is an analysis of the prevailing literary habits of the *Histories*.[10]
Explications of individual passages and apparently contradictory texts appear
in chapters 8 and 9, but this book focuses more on rhetoric and poetics. For
this approach, Homer offers more relevant comparisons than later histo-

rians. My reading of this superficially simple, but, in reality, demanding and difficult text will reveal the patterns of presentation, *apodexis*, that inform, pace, and unify the *Histories*.

Part 1 presents some of Herodotus' characteristic literary methods and most important structural procedures. Part 2 concerns methods that distinguish his work from that of later historians. These three chapters look at several intellectual strategies for recovering the past and his categories of inclusion. Part 3 explores the manner by which Herodotus integrates various snippets and large chunks of information into his book's major themes. We move from discrete facts to organizing principles and themes: the role of chronology in his thought and his presentation; limits or boundaries and their violation as a recurrent theme in many modes; the principle of polarity in the realms of nature and man to define and distinguish essential qualities; and the function and technique of a privileged passage, the 'constitutional debate' (3.80–2), that establishes a pattern, organizing previous histories and setting up the reader's expectations for the rest of the text. These four topics reveal a conceptual sophistication in the apparently haphazard assemblage of reports and observations. Part 4 considers how events are explained and the meanings that Herodotus found and transmitted in his chosen material. Such interpretation probably developed as part of the act of literary, historiographical creation, because historical meaning simply does not exist before a historian finds it. The uniqueness of Herodotus' approach and accomplishment are considered in the last chapter. The seminal *Histories*, although they embody an approach that Herodotus' ungrateful progeny rejected, require such full consideration.

The 'Difference' of Herodotus

'History is not what you thought. It is what you can remember. All other history defeats itself.'[11] Great historians or mediocre ones, Herodotus and Gibbon or Suetonius and Parson Weems, can fix the standard history of a people in writing. Even allowing for the irrepressible and potent oral tradition of a people, a single writer often produces the canonical view of a nation's past. The more accessible and acceptable a narrative and explanation of the past, the more useful it is to a public that desires a master personality (Cromwell, Lenin, Hitler) or 'key' analogy or metaphor (the growth of Rome, decline and fall, the rising middle class) or polarity (freedom or slavery, capitalism or communism). For any audience, comprehensibility matters more than comprehensiveness, and any attempt to present 'all the facts' is an unattainable ideal. The great historian creates an artistic narrative, shrinks the details of history into a simpler story, and simultaneously freezes certain incidents that validate a nation and its past for itself, for posterity, and for others. 'To write history is so difficult that most historians are forced to make concessions to the technique of legend.'[12] This formulation understates the degree of distortion in historiography.

Herodotus, impressed by the astounding fact of Hellenic victory in 490 and 480–479, wished to create a permanent record that would reveal and display the past histories of the peoples concerned. The examination of near and far cultures and the forces that shaped them was his intellectual proclivity before he turned it into a literary genre. Thus he calls his work 'a demonstration of his research,' ἀπόδεξις ἱστορίης, rather than 'research' itself or 'history' in the sense of 'what happened' (τὰ γενόμενα). Herodotus asserted that his purpose was to forestall the deformation of the record by forgetfulness, partiality, and false accretion (proem; 7.152.2; 2.23.1, 45.1). Investigation of the facts (another legitimate rendering of *historie*), would help him to prevent this all-too-human process of falsely elaborating or discrediting the marvellous. But great events are never left merely to historians. From sundry speeches preserved in Herodotus and Thucydides, it is clear that the notorious Isocrates (*Panegyricus* 9) was not the first to consider history a useful tool of the propagandist.[13] The moralist Livy, as his preface says, also wanted to consecrate the past and instruct posterity about manners and men worthy of imitation more than to ensure the accuracy of his account. Plutarch, with a similar instructional aim, objected to Herodotus' objectivity and called him 'a barbarian lover,' φιλοβάρβαρος (*De malignitate Herodoti* 12 857A). To record and explain with accuracy was no longer enough. 'Wie es eigentlich gewesen ist,' von Ranke's oft-quoted phrase may be one popular perception of how to write history, but literary theory has shown that there is no such thing as an 'artless' or unprejudiced narrative. The question is, can an author fulfill the demands of art without sacrificing the truth as he sees it?

Herodotus tried to preserve the essential, salvageable facts of an important, recent, climactic historical contest by creating a studiously fair account, the accuracy of which would render it the more convincing and memorable. The opening sentence, a kind of 'title page,' states this intention.[14] What Hegel said of Thucydides is equally true of Herodotus: 'his immortal work is the absolute gain which humanity has derived from that contest.' Yet he failed to satisfy the readers of antiquity and the modern age; as Momigliano has said, 'Dionysius is in fact the only ancient writer who never said anything unpleasant about Herodotus.'[15] Our second task, therefore, is to save Herodotus' reputation from the friendly condescension of later historicists and scholars of prose-style, to concentrate on the unique investigative and aesthetic merits of his book. He transcended the apparently flat catalogues and closed-ended descriptions of his logographic predecessors and contemporaries who recorded and often rationalized lands, peoples, myths, and related beliefs, but failed to trace their historical development.

Herodotus created a new realm for investigation. This new territory contained more than discrete particulars, facts meaningless in themselves, even though this area was not subject to scientific generalization, to the laws of the positivist historian. Herodotus differs from his predecessors and successors both in his organization of subjects and in his literary and scientific attitudes towards the material. He avoided some of the pitfalls of Thucydides and other successors by not reducing his subjects to simple political or ethical analysis. Herodotus' concepts of time, power, society, even cause, while not the same as ours, directed historical research into paths that it still travels, albeit sometimes reluctantly.

Let us pursue this question of scope, Herodotus' concept of what is worth knowing, what one can know of it, and how to explain it. Persistent criteria of presentation provide *differentia* that have isolated and preserved this exotic work two and a half millennia after all 28 rolls of it were first rolled up.

Ἡροδότου Ἁλικαρνησσέος ἱστορίης ἀπόδεξις ἥδε, ὡς μήτε τὰ γενόμενα ἐξ ἀνθρώπων τῷ χρόνῳ ἐξίτηλα γένηται, μήτε ἔργα μεγάλα τε καὶ θωμαστά, τὰ μὲν Ἕλλησι, τὰ δὲ βαρβάροισι ἀποδεχθέντα, ἀκλεᾶ γένηται, τά τε ἄλλα καὶ δι' ἣν αἰτίην ἐπολέμησαν ἀλλήλοισι.

After name and ethnic, Herodotus tells us what is to come. 'This is the account of Herodotus the Halicarnassian, written so that the past will not be forgotten, so that great and amazing deeds of Greeks and barbarians will not lack celebration, particularly the Persian Wars.' Yet this does not translate the text, because it omits at least three essential elements: *apodexis*, 'presentation,' *ta te alla*, '[all] the other relevant information,' and *aitie*, or cause. The subject is not stated to be 'The War' or 'Wars.' Herodotus promises to describe Greek and barbarian, big and marvellous accomplishments in detail, but especially, the *aitie*, cause or explanation, of their going to war. In truth, he bestows more description on causes, in the widest sense of cultural background and differences, than to The War, even in the last books of the war's narrative.

The literary text sometimes clearly reveals oral origins, as when Herodotus mentions informants on ethnic traditions and conversations with eye-witnesses to historical events. The text sometimes clearly betrays its pioneer status among extended prose books in its struggle to digest a congeries of data: itemized itineraries and postal stations, all the names from some ruler's family tree, lists of luxury products from exotic lands, and inventories of imperial troops and revenues. Such tabulations are now known to characterize written documents, not off-the-cuff, word-of-mouth accounts. Herodotus knew from experience, what twentieth-century students of literacy have rediscovered,[16] that utterances vary substantially over short distances and short periods and by audience addressed. The 'flexibility' of the historical accounts that Herodotus encountered created an anxiety to preserve 'facts,' the truth that quickly dies. The possibility of writing down that information for a newly literate reading public, however small, may have inspired him to undertake for posterity the unprecedented task of a permanent record of recent history. Writing down different versions, the new technology for history, also brought distance from the easy but false certainty of unquestioned local traditions. The result combines oral and written aspects of his activities, aspects that certainly reflect the work's genesis and are likely to reflect the author's consciousness of the new power of writing as much as expectations of his audience's interests.

Historie, apodexis, and *aitie* were relatively new terms: Herodotus draws attention to his invention. Ἀπόδεξις ἱστορίης suggests that the written report is at least two steps removed from τὰ γενόμενα, the events not to be forgotten on account of the passage of time, μήτε ... τῷ χρόνῳ ἐξίτηλα. His report cannot replicate the event itself, of course, or even the descriptions that others purveyed; it can only provide a synoptic summary. Nor is his report all the accounts that he heard, all the research that he conducted, for even the most restrictive annalist assimilates, digests, discards, reorders his assembled notes and data. His report is the production-display-performance-proof-declaration-publication of his labours, to put it awkwardly but more adequately.[17] He implies that time, his own mind, his informants' prejudices, and the exigencies of creating an account of men's actions all intervene between the 'then' of the raw materials and the 'now' of Herodotus, and the later reader. The phrase ἀπόδεξις ἱστορίης assumes an objective correlative to historical research and admits the subjective nature of historical thought and reports.[18]

Herodotus' proem as a whole emphasizes the commemorative task. By contrast, that of Hecataeus (*FGrHist* 1 F 1) emphasizes an objective truth independent of all testimony:

Ἑκαταῖος Μιλήσιος ὧδε μυθεῖται· τάδε γράφω, ὥς μοι δοκεῖ ἀληθέα εἶναι· οἱ γὰρ Ἑλλήνων λόγοι πολλοί τε καὶ γελοῖοι, ὡς ἐμοὶ φαίνονται, εἰσίν.

'Hecataeus the Milesian gives his account in the following way. I write up these matters as they seem to me to be true. For the accounts given by the Greeks are both numerous [ie, contradictory] and laughable, so they seem to me.' Hecataeus, both learned and hypercritical, seems to have created a remarkable instrument of analysis, but he did not develop a sound method for his rationalist and rationalizing criticisms. His works seem to lie closer to the Xenophanean tradition in Presocratic philosophy than to history. A translation of Herodotus' proem will suggest his more modest and epistemologically sophisticated intention: 'This is the presentation of the investigation of Herodotus of Halicarnassus, provided in order that the actions and sufferings of men should not be effaced by time and that men's great and amazing accomplishments, some of them produced by Greeks and others by barbarians, should not be without renown, their many other accomplishments included but especially the explanation of why they came to fight with one another.' The problem of survival requires a detailed but not unselective narrative;[19] the answer to the only question explicitly posed lurks in the hundreds of pages of the *Histories* that follow.

Hecataeus emphasizes his own intervention, his righting of fabulous wrongs and 'myths,' his light of truth in the misguided Hellenic darkness. He introduces himself as subject by name or first-person pronoun three times, by one first-person verb, and by two virtually equivalent third-person expressions. This is, then, Hecataeus' truth, opposed to various Greek falsehoods and childlike fibs. Herodotus, on the other hand, places himself in a possessive genitive clause, reports his purpose as commemoration and recognition rather than rectification, stresses human achievements and the causes of the wars rather than an indefinite variety of undifferentiated divine and earthly stories (*logoi*), and by the name that he gives to his activity suggests a distance from the events he relates.

His demonstration (*apodexis*) nevertheless intends to represent in a faithful manner the demonstrable actions (ἔργα ... ἀποδεχθέντα) of his chosen subjects. When he speaks of correctness, he offers not Thucydides' ἀκρίβεια, 'precision,' a word not found in this text, but ἀτρεκείη, an account without purposeful distortion or deflection.[20] He reports as directly as possible what he has heard and seen, and then attempts to make historical sense of partial, contradictory, and incomplete accounts. For instance, he will not attribute victory in the great war to Athens alone, nor will he deny that city any credit whatsoever, each view being a current drastic simplification of an intricate truth. He presents the more objective, and less glorious or defamatory, complexity and paradoxes of Hellenic victory.

PART ONE

Rhetoric:
How Herodotus Recreates
the Past

1

A New Genre,
a New Rhetoric

The Promise of the Proem

Before our century, Herodotus was often considered a charming but inaccurate and gullible historian.[1] In the last seventy-five years, however, scholars have more profitably attempted to comprehend what Herodotus has done, not what the later Thucydides thought a historian ought to do, and have vindicated Herodotus' paradoxical position as the childless 'father of history.'[2] The maverick genius had created a subject and a method, but the later practitioners of the art immediately disowned their progenitor. No matter which clever structure and divisions are attributed to his unique mode of organization – and no two scholars' schematic summaries are even encouragingly similar[3] – the reader is still baffled by bizarre dislocations of time and place, infusions of legend, folktale, and saga, and frequent excursuses that run from one paragraph to seventy pages. Rather than the organic unity of the poets, the dramatists, or some philosophers and historians, one encounters surprising facts, lengthy descriptions, comic anecdotes, and seemingly irrelevant histories, sorted and organized but often without specific justification or explanation. The unwieldy length of the work made it inaccessible to most of those who might wish to hear it read or to those few rich and literate men who might buy it. The text was a monster. We must consider what shapes it and how it works.

'Historical knowledge in Herodotus moves on three levels: events, traditions about events, and the historical work which interprets these traditions.'[4] He invented a craft to handle the perceptions of those who were transmitting the facts about the past so as to ascertain a reality worth conserving, and he invented a form of writing to fix his results permanently, for future generations. Modern methods for presenting facts and their interpretations were alien to Herodotus, as his methods are obscure to the present day. Herodotus so infrequently talks of his method that one scholar's excursus is another's paradigm, counter-example, foreshadowing, or essential element of a major theme. Modern analyses and criticisms of the Egyptian *logos* exemplify this inconsonance of analytic schemes.[5]

Whereas some readers find Thucydides' *History* excessively narrow in its range of topics, and, at the least, requiring sympathetic explanation of his compression and excisions,[6] most critics find Herodotus' scope incomprehensibly vast and amorphous. Can we define his subject(s) and technique in the absence of an explicit methodology? Just as solid buildings based on an intelligent conception exist before blueprints and architectural theorists, so too solid history based on perceived patterns and traditional literary structures can be discovered in the *Histories*.

Herodotus' opening sentence, already considered above, may now be seen as an advertisement for a new kind of literary prose as well as a new historical method.[7] Herodotus presents four rhetorically balanced phrases which exhibit parallelism, isocolon, and paronomasia. The four balanced phrases are μήτε τὰ γενόμενα ... μήτε ἔργα, ἔργα μεγάλα τε καὶ θωμαστά, τὰ μέν Ἕλλησι, τὰ δὲ βαρβάροισι, and τά τε ἄλλα καὶ δι' ἣν αἰτίην. They are deployed in a threefold division of clauses, by syntax and sense (the first five words, the last nine words, and the long ὡς μήτε ... ἀκλεᾶ γένηται clause between). The threefold division of sense units falls into the following sections: the basic data for a Greek book (author, ethnic, and title), then the author's subject and purpose, and finally, a refinement of the specific subjects that also promises an explanation of the events as well as the deeds themselves. This sentence successively narrows the focus from the most general to the very particular, and from the potentially knowable to the actually known. The second μήτε clause, for instance, makes the first more explicit. τὰ γενόμενα would theoretically include all human practices, customs, beliefs, and historical actions, but the phrase ἔργα μεγάλα τε καὶ θωμαστά[8] refines the scope to include only practices, *nomoi*, and beliefs of unusual interest, and unique events of historical significance.[9] The last clause ensures that no matter how extensive the surveys and reports of their *other* activities are,[10] the organizing idea will remain the reason(s) that the Greeks and barbarians came to fight each other.

Herodotus soon says (1.5.3) that he will proceed 'equally' through small and large cities, because this year's village was significant in a previous epoch or may be so in the next, but ἔργα of magnitude, concrete or abstract or in process ('deeds'),[11] chiefly occupy his thoughts. Such remarkable ἔργα have been produced by both Greeks and barbarians – that is, by many nations. The initial antithesis of the proem rejected a provincial or partial Greek standpoint for an objective appreciation of all human achievement.

Human History, that is, has been defined as *Great and Wonderful Deeds*, which is restated as both *Greek and Barbarian Deeds*, which is then explained to be *Other Matters* (including the prior ethnic histories, chief combatants, and the actual battles of the Persian Wars), but especially *The Cause* for the series of *Wars*. Ἱστορίη, following epic (*Iliad* 1.6–8) seeks to record the special and paradigmatic event and explain its meaning, and here we have quickly reached the motivating concern for Herodotus' vast project. Paratactic form in Homer, Hesiod, or Herodotus does not prevent an author from clarifying his focus. 'Cause' (αἰτίη) in the proem is immediately connected to and reflected by 'responsible parties' (αἰτίους, 1.1.1) in the next line. 'Especially the explanation of the war,' the climax of the majestically articulated first sentence, provides the explicit motivation for the author's presentation of his research. The first five books and much of the remainder explore the nature of the cultures that were to conflict.[12] The *nomoi* of the principal combatants give the explanation of their various conquests and defeats, including the 'great and marvellous deeds of Greeks and barbarians' in the Great War itself that the final three and one-half books record.

Because the varied annals of despotism only can have meaning in contrast to a reality of freedom, the successful and unique Greek defence of liberty preserved significance for τὰ γενόμενα, which otherwise would have become only the unobjective chronicles of universal despotism and slavery, an unedifying and depressing glorification of the unstoppable progress of human servitude. The proem's explicit concern with preservation and commemoration indicates a clear and coherent purpose. Ἐξίτηλα and ἀκλεᾶ, words that justify the entire enterprise, appear only here. Herodotus' opening paratactic sentence has stated and progressively refined that purpose with an emphasis that elucidates those matters most necessary to explore.[13]

However cunningly the *Histories* are organized and the subject stated, Herodotus admittedly leaves himself more latitude than most subsequent historians.[14] From 1.170 to 5.17, more than a third of the text, there is no systematic warfare of Persian against Greek. Herodotus justifies the last third of his work on Xerxes' invasion by the unique size of the invading army (7.20.2–21.1) and the threat posed to the idea of autonomy (7.8 γ2*, 102.2*, 104.4*). The first two-thirds is justified by explaining how such a force came to be and how Hellas and Persia developed their irreconcilable hostility. An unexpressed justification for the entire enterprise may be found in his desire to illuminate imperialism and the ongoing war of the final years of the fifth century,[15] but the preface says nothing of this.

For the relentless curiosity of Herodotus other things than war and its causes are worth knowing, even if some are less relevant and decisive for the war, for the great event, when considered one by one.[16] The Pyramids,

Cyrus' rebellion against the Medes, Croesus' wealth, Egyptian daily habits, Solon's wisdom: each offers something to the understanding of humanity, although less individually than the great war that tested all the resources of the cultures involved.

The Persians threatened the Mediterranean world with 'an excess of unity' – a threat whose consequences are clearly presented in the *Histories*. A variety of national customs and institutions is both natural and beneficial for all, according to Herodotus, since different geographical and historical circumstances should prompt different responses, and all men can profit from nature's and humanity's diversity.[17] Herodotus expresses and endorses this open attitude and comparatist approach by giving each nation's individual character its due description and history.

For example, if unlike the Greeks Egyptian men sit and women stand when urinating (2.35.2–3), Herodotus does not condemn them as 'savages, the lower races, uncivilized.' While he here fails to explain their habits by the modern academic disciplines of psychology, history of religion, and anthropology, his motive for recording the fact lay in a cultural antinomy, not sexual curiosity:[18] it illustrates his thesis that the Egyptians 'established habits and customs opposite in nearly all respects to the rest of mankind.' However trivial the particular item, it contributes its mite to the arresting and useful picture of a society 'poles apart' from the Greeks. Ethnography contributes much to αἰτίη.

Ethnographic information in the *Histories* is neither shapeless nor only there to charm; rather it is documentation deployed to assert an historical thesis, namely that mankind has benefited from ethnic and political separation and self-determination. The practices, institutions, dilemmas, and conflicts of every society help to explain its political decisions and efficacy. For Herodotus, the political freedom of citizens in the autonomous city-state unit seems characteristic of the Greeks, whereas deference to an authority more than earthly and unquestioning service seem typical of many oriental communities. Herodotus' scope is a function of his belief, not a symptom of naiveté or disorganization. He searches for something not obvious; he discovers more questions than answers. He inquires into the explanation of a remarkable historical event. Thus Herodotus bothers to defend his inclusion of smaller cities and peoples, and does not assume that the reader would understand his new method without comment.

Herodotus, however, is hardly all-inclusive: he does not consider the legendary histories of most of the Greek city-states worthy of inclusion, nor does he tarry over stories about the gods, because they and semi-legendary beings such as Minos are beyond the evidence that history can deliver or explain. They are generally obscure in their workings and not part of the 'human epoch,' ἡ ἀνθρωπηίη λεγομένη γενεή (3.122.2). Their stories are omitted, curtailed, or told only to be dismissed.[19] Herodotus promises in the Proem exactly what he delivers – or perhaps, more modestly, we can say he promises an account less comprehensive than what he finally produces. A new way to look at human experience appeared, not his predecessors' unsorted observations, fantastical tales of distant eras, or idiosyncratic reactions to exotic oddities, but history – a synthesis of recent world events that demonstrates the value of political independence, a hardy way of life, and moral courage.

The following considerations of Herodotus' narratives, descriptions, and reports of speeches and gestures canvas some habitual features. We examine his sometimes idiosyncratic uses of direct and indirect speech, and of nonverbal behaviours, his manner of bringing in the audience by second-person verbal forms, and the deployment of the particles κως and κου to establish near and distant relationships between himself, his material evidence, and his audience. The topics comprehend both easily isolated phenomena and pervasive tones and structural techniques. When feasible, all examples are discussed or at least listed. Important examples are selected from categories that do not lend themselves to quantification (irony) or that are ubiquitous (direct speech).[20] Later chapters (2–4) include inventories of quantifiable phenomena. By observing the varieties of historical rhetoric, literary habits, and narrative structures, along with the reasons for and the frequency of their appearance, we may discover the meanings that Herodotus intended the reader to draw from his unique exposition.

The Rhetoric of History: Narrative and Speech

Narrative

[Herodotus'] achievement, measured by what we know of his predecessors, marks, I believe a greater advance than any other Greek prose writer achieved ... Perhaps their [previous logographers'] most important function is to make us realize how much concealed art underlies the seeming artlessness of their great successor ... Herodotus is an unaccountable phenomenon in the history of literature. He is in the direct line of succession to the logographers: but while they, apparently, had no technique at all, he had a technique at once effortless and adequate to any demands he chose to make upon it.

J.D. Denniston *Greek Prose Style*

A thorough study of Greek historical rhetoric should constitute a branch of ancient historiography. Historical scholarship, however, from the beginning has been loath to admit the necessary mediation of the historian's selectivity, organization, and rhetoric – in short, his narration – between the events of the past and the present audience. Authorial voice and distance, order of events and their duration in the narrative, achronic descriptions of communities, frequency of shifts in the field of action, the relation of data to preconceived patterns of behaviour, these problems of historiography had yet to be formulated when Herodotus wrote and are hardly precise today.[21] Every historian, even the first, consciously and unconsciously shapes narrative and judgments so as to communicate a perception of his subject in a persuasive manner. Already the noun ἀπόδεξις in the proem asserts a mediating intelligence, the personal intervention of Herodotus in the presentation of the facts of the past. The historian has the power to distance himself or the reader, or both, from the events recorded, or to invite the audience to observe the researcher at work or to participate in the drama.

The *logopoios* 'makes hearing sight' ([Longinus] *De sublimitate* 26.2); he introduces conversation, attendant gestures, and even unvoiced thoughts. Vivid presentation has always enhanced intellectual impact and literary survival. The linearity of prose theoretically allows an 'ideal' narrative in which one page describes one event, but the historian's interpretive and literary vision requires acceleration and deceleration of events. Furthermore, retrospects, prospects, and anticipations complicate the progress of historical narratives. Herodotus 'complicates' the rhythm of his history by 'inflating' incidents that he tells with dramatic detail and 'deflating' episodes, even centuries and epochs. The main progress is 'interrupted' by privileged scenes that develop principal themes and by discontinuous anecdotes as well as seemingly irrelevant anthropological surveys whose significance may become apparent only hundreds of pages later. As in the *Iliad*, the steady revolutions of the sun come to a halt for the historically significant moment.

For example, Herodotus wants the reader to see what Xerxes alone of rulers saw and accomplished, the uniquely grand and numerous Persian army crossing the Hellespont (7.54–6). To place us there also, Herodotus has a local Hellespontine watch Xerxes' parade, gape and speak (7.56.2), just as he, or we, might have spoken in awe at seeing such a tremendous task accomplished and Hellas threatened with desolation. The story is told as if for the first time, and the 'man in the street' anecdote heightens an already familiar theme. Occasionally, Herodotus interrupts a speech to make certain that the audience follows the story in the right way. In the middle of Aristagoras' dramatic, direct-speech sales-pitch to Cleomenes, the narrator suddenly interjects: 'While speaking, he was pointing (δεικνύς) to that map, the one [I mentioned] engraved on a bronze tablet which he carried about with him' (5.49.5). Herodotus' *apodexis* points to Aristagoras' *deixis*. Both expositors required close attention and knew how to get it.

The modern historian also arranges narrative in dramatic form, but employs footnotes to show the workings, the raw data and their basic manipulations. Notes permit citations of sources, the presentation of tangential information, and the cumulation of proofs. They also provide an important rhetorical tool for persuading an audience of an arguable truth. The writer keeps the forest in view while examining particular trees. This double view is managed by means of a technical fiction, namely that the footnotes do not interrupt the flow of the narrative. Herodotus had no such convention of footnotes (or pages, chapters, or appendices), so his digressions needed to be inserted more carefully and related more clearly to the larger narrative. He wanted to distinguish the thematically significant from the inessential. He thus develops the arts of digression and explicitly defends their employment.[22] Consequently he is not bound to the distinct concentration on one or two characters or incidents found in Sophocles or Homer's *Odyssey*.

For Aristotle (*Rhetoric* 3.9.2 = 1409a), Herodotus wrote typical λέξις εἰρομένη, paratactic and relatively plain prose. Yet Herodotus' real importance for Greek literature is to be found in his having been the first writer of an extended prose narrative to develop a prose style characterized by extended periods and rhetorical figures (such as anaphora, antithesis, and ascending length of cola).[23] The logographers, if we judge from the surviving fragments, did not employ a periodic or a markedly personal style. Herodotus' narrative style supersedes the old austerity with a new ease, intimacy, and comprehensive control of presentation. For this we have principally the structure of epic and the forms of analysis of the Sophists to thank. Epic poetry, much more than contemporary tragedy, influenced both his way of structuring events and his style, especially diction, imagery, and vividness. The author of *On the Sublime* and Hermogenes (*De sublimitate* 13.3; *De ideis* II, 421 Sp.) both expressly remark on Herodotus' debt to Homer, so extensive and pronounced that he seems to wish to advertise it.[24] His 'east Ionic' dialect, an elevated literary medium, at least by contemporary Attic standards, presents a personal amalgam of words and constructions, a spectrum of diction suited to the variety of tone and mood demanded by his stories. His speeches present antilogical debates in pairs, triads, and larger numbers that account for major historical decisions and discuss ethical and political problems in terms first posed in his own day by the Sophists.

Speeches

And yet I often think it odd that it [history] should be so dull, for a great deal of it must be invention. The speeches that are put into the heroes' mouths, their thoughts and designs – the chief of all this must be invention, and invention is what delights me in other books.

Jane Austen, *Northanger Abbey*, Book i, ch. xiv

Without absolutely condemning the composition of speeches so familiar to the ancients, I shall presume to impose the three following laws on this species of historical fiction. 1. That the truth of the leading fact, of the council, debate, orations, etc. be positively ascertained. 2. That some natural means be suggested through which, the historian (who cannot plead the inspiration of the Muses) might derive his intelligence. 3. That the language and ideas be strictly adapted to the national and personal characters of his Dramatic speakers. On these principles it would not be easy to justify the orations of Xerxes, Mardonius, and Artabanus.

Edward Gibbon 'Marginalia in Herodotus' on 7.8

The speeches presented directly in the later books of the *Histories* have a serious purpose: to convey a real person's real problems and to present real policy choices. By their psychological and political insight they also carry the author's interpretation of events. As a modern historian aggressively expressed it: 'The many speeches ... do not claim to reproduce faithfully what the speaker said, if indeed he delivered a speech at all ... They are invented to reveal character, to explain the grounds of a policy, or to elucidate strategical considerations ...'[25] 'Herodotus must be credited with the words, the thoughts and the structure of the speeches'[26] in the Persian council scene (7.5–11) as well as in many other assemblies and colloquies.

Oratio recta, in both the progression of thought and the verbal expression, is the writer's own reconstruction, for Herodotus could not have had sound authorities for the intimate and sometimes trivial thoughts and conversation of kings in high council, at table, or in bed.[27] *Oratio recta*, so unlike the canonical modern use of quotation marks, was intended as a sign of the author's intervention, not meant to be read as a sign of the author's gullibility.

Herodotus' interest in dramatic and persuasive debate is faithful enough to the limited evidence available and to the situation of the individuals being characterized.[28] To profess that every Herodotean speech rests at least on some actual report, does not, of course, prove the veracity of that report. The ultimate absurdity among reported speeches, namely the eighty-seven word 'inscription' that Themistocles caused to be carved in stone near Artemisium for the Ionians to find (8.22.1–2),[29] reads like a speech, for its presumptive purpose was to persuade (as its historiographical purpose was to explain), not, as with other inscriptions such as the epitaphs at Thermopylae (7.228), to commemorate or make a permanent record. It presents an extension of the creative use of *oratio recta*, a technique used to explain known events in the historical record.

Speeches in *oratio obliqua* are, as a rule, more likely to represent accurately the gist of actual words and discussions. This is the form in which Herodotus will first have learned the contents of all verbal communications (eg, 7.143, 145; 9.106.2–4), before he elaborated the main points of some of them for thematic and dramatic purposes. Short addresses and dialogues in *oratio recta*, on the other hand, seem especially dramatic because of their conversion to direct speech (eg, 1.45.2*, 7.136.2*, 7.234–5*). All speeches in the earlier books, which deal with more distant epochs, are more likely to be embellished and thus often appear in *oratio recta*.

The author of *On the Sublime* comments on the dramatic efficacy of this method: 'The words [of Phocean Dionysius, 6.11] do not seem rhetorically composed [by Herodotus] but rather forced out of him' (22.2). By comparison, Thucydides' speeches are less like real talk, less believable as words actually spoken, and therefore from the point of view of historical credibility, less successful. Longer speeches and dialogues in the *Histories* may be equally dramatic, but often present historical analysis (eg, 3.80–2*, 5.92*, 8.100*, 8.142–4*), frequently where today historians would provide 'might have been's' or 'ought to have done's.'[30] Both historians have utilized a helpful convention of Greek epic, namely the explanation of policy and action by the reflections and utterances of characters, even though trustworthy evidence for such evaluations and justifications by the historical participants is often thin or non-existent. Furthermore, what the historians give as historical data often represents only their present best possible reconstruction of past events. As Herodotus realized, there are no 'bare facts'; facts are always dressed.

Demaratus' response to Xerxes (7.104.3*), that he would not claim to be able to fight ten or two men, nor willingly (ἑκών) even one, seems both individual *and* general, since it embodies an attitude which seems somehow un-Spartan, yet this fugitive from Lacedaemon expresses most powerfully the Spartan creed and *ethos*. The colloquy between Demaratus and Xerxes (7.101–4) has been called 'lo svolgimento di questa intuizione [ie, regarding the barbarian-Greek antithesis] umana e storica,' which Herodotus 'non ha scritto per il momento ma per l'eternità: prima di Tucidide, come Tucidide.'[31] The conventions concerning the presentation of thought and speech permit the narrative itself to carry an interpretation without the author's obvious intrusion.[32] In other words, just where anxiety for Herodotus' fidelity to historical truth has been greatest, there paradoxically one discovers his most ambitious efforts to elucidate the meaning of historical facts and processes.

Herodotus will distance himself from a report, or draw the audience into high councils, or estrange the reader's sympathies by skilled use of direct and reported speech – and all other tools of Greek rhetoric. His stance is generally unpartisan, although he takes the side of an unappreciated Athens (7.139) or of even the wicked but remarkably successful tyrant Polycrates who died in such miserable contrast to his achievements and ambitions (3.125.2). Like Solon (1.29.1), in exile Herodotus travels for θεωρίη, observation of strange lands and customs; like Otanes (3.83, especially § 3), he extricates himself from immediate, political pressures and maintains a solitary and precarious freedom as long as he does not transgress his society's nomoi. The historian does not disbelieve, or believe, reports entirely (4.96.1), unless he can verify information. His detachment too often goes unnoticed. His acknowledgment of irresolvable conflicts in the versions of some events (eg, 6.14.1, 8.87.1) should increase the reader's confidence when he does not complain about the state of the evidence for other events.

Herodotus does not scribble whatever he is told; he recognizes that men can be mistaken or ignorant (2.19.1, 4.187), that they will lie and magnify in order to save face (3.16.7, 6.14.1) or to glorify their ethnic heritage (1.95.1, σεμνοῦν, only here and 3.16.7). But by quizzing local logioi, those versed in their native traditions, and ordinary folk, he thinks that he can both approach the truth and preserve a diversity of thinking dear to his ideals.[33] Such historical traditions are worthy of report, even when some versions are flatly condemned as untrue (5.86.3, ἐμοὶ οὐ πιστὰ λέγοντες; 3.3.1, ὅδε λόγος, ἐμοὶ μὲν οὐ πιθανός ...).

Λέγεται, 'it is said,' separates the historian from a report, for instance the explicitly disbelieved tale of Xerxes' homeward voyage: 'It is said that Xerxes, once he heard the captain, answered ...' (8.118.3). He employs this convenience for 1) what he has not seen and deems most unlikely, 2) what is divine or miraculous (6.117.3, the tale of Epizelus illustrates the historian's nervousness), 3) what seems best or worst or otherwise superlative, and 4) when more than one account of a given event is current and no secure resolution is discernible.[34] These four categories represent what he does not know, what he cannot know, and what cannot be known by anyone. Legetai therefore is a legitimate warning, easily passed over, that Herodotus does not vouch for what followed (cf the tables in chapter 2). When he presents more than one account, logic demands that he thinks at least one to be false, and thus the two or more versions demonstrate his reservation of judgment. Herodotus expresses serious doubt quite often with other, more parenthetical phrases such as 'if indeed the story be true' (eg, 5.32, 8.8.2).

G.L. Cooper has demonstrated a way in which syntax serves historiographic subtlety. 'The intrusion of oblique infinitives into certain O.O. [=

oratio obliqua] constructions where they do not regularly occur indicates an attempt on the part of the reporter to indicate reserve vis-à-vis the reported speaker, ... to avoid responsibility for the matter or opinion ... represented.'[35] Herodotus' explicit cautionary statements (introduced by λέγεται or parenthetical clauses like εἰ δέ ἀληθής γέ) must be supplemented by several other sorts of warnings, including the seventy-seven examples of these infinitives 'intruding' in subordinate clauses, appearing after ὅτι or ὡς, and showing up in a few passages without any ruling or introductory verb. The reporter withdraws confidence or delivers a story with studious irony.

The oblique infinitive when intrusive, by disappointing the hearer's expectation of a normal (oblique) *finite* verbal form, signals the reporter's reserve. It is common in alternative versions, where authorial doubt often surfaces, even when Herodotus expresses a preference. A cogent example occurs in a *rejected logos* at 8.118.1–4. Xerxes' return to Asia certainly took place, so even the rejected version (οὐδαμῶς ἔμοι πιστός) receives indicative verb-forms for the trip as far as Eion, for the bestowal of an army on Hydarnes, and for the boarding of a Phoenician vessel. As soon as the storm hits, however, Herodotus switches to intrusive oblique infinitives that carry him through the rest, through the waves, Xerxes' conversation with the helmsman (note the *oratio recta*), the grandees' leap, Xerxes' safe arrival, and the helmsman's ambivalent reward, a gold crown for saving the king and the loss of his head for destroying his court. Here, not for the only time, Herodotus explicitly rejects an intriguing tale of oriental wilfulness, barbarity, and idiocy.[36]

This 'extra-grammatical idea of citation or quotation,' by which the historian wishes to safeguard himself against charges of gullibility, finds clearest proof in examples where there is little or even no parenthetical preparation for *oratio obliqua* infinitives.[37] The story of Pan's message to Philippides and Croesus' narrow escape from the pyre deserve inclusion because the stories were commonly believed and told by his contemporaries. Furthermore they are good stories; that is, they provide interesting and important information about those who retell them. Nevertheless, Herodotus insulates himself from seeming to believe them and encourages his audience not to believe them by indicating, with more than sparse, general caveats, his weak or strong doubt that the story has a factual basis, an *historical* merit in our modern sense. Herodotus also follows this distancing method when he preserves local beliefs, legends, folktales, and pseudohistory, without compromising his expressed concern for historical facts, so far as they can be determined.

As we turn from narrative style and reported speeches to other aspects of

Herodotus' historical rhetoric, we note that historiographers have always attended more to apparently irresolvable epistemological problems in history than to its less visible but more easily studied rhetoric, more to history's claims of truth than to its techniques of persuasion. In a field so open, this section may only probe some leading forms that persuasion assumes in the work of the first historian. Having first explored two pervasive and recognized elements of his rhetoric, his programmatic statements in the preface and then the subject to which the words 'historiographical rhetoric' most naturally apply, namely speeches, we may now examine how Herodotus gains the reader's confidence in other, less familiar ways. The reader's active co-operation is necessary for understanding the *Histories*; the author's guidance is generally indirect rather than explicit.

The use of nonverbal behaviours provides a clear example of Herodotus' unusual historical 'rhetoric.' Two literary sources stand behind it: the ethnographic tradition for relatively neutral descriptions of alien societies and the epic tradition for highly charged, dramatic incidents. The former category appears in the *Histories* as flat catalogues of exotic practices with little or no structure and occasional comparisons to Hellenic *nomoi*; the latter category of description of nonverbal communication occurs in many of the *Histories'* most memorable moments when leading characters scream, fall to the ground, chuckle, strike one another, or speak in signs. These scenes of high emotion, crisis, and self-revelation are often articulated by the description of nonverbal behaviours not merely for ornament, excitement, or audience enjoyment. They appear precisely where the modern, superficially more objective, method steps back from the rush of events in order to proffer psychological analysis of principal personalities, to reflect on personal or national character, or to formulate other non-narrational, non-sequential analyses of the causes of major happenings.

That is to say, nonverbal behaviours in these privileged scenes, where the action decelerates and the attention of the text focuses on individuals, enrich both the literary and the historiographical texture. Drama and history complement each other: the narrative of the past is now more interesting because it is more human, and more significant because the roots of men's actions are exposed.

Furthermore, nonverbal behaviours often surface in dramatic scenes lying behind important events for which evidence and explanation are particularly thin. Where Herodotus cannot transmit verifiable facts or adequate recollections but requires some account of how events came to pass, the reader is offered explanatory incidents, based on received reports but insulated from the author's endorsement of every detail by their elaborately dramatic nature (conveyed by direct speech, gestures, paralinguistic noises, etc). That is, Herodotus offers the reader a choice: I will lend you my best re-creation of the past, a vehicle for understanding how known outcomes arose; you may accept it along with more testable data and find my narrative and explanation cogent, or you may reject those insulated segments for more persuasive, if equally imaginative, re-creations of the origins of events and their meanings provided by other historians. The implicit negotiation recognizes the limits of his ability to substantiate all his 'facts,' especially those long ago, far away, or performed in secret. The greater the aura of verisimilitude, the more mimetic a story, we may say, the less credence the author seems to give it. Thus we consider scenes dense with dramatic technique including nonverbal behaviours to be intended as both persuasive and monitory. Herodotus warns the audience of factual uncertainty while entertaining it with dramatic skill.

Herodotus frequently breaks into his narrative and analysis to negotiate with the reader an understanding of his method or his posture on a specific question. As a mediator between the familiar and the unknown, he wants to convey simultaneously a detailed account of other societies and a holistic picture of how foreign and strange societies compare to his own Hellenic world. Otherness is to be a tool for self-understanding, for realizing the parochial limits of the Hellenic world-view – indeed for realizing the limits of any world-view. Apparent absurdities, at least from the Hellenic point of view, are not mocked but provided to show the culture-bound parameters of Hellenic consciousness. The power of strangeness will enable a reader to reinterpret from a different perspective much that is thought familiar and natural.

Herodotus realized that such a major challenge to Hellenic complacency and such an audacious program of edification required some guidance for the reader. The mode, as we show below, is often conversational, but the purpose is serious. Herodotus wants to implicate the audience in his re-search and re-creation of the past. A thorough study of the relationship between writer and reader in the *Histories* requires attention to all forms of the stems ἱστορ- and λογ-, all first- and second-person pronouns and verbs (excepting those appearing in *oratio recta*), everything praised, blamed, compared, wondered at, or doubted.[38] Furthermore, it must consider topics that are explicitly included, excluded, argued, expanded or contracted, postponed or otherwise taken out of some 'natural' order, subordinated or handled only to be rejected (see part 2 for some of these matters).

Here we only probe the rhetorical postures the historian assumes in order to gain the reader's assent. A rhetoric of familiarity and uncertainty rather than of authority and omniscience emerges. Herodotus minimizes the distance from his reader whereas Thucydides maximizes it, often objectifying even himself as general and author by third-person grammatical forms. Irony and parody provide two more bonds between author and reader, as both share a distance from the 'certainties' of the misguided actors, playing off the historical record against imagined eternal verities. The *Histories* provide many other perspectives and the reader is invited to share in the relativist adventure. This openness to barbarian and iconoclastic attitudes and interpretations appears in the historian's interventions in the text that directly address the audience or imply an intimate, perhaps face-to-face relationship.[39]

Another rhetorical problem or opportunity will be explored: how Herodotus entered and exited specific *logoi* small and large. The author had to delimit and shape the whole and the parts. The nature and extent of his work may be clarified by studying when, where, and why he began and closed his book. Every tiny narrative within the grand narrative requires its own defining entrance and exit; more and less artful transitions, as well as typical introductory and final incidents, deserve separate study.[40] That manner necessarily includes fitting the sloppy data of history into clarified, even familiar forms that the ancient Greek reader, and the modern as well, can comfortably assimilate. Narratives need a beginning and end.

These essays may clarify both the great power of any historian to shape our perception of the past chosen for study and this historian's manner of making his perception seem the right one. Herodotus violates both the philosopher's canons for mimetic literature in his comments to the reader, and the later historian's canons for including only trustworthy and somehow testable statements in his dramatic incidents, but this apparent temerity serves to remind us that Herodotean history, if not all history, is inevitably situated somewhere in the mine-strewn borderlands of δόξα, appearance, between the untestable particularities of myth re-enacted or recited (drama and epic) and the eternal universalizing generalities of philosophical truth, abstract notions ever present but shorn of flesh and blood.

Nonverbal Behaviours

[Artabanus] yelled, leaped out of Xerxes' bed, sat himself down by Xerxes, and related the vision of his dream. Then he said: 'King ... I've already seen many great states brought down by lesser ones ... I know that always desiring more is a bad thing.'

Herodotus 7.18.1–2*

Anthropology, linguistics, folklore, and photography have convinced this century of the meaningfulness of gesture and other nonverbal behaviours. History, a verbal art, records few of them, however, because they seem trivial and resist verbal analysis or even bare description. Description of bodily movements, postures, inarticulate shouts and groans of epic and lyric, drama and fictional prose, have always been uncommon in historiography, although such events were actual occurrences, because historical prose generally consists of narratives of significant actions, reports of speeches and plans that changed history, and reflective analyses isolated from the narrative. Human character is exposed only insofar as it can be deduced from actions, or so it is suggested.

Gestures, reported with detail as if from an eyewitness, dramatically reveal emotions and thought in the *Histories*, when speech is inadequate.[41] They offer a technique of persuasion that is not argumentative; the reader creates his own connections from reported acts. Herodotus' demonstration employs a rich variety of literary enticements and does not disdain nonverbal communication, the language of the body. His innovative prose technique encompasses all the strategies that Greek literature, especially epic, had developed before generic distinctions ossified.

Herodotus' objectionable μυθῶδες (fiction-like quality, Thucydides 1.22.4),[42] allows smiles, tears, rude noises, and even obscene gestures. Nonverbal communication in Herodotus generally reports two quite disparate classes of behaviour: customary (ethnic) practices[43] and unique or individual pain or painful insight. Especially when suffering escapes the limits of ordinary expression, a gesture provides some unmediated expression of emotion for the victim and a powerful signal to the reader. The *Histories* thus report gesture in their most objective, reportorial mode (ethnography) and in their most subjective, dramatic and interpretive mode (folkloric, historical, and paradigmatic stories).

Greeting and parting rituals may serve as instances of customary practices. They regularize and convey sentiments about difficult moments in social intercourse, especially between participants of different status. Arbitrary forms of communication such as a few 'meaningless' words (our 'hail, hello, goodbye'), a kiss or embrace (1.134.1 with relative status discussion; 2.41.3), tears of sorrowful loss, or the submissive posture of the entire body (eg, *proskynesis*, nine occurrences, especially 7.136, where ethnic customs are compared) symbolize relative status: the more one disturbs the body to initiate or terminate an encounter, the lower his relative status. Those who are allowed to approach the Persian king must demonstrate their recognition of his social superiority; italicize, so to speak, his superiority by their bodies as well as their words. The nuances of posture, gesture, and relative position (first to approach and speak, distance gap, relative elevation of the person) clarify status in meetings between equals and non-equals. Body language introduces, complements, and ends our verbal messages.[44]

The other major class of nonverbal communication, where emotion transcends or precludes articulate response, allows Herodotus to manipulate the dramatic techniques of epic. Croesus on the pyre suddenly remembers and appreciates Solon's wisdom; he heaves a sigh, moans, and thrice cries out the Athenian's name. Astyages suddenly puts his facts together, perceives who the young Cyrus really is, and falls dumb. Cambyses on his death-bed is struck by the truth (ἔτυψε ἡ ἀληθείη) and learns that in vain he killed his own brother.[45] Men cry out in fear or openly weep,[46] sometimes groan in frustration at their foolishness, exhaustion, or the failure of their dearest plans.[47]

Pheros spears a river in his anger (2.111.2); Demaratus retreats to a passive grief in which he wordlessly wraps himself away in his cloak (6.67.3). The boundless anguish of the defeated and deposed Pharaoh Psammenitus results in much weeping, but the King himself, bent double with sorrow (3.14.3, ἔκυψε ἐς τὴν γῆν) is beyond tears (3.14.10*). The misery of one poor friend, however, finally resolves his emotional paralysis so that he attacks his own body (3.14.7).

Laughter and smiles in the *Histories* convey not benign happiness, joy, or pleasure, but scorn, arrogance, or self-delusion.[48] Laughter is ascribed to powerful men so pleased with themselves that they become blind and too self-assured for human security. The gesture reveals by its pattern in the *Histories* a character's self-destructive tendencies. Individuals who are destined to die in peace do not laugh in this text.[49] Those who are at one moment described as 'mightily pleased' (περιχαρής) with their lot soon after meet with disaster: Astyages, Cambyses, the Babylonians, Oeobazus, Aristagoras, Xerxes, Mardonius, and Artaÿnte, a list of the doomed.

Sometimes words are insufficient to express the scorn and contempt one party feels for another. Characters in Egyptian stories in the *Histories* especially, for instance in the tale of the wily thief and Rhampsinitus, tend to be uninhibited this way. Psammetichus' soldiers react negatively to his request for them to return to his service and their families: 'one of them is said to have pointed to his penis and said, "wherever this should be, there too will be both wives and children"' (2.30.4). When Pharaoh Apries sent an honored courtier to bring back the rebel Amasis, the latter 'raised himself on his horse and farted and told Patarbemis to take *that* back to Pharaoh' (2.162.3).[50] Between speech and gesture come words that describe nonverbal reactions. The Scythian King retorted to Darius' emissary (4.127.4*): 'My response to your statement that you are my master: I say "nuts".'[51] The contemptuous expletive borders on a nonverbal grunt.

Besides grief, laughter, moments of inadvertent movement, and expletival contempt, speechless communication includes 'sign language.'[52] This comprehends not only hand signs, but also the unusually frequent inventories of historical monuments like the chains hanging on the Athenian acropolis with which the Boeotians and Euboeans once were bound (5.77.3; cf 1.66.4; 4.81.3); rarely paralleled reports of grooming customs like the opposed Spartan and Argive hairstyles that commemorated the battle for Thyrea, or the dress requirements imposed on Athenian females following the disastrous war with Aegina (1.82.7–8; 5.87.2–3); and the remarkable inclusions of momentarily significant objects. When, for example, the Spartans replied to the Samian exiles' impassioned speech requesting military aid by saying that they had forgotten the beginning and had not understood the end, the Samians next time brought in a sack, and limited themselves to one phrase, 'the sack needs barley.' Even this speech seemed too wordy to the laconic audience (3.46). Similarly, by a simple display (δεικνύς), Pausanias wordlessly compares Persian luxury and Greek frugality at table in the royal Persian tent at Plataea (9.82).

Herodotus frequently notes threats and punishments that advertise the unlimited power of potentates. 'To encourage the others,' soldiers and labourers are whipped (7.22.1, 223.3; cf 4.3.4), and bodies are variously mutilated (4.202.1; 9.112; 3.16; 7.238, 39.3). Mass deportations (eg, 2.154.3; 5.15.3; 6.3, 119) and other mass punishments, as well as the individual disfigurements, tortures, and executions send a message by nonverbal means that is impossible to misconstrue. For the slaves of despots, the acts of autocrats displayed their own powerlessness; for the reader, the message conveys the irrational and whimsical nature of noninstitutional régimes. The nonverbal behaviours ubiquitous in epic help the *Histories* to describe and colour important actions.

Dumb-shows replace words when talk is dangerous or when symbolic actions are used as a standard language of diplomacy. Thrasyboulus says nothing to Periander's messenger; he simply cuts down the highest ears of grain in a field and 'appends not a single word.' To the messenger he seemed a fool, but 'Periander comprehended what had been done' (5.92.ζ2–η1*). The Persians asked for proof of submission from the European Greeks by demanding earth and water, symbolic surrender (4.126; 6.48.2; 7.32, 133.1). The king of Ethiopia rejected Cambyses' gifts and returned to him a meaningful object, a stiff bow; only when the Persians could easily bend and string it, should they try to subdue independent Ethiopia (3.21.3*, an obvious echo of the *Odyssey* and certain other testing folktales, but not therefore unfactual).

Herodotus reports one gesture that may have been unintentional. A messenger from the satrap Oroetes reached the tyrant Polycrates at dinner with Anacreon; Polycrates did not turn around to face the speaker or give any answer 'either because he despised Oroetes or by chance' (3.121.2; cf 3.53.2). The author attends carefully to this ambiguous nonverbal moment, but does not resolve the historical issue of whether it actually happened.

The wily Scyths dispatched to their pursuer Darius the most complex nonverbal communication reported in the *Histories*. 'They sent a herald with the following gifts: a bird, a mouse, a frog, and five arrows. The Persians asked the bearer what intention did the senders have. He replied that he had no further orders than to deliver the objects and return as quickly as possible. He bid the Persians themselves, if they were clever, to determine what the gifts were meant to convey (γνῶναι τὸ θέλει τὰ δῶρα λέγειν). Hearing this, the Persians pondered the gifts.' Darius thought that the gifts amounted to a symbol of surrender, equivalent to earth and water. Gobryes, however, by the same process of inferential comparison (εἰκάζων), determined that they signified the impossibility of the Persians ever effectively cornering the Scyths (4.131–2). When the Scyths mobilized against the Persians, Darius had to accept Gobryes' interpretation (4.133–4.2). Objects, like historical accounts, can mean different things to different people, a point Herodotus makes repeatedly.

Herodotus' story offers more than this kind of riddle so pleasing to the Greeks – it is another opportunity to show the monomaniacal desire of despots to expand their empires and the deterioration of their strategic thinking after extended success. Like Croesus with his river-crossing oracle, Darius reads into ambiguities anything he wishes to find. This time, he is barely saved from disaster by a wise adviser. There is a gap between the signifying 'message,' what it is meant to signify, and what the recipient understands. The reader also feels this gap and thereby participates in the historical process, erring for a moment perhaps as the king has erred. Nonverbal behaviours externalize psychological attitudes and emphasize the drama of the important moment.

Talking to the Reader

Herodotus also draws his reader into his text by employing conversational second-person singular verb-forms. With reference to his (fallacious) belief that all Persian names end in '-s,' he writes 'If *you* investigate this matter, *you* will find that all, not some, end in the same way' (1.139). Referring to Babylonian religious prostitution, he alleges 'Once she has intercourse with a man, she has discharged her sacred duty and goes home; thereafter *you* could not seduce her, however much *you* offer' (1.199.4). The colloquial second-person suggests sometimes the intimacy of personal observation and sometimes the truculent tone of someone who has met disagreement. (See the list of polemical passages appended to chapter 4.)

Herodotus thus appears to permit his reader to believe differently by reifying the possibility of another point of view, a form of presentation rarely found in other historians. This conversational manner confirms Denniston's observation that 'Herodotus is fond of divesting himself of the historian's omniscience, and assuming a winning fallibility.'[53] Elsewhere Herodotus dismisses a person or subject with an impatient third-person imperative (eg, ἐχέτω ὡς καὶ ἀρχὴν ἐνομίσθη, 'let them keep their old custom,' 1.140.3). Herodotus the *histor* intends by his colloquial apostrophes to the reader to perpetuate the fruits of his research,[54] even though sometimes his 'button-holing' consisted only of road directions, for instance, how to reach Meroë in Egypt: 'You'll sail upriver from Elephanttown and then you'll come to a smooth plain' (2.29.2–6). 'All such appeals with a direct personal application set the hearer in the center of the action.'[55] With a similar pose of conferring with the reader, he appears to doubt whether he can speak openly about Medizers (8.73.3 *fin*). The example of the Athenians fining Phrynichus for reminding (ἀναμνήσαντα) them of their ill-fortune and the consequent condemnation of the *Sack of Miletus* never to be shown in public again (6.21.2) justified his (rhetorical) hesitation.

Digressions are often linked to the main narrative by a casual guideword that seems suddenly to arrest his attention and story, and to plunge the reader into a sometimes distant account, that only returns at its end to the point of departure, the leading subject. Frequent asides, introduced by γάρ, provide informal, momentarily necessary explanation. These can offer the grounds for a belief or a series of causes (eg, 3.80–2: eighteen examples, mostly beliefs of the interlocutors followed by a 'cause'; 4.1: eight sentences, six opening with causal γάρ; 6.61, digressions within digressions).[56] Chains of δέ clauses suggest that a story rushes the author along too fast to stop in order to put the details together with a more careful articulation of sequence or cause (eg, 5.119–21 *init*: ten sentences with δέ eleven times). Anecdotic, dialogic, novelistic, digressive, the style of Herodotus' historical discourse sometimes bewilders the seeker of plain fact but always intrigues the student of complex literary structures.

As the formal doubt of the rhetorical question can extricate Herodotus from full responsibility for a report, so he may use indefinite adverbs for similar protection, particularly κως for 'hesitant statement,' and κου (που) which claims only approximate truth. These words 'admirably suit the easy, colloquial style of Herodotus' because they suggest 'a feeling of uncertainty in the speaker.'[57] Broad generalizations on *divine* arrangements (3.106.1, 108.2; 6.27.1) and uncertainty concerning the *reason* for the beauty of the whores of Naucratis or for the seniority of the Eurypontid house at Sparta (2.135.5; 6.51; no other examples) receive a vernacular *kos*. With *kou* also, Herodotus liberates himself from responsibility. 'The Paeonians conjectured that this is what the oracle meant, and said, I suppose (κου), to each other: "This now could be the oracle's fulfillment ...".' (5.1.3*; cf 1.87.4*).

'The primary gain ... from the oral fiction is an immediacy through which tradition appears to reflect events directly, and without the intrusion of the historian's own thought.'[58] This mirage of a history without a historian may sometimes be intended, but Herodotus generally wants the reader to see and see through the 'fictions' that explain his facts, to know his imaginative devices for what they are, means to transcend the limitations of the chronicle, and to reach 'the higher imaginative level we associate with the drama.' His *Histories* rarely, if ever, degenerate into a naked sequence of political events, because he discovered an historiographically legitimate means of creating 'a poetic and philosophic dimension.'[59] Speeches reported directly do this, so do remarks like the parenthetical ὡς ἐγὼ δοκέω which, after Harpagus unwittingly ate of his own progeny (1.119.7), 'transforms the omniscient historian into the spectator, horrified and ignorant of the issue ...'[60] Herodotus, however, does not pretend that all his reported folktales, propaganda, and fictions were historical fact.[61] Rather he often chooses to indicate the limits of his knowledge, and he reminds the audience of his interference or uncertainty on every page. Thucydides, by contrast, never uses the inexact and colloquial που in his own narrative,[62] but then he generally avoids the history of the uncertainly known past, regarding all periods before his lifetime as incapable of reconstruction in any detail.

Herodotus finds *kou* especially useful for numerical approximation where precision is not at all essential, such as the age of Harpagus' son ('about thirteen at most'; 1.119.2, cf 1.209.2; 3.3.3), or the fraction achieved of a famous climb up a tower ('about halfway up,' 1.181.4), or a geographical distance (7.198.2).[63]

C. Rubincam has explored in detail Herodotus' treatment of numbers. Her preliminary survey indicates that he offers many figures and statistical calculations, often clustered in lists. Most frequently he records by numbers the passage of time or the strength of military forces; less frequently distance, the size of civilian populations, and financial statistics (all in that order). Herodotus spreads his numbers more evenly into all these categories than Thucydides, who concentrates 63 per cent of his into military counts. While ethnic catalogues have Homeric antecedents, the historian's regular grand totals of contingents and distances do not. These totals (eg, 3.95; 4.86; 5.54.2; 7.60.1, 87, 89, 185; 8.2.1; 9.28–30), and his occasional conversions of monetary units to a more familiar Greek system, or translations of units of time into units of distance (3.95; 5.54), reflect an intention to report meaningful numbers (effective fighting forces, known 'currencies,' a more precise way to denote space), in order to produce a synoptic account. They are not part of his ancient and oral poetic heritage but part of his interest in accurate knowledge and its written tabulation and inventories, a concern shared with contemporary medical and scientific writers. The difficulties of getting *any* numbers right in his circumstances should not be underestimated.

Herodotus offers numbers with a frequency that places him in the middle of extant Greek historians, slightly more often than Thucydides, slightly less often than Xenophon in the *Hellenica*. He rarely qualifies their accuracy or exactness ('about,' 'more than,' etc) but this may reflect an awareness that such figures, reported long after the event, were, at best, popular estimates of the time or, as figures, the element most likely to be distorted by the subsequent tradition. Thucydides qualifies numbers much more frequently, but he also has the advantage of contemporary data and he also rounds off more often to tens, hundreds, and thousands – without his reputation suffering for it. In brief, Herodotus' use of numbers is similar to the practice of later historians and does not indicate, statistically or otherwise, that he means to deceive or is himself frequently deceived by others in the tricky business of recording numerical data.[64]

Occasionally he uses the adverb κου to indicate to his audience a gap in his information or some inessential fact: Cyrus had *some* earlier name (οὔνομα ἄλλο κού τι, 1.113.3); Cyrus made *some* child play the King' Eye (1.114.2); Phanes ran away from Amasis because the latter had blamed him for *some* act (μεμφόμενος κού τι, 3.4.2). The art of the effective storyteller and not dishonest historian should not be mistaken for laziness or indifference to truth.[65] The essential persons and national characteristics have been highlighted; the relevant context indicated as far as it can be, or needs to be, for the historical narrative.

Irony, Satire, and Parody

'Gibbon might have taken lessons in the art of irony from Herodotus ...'[66] Sometimes Herodotus casts doubt on the historicity of an incident, sometimes he shows reserve towards the tradition of an entire folk,[67] sometimes he advertises his incredulity, towards, for example, the belief that 'god is on our side.' Herodotus' own desacralization of the past is implied by his note that the Athenians consecrated a shrine to Pan only after the victory at Marathon (6.105.3), and in incidents like Xerxes' too precipitate joy in the seers' interpretation of an eclipse as portending the defeat of Hellas (7.37.3), or the Magi's *post hoc propter hoc* fallacious 'success' in stopping the gale of 480 by sacrifices to Thetis and the Nereids (7.191.2; cf 189.2; 8.94.4). Herodotus invites us to contemplate the flawed vision of people swept away in their enthusiasms.

Often alternative versions suggest an ironic note: 'Whether this story is true, I don't know, but I write what I'm told' (4.195.2). 'About Salmoxis and his underground den, I neither disbelieve nor believe it more than one should ... Whether Salmoxis was some man or some spirit native to the Getae, let us anyway say farewell to him' (4.96). Indeed the ethnographic tone is generally one of personal reserve but determined purpose: to record what men believe and say. *Oratio recta* and *obliqua*, source citations, and various indications of caution constitute Herodotus' most frequently employed techniques of insulating himself from information reported. Chapters 2, 3, and 4, discussing selection, alternative versions, and polemic, show that ironic or caustic statements are frequent. Man's not quite total inability to learn from others' experience and his own, constitutes a favourite theme that recurs in each major narrative. What is tragic for the autocrat offers ironic confirmation of the historian's belief in the perils of prosperity and universal mutability in human affairs.

In addition to irony, Herodotus also presents satire and parody in the *Histories*. One probable parody of gender or youth is found in the speech of Periander's daughter (3.53.3–4), where tired *gnomai*, artless anaphora, and choppy phrases in asyndeton characterize the young female's impotent attempt to sweeten her father's bitter pill, and to meddle in men's business.[68] As for the longer narratives, the first story of legendary rape and silly (ἀνόητος) counter-rape leading to intercontinental warfare shows humorous intent (especially the rationalizations of 1.4.2), and the 'Taming of the Amazonian Shrews' (4.113) displays a similar, satirical attitude towards women and their manipulation of male sexuality. Both these stories attribute to men also irrationality and foolishness in sexual matters, a frequent topic for Herodotean satire and pathos. Caution and evidence are always needed when one attempts to show satire or parody in a generally serious text, but inflated speech, undercutting comments by the author, and inherently ludicrous situations often clarify the tone of a tale.

Observable stratagems like irony and parody should encourage audience confidence in the author's control of his presentation. Such micro-level techniques of rhetoric, one step beyond the familiar figures of speech, are not incompatible with ferreting out historical truth and bringing it home to the reader. We next approach more perplexing and far-reaching literary problems. The historian, like any other narrator, must determine where and how to commence and conclude his main and subsidiary stories. Beginnings and endings in historiography have been unduly neglected, and to these subjects we now must turn.

Beginnings

Herodotus clearly wrestles with the beginning of each account or tale, *logos*: Where and when does a certain chain of events commence (the historical problem)? How might this chain be begun dramatically with some noteworthy moment (the literary problem)? He needs to define, for aesthetic and practical reasons, many 'beginnings,' since every new story should be attached to the preceding and yet have its own demarcated origin. Major sequences may begin with explicit recognition (αὗται δὲ αἱ νέες ἀρχὴ κακῶν ἐγένοντο ..., 5.97.3); sometimes abruptly with asyndeton (Κροῖσος ἦν Λυδὸς μὲν γένος ..., 1.5.4–6.1); often with no more than a particle's pause after the conclusion of the previous *logos*.[69]

Herodotus reports the first known action in each set of political events, one simple but essential kind of historical cause.[70] The deeds (ἔργα) that the proem promises include beginnings (ἀρχαί), and beginnings often adumbrate or include cause (αἰτίη), as in the stories of Croesus and of the Athenian warships sent to aid the Ionians (1.5.1,3 and 5.97.3). The settling of historical credits and debts is part of Herodotus' task. He almost always traced events, institutions, and devices back to a human originator, rejecting common stories of the beneficence or malevolence of gods and heroes. The frequent phrase 'the first of whom we know' (34 occurrences) is thus polemical in itself, a firm distinction drawn between human and mythic history, in contrast to the unhistorical practices of writers in other genres such as Homer and Hecataeus, and in contrast to various ethnic traditions. In wars large or small, Herodotus sought to record the first aggressor: the first chapters shuttle blame back and forth between Greece and the East until Herodotus shreds the lovely but unverifiable fables by rejecting both Persian and Phoenician versions for his own more demonstrable, non-mythical, and original aggressor, Croesus.[71]

Many *logoi* begin with women. The Mermnad dynasty, Astyages' intent to murder Cyrus because of a dream about his daughter, Cambyses' Egyptian expedition, the exposé of the Magus (3.68), Darius' Scythian and Paeonian expeditions (3.134, 5.12–13), not to mention the Trojan war and the hint of Xerxes' death, all have a popular ultimate origin, obscure to Herodotus, in the prominence of a princess or queen. The 'Persian sources' state that one should not pay much attention to women, and that women who run off with strangers probably go willingly (1.4.2–3). Yet the Persians' own version of their history refutes this professed unconcern. They, more than the Greeks, seem to 'gather together great expeditions' and wreak international havoc 'for the sake of a single woman.' The prominence of women in the narrative often betrays folklore, the presence of 'popular explanations,' ethnic artefacts rather than political history.

Such stories comprise part of the multi-faceted condemnation of one-man, totalitarian governments.[72] The omnipotent Great King proved his high status by acting in ways beyond the comprehension of his subjects and enemies. What struck Greeks as irrational and overly secretive is part of the essence of despotic power. Where one man is the law, his passions may determine state policy, frequently to the great cost of his subjects, one point of the two stories about the wives of Candaules and Masistes emphatically juxtaposed to the beginning and to the end. Darius initiated campaigns in Europe, we are told, because Atossa made a promise to her Greek doctor and wanted European serving-girls, and because later Darius fell for the scheme of two would-be Paeonian tyrants who pretended that their sister's willingness to labour was a Paeonian norm. A woman, however, is never paraded as all the reason; these superficial motives of sexual lust, selfish desires, and deceptions afford Herodotus a point of departure, an available entrée into his more taxing and complicated business of adequately explaining government policy and national behaviours.

Croesus is emphatically termed 'the first beginner' of unjust deeds against the Greeks. This beginning is the first of many documented beginnings and one of the few introduced with a flourish that commences a major complex of events. Herodotus judged the Ionian revolt led by Naxos and Miletus 'to have begun a second series of evils for the Ionians' at the hands of the Persians, and the Athenian and Eretrian allied expeditionary force was 'the beginning of evils for both the Greeks and barbarians' (1.5.3; 5.28 with 6.32 and 5.124.1; 5.97.3; cf 6.98.1)[73] In the third instance, with a Homeric phrase Herodotus himself faults some Greeks, especially the Athenians, for precipitating the conflict, a terrible mistake. Although actuated for their own different and often self-exculpatory reasons, so likewise Darius, Mardonius, Xerxes, and the Spartans blame Greeks for beginning the hostilities (6.119.1; 7.5.2*, 9.2*, 8β2*; 8.142.2–3*). The very verb ὑπάρχειν, when it means to 'start something,' denotes actions that are deemed by the author or his speaker to be unjustified (1.5.3; 4.1.1; 6.133.1; 7.8β2*, 9.2*, 11.2*; 9.78.2*) Herodotus thus argues that some Hellenes brought the Persian war-machine on themselves, initiating the final stage of the conflict not with Croesus or even Cyrus, but with the Ionian rebellion and Athenian intervention in East Aegean affairs at that time. The Hellenes are far from blameless.

Where to begin? The procedure of two later, more explicitly methodological, historians may elucidate how and why Herodotus has begun his account where he has. Polybius remarks that to understand fully his account of the fifty-three-year progress of the Roman empire, a certain *prokataskeue* or 'preliminary sketch' will be necessary (1.3.10). This sketch extends to two books, about two hundred pages. The background is necessary for those who knew little of Rome and Carthage, for those who have not perceived the interconnectedness of events (1.3.7–10, 1.4.2–11), and for the work itself which must begin somewhere or there will be no clear basis for the remainder (ἀνυπόστατος, 1.5.3). A history must begin with an event whose primacy in time and importance is generally accepted (1.5.4–5). This moment is the Romans' first 'overseas' expedition (264 BCE), which also marked the end of Timaeus' history. The date was familiar to Greek readers and self-evident, in the sense that with it one could avoid an infinite regress and not confuse the reader.

Before commencing at this rational point, however, Polybius nervously drops back to 387/6 BCE, the year of the Peace of Antalcidas, an even more widely recognized epochal year for Hellenes. Chapters 6 through 12 move the reader from 387/6 to 264, the 'natural starting-point' (1.12.6), but one that required its own elucidation. So, even when the procedures of historiography have been clarified by generations of historians, every rupture of the seamless fabric of events presents a problem.

Thucydides' first book reports the events immediately previous to the War of 431–404 BCE, the affairs of Corcyra and Potidaea, in order to explain how the war began (1.24–66). To explain them, although he disapproves of trying to recover the history of an epoch when the historian was not yet born or of age (1.21.1, 5.26.5), he summarizes the 'Growth of the Athenian Empire' and its enemies' growing concern (1.89–117), and to explain this, more fundamental cause of the war, he has already presented the general diagnosis of essential factors in political history, especially imperial growth through seapower in the 'Archaeology' (1.2–19). He also tries to explain his method and magnifies the extent of his war (20–2; 1, 23). If he thinks of an epochal event, it is the end of Spartan involvement in Aegean power politics, the beginning of the Athenian hegemony (1.95–8), which provided, not coincidentally, the end of the historical progress of Herodotus' *Histories* (9.106). Thucydides' own war does not commence until book 2, after nearly one hundred pages. This approach reveals that Thucydides is obeying, although not stating, principles like those of Herodotus and Polybius. But since Herodotus had no predecessor for a full-scale history, the search for an ἀρχή, a beginning, was then more difficult. Painfully aware of the connectedness of events, he yet had to sever the web in order to make a beginning for his history.

There are many beginnings in Herodotus, but, as in reality, no one common beginning for all relevant events. A false start (1.1.1–1.5.1) reports a Persian version of the 'beginning of the hatred,' the ἀρχὴ τῆς ἐχθρῆς. Herodotus rejects this sterile and banal answer in a parody of Hecataean mythological investigation,[74] preferring to such silliness a man, a time, and an event more certain in *human* history (1.5.3), he who demonstrably initiated the series of injustices against the Greeks, Croesus. Thus he reacts to three existing conventions: he rejects the epic convention of beginning *in medias res* and the cosmological and theogonic convention of beginning 'in the beginning', and he curtails the logopoetic-genealogical convention of seeking mythical ancestors for historical persons. He has no sooner begun, however, with Croesus than he speaks of the pre-Croesus epoch (1.6.3), and, at 1.95, the reader finds himself at least two hundred years earlier among the 'Assyrians', c 1,000–750 BCE. The Egyptians convinced Herodotus of a chronological span for human history beyond the conception of most Greeks, for they told him of human kings eleven thousand years earlier (2.99.2–100.1), and of Heracles (2.43.4, 145.2) on earth seventeen thousand years before Amasis (the latter reigned c 569–26 BCE: 2.182, 3.1). Such chronological perspectives, however, hardly related to historical human events that he could verify in some way (τὰ γενόμενα ἐξ ἀνθρώπων).[75] I have no new answer to the vexing 'genetic' questions: when did Herodotus begin to write, what did he then write, and when did he 'realize' what in the end he would write, yet I believe one can fruitfully suggest the reasons for the shape of the final version.

The perceived need to find a clear basis for subsequent events drove Herodotus back to two decisive moments.[76] The shorter chain[77] led back to Athenian and Eretrian aid for the Ionian revolt, which calls forth the Homeric prhase 'the beginning of woes' (ἀρχὴ κακῶν, 5.97.3; *Iliad* 5.63, 11.604). This limited *arche* serves more as an historical and moral judgment (cf 5.28, where Ionian prosperity appears but a pause [ἄνεσις, conj] before a second era of troubles; 6.67.3) than as a universally agreed-upon starting-point. Herodotus himself obviously prefers the longer chain, the *arche* specified immediately after the travesty of the Persian antiquarians, λόγιοι, the strongly emphasized starting-point:[78] Croesus' policy of total and profitable subjugation – not another raid – of the Ionian Greeks (1.6.2–3). Herodotus deals with important, persistent kinds of change,[79] and the Lydian *logos* provides this for East-West conflict. This is the first independent *logos* in the text with beginning, end, and ethnographic survey.[80]

The self-sufficient unity of the Lydian *logos*, however, is subordinate to its function as an introduction to Herodotean historiography. This *logos* introduces the main conflict, the wars between barbarians and Greeks; and more generally the themes of the instability of human affairs and blindness to danger. It offers a preview of Herodotus' method and his understanding of history. The author labels Lydia 'first' chronologically, in terms of systematic injustice perpetrated against the Greeks.[81] Lydia provided a relevant test case, a complex of events significant for cultural exchange and political conflict, centrally located as buffer and conduit between the oriental powers and the Greeks. Once introduced in this *logos*, all these matters maintain their prominence in the narrative. Indeed, the persistence and pervasiveness of the theme of differing political structures leading to military conflict support the argument that the Lydian *logos* obtained its present elaboration after the general plan of the work had been determined, becoming, in part because of its initial position, a complex and unusually symbolic narrative.[82] It constitutes an exposition *in nuce* of one type of Herodotean causation, a key such as Thucydides offers in the 'Archaeology' (1.2–19).

Herodotus himself makes Croesus remark that Solon's words applied not only to himself but to the entire human race (ἐς ἅπαν τὸ ἀνθρώπινον, 1.86.5). The Lydian history is, however, more oblique than Thucydides' introduction, because it embodies particulars rather than historical general-izations (except for Solon's words), and because it does not impose an all-purpose interpretive theory of history. Herodotus is more wary of generalized explanations than Thucydides, who seems to expect to find *some* laws at work in human events. The Lydian history was fashioned into an ideal starting-point,[83] a historiographical convenience locating the events, the author, and his audience in time, space, and power relationships. It is a door through which the reader is made to pass, and he emerges with a new kind of insight – historical knowledge.

Herodotus has an interest in chronological problems,[84] but the importance of absolute dates and even sequence is subordinate to more compelling relationships.[85] Chronology does not explain anything: some current historians' obsession with it obscures the advantages that Herodotus gained at times by ignoring it. By not beginning at 'the beginning,' the historian (like a novelist) was able to commence with something more important, the Janus-figure Croesus, who pointed back to a free Ionia and forward to the inevitable conflict of Persia and the Greeks. Herodotus will compress 11,000 years, that is ninety per cent of his span of Egyptian history, into less than a page (2.100–101.1), yet allow five pages to Socles' speech on institutions, an obscure event to which he gives prominence (5.92) because it explains something essential about the Greeks.

Like all his successors, Herodotus does not always correlate historical time and literary time, either with reference to sequence or duration. For him, time does not determine events, time does not even always 'move forward,' as the Greek and English idiom has it. Of 'the great deeds accomplished by barbarians,' there were none in Egypt during those eleven thousand years (οὐδεμίαν ἔργων ἀπόδεξιν, 2.101.1). In that epoch *ta genomena* deserved, or – at best – encountered obscurity. Given enough time, anything *might* happen (5.9.3; cf 4.195.2), but little of what in fact had happened in Egypt during these many centuries requires his commemoration. Herodotus is very selective.[86]

The idea of analytical history or its invention by Herodotus was not inevitable. Commemoration of recent historical events was rare even in the late fifth century BCE. Unmistakable reflection of particular events in the recent past can be discovered in ceremonies for the founders of colonies (6.38.1; cf Thucydides 5.11.1), on a few issues of coin in Athens and in Syracuse, in a rare painting or sculpture (eg, the Stoa Poikile, statues of the Tyrannicides), and in private and public dedications (4.88, Mandrocles; 5.77, the Athenians' victory), but a preference for the general, the eternal, and the ideal dominated Greek art and thought well into the fourth century and beyond.[87] There exists no prior comprehensive attempt to explain or account for recent human actions in predominantly human terms.

The *Histories* embody inquiries and results intended as a possession for all time and constructed without much, or sometimes any, help from written sources.[88] While any contemporary scribbler can write some history of the Peloponnesian War, few historians have ever faced so thorough a lack of relevant written materials for the period they wished to record. Herodotus made the story of *past* events, rather than visible topography and creative genealogy, the best kind of 'history'. These events, moreover, are made to delimit the rest of the various kinds of information that he conveyed to his fellow Greeks. No one would expect the variety of information, biological, anthropological, and even geological, that Herodotus proffers after his explicit programmatic statement. When Dionysius asserts that τὸ γὰρ αὐτὸ προοίμιον καὶ ἀρχὴ καὶ τέλος ἐστὶ τῆς ἱστορίας, he means that Herodotus' proem encompasses all that a historian might consider germane, or less probably but not less usefully for this point, that the proem encompasses all that Herodotus' work contains, when understood properly.[89]

An ancient preface, as distinct from a proem, usually consists of more than a paragraph, a page, or even a modern chapter. It generally follows a sentence-long proem that 'shows the way' with the name of the author, an ethnic, the title of the work, its subject, and perhaps some remark on purpose. The preface thereafter introduces and explains the scope, background, intent and method of the work in hand. Two problems complicate the task of identifying the limits of Herodotus' preface: first, a 'running style' makes all division difficult, and second, the author nowhere states his theme in a manner sufficiently explicit for modern investigators to agree on. The proem apparently says too much or too little.[90]

The proem offers a prose imitation of the form and substance of epic proems; it voices the theme of great deeds and warfare, fear of oblivion (ἀκλεᾶ), connects itself to the first episode through a key word (αἰτίη/ αἴτιοι), and more ambitiously expresses Herodotus' belief that his efforts have produced something new, a permanent record of major events. He implicitly criticises both Homer and Hecataeus for disregarding the limits of reconstructing events far in the past (τῷ χρόνῳ ἐξίτηλα), and he implies that no one before has accounted for the recent past combining ethnography, geography, genealogy, and political-military events in a way that is adequate to the demands of both truth and art.[91] The proem defines the theme (in the ὡς μήτε clauses) broadly and then more specifically as Greek and barbarian achievements, especially their Great War. Its information about participants, subject, and the author's task is completed only at 1.5.3–4 with further elucidation and justification of the historian's scope, method, and intent.

Where ends the preface, post-proem matter introductory to the main string of narrative? In antiquity, the initial paragraph of a prose text functioned as the bibliographic data for the volumes, and, in this case, as the introduction of a new approach to past achievements, and as the first reminder of the problem of accurate knowledge of the past in the present. The two fragile bonds that connect past and present are said to be monuments and memory. This proem has immediately raised the problem of the survival of human knowledge and expressed the belief that even these two bonds will fail to fulfil their function unless ἀπόδεξις ἱστορίης intervenes. The preface first presents an inappropriate example of human tradition and explanation and then a proper and relevant counter-theory, first the tales of woman-stealing and then the history of Lydia.

Arguably the preface formally ends with the proem, when the aetiology of guilt offered by 'learned Persians' begins: 1.1.1. However, this view fails to distinguish the proem from the preface (in the way described above) and disregards the fact that the Persian story is an historian's parody of epic and popular explanations; it is to be discarded by the wary. It illustrates what the *Histories* will *not* purvey.[92] In fact, the woman-stealing of 1.1–5 is a false scent, a first lesson in how *not* to read reports, by which Herodotus showed his disdain for the inadequate explanatory processes of epic poetry, for the subjective sort of rationalization dear to Hecataeus, and for fictional, impossible chronological pseudo-precision.[93] Herodotus mocks the Greek predilection for linear patterns and for a single definite cause, often one man, of multiple and complex phenomena, which sometimes require complex explanations.

Folktales of woman-stealing appear to be part not of the proem but of the preface. All history is revisionism, even the first historian's first story! He encourages our caution by a witty but firm rejection of the tradition, and of trusting in charming 'historical' tales told by Greek and barbarian λογοποιοί.[94] Herodotus shoves these mythic stories aside (1.5.3) with a refusal even to pass judgment. He now returns to a synoptic recapitulation of what is to come: the story of the first man known for certain to have wronged the Greeks in a systematic way followed by the relevant historical narrative of both the small and great cities of men. The end of 1.5 (from τὸν δὲ οἶδα ...) completes the proem. Herodotus emphasizes the instability of fortune, a topic even dearer to later historians' proems (eg, Polybius 1.4.1–5).

Author, title, subject, and purpose provide the proem. Then the explanations and statements of others, followed by expressions of the author's disagreement or even contempt, and a counter-proposal give a standard sort of justification that subsequent ancient prose prefaces follow. Thus the Lydian *logos* opens the preface for a second time and in a better way.

Since Croesus is shunted aside for pre-history almost as soon as he appears (1.6), only with his reappearance did Herodotus go forward in chronological sequence with that story: προβήσομαι ἐς τὸ πρόσω τοῦ λόγου. Thus, 26.1 marks a recommencement of the *Histories'* promised narrative after a rapid survey (*prokataskeue*) of obscure 'earlier times,' and, when Solon lays out his views on human happiness (1.30–3), history can unfold in an intelligible manner. Solon's wisdom seems as close to Herodotus' world-view (eg, 1.5.4, 13.2) as any reported analysis that follows, but, typically enough in these *Histories*, Croesus – his audience – learns nothing. This human frailty provides another pattern for the reader alert to prefatory warnings and structures. He tells us the rules of the game and the limits to his assistance to the reader who must himself wrestle with knotty historical problems.

The mere outline of the events of Croesus' reign has been enriched by an historical logic and meaning. This enrichment of Lydian 'annals' justifies the chronological displacement of the Lydian *logos* (from 1.130.3, a cross reference; or 1.141.1). Only after Solon's visit and the death of Atys (1.46) does attention focus on Croesus' relationship to the Persians and the Greeks. Henceforth events are part of political history as well as dramatic and paradigmatic. Similarly, after his proem Thucydides includes prehistory in his introductory book as a paradigm of historical forces and an example of his new method, but also the previous 'fifty years,' and the events immediately preceding his chosen war.

I would therefore divide the proem from the preface, and the long preface from the main narrative as follows: the first break comes at the end of the first sentence which is the proem, the second at the end of 1.94. The long preface itself, a kind of prolegomena, then falls into four unequal sections: silly stories of the cause of the war (1.1–5); the prehistory and rise of Lydia, largely dramatic and paradigmatic tales (6–45); the account of the fall of Lydia to Persia (46–92); and the first ethnographic survey of a barbarian folk (93–94). The conclusion of the first part of the preface, 1.5.3–4, restates the proem's concern with initiating cause (πρῶτον ὑπάρξας) and great deeds (μεγάλα, ter), and offers the revised statement on method and the first appearance of the μνημ- root – remembrance. These clauses not only pick up the concerns of the proem, but, with the asyndeton at 1.6, allow a very different second beginning, the right historical background to the work, the history of Lydia.[95] Herodotus knows and will recollect and mention (ἐπιστάμενος ... ἐπιμνήσομαι) what is wanted.

The preface now presents the essential narrative of Croesus and his predecessors, and details the first involvement of Greeks with Lydians and Persians. The preface includes a mini-version of the rise and fall of empires and ends at 1.95, with the start of the history of Cyrus and the Persian nation. Herodotus has reached one of his vital concerns, the nature and growth of one of the leading combatants who came to fight the war between Greeks and barbarians. Half of the *Histories* is articulated by an organized account of the expansion of the Persian empire. The last third, the Hellenic defeat of Persian invaders, has an equally strongly marked first sentence, the ἀρχὴ κακῶν (5.97.3).

I would then propose that, in the final version, the prehistoric rapes and the entire story of Lydia provide the preface or introduction to the whole work (1.1–5.3 and 1.6–94).[96] The story of the Median empire, in contrast, is only one part of the prehistory of Persia, and the rest of book 1, including the birth, accession, conquests, and death of the semi-legendary Cyrus, provides a necessary account of the sudden rise of the Persian people to prominence. Few have considered all of book 1 to be a preface,[97] although we recall that Thucydides reserves 88 modern pages of type or one full book, and Polybius two books for events distantly and immediately prior to their subjects proper. Herodotus' central subject, being less clearly circumscribed, is harder to separate from its preface. Indeed, all of the work up to the Ionian revolt can be said to provide prefatory material necessary to understand the causes of the Helleno-Persian Wars, but by now the sane critic may think this analysis has yielded what fruit it will. Modern concepts of relevance, generic propriety, and topical division in a preface do not apply to Herodotus' achievement, but we have seen the plan undergirding the presentation of his first *logoi*.

Endings

'You've got to look for the *end* of everything, how it will turn out.'

Solon in the *Histories* 1.32.9*

Having surveyed inception in Herodotus' historiography, we turn to conclusions, especially to the last page preserved in all the complete manuscripts. Herodotus attends to 'archaeology' and 'teleology,' beginnings and endings in the historical process, and to effective presentation. Solon's speech to Croesus, generally recognized as reflecting upon the entire *Histories*, sums up human wisdom thus: σκοπέειν δὲ χρὴ παντὸς χρήματος τὴν τελευτὴν κῇ ἀποβήσεται (1.32.9*; cf 7.157.3*).[98]

Every ending begins something else in the *Histories*. Transition from one topic to another requires some stock-taking, a summary or pause, generally introduced by a phrase such as μὲν νῦν, μὲν δή, οὕτω μέν, and often exhibiting a pluperfect verb-form, eg, Λυδοὶ μὲν δὴ ὑπὸ Πέρσῃσι ἐδεδούλωντο (1.94.7, 'And so the Lydians had been conquered by the Persians ...').[99] The following phrase introduces the new protagonist, drawing the previous and the next topic into some meaningful relation.

Occasionally Herodotus leaves a topic with impatience because the story just related seemed fanciful or impossible to verify, or its telling has now begun to exceed its interest. In these cases, he dismisses the topic with a third-person imperative: χαιρέτω,[100] ἐχέτω,[101] or, most common, εἰρήσθω:[102] ταῦτα μὲν νῦν ἐπὶ τοσοῦτον εἰρήσθω. Six of the twelve examples concern myth, four, natural history. Only one is historical (Croesus) and one other describes a custom, the Magi's permission to kill any animal except dogs and men. He abruptly leaves this unseemly topic saying: 'Well, it's an ancient custom, so let them keep it' (1.140.3, de Sélincourt). This locution betrays more feeling than the usual εἴρηται, eg, 7.153.1: 'That's the story on the Argives,' but even that word can express engagement, eg, 2.120.5 on Troy's divine punishment: 'the story has been told as I see it.' These formulae of closure remind the reader of the author's presence and power, his control of what the audience can hear or see. They appear when stories ought to end or accounts are sufficiently full – in the author's opinion. Thucydides, by way of contrast, chops up events that are organically connected by his calendrical approach (eg, 2.68.9–69.1, 'so much happened during the summer; the following winter the Athenians ...').[103] This mechanical principle of the younger historian, however sound for chronology, is hard to follow and lacks any literary virtue. Herodotus' more natural manner, even if it be another artifice, enables a hearer to follow the account and a reader to apprehend the thread without constant cross-reference.

Herodotean endings sometimes consist of mechanical tags (eg, 4.82, 2.135.6), but more often mark an event's significance (1.214.5, 7.107.2, 8.13), emphatically present an event's final stage (eg, 1.45.3, 1.119.7), or – most common – summarize the previous action (eg, 1.14.1, τὴν μὲν νῦν δὴ τυραννίδα οὕτω ἔσχον οἱ Μερμνάδαι ...; cf 3.75.3). Even the crudest indication of closure, such as 'that's that' (4.82, τοῦτο μὲν νῦν τοιοῦτον ...) points forward, generally with a particle or another attached clause, such as here, 'and I'll proceed to the story I first promised to tell' (... ἀναβήσομαι δὲ ἐς τὸν κατ' ἀρχὰς ἦια λέξων λόγον). Thus some critics believe that Herodotus has not put the finishing touch to his work, because the annalistic formula that generally introduces information for the *following* year, 'nothing further happened in that year' (9.121), appears at the end where it presents an inelegant conclusion for the events reported.[104]

Since Thucydides' *History* lacks its last books and conclusion, the best elaborate prose conclusions to a series of events available for nearly contemporary parallels are the Athenian historian's evaluations of individuals,[105] and of the *pathos* experienced by the people of Ambracia, Mycalessus, and the Athenians in Sicily (3.113.6, 7.30.3, 7.87.4–6).[106] These passages stress the impossibility for the historian of obtaining accurate statistics, the immediately consequent panic and loss of confidence in the afflicted communities. Most of all they dwell on the shocking magnitude of the loss of life and able-bodied citizenry. The measured summary of the Sicilian debacle may be quoted: 'All of the enemy [the Athenians and their allies] were captured, no less than 7,000, although it is difficult to report with exactness. This was the greatest action (ἔργον ... μέγιστον) to occur in this war, indeed I at least think the greatest Hellenic deed that we know of even by report (ὧν ἀκοῇ Ἑλληνικῶν ἴσμεν), most glorious (λαμπρότατον) for the victors and most catastrophic for the destroyed. Conquered completely in every way and suffering horribly in all respects, both army and navy were totally wiped out, nothing and no one survived, so that few out of many ever journeyed back home.'

Such a highly wrought conclusion satisfies some ancient and many modern literary expectations. In Herodotus a different sort of closure prevails (call it 'archaic,' if you will), such as the quiet discussion of *aristeia* and the epigrams that follow upon the last day at Thermopylae (7.226–8). A less well known example is found in Lampon the Aeginetan's praise of Pausanias' achievement at Plataea which functions as part of an epilogue after the battle (9.78–9*). Lampon states, 'Son of Cleombrotus, you have accomplished a deed of miraculous greatness and nobility (ἔργον ... ὑπερφυὲς μέγαθός τε καὶ κάλλος), and, for defending Hellas, god granted to you to store away the greatest reputation for valour (κλέος μέγιστον) of any Greek of whom we know (τῶν ἡμεῖς ἴδμεν).' The greatest deed, the greatest deserved fame, the limiting clause ('limits of knowledge') that rather curiously magnifies the thought – these elements occur in both epilogues. The reflections of the participants estimate the achievement and echo the author's own high opinion of Pausanias (9.64), one that here ignores later allegations of treason (8.3.2).[107] This technique also encourages the reader to estimate for himself the meaning of what he has read.

That meaning includes both magnitude of effort expended and moral values. After praising the victor, Lampon suggests revenge, *tisis* in the form of decapitating Mardonius in return for the decapitation of Leonidas. The idea is described as sacrilegious and 'barbaric' by Pausanias and Herodotus, for the true *tisis* was the Greek victory itself. Such atrocities would make the Greeks no better than their enemies. This colloquy, consisting of praise and a reply worthy of even greater praise, offered Herodotus another chance to underscore an important aspect of Greek superiority (not always observed, of course), the recognition of limit, the decent treatment of the defeated.

Since Herodotus compares and evaluates events and offers explicit judgments more frequently than Thucydides, why did he not close his narrative by restating the awesome and unparalleled magnitude of his war, an assertion elaborated at 7.20.2–21 (στόλων ... τῶν ἡμεῖς ἴδμεν πολλῷ δὴ μέγιστος οὗτος ἐγένετο)? The answer may lie in the proper identification of his subject as well as in an unbombastic style that avoided flashy and explicit finales. That subject was not originally – or later – only the Persian wars themselves, but human achievements, the great and marvellous deeds of Greeks and barbarians, especially the reason why they came to war against each other. If he had focused attention on the combat at the very end, he would have deprived the longer description of the combatants' cultures and societies of its determinative role and due honour.

The evidence suggests that the *Histories* reach their intended term, although the hypothesis cannot be proven. The story of the wife of Masistes, a harem-intrigue of lust, mutilation, and death, balances in its penultimate placement the 'peninitial' story of the wife of Gyges. Both dramatic tales of arbitrary despots test the fidelity of the men's dearest 'friends,' both involve persons whose bad end the author certifies, both stories are stained with fear, a laughable yet tragic freedom of choice, and an enforced compliance.[108]

Outside these two frightening palace narratives providing implicit contrasts to the generally milder mores of Greeks when free from despots (but see 5.87; 9.5, 120.4 on Athenian atrocities) are the initial accounts of contact and injustice between Europe and Asia, and the final revenge visited on the arch-polluter of Greek holy property, Artaÿctes (9.116.1). The despot's agent is caught and crucified for his crimes by the Greeks, once the continents are properly cut asunder. He dies at the end of the *Histories* in the very spot where Protesilaus long before had been the first European victim of Asiatic weaponry. Here began international and even inter-continental warfare, exactly where Xerxes later constructed his sacrilegious bridges. Artaÿctes furnishes the concluding paradigm of the abuse of power that Persian social structure encourages. Balance is restored, as another circle closes on itself.[109] One cycle of transgression is complete, another began with the entry of Athens into Asiatic affairs on land and sea. From 479 on, they claimed that the peoples of the litoral of Asia Minor were theirs to worry over, counsel, organize, and defend (9.106.3). For an East Greek writing in the 440's and later, this moment marked the end of the previous epoch and the beginning of the present one.

Wilamowitz believed that the *Histories* 'must' have continued down to the founding of the Delian League. This idea has become one of the curiosities of scholarship, because, although 'in abstracto ist ja alles möglich' (Meyer), the evidence from Herodotus' style and from other narratives argues that nothing more should be expected.[110] The brevity and military unimportance of the Artaÿctes/Protesilaus episode dissatisfies rhetoricians, because the seeming absence of a concluding epochal event to provide a definitive literary climax, a summary that would allow no further attachment, distresses modern notions of closure. No ancient critic, however, voiced a similar complaint. In fact, this last scene in the historical progress does mark an epochal moment in the warfare of the continents, as we have argued above. Below we consider the very last chapter, an epilogue.

Although Herodotus ended his story at the year 479/8 BCE and Thucydides reached back to the same date for a beginning, the fifth-century Ionian knew well that Mycale marked merely the beginning of a series of wars against the Persian Empire: 'And thus for the second time Ionia revolted from the Persians' (9.104). The full and final story of these wars cannot be read in his pages. The year 479 was less a limit than a pause, although the momentum of victory did produce a change in the nature of the continental conflict. Artemisia wryly remarks to Xerxes: 'While you and your house live on, the Greeks will often contest with you over their own fate' (8.102.3*). Eurybiades the Spartan and Herodotus (8.108.4; 8.3.2) refer prospectively to further fighting against the Persians for Asiatic possessions. Herodotus had earlier mentioned Persian outposts in Europe in a manner that indicates that he had no desire to expatiate on their long survival or capture (7.106–7). The thinker who connected the three generations from Darius to Artaxerxes, from 522 to 424 BCE, emphatically and explicitly eschewed false periodizations and clean boundaries to history, although his account required some signposts.[111]

No reason urges belief that Herodotus intended to narrate the capture of

Byzantium, Pausanias' odd behaviour, or the founding of the Delian League. If one concurs with Pohlenz' judgment that 'we have no true conclusion [to the action] in form or in substance, such as we have a right to expect from Herodotus' entire literary technique,' he must answer Immerwahr's question, 'How else should Herodotus have put this idea [sc., of the unbroken continuity of warfare and hostile diplomacy?]'[112] Another form of the end to this narrative can be conjectured, but Herodotus' solution has a historical and literary logic. He ended his sequence of events after a moral climax, an event chosen for artistic and symbolic reasons but 'not unscientific' either. Grote, Meyer, the *Cambridge Ancient History*, and Burn, to mention a few, follow his example. *Persia and the Greeks* devotes only eleven pages to the next forty years of Asiatic-Greek relations, a paucity justified not by the brevity of Herodotus' and Thucydides' accounts, but by a significant alteration in the nature of the conflict.

The actions of the greatest campaign in history end with the Greeks returning home with their booty (9.121), but the *apodexis* ends one chapter later, with Cyrus' advice for the Persians, to choose hardship so as to rule others or learn a life of ease so as to become slaves. Cyrus is not the first ruler in the *Histories*, but in the opinion of Herodotus, it was his thorough subjugation of Asia Minor that made a decisive struggle between old Greece and much of Asia inevitable. So, the choice posed in the Epilogue for the Persians between freedom and hardship on the one hand and slavery and luxury on the other, returns to the theme of freedom and to the 'first initiator of unjust acts (1.5.3) committed against the Greeks,' the distant origin of a long and connected series of wars.

This epilogue, the very last paragraph in the *Histories*, narrates Cyrus' pessimistic projection about the Persians, if they should ever leave their harsh and infertile homeland. This paragraph eloquently echoes many choices, decisions, and events, and concludes the work. The punishment of Artaÿctes is retailed just before Cyrus makes this final appearance. Since Artaÿctes' ancestor, Artembares, serves as Cyrus' interlocutor,[113] we may be confident that these two stories were meant to appear together. They both deal with self-indulgence and imperialism: the incompatibility of such qualities. The words are presented as an historical prediction, but literary placement makes them retrospective for author and reader. As the opening pages go back in time but look forward to the Persian Wars, so the ending, having advanced to 479 BCE, looks back momentarily in order to intimate how the Persians reached their present predicament. It recapitulates what has preceded by drawing on a reservoir of meaning created by the thousands of particulars that the reader has absorbed.

Cyrus, furthermore, endorses the Sophistic doctrine of environmental determinism that Herodotus has presented more than once. Like Darius' ghost in Aeschylus' *Persae*, or Croesus and Psammenitus after they cease ruling, Cyrus is now available to speak wisdom in the *Histories'* last retrospect. He advises his fellow Persians to avoid gentle climates and fruitful soils insofar as living there (not ruling such lands) would threaten the Persian martial way of life and national character. The Persians, however, did come to enjoy leisure and luxuries whose fruits included the degeneration of Persian courage (cf 1.133.3–4, 135; 3.20.1–22, Cambyses' seductive gifts to the Ethiopian king, and his reaction). Sandanis had noted with a caution for Croesus the rude, poor, but manly life of the Persians under Cyrus (1.71.2*; cf 71.4, 89.2*). Demaratus and Tritantaechmes praise the Greeks for poverty enforced by nature and seconded by a noble indifference to material wealth, the commodities of luxury (7.102.1*; 8.26.3*). Croesus himself advises his master Cyrus to end the threat of future Lydian uprisings by feminizing the Lydians: encourage effeminate undergarments, education in music, unwarlike occupations, and the joys of civilian life (1.155.4*). His advice about how to make men soft (and servile) is the complement to Cyrus' on how to keep them hard (and free).

Herodotus believed that the Persians lost their freedom-loving and manly qualities and sank into luxury and self-indulgent frivolity (7.135, 210.2; 8.68α1*, 88.3; 9.82.3*; cf 7.102* with its recognition of πενίη), Xerxes their monarch not least (cf 9.82, 108–13). The *Histories* thus end with Cyrus' prognostic because the defeat of oriental expansion and megalomania, not the growth of Hellenic power, constituted Herodotus' concern and goal.[114] The Greeks, Herodotus has implied, were the agents of an eternal balance as well as a determined and intelligent people fighting for freedom. No land or man can monopolize all the advantages of life (9.122.3*, 1.32.6*). The more power and goods an individual or a nation acquires, the more numerous the seeds of degeneration and destruction. In Cyrus' day, the Persians had chosen a hard life and achieved a ruling power.[115] Their success was so great that their desires, when no limit seemed to apply, were bound to meet disaster.

As Xerxes' empire declines, Greek power ascends; the *kyklos* (1.207.2) thus revolves. Yet, even for Xerxes, life continues; the sorry tale of the wife and daughter of his brother Masistes points to the unhappy future and the assassination of the despot, but leaves it unsaid. Similarly, Herodotus shrouds Pausanias' future after Plataea and the plans of Pericles' father after the capture of Sestos. This avoidance of explicit discussion of the major issues posed by Athenian imperialism results not from a prejudice in favor of that nation's enforcing its will on others[116] – something contrary to the entire tenor of the *Histories* – but from a willingness to let his readers apply the lessons that he has offered. His silence speaks volumes. The Persian invasions had ended, but 'the deeds of men, both Greek and barbarian' and their tragic mistakes continued with only a barely perceptible shudder of the wheel on the axle.

Therefore, we believe that the epilogue with Cyrus is in its proper place serving its intended function.[117] It provides a resting-place with a dramatic anecdote. It would be hard to explain what it is doing here, if it is not meant to end the book. It balances the opening statement of Herodotus in its brevity and its long view of human efforts, and it magisterially confirms central themes: the positive values of liberty, modest homelands, and minding one's own business; the negative lessons of the blindness of humans in the face of temptation, the unavoidability of doing and suffering wrong, and the ubiquity of imperialist ambitions. The story of imperialism's latest and most spectacular, if momentary demise, the object-lesson that the Persians furnished, stops ironically with the recipe for success offered by their founding hero. His advice was ignored and Herodotus suggests that such advice always will be.

The preface promised to explain the fundamental cause of the Helleno-Persian conflict. The entire narrative contained in the *Histories*, minus the two invasions themselves, constitutes the answer, although not in the form of a single explanatory cause, or series of causes. The last 'legendary' paragraph offers that cause, not by logical argument or synoptic analysis, but by an anecdotal recapitulation of leading themes. Wealth and despotism may extend and multiply material goods and human subjects – in short, power – but they also corrupt and eventually destroy the individuals and communities that enjoy them. Xerxes' attack was a monstrous injustice committed against substantially innocent men. The attack itself captured the Greek imagination, but the even more important cause of that attack (αἰτίη) – though less glorious for the Greeks – not only continued to operate *on* the Greeks but also, once Xerxes was put on the defensive, began to operate *in* the Greeks. The αἰτίη, therefore and then, transcended Greek self-satisfaction and invited the consideration of all men. The examination of the concepts of limit, polarity, and narrative patterning in part 3 will substantiate this assertion.

Conclusion

Ἀπόδεξις ἱστορίης, 'the presentation of [the results of] research,' in this text has been found to mean the author's own creative shaping of the past, what he has discovered of men, their past deeds, their beliefs and habits in other times and places. As with the comparable *apodexis* that kings presented, deeds and monumental structures (eg, 1.207.7; 2.101–2; 2.148.2), such activity justifies personal pride and offers a way to escape merely provincial recognition and a transitory mortality. *Nomos* is king of all (3.38.4; cf 7.152.2) – except that he who knows this truth is already semi-detached from the shackles of his society. The privileged few include Herodotus and anyone willing to be liberated by his work from the tyranny of parochial values.[118] Those who know many *nomoi*, not one *nomos*, may preserve independent judgment. The arbitrariness and diversity of *nomoi* do not in themselves invalidate them, as Herodotus understood better than some Sophists, because each set functions admirably for its community. He does not disparage divergence. Indeed, Herodotus believed that preserving this very variety, conserving human diversity and its consequent frictions, promoted the desirable survival of free men and institutions. The autonomy of a nation and the rule of law rather than men were his two touchstones of admiration in the sphere of human political life. Disunity and even internal political strife and military insubordination sometimes promoted European liberty (see chapter 8). Maintenance of local identity, achieved through local autonomy, therefore benefited the human collectivity.

In addition, he considered the establishment of personal repute among men, κλέος, a worthy goal (Proem, 7.220.2,4; 9.78.2*). Herodotus' ἀπόδεξις ἱστορίης like the ἀπόδεξις ἔργων of kings, created a memorial that transcended transience and mortality and separated him from ordinary men and from those 328 deedless, therefore nameless, Egyptian kings (2.101.1). His glory may even be superior, since the fame of great kings also is obliterated, unless a Herodotus appears to point it out. Herodotus supplied for the recent past what epic had done for the distant past: commemoration of outstanding human achievements.[119]

Herodotus recorded the greatest trauma that the Greek people had ever known, an attack that threatened their political independence and social fabric. He values and therefore highlights in his story some of the very qualities that were endangered. These include spiritual freedom, interest in free inquiry, a relativist perspective on human institutions, inquisitiveness about the limits of human moral and physical endurance, and a respect for human dignity, law, and liberty in the face of overwhelming temptation and force. The traumatic disturbance created the desire to memorialize the combatants and their worlds. Herodotus then invented a structured, analytical form of non-fiction, history, a worthy literary means to preserve that evanescent record. Like one of his minor but memorable characters, Herodotus saved the precious object, and now reveals and displays his large and well-shaped charge to us (1.112.1, ἐκκαλύψας ἀπεδείκνυε ... μέγα τε καὶ εὐειδές).

The Presentation of
His Research:
The Historian's Power

INTRODUCTION TO PART TWO

Historical truth remains an elusive abstraction for working historians, except as an intellectual standard to which all allege fealty. The historical-critical method, not to mention current philosophical and literary movements such as phenomenology, hermeneutics, and deconstructionism, realizes that different generations need, or will recognize, different accounts of the past as well as different interpretations. The invention of historical consciousness may justify our according to Herodotus the epithet 'genius,' but students of Greek historiography and Western thought may reasonably desire a detailed analysis of his method, an explanation of the epistemological sophistication that can be alleged for a work that others have found to embody an apparently naive and uncritical method of jotting down stories.

Part 1 looked at the invention of a new literary genre, dependent necessarily on prehistoric conventions of story-telling as well as on more recent Homeric epic, yet seriously attempting to produce a veridical record of the recent past. Explicit remarks of the author about investigating the past as well as his conscious method and unconscious habits presented a wealth of methodological material to explicate.

This part considers the historian's treatment of issues of truth, reliability, and accuracy. Beginning again with explicit remarks about intentional omissions, controversies among his informants, and his own disagreements with written sources, we inventory all instances of explicit remarks and discuss the principles that govern their appearance. This part argues that Herodotus developed a novel way of co-ordinating accounts of real events under *appropriate* conceptions of truth, given the essential and unavoidable fact that the events that he wished to preserve had occurred in the past. The result of his new method for recovering the past – a self-disciplined collection, selection, and presentation of recent facts, and a self-conscious clarifying of recollection – was the creation of a secular meaning for mankind's immediate past.

These chapters will demonstrate the character of his method,[1] some procedures of his research that refute the idea that his work is a hodge-podge of oral reports and an undiscriminating application of the religious clichés of the archaic era. He did not often claim that he had found the only true account, and he invited the reader's participation in the search for what actually happened. The past offers a bristling resistance to the present, mesmerized by its own concerns. This open-ended approach is less arbitrary, less cerebral than Thucydides' but not for that reason inferior. Rather than finding universal laws, he savours singularity, he remains planted in concrete particulars while he organizes opinions and discussable issues. This polyphonic largesse signals a tolerant recognition of the irremediable subjectivity of human knowledge and his willingness to work with relativism without abandoning the realm of experience and knowledge. Although the intrinsic laws of his new literary subject and his new interpretation of human experience often remain tantalizingly implicit or even slippery, analysis and synthesis of contemporary accounts of past events are integral concerns, not an occasional aside. As he says about a particular problem where information is sketchy, he wishes to learn that which can be known from the evidence available: θέλων δὲ τούτων πέρι σαφές τι εἰδέναι ἐξ ὧν οἷόν τε [ἐστιν] (2.44.1).

No one can make explicit all Herodotus' assumptions and principles, because he never supplied a comprehensive statement of method; moreover the scattered indications that do appear are not only prone to misinterpretation but are also liable to be regarded as inapplicable to the whole work or even to the passage in which they appear. Would Herodotus have preferred to be considered dishonest, incompetent, or unconscious of historiographical issues? It is the rare historiographer who recognizes that Thucydides and later historians only elaborated the fundamentals of historical criticism already implicit and sometimes explicit in the *Histories*.[2]

Three times he states, guarding himself against a charge of gullibility, that he reports what he heard without necessarily believing a word of it (2.123.1; 4.195.2; 7.152.3). These explicitly programmatic caveats in a long and pluriform text are sometimes ignored, sometimes used to imply that he recorded all that he was told and that he served as a mindless stenographer for his more than three hundred listed informants. Here we thoroughly refute the last notion by discussing his explicit omissions (chapter 2) and justify, on good historiographical grounds, his inclusion of alternative versions (chapter 3). The last chapter of this part (chapter 4) explains the inherited Greek conventions for literary controversy and some new rules for taking issue with the opinions of others about past events and present customs.

These studies of his data are not exhaustive; for instance, no analytical survey of his travels or of his use of inscriptional evidence appears. Further, I include no tabulation and analysis of his recording of his sources' ethnics, 'statistics,' and other uses of numbers, or the word *logos*, which often indicates self-reflexive comments or methodological problems. These worthy issues have been treated by others, as the notes indicate, and they are peripheral to the present concern, which is to demonstrate the author's exceptional desire to discover and communicate the best available current versions of past events, and to document the originality and thoroughness of his presentation.

His modes of determining historical truth and of distinguishing the knowable from the merely probable, the improbable, and the demonstrably false, and his techniques for separating deceptive and self-justifying statements from objective ones are pre-formal, in that no theorist of historiography preceded him and provided rules. His standards, however, are neither unpredictable nor irregular nor plainly shared by his contemporaries, so we cannot call his method unformed or informal or the common property of his generation. To an unexpected degree, archaeological progress in the Orient and in Greece has confirmed the named individuals, the topography, and the institutions that he has reported, although naturally his dependability and accuracy decline the further from him in time and space his subjects recede. His dedication to personal observation, verification, sceptical questions, and predominantly human explanations produced a shrewd exercise in impure historical reasoning.

Nevertheless, when available information is distant in time or space from the person or thing to be described, the historian's tools are limited.[3] Herodotus utilized a self-conscious method of critique and independent verification (γνώμη καὶ ἱστορίη, 2.99.1), whenever possible, but often he could do little more than report and express doubt on traditions, even *prima facie* fabulous accounts of far-distant phenomena (eg, 2.123.1; 3.9, 116.2; 4.16.1–2, 25; 6.137; 7.15, 152). Insofar as the continuous narrative of Xerxes' invasion described events of a half-century earlier, oral and written accounts had to predominate in the exposition over personal experience with the data. Even so, Herodotus has more ways than have yet been explored for distinguishing trustworthy information from unreliable rumour. As opportunities for *opsis* decreased, explicit omissions, alternative versions, disagreement with sources indicated by first-person pronouns and verbs, particles and adverbs of doubt, and (as we saw in chapter 1) other distancing techniques such as direct speech and authorial words of warning (*gnome, doxa*, etc) provided a supple set of procedures for indicating reserve, caution, or disbelief.

Herodotus and Thucydides, in their legitimate reaction to the speculative ruminations of philosophers and fabulists, overrated the significance of autopsy for determining the facts of history. The method has inherently crippling limitations for investigating times gone by.[4] The later historian, seeking constants in human behaviour and political processes, abandoned the field of early history as insufficiently knowable and, in any case and for various reasons, it was not what he really cared to report and analyse. The earlier historian was motivated by a different concern. He wanted to save witnessed fact from being sentimentalized, universalized, ornamented so as to be turned into epic poetry. The Greeks would seek to transfer those deeds to some realm beyond history, more exalted and perfect than that irregular, gritty, quarrelsome one recorded by the conflicting testimony of the participants. Often in his account, noble achievements result from base motives, and one action presents two faces, as different communities report it. Impelled by his desire to record the accomplishments of the previous generation, he developed a method that tested assertions when it could and recorded untestable assertions where it had to, complete with warnings to the reader. Herodotus the historian closes in on, and distances himself from, events and their reporters.

This method, alternately empirical and transcriptional, produced the first coherent vision, based on historical data, of the human condition in various places and times. The *Histories* were also, when finished, the longest and, perhaps, the most difficult and original book ever written in Greek, an intellectual anomaly that has invited both the appreciation and the misunderstanding of posterity. For the moment, it will be enough to analyse some of these essential innovations, and later (in chapter 10) we shall consider his differences from later historians.

2

Selection: Explicit Omission

The previous chapter sketched Herodotus' conception of the nature of both his investigations and of the writing of history. Every historian defines a field of inquiry, and Herodotus observes an economy of scope for the sake of his thesis. Studies have discussed what he thinks deserving of inclusion,[1] but none has yet explored what Herodotus does *not* report, where and why he is reticent, or why he consciously obliterates the memory of certain actions. There are two main categories. On the one hand, the historian's powers of *apodexis* are limited by evidence and ignorance; on the other, sometimes he chooses not to record information, impelled by disinclination to report religious matters, by a judgment of historiographical insignificance or distaste for repetition, or by moral aversion to commemorating a wicked person. Explicit silence on the author's part helps to define what he considers necessary and proper to discuss.

The investigation of Herodotus' scope is hampered by the obscurities of his principles. Unlike Thucydides (1.22) or Polybius (12.25e), he rarely makes explicit his methodology, with the exception of the repeated statement, that he will report what he was told without necessarily believing it (2.123.1; 2.130.2; 4.173; 4.195.2; 6.137.1; 7.152.3).[2] One properly does not expect to hear, however, everything that the investigator was told;[3] nor did he learn all that he wished to. At 2.19 he reports having questioned priests and others about the unique properties of the Nile river. His eagerness (*prothymos*) and careful inquiry (*historeon*) were here in vain, although elsewhere his careful investigation (ἐπιμελὲς γὰρ δή μοι, 2.150.2) brought him satisfactory, if incorrect, results.

The usual approach to investigating Herodotus' selectivity is to examine what he does choose to tell the reader and why: *Erga megala te kai thomasta*, 'great and wonderful achievements.' Croesus' *krater* is 'worthy of remembrance' (1.14.1), the Greek temples of Ephesus and Samos 'deserve record' (2.148.2), certain deeds of Alyattes the Lydian and Cyrus the Persian and the nature of two Egyptian temples 'deserve recounting' (1.16.2; 1.177; 2.99.4; 2.137.5).[4] Of Cyrus, Herodotus informs us that he will omit hagiographical accounts and many minor campaigns in order to focus on the reliable histories and most noteworthy campaigns. Three times, with regard to this figure of legend, Herodotus excuses himself from telling all that he had heard (1.95.1, 177, 214.5).

After the proem, the main subjects and theme need not be stated again. Herodotus' inclusiveness threatens any modern attempt to abstract his subject. Nevertheless, Greek and barbarian events, achievements and conflict – the stated range – do not prepare us for the actual breadth of coverage or for any particular lacuna. His comprehensiveness, asserted at 1.5.3 when he promises to 'touch on small and large cities alike,' reflects, on the one hand, his cyclical view of history, and, on the other, a subversive willingness to find significance in what might not seem important to his contemporaries or posterity. A list of relevant topics cannot be surmised from programmatic statements but can be deduced from the text.

Why does Herodotus neglect the relevant history and conquest of Phoenicia?[5] The omission of certain other important subjects can be justified by their irrelevance to the immediate purpose, such as the absence of the interesting histories of Etruria and Carthage, two western barbarian powers that threatened Greek interests, or the history of Ionian colonization. Punic matters are slighted throughout, a consequence perhaps of Herodotus' travels, or their inclusion may have been perceived as a threat to the *Histories'* centre of gravity. Two relevant and major epochs of East-West conflict, the Trojan War and Greco-Persian relations after 479, are minimized or ignored, one because it precedes 'human' history, the other because it follows the date at which Herodotus chose to end his work. All these topics interested Herodotus, but the economy of his narrative impels him to curtail or exclude a full consideration of them.

One cannot compile a list of the *inexplicit* omissions in Herodotus.[6] Frequently he briefly glides over topics not immediately germane to his conception of his subject, such as Croesus' alliances with states other than Sparta (1.77.1–3, 82.1), his conquests of Asiatic Greek communities other than Ephesus (1.26.3), his subsequent acts of state until Cyrus became a threat (cf 1.46.1). When Athens first enters the *Histories*, he forbears to mention many details of Athenian constitutional history that he will relate subsequently (1.59–64).

The following pages proceed in another direction and will consider what Herodotus explicitly omits. The two main categories consist of omissions forced on the author by his method and matters that he prefers to leave out of his narrative. The former category is a consequence of the information currently available and needful; the latter category contains subjects inherently incapable of investigation, or excessively trivial, or purposefully excluded to deny them commemoration.

Research Problems

Ignorance Universal[7]

Herodotus is interested in boundaries: physical, political, and epistemological. In his geographical researches in every direction, he comes to points beyond which informants are no longer helpful, beyond which answers to his questions are no longer reliable. South of Ethiopia, east of India, north of the Borysthenes, or west of Gibraltar, all is, at best, conjecture. The source of the Nile or the Borysthenes cannot be determined. For instance, Herodotus submits concerning the Nile: 'These facts concerning the river are what I could find after having conducted my investigations as far as possible' (2.34.1; sim 4.16.2). For the names and boundaries of the continents he can find no explanation or account (4.45.2), but he seems to hold current Hellenic ideas on the subject in the same contempt that he shows for Hellenic views on Egypt (2.45.2). Books 2 and 4, since they are the richest in geographical research, contain most of the admissions of despair, typified by his outburst on Europe: 'Europe is clearly understood by no one, in particular whether it is surrounded by water to the west or the north' (4.45.1). When he does not have eye-witness information on geography, he will not comment on the veracity of his account (2.29.1; 3.115.2; 4.16.1: the only uses of αὐτόπτης, 'eye-witness,' other than two in direct speech). A similar caution, not always observed (2.66; 3.101.2, 107.2; 4.30), is evident in his zoology (2.73; 3.105.1, 116.2; 4.25.1, 192.3): τοσαῦτα μέν νυν θηρία, ... ὅσον ἡμεῖς ἱστορέοντες ἐπὶ μακρότατον οἷοί τε ἐγενόμεθα ἐξικέσθαι.[8]

Certain passages in which ignorance is admitted need further clarification. In 2.126.1, Herodotus confides that the priests 'did not indeed (δή) tell the exact price (γέ)' which the daughter of hated Cheops charged for prostituting her body to all and sundry. Here ignorance is a transparent mask for utter disbelief in the story. Occasionally he expresses a willingness to mention – at least for consideration – any tradition that he wants for his narrative: of Timoxenus' treachery, he says (8.128.1): 'How he conspired with Artabazus, I at least cannot say – for there is no story reported – but the following was the upshot.' At other times, he will admit ignorance but hazard a guess, for instance, on a distribution of booty to the best warriors after Plataea

(9.81.2; *sim* 8.133). At 9.32.2, Herodotus notes that no one knew, because no one had counted, Mardonius' Greek allies at Plataea. Although he conjectures fifty thousand, one should note that Herodotus declines to offer information without some basis in evidence or report. Herodotus always likes to describe as well as list, to give a context as well as a name. This is his method and his style. When the data do not permit, the method prescribes a note to that effect, and his technique admits the occasional acknowledgment that his sources are silent. In accounts of recent history, the effort to be precise is serious; in his reportage of folk-tales and popular legend, the seeming precision is the pseudo-precision of fiction, a lively and innocent diversion. A Herodotean confession of ignorance, then, may serve rhetorical as well as epistemological purposes.

Certainty Impossible

More frequent than confessions of complete ignorance are those of uncertainty. Some things men perhaps know, but not beyond doubt or not with exactness. Herodotus is cautious, the very opposite of gullible, although, unlike Thucydides (and perhaps Hecataeus), he refuses to lose the *logos* because of confidence in his own *a priori* views (eg, see on Scyllias the diver, 8.8.2). The *logos* itself is part of *ta genomena*, human events and ideas deserving of preservation, cultural artifacts. His world is full of wonders; Hecataeus' mistrust can be more damaging to historical science than Herodotus' willingness to hear or be shown. Most instances of uncertainty pertain to geography or ethnography. A good example is provided by the untestable accounts of the source of the Nile's waters (2.20.1–23). At other times, Herodotus acknowledges a lack of relevant 'hard' or 'soft' historical information. For instance, he cannot calculate the numbers of Scythia's population or relate from any source the size of the contingents of Xerxes' army (4.81.1; 7.60.1; cf 2.75.1). In calculating the total manpower of Xerxes' invasion, he diffidently states (7.185.1, cf 9.32.2;): 'One must offer a guess.' Elsewhere he reports an absence of dependable data, caused by the passage of time: the language of the Pelasgians or the antecedents of Isagoras (1.57.1; οὐκ ἔχω φράσαι, 5.66.1). On occasion he implies that partisanship in his informants precluded the historian's proper judgment: why did the Aeginetans not fight the Athenians? or which Ionian contingents were brave at Lade? (5.86.2; 6.14.1; cf 6.82.1, the story of Cleomenes in Argos; 6.137.1, the Pelasgian expulsion). Sometimes, he grants the inaccessibility of a man's motives (7.54.3, Xerxes' sacrifice at the Hellespont), or a lacuna in the record (1.160.2, the price to be paid for Aristodicus; 7.26.2, the victorious commander at Sardis in a competition among army units).

εἰδέναι ἀτρεκέως, 'to know with certainty', is most desirable, but on the 54 occasions when ἀτρεκ- words appear, most often Herodotus signifies the limits of his certainty. North of the Ister, nothing certain is known (5.9.1). Was Cleomenes truthful? Who of the Athenians sent the signal at Marathon? No one knows. In the case of Mardonius' body (9.84.1–2), Herodotus could not learn who really buried it, although he heard that many already had made the claim and knew that many had been rewarded for it.

At times, in passages obviously emphatic, certainty is asserted.[9] Herodotus contrasts the period of Egyptian history before Psammetichus – that is, before the arrival of the Greeks – conveyed to him by the priests, to that period about which 'we know all with certainty' (2.154.4). The inquiring reporter must always fear informants speaking *ad maiorem Aegyptiorum gloriam* or those glad to find a dupe: the Saite temple treasurer 'saying he knew with certainty [the source of the Nile] seemed, to me at least, to be joking' (παίζειν, 2.28.2).[10] At 1.140.1, in a discussion of Persian custom, Herodotus explicitly moves from the known to the unknown. On occasion, he emphatically rejects accounts: '*Me* they do not persuade saying this [about men briefly becoming wolves], but they certainly do say it and they swear it up and down' (4.105.2). At 6.43.3, Herodotus counterattacks those who rejected the report that Otanes called for 'democracy' (3.80.1). He provides a 'greatest marvel' for his opponents to digest, the brute fact that the Persians through Mardonius did establish democracies in Ionia after the rebellion. The logic is unsatisfactory, but the polemical point and method are noteworthy: the truth about past events can be found by argument. Circumspection about knowledge of the past can lead to trustworthy results.

Non Constat *at Present*

Overlapping the category of the insufficiency of evidence conscientiously sought out, the category of topics dismissed as unsuitable for further research at present deserves attention. This indication most often betrays Herodotus' disbelief in the matter at hand. The prototypical passage is his leave-taking of the legendary rape and counter-rape tales: οὐκ ἔρχομαι ἐρέων, 'I'll say no more' (1.5.3). Consonant, however, with the principled rejection of Greek mythology (eg, 4.36.1) is his impatience with Minos and any others who precede 'the properly denominated age of men [3.122.2; cf 2.15.3] among whom Polycrates was first to conceive of a thalassocracy.' Twice he bids adieu, χαιρέτω, to unprofitable topics (2.117, Homer and the Cypria; 4.96.2, Salmoxis' nature). More often, he plainly indicates the incredibility of a story, such as that of the Phoenix (ἐμοὶ μὲν οὐ πιστὰ λέγοντες, 2.73.3),[11] or he suggests doubts, for instance, whether Helen was the cause of the Trojan War, or whether the Phoenicians circumnavigated Africa (2.120.3; 4.42.4). Even though *non constat* is often his historical judgment on them, a conscientious investigator may report sundry folktales and curious accounts (2.123.1; 2.130.2; 4.173; 4.195.2; 6.137.1; 7.152.3). He has numerous ways of dissociating himself from fantastic stories,[12] including expressions of uncertainty (4.187.3, an unlikely nostrum), ascription of views to others, sometimes with an ironical δῆθεν to expose error (eg, 9.80.3, fool's gold) or an ironical δή (4.191.4, ὡς δὴ λέγονταί γε ὑπὸ Λιβύων). Elsewhere the author grants permission to believe at will (2.146.1 on Dionysus), or uses rhetorical questions (see pp 72–3).

Rhetorical questions also served to free the author from committing himself on a matter that he could not settle. There are thirteen Herodotean questions to the audience,[13] eight of them in the Egyptian *logos*, where appeal to the ordinary man's taste for quantity and paradox is most evident. Egypt radically altered Herodotus' and therewith the Greeks' perspective on time, customs, religion, and ethnocentric judgments. No other book has more than two such queries. The powers of the Nile, the source of the Nile, the antiquity of man, the religiosity of the Egyptians, the powers of the man Heracles, the birdlike talk of an alien woman, the expense of Cheops' pyramid, all evoke the emphatic question which is, of course, a kind of statement, eg, 'How could the [scrupulously religious] Egyptians sacrifice men?!' They could not (2.11.4 *bis*; 22.2; 15.2; 45.2; 45.3; 57.2; 125.7). Herodotus put one question in the mouth of an imaginary interlocutor, astounded at the number of Greek pots in Egypt (κοῦ δῆτα, εἴποι τις ἄν ..., 3.6.2). Once Herodotus allows himself the epic poet's astonishment at the beginning of a catalogue: 'What nation did Xerxes not lead from Asia against Greece? What sort of river was not drunk dry, save the greatest?' (7.21.1; cf *Iliad* 1.8, 2.484 ff, etc). The answer implied is 'none,' but the device earns mention here because of the formal doubt or appeal. The practitioner of *historie* in Egypt relies on the common Greek's common sense for his rhetorical point. Alternatively, he who gives the reader *apodexis* emphasizes the magnitude of his task by the question which can find no answer. A rhetorical question disguises an unchallengeable declaration.

Reticence

Disinclination to Probe Religious Matters

The first category of omitted matters consists of historical topics that could not be fully investigated, related, or explained by the historian. The second category comprises topics that deserve tact or discretion. Although Herodotus writes in detail about many cults and mankind's religious practices, he does not pontificate about divine matters or 'facts' about the gods. He never disparages the religious beliefs of others. In the special case of religious mysteries, Herodotus respects the initiates' silence. With Osiris' mysteries at Saïs as with Demeter's at Eleusis (2.171.1–2), Herodotus observes the custom of silence, either as a believer or, more likely, because arcane religious doctrines and rituals do not illuminate his proper subject, immediate (the civilization and conquest of Egypt) or perduring (human achievements). Such 'mystery' items are 'unbecoming' or 'impious' to mention (2.47.2, 86.2, 170.1), an elegant excuse for avoiding an excursus into the irrelevant. At 2.51.2, Herodotus refers to the Samothracian mysteries in a way that clearly suggests detailed knowledge (not necessarily initiation), but he reveals no secrets. The real reason for such prudence seems evident from the programmatic passages 2.3.2 and 65.2, in which Herodotus declares that he especially avoids relating divine business, τὰ θεῖα πρήγματα, except when his account demands them. This comprehensive category is not limited to 'mystery' materials; theology, myth, and the personal psychology of the gods do not come under the decisive rubric of the proem, τὰ γενόμενα ἐξ ἀνθρώπων, ἀνθρωπήια.

References to the gods, their names, and their cults, are frequent in Herodotus, especially in book 2, but rarely are the gods described as intervening in human affairs.[14] Herodotus, like Thucydides, will append a tale from myth to a geographic note (eg, 7.193.2, 197, 198.2; cf Thucydides 2.68.3; 3.88.3; 4.24.5; 6.2.1), but this Ionian touch stands far from the lengthy mythological discussions that Hecataeus devoted to geography and genealogy. The austerity of his handling of myth is more remarkable than his decision not to banish utterly τὸ μυθῶδες, the extreme of a restrictive policy that Thucydides knew he had to defend (1.22.4).

Herodotus chose not to tell a myriad of fictions about Greek and alien gods because there was no rational way to control these stories, no tangible evidence, no system to distinguish true from false (οὐκ ἔχει ἔλεγχον, 2.23, on geographical theorizing and poets' inventions). Consequently, Herodotus says: 'I think that all men know an equal amount concerning the gods' (2.3.2), that is, all men have beliefs and rituals which satisfy them, and they are inaccessible to testing for objective truth. This disclaimer of special knowledge and his avoidance of extensive reports result not from religious belief or fear or literary suitability for the text,[15] but from Linforth's 'historiographical principle.' Those things which Herodotus cannot prove or disprove, topics that afford the historian no suitable, 'down to earth' evidence, do not present material for *historie* as he understood it. Sourdille's argument for pious 'religious scruples' may be rejected: an imputed wish to cloak in silence Greek and Egyptian esoteric doctrines relating to Orphism, Pythagoreanism, and Dionysus does not correspond to the evidence of the text.[16] To speak of Osiris (2.48.3) might reveal Greek Dionysus, but Herodotus' discretion is equal to the task. His Egyptian *logos* must speak of religious matters (2.3.2, 65.2 ἀναγκαίη), because he was trying to prove the chronological priority of Egyptian to Greek practices, religious and otherwise (49.3).[17] The outlandish qualities of Isis, Horus, and Osiris are not relevant here; Osiris' name is sometimes avoided (61.1, 86.2, 132.2, 170.1–2), but not everywhere. Sayce's argument, that Herodotus does not mention Osiris' name because he 'had not caught [it] when taking notes,' represents well the extravagances of hyper-criticism in the late nineteenth century.[18] Herodotus shies away from stories without evidence. When exceptionally, a god is credited with earthly action, Herodotus cites an earthly source to hedge the bet. He follows Xenophanes (*Vors* 21 B 34, cf 35): 'Now no man has ever seen and no man ever will know certain truth (*to saphes*) about the gods …'; and Alcmaeon (*Vors* 24 B 1): 'Concerning things both unseen and mortal, the gods have sure knowledge but men can only conjecture.'

Herodotus likes to poke holes in traditional Greek myths. These were a creation of Homer and Hesiod, he says, less than four hundred years prior to his own day (2.53.2). His generous accounts of Heracles' adventures result from the opportunity to show again the puerility of Greek reflection on the past. He is sceptical not of the existence of divinity, but rather of human knowledge about it (50.2). Descriptions of gods are usually prompted by peculiarities of visible cult. He avoids elucidation of the permanent, invisible nature of the gods and reports of their mythical adventures.[19] His implicit reluctance to accept the tale of Pan's encounter with Philippides provides a paradigm of his reserve (6.105.1). There Herodotus explains that the runner and the Athenians were the source of the story, and he shifts responsibility for the account by telling the doubtful part of the story in *oratio obliqua*, presenting the reader with Cooper's '*oratio obliqua* infinitive intrusive in finite-form narrative.' This infinitive has no grammatical connection with the verb initiating *oratio obliqua* (κελεῦσαι, 6.105.2; cf 3.105.1; 5.10; 6.54). At the end of the incident, Herodotus reports with some irony that 'the Athenians believed this [report of a divine encounter] was the truth, when their independence was assured …' (6.105.3; cf 7.189.3).[20] A similar detachment appears often when gods are invoked by participants or their interference is claimed by men. The Magi reduced the storm off the coast of Magnesia by incantation and prayer – or it fell quiet some other way (ἢ ἄλλως κως, 7.191.2).

Herodotus nevertheless occasionally reports divine interference in human affairs. The list is brief. He speaks of divine nemesis destroying the self-satisfied Croesus (1.34.1); the author formulaically requests the favour of gods and heroes (εὐμένεια, 2.45.3, only here); he confirms two divine revelations (Chios, 6.27.1; Delos, 6.98.1); he suggests that the divinity wished to make more equal the opposing Greek and Persian fleets (8.13); he accepts the Potidaean explanation of the tidal wave as sent by Poseidon to punish Persian impiety (8.129.3); he allows a heavenly explanation of the rumour at Mycale of a Greek victory at Plataea (9.100.2; cf 1.174.4–5, 9.65.2) and he expresses little caution before Delphi's miracles (8.37–9). Nevertheless, he generally omits the gods from his own explanations of historical events, he stresses human autonomy, and he presents human and political causes for the events he believes historical. His stated reluctance about delving into the *thoma* of the absence of Persian corpses at the sanctuary of Demeter at Plataea is the exception that proves the rule: he prefers not to explain what seemed to him inexplicable; under pressure he threw out a *merely* divine explanation (9.65.2). Divine interest does not counter the order of nature.[21] The neuter substantive τὸ θεῖον provides a comprehensive abstraction to invoke, when coincidence is hard to accept, when human aetiologies seem inadequate, when available explanations can go no further (1.32.1*; 3.40.2*, 108.2; 7.137.2; 9.101.1).[22]

Other Historiographical Principles of Exclusion

Occasionally Herodotus states that he will not present certain information he possesses, not because its truth is uncertain, but because his *logos* finds it superfluous.[23] Not all *historie* is proper to his narrative's economy; certain information finds commemoration elsewhere.[24] Explicit omissions generally occur when the historian is indicating exactly what instead he will soon recount. The abstention rhetorically highlights and embellishes the truly significant: so the minor deeds of Gyges, Cyrus' minor conquests, the fellow commanders of Artemisia are all passed over in favour of what is historically important (1.14.4, 177; 7.99.1; also 8.85.2). Similarly he restricts himself to the one interesting Lydian *nomos*, to the one true version of Cyrus' early life, to two rivers only which create silt (the Nile and Acheloüs), to the only two Egyptian monarchs from a roll of 330 who left a monument or distinguished themselves, and to the one best story of crocodile hunting (1.94.1 [cf 1.196.1 with 5], 1.95.1, 2.10.3, 2.101.1 with 102.1, 2.70.1).

The size of Babylonian sesame and millet is so impressive that those who have not seen the grains will not believe the report (ἀπιστίη πολλή, 1.193.4). Therefore, Herodotus, although he knows the dimensions well,[25] will not record them. The *praeteritio* does not result from a fear of controversy; at 3.80.1, 6.43.3, 6.121–4, and 7.139, Herodotus fans the controversy his opinion will surely engender. Here the rhetorical flourish flaunts his exotic knowledge without burdening the text with a trivial fact that would produce disbelief. The posture encourages (or reflects?) intimacy with his audience.

Other information is simply too tedious for the historian to report, although perhaps known to him: the exact contributions in taxes of Darius' subjects, the generally known facts about the camel, the Athenian rights not possessed by the Gephyraeans, the names of the Persian commanders with Xerxes (3.95.2, 3.103, 5.57.2, 7.96.1). Less trivial but still inappropriate for his memorializing are the great deeds of the Delphian Timesitheus (5.72.4) and the foul treatment of Polycrates, a murder that, in some unspecified way, is 'unworthy of repeating.'[26]

This forbearance that selects the relevant for commemoration and rejects the rest, is clarified by his account of early Athens: 'I shall now recount *as much as is worth recalling* of what the Athenians did and suffered once they were free of the tyrants and before Ionia revolted from Darius ...' (5.65.5).[27] At 6.55, Herodotus passes over the relevant story of the 'Egyptianization' of the Peloponnese for a different reason; it had been adequately treated by others.[28] In other words, Herodotus wished to draw attention to something worthy of recording and as yet unrecorded. His principles of inclusion puzzle every reader – some items would have to be elaborately explained, were we to try to maintain the thesis of an always observed Master Plan.

One implied exclusion remains to be explained: in the conclusion of the Thermopylae narrative, after the fate in store for the last Spartans becomes clear, Herodotus interjects, 'Leonidas perished in this ordeal, having proved his bravery, and other notable (ὀνομαστοί) Spartans whose names I inquired about, because (ὡς) they were men worthy of the effort. In fact I inquired and learned the names of every last one (καὶ ἀπάντων) of the three hundred' (7.224.1).[29] Why has Herodotus gone to the trouble of procuring the names and mentioning the fact, but then omitted the result? These free citizens freely chose to encounter a tremendous number of enemies come to enslave them (7.102.2*, 104.4*). Demaratus says 'Don't inquire their number,' ironically using the same verb (*pynthanomai*) that Herodotus employs for his inquiry into their names and number. What was simple curiosity for the despot Xerxes, became (I believe) a sacred task for the commemorator of the greatest deed – at least symbolically[30] – of the greatest war ever fought. Generals who are slaves to despots can be safely forgotten (7.96.2), but even if the Spartan three hundred are here nameless (in the absence of modern appendixes), Herodotus decided to learn their names and to tell readers he had done so. This was the historian's tribute, and they do not lack their due glory for a 'deed great and marvellous.'

Personal Disinclination

Herodotus occasionally employs the rhetorical fiction that he is compelled to relate certain things. Sometimes the *logos* itself compels,[31] sometimes necessity is more abstract;[32] on occasion the *logos* requires Herodotus to ignore strict relevance.[33] Twice, however, Herodotus chooses to tell the reader that he will *not* relate what he knows well, although neither religious nor historiographical principle interferes. The Egyptians provided the historian with a kind of precedent for *damnatio memoriae*. The Egyptians wished not even to name the hated Cheops and Chephren, and purportedly called the pyramids after a shepherd, Philitis, in order to extirpate the memory of the Pharaohs. Herodotus writes in a similar vein that he knows well the name of the Delphian who surreptitiously engraved the Laconian ethnic on Croesus' dedication, but he will not mention it (ἐπιστάμενος ... οὐκ ἐπιμνήσομαι, 1.51.4). Similarly, although he knows the name of the Samian who robbed Sataspes' eunuch, he will gladly forget it (ἐπιστάμενος ... ἑκὼν ἐπιλήθομαι, 4.43.7). In these two instances, the commemorator of great deeds consigns the perpetrators of dastardly but trivial crimes to oblivion. One meets the reverse of the memorializer (ἐπιμνῶμαι, as in 1.5.4, 14.4, 177). Moral inclination, or even the anticipation of criticism, does not silence Herodotus. The great crimes of despots and tyrants are frequently narrated. In these two cases a purposive desire to consign a small, foul act to oblivion is decisive. The reserved historian can deny or tease his audience as well as gratify it with knowledge. His choice of what to omit and include reflects his ideas about reliable knowledge and its sources as well as personal considerations.

Inventory

Research Problems

Occasions on which Herodotus tells the reader that (A) information fails completely, or (B) is insufficient for certainty, or (C) the subject does not currently reward further research. Categories B and C sometimes overlap.

A Ignorance Universal

1.2.1	Names of the prehistoric rapists
1.47.2	The rest of Delphi's answer to Croesus
1.49	Croesus' oracles from the sanctuary of Amphiareus
2.19	The causes of the Nile's peculiarities
2.28.1	The sources of the Nile

2.31	What lies south of Psammetichus' deserters
2.34.1	The limits of knowledge on the source of the Nile
2.126.1	Price of the body of Cheops' daughter
4.31.2	Limits of knowledge of farther Scythia
4.40.2	What lies east of India
4.45.1	West and north of Europe: a body of water? (cf 3.115.2)
4.45.2	Names and boundaries of continents
4.53.4	North of Borysthenes river (the Dnieper)
4.53.5	Source of the Borysthenes
4.180.4	Did the Auses have armour before the Greeks?
4.185.1	Peoples west of Gibraltar
7.153.3	Source of Telines' *sacra*
9.32.2	Accurate tally of Mardonius' Greek troops
9.81.2	Was booty distributed to the Greeks after the battle of Plataea?

B Certainty Impossible

1.57.1	Pelasgian language
1.160.2	Money for Aristodicus' delivery
1.172.1	Carians and Caunians: who resembles whom?
2.75.1	Number of snake bones
2.103.2	Sesostris' Scythian settlers
3.98.2	Only one bit of certainty on the eastern Indians; the rest is conjecture
3.115.1–2	The ends of Europe
3.116.1	Gold in northern Europe
3.122.2	Tales of pre-historic Minos *et al* rejected from the text
4.16.1	Beyond the Scyths there has been no autopsy
4.17.2	Beyond Neuri
4.18.3	Beyond Androphagi
4.20.2	Beyond Melanchlaini
4.25.1	Beyond Argippaei
4.81.1	Tally of Scythian population
4.197.2	Only four known tribes of Libya; others remain unknown
5.9.1	Beyond the Danubian Thracians
5.66.1	Isagoras' antecedents
5.86.2	Aeginetans unclear on why they did not fight
6.14.1	Lade: brave men and cowards in battle now undeterminable (οὐκ ἔχω ἀτρεκέως συγγράψαι)
6.82.1	Was Cleomenes truthful?
6.124.2	Who showed the 'shield signal' at Marathon?
7.26.2	Who took the 'best contingent' prize at Sardis?

7.50.2*	Xerxes himself states the unknowability of future events (cf 1.32.7*)
7.54.3	Xerxes' motive for Hellespont sacrifice
7.60.1	Xerxes' army numbers (cf 7. 187.1)
7.111.1	Thracian Satrae never yet subjugated, as far as we know
7.185.1	The number of Xerxes' European soldiers
7.187.1	Grand total of Xerxes' men and pack animals
7.189.3	Boreas' aid to the Athenians
8.8.2	How did Scyllias reach the Greeks
8.87.1	Actions of the various contingents at Salamis
8.87.3	Were Artemisia and the Calyndian commander enemies already?
8.112.2	Did other islands contribute to the Greek funds?
8.128.1	How Timoxenus betrayed Potidaea
9.8.2	Why the Spartans stayed calm during the second invasion of Attica
9.18.2	The purpose of the Persian cavalry's encirclement of the Phocians
9.84.1–2	Who buried Mardonius body? Many claim credit; Herodotus cannot say

B Appendix: Certainty Explicitly Achieved

1.140.1	Herodotus knows so much of the Persians with certainty
1.140.2	Herodotus knows at least this practice of the Magi
2.28.2	A certain pretence of knowledge, but really an informant's 'joke'
2.154.4	Egyptian history in its outlines, since Psammetichus
3.80.1	The Persian conspirators discussed the future regime (cf 6.43.3)
4.152.3	Largest commercial profit
5.54.1	More certain information on distances within Persian Empire
6.43.3	Mardonius disestablished Ionian tyrannies and set up democracies (unusually emphatic)
6.124.2	A shield was shown at Marathon
7.214.3	Ephialtes was the guide for the Persian troops

C *Non Constat* at Present (Responsibility Disclaimed)

1.5.3	Origins of Greco-Barbarian hostility
1.75.6	Did the old Halys bed dry up?
2.73.3	Doubts on story of the phoenix

2.117	Homer and the *Cypria*: topics dropped
2.120.3	Distrust of epic versions
2.123.1	Distrust of Egyptian details, but 'so they say' (reaction to 2.122, where his own reticence is violated)
2.130.2	Ignorance concerning identity of Egyptian female colossal statues, but Herodotus reports τὰ λεγόμενα
2.146.1	Concerning Dionysus, let each believe as he will!
2.167.1	Did Greeks learn to scorn crafts from Egyptians?
4.42.4	Disbelief for Phoenician circumnavigation of Africa
4.96.1–2	Salmoxis: demon or man? topic dropped, along with *logos*
4.105.2	Herodotus does not believe that the Neuri briefly become wolves
4.173	Doubts on Libyan story of how Psylli perished, but 'so they say'
4.187.2	Confession of ignorance on whether all Libyan nomads practise certain reported rites
4.187.3	Confession of ignorance on whether head-singeing responsible for Libyan health, but Herodotus reports τὰ λεγόμενα
4.191.4	Dissociates himself from Libyan animal stories (cf 4.192.3, *fin*: limits of knowledge)
4.195.2	African versions of gold-mining: Herodotus writes what he hears
6.137.1	Athenian removal of Pelasgians from Lemnos justified? Herodotus writes what is said.
7.152.1	Uncertain whether there were Argive envoys to Artaxerxes
7.152.3	Argive politics in Persian Wars: Herodotus writes what he hears
8.133	Why Mys was sent to oracle: οὐ λέγεται ('it is not said'; ie, there is no reported explanation).

c Appendix: Rhetorical Questions in the *Narrative*
(Not in Speeches)

κοῖον

7.21.1	Which river did not fail Xerxes' army?

κόσος

2.125.7	What was the likely expense of Cheops' pyramid?

κότε (*nil*)

κοῦ

2.11.4	Where is the gulf which could not have been filled up by the silt of the Nile?

3.6.2	Where are the Greek pots in Egypt disposed of?

κῶς

1.75.6	How could one cross the Halys?
2.22.2	How could the Nile form from melting snows, if it comes from hot areas?
2.45.2,3	How could the Egyptians sacrifice men?
2.45.3	How could the *man* Heracles kill myriads of Egyptians?
4.46.3	How could the nomadic Scyths be other than poor and unwarlike?

τίς, τί

2.11.4	What will stop the Nile from altering its course?
2.15.2	Which race of men is oldest?
2.57.2	How could a bird employ human speech?
7.21.1	Which men did Xerxes not take with him?

Reticence

Occasions on which Herodotus declines to tell the reader what he seems to know for (A) religious, (B) historiographical, or (C) personal reasons. These categories are not mutually exclusive.

A Disinclination to Probe Religious Matters

2.3.2	Herodotus is not eager to report τὰ θεῖα of Egypt; (for ὅσα δὲ ἀνθρωπήϊα, see 2.3.2, 2.4.1, and proem)
2.46.2	Not pleasant to mention (οὐ ... ἥδιον... λέγειν) the reason for Pan's goat image
2.47.2	Unbecoming (οὐκ εὐπρεπέστερος) to mention why no swine are slaughtered on holiday, although Herodotus knows the reason ('a tale')
2.48.3	The large genitals of Dionysus have a 'holy tale'
2.51.2	Details of the Samothracian mysteries; cf 51.4: Pelasgian 'holy tale'
2.61.1	Detail of the festival of Isis [Osiris beaten]; not 'lawful' (ὅσιον) to report
2.62.2	Why the night of the 'feast of lights' has honor: a 'holy tale'
2.65.2	Herodotus wishes to avoid τὰ θεῖα, whenever possible (programmatic)
2.81.2	The prohibition against the wearing of wool in burial has a 'holy tale'
2.86.2	Embalming [Osiris]; not 'lawful' to name the god in this connection

2.132.2   Mourning at Busiris [Osiris]; I will not name the god involved in this matter

2.170.1   Sais tomb [of Osiris]; not 'lawful' to mention the name of the god involved in this matter

2.171.1–2   Suffering [of Osiris]; Herodotus knows the details of the Mysteries, but maintains silence

2.171.2   Mysteries of Demeter will be left in silence, except what is 'lawful' to mention

6.53   Herodotus omits divine ancestors of Perseus; no certain information possible

9.65.2   Herodotus reticent about having an opinion on a matter of divine interference (θῶμα); if he must surmise about divine matters, he will offer an idea.

B Other Historiographical Principles of Exclusion

1.14.4   Herodotus will omit (παρήσομεν) the minor deeds of Gyges

1.94.1   The Lydians have only one interesting custom; they are otherwise Greek-like (implied *praeteritio*)

1.95.1   Three less likely stories about Cyrus omitted

1.106.2   Assyrian *logoi* (cf 1.184)

1.177   Herodotus will omit (παρήσομεν) Cyrus' minor deeds

1.184   Other Assyrian kings will be mentioned elsewhere

1.193.4   Size of Babylonian sesame and millet (ἐξεπιστάμενος μνήμην οὐ ποιήσομαι ... ἀπιστίην)

2.10.3   Rivers which silt up other than the Nile and Acheloüs not mentioned

2.70.1   Only the best story about catching crocodiles will be told

2.101.1 and 102.1   Herodotus passes by (παραμειψάμενος) the 328 Egyptian kings who accomplished nothing great

2.123.3   False Greek claimants to the doctrine of metempsychosis; names omitted

3.95.2   Herodotus ignores the small change of Darius' total revenues (ἀπιεὶς οὐ λέγω)

3.103   Herodotus does not write up (οὐ συγγράφω) what all Greeks know of camels

3.125.3   Manner of Polycrates' murder is not worthy of recounting (οὐκ ἀξίως ἀπηγήσιος)

4.36.1   Herodotus rejects Abaris legend

5.57.2   Gephyraeans at Athens did not enjoy a few rights not worth mentioning

5.65.5	(By implication) many Athenian deeds are not worthy of note
5.72.4	Herodotus could recount the deeds of Delphian Timesitheus (τοῦ ἔργα ... ἔχοιμ᾽ ἂν μέγιστα καταλέξαι)
[6.19.3	Cross-reference to mention of Didyma offerings (1.92.2; 5.36.3)]
6.55	Herodotus leaves aside (ἐάσομεν) the story of the Egyptians in Greece; others have told it.
7.96.1	Herodotus passes over (οὐ παραμέμνημαι) the Persian commanders; it is not necessary to name them
7.99.1	Other Persian taxiarchs passed over; not necessary to list
7.213.3	Herodotus promises to explain elsewhere Athenades' killing of Ephialtes
7.224.1	Three hundred Spartan fighters at Thermopylae known by name; Herodotus learned them all, but does not list them
8.85.2	Names of all but two Persian naval trierarchs who captured Greek vessels omitted
9.43.2	Herodotus knows other oracles concerning the Persians, but omits them

c Personal Disinclination

1.51.4	Herodotus knows but does not report the name of the Delphian who forged Lacedaemonian name on Croesus' gift (ἐπιστάμενος ... οὐκ ἐπιμνήσομαι)
4.43.7	Herodotus knows but gladly consigns to oblivion the name of the Samian who robbed the eunuch (ἐπιστάμενος ... ἑκὼν ἐπιλήθομαι)
cf 2.128	Egyptians wish to forget cruel Pharaohs; purposely assign wrong name to pyramid builders. Herodotus reports that others also practice *damnatio memoriae*.

3

Alternative Versions:
The Reader's Autonomy

Thucydides established the rule that ancient historians endorsed when dealing with the events of the very recent past: the historian must not accept the random informant's version or what merely seems plausible to him, but must base his published account on eye-witness reports which are meticulously compared, since memory and allegiance (not to mention limited perspective on the battlefield) produce conflicting versions (1.22.2–3). These enunciated principles met no objection or refutation, whatever later historians practised. An unnecessary corollary of this ancient method impedes the modern critic. Thucydides generally eschews reporting the name, position, or ethnic identity of those who had provided his information. We have therefore no control over the quality of his sources. We can only trust him. Moreover, he seldom reports more than the one version of events or the causal explanation that he finds most satisfactory.[1] Speeches in Thucydides may remind the reader that events can be variously interpreted, but these passages reflect political exigencies and problems of prediction in wartime as much as historiographical issues.

Thucydides is more pessimistic than most about the possibility of recovering the history of even the not-so-distant past. His excursions into periods for which there were few or no witnesses are hedged with caveats about the limits of accuracy (eg, 1.1.3, 20.1, 21; 6.2.1), as are Herodotus' (see chapter 5). His comments about the previous one hundred years are intentionally limited (eg, 1.89–117, 6.53–9). His methodological caution may be read as criticism of Herodotus, who attempted to capture waning memories and to reconstruct at least a century of Aegean history. Herodotus had interrogated all the sources that he found (not always the best), including eye-witnesses, hearsay, oral tradition, and physical monuments. Thucydides certainly recognizes that the criteria for reconstructing the past must be different from those for contemporary history, but his comments and example stifled the use of Herodotus' method – one far removed from the later bookish and sedentary histories of Ephorus and his progeny.

The present chapter aims at explaining one tool that Herodotus employs to preserve the memory of human achievements: the frequent report of his informants' alternative versions. The technique does not abjure critical evaluation, and the second aim of the chapter is to survey the historian's methods for indicating the varying credibility of different reports and reporters. The historian may sift oral traditions in order to approach the truth;[2] like the modern anthropologist, he may find material worth preserving even in tendentious narratives (eg, 7.152 on the Argives) and false stories. The historian finds cultural meaning and historical significance even in fictions. He has many ways to devalue the suspicious tale and the distantly authenticated story. However untrue some parts of Homer's account of the Trojan War may be, the reported events were real to the Greeks and shaped their beliefs and customs. Especially when dealing with the distant past, Herodotus determined that one often cannot decide with confidence between contradictory versions of the same event.

False or inadequate histories can contain valuable truths and preserve illuminating false opinion. Veracity is only one historical criterion. History is what men think, as well as what they do. Thus the unbelievable stories about Xerxes' return voyage to Asia (8.118–19)[3] and Salmoxis' activities (4.94–6) deserve inclusion despite Herodotus' disbelief and suspension of disbelief. Scepticism is not allowed to interfere with dramatic impact and thematic utility. Only *after* Xerxes' safe return to Asia Minor, made possible by the jettisoning of his highly noble companions, does Herodotus report that the story is completely unworthy of credence.[4]

We shall not here attempt to reduce to a simple system the many ways by which Herodotus indicates certainty, preference, and doubt. Nor shall we consider the most important vehicle of his presentation of alternate versions, the varying opinions expressed in direct speech by his speakers, most importantly the formal dispute among Mardonius, Xerxes, and Artabanus discussing the wisdom of the Hellenic expedition. Antilogies clarify, especially through express contradictions, his characters' different motives and policies, and the relative expense and consequences of their recommendations.[5] The narrative may afterwards endorse one or another speaker. The following analysis offers a list of alternative versions, distinctions among types of alternatives, and a consideration of the historian's intention in his peculiar proceeding. The list could be analysed into categories defined by Herodotus' belief and disbelief, choice and suspension of choice, and historical, logical, and trivial/fictional alternatives. The analysis ponders the historiographical significance of the decision to include alternatives at all.

Herodotus offers alternative versions on more than 125 occasions (see list at end of chapter). These include the discrepant accounts that he collected from sources, conflicting analyses in his sources, and alternatives that arose from his own analysis. The relative importance of different kinds of variations may be suggested. The list below does *not* include (1) simple imprecision (a necessary vagueness) or those occasions when Herodotus chooses to avoid a misleading and unjustified precision. Rather it records all the times when (2) informants differ in their reports of events (the main concern of this chapter) and when (3) Herodotus disputes the analyses of others. This last category includes divergence of explanation that Herodotus encountered from others, as well as divergence or a new hypothesis produced by his own analysis. For instance, he sometimes identifies one existing hypothesis as preferable (eg, 4.11.1; 7.220.2), sometimes he supplies his own (for examples, see note 15).

1 Simple imprecision, that is, slight degrees of difference in time or space where pseudo-chronological, novelistic concern outweighs any possible knowledge, are only formally part of this topic. In this category are phrases such as: 'Five *or* six' days after the Phoenicians arrived in the Argos of myth or after Polycrates hurls his beloved ring into the water; or 'three *or* four days' after Solon reached Croesus' palace. The reader finds Gorgo's age reported as 'eight *or* nine,' and is told that Rhampsinitus' thief pulled on 'two *or* three' wineskin necks. Similarly exact or inexact is the 'eighteen *or* twenty stade long' field of Acanthus which Cyrus used for an experiment.

Occasionally exact measurement is impossible because of real and persisting local variation, and one can only report within the degree of accuracy obtainable: the Nile now must rise 'sixteen *or* fifteen cubits' before it floods the land; the corpses of Egyptian women arrive at the mummifiers 'three *or* four days' after they die.[6] These variations are all historically immaterial, and they signify that the historian has momentarily left the realm of the ascertainable datum.

Sometimes alternatives are posed only to be dismissed immediately, because the issue is unimportant or unresolvable. The narrative progresses while it sidesteps perplexities of no consequence. Of this nature are incidents about which Herodotus says 'it happened this way – or some other way we don't know of (ἄλλως κως)': this category includes the 'rape' of Io and the detailed report on the methods of Egyptian desiccation. Similarly 'Homer *or* some other earlier poet' invented the name Ocean; Priam would have surrendered Helen as soon as 'two *or* three or more of his children died in battle.'

Similarly, he will postulate variations when he cannot obtain accuracy. In his account of Xerxes' navy, he adds eighty men for each penteconter, allowing that in any given boat there may have been 'more or less.'[7] Thucydides used the same sort of unavoidable approximation in calculating the number of Greeks who went to Troy (1.10.4–5). These variations also are not tabulated below.

2 Herodotus rarely speaks of his criteria of inclusion for discrepant reports and never with more than a single remark. When rejecting an assertion that the Argives sent envoys to Susa, he interjects that 'I have an obligation to report what is reported, but no obligation to believe it all – let that apply to my whole *logos*' (7.153.3). When rejecting an Egyptian tale of wolves guiding a priest once each year, he tells us 'throughout my *logos*, it is a principle that I write what is said, as I hear it' (2.123.1). The Psylloi were lost in a sandstorm – perhaps, but 'I say here just what the Libyans say' (4.173). On the island of Cyrauis, local girls have a strange method for mining gold – 'whether this story is true, I don't know; but I write what is reported. It may all be true, for I have myself seen [something similar] in Zacynthus' (4.195.2). Of the justice of the Athenian expulsion of the Pelasgians, 'I cannot say, I can only report what is said' (6.137.1). 'Let me report information as I have heard it' (2.125.5).

These remarks on method comprehend the most explicit, yet they do not constitute a method. Herodotus prefers to leave certain questions to his reader's judgment (3.122.1; 5.45.2) and to record unlikely traditions even when falsity is patent (3.9.2). He is conserving accounts, not imposing interpretations or even a rationalized, tested 'best version.' Sometimes he reports two full versions (1.75.3–6, 3.86–7, 7.150); sometimes he reproduces only one full version and another less credible in summary form (2.2.5, 21; 3.45; 7.3); sometimes he refuses to include variant versions (eg, 1.95.1). Versions may be suppressed or rejected for their hagiographic, miraculous, or overly patriotic tone (1.95.1; 3.2, 16.5–7; 5.86.3).[8] The mature method appears in his account of the Argives' behaviour before Xerxes' invasion (7.148.2–152.3): he reports the Argive version (with a καίπερ *caveat*, 149.1), a common Greek version (with a συμπέσειν argument in support, 151), and, briefly, a third malicious version. The second, serious alternative is qualified at once by an expression of historical uncertainty, a comment on political prejudice, and a reminder that the recording of alternatives does not amount to endorsement (152).

Herodotus can select either explicitly as in the case of Cyrus' birth and death (four known versions at 1.95.1; many known versions at 1.214.5), or implicitly, for instance when he presents narratives without comment, some of which were certainly contested by his contemporaries.[9] Occasionally he expresses no preference among conflicting accounts (*non liquet*: 5.44–5; 6.137), but generally he tries to choose intelligently (2.146.1; 3.9.2; 4.11.1, 77.1; 8.94.1–4, 119).

A version need not be rejected outright in order for the reader to sense the author's distance from a report. By using intrusive oblique infinitives or optatives in ὅτι and ὡς constructions in primary sequence, Herodotus expresses irony, scepticism, or disbelief without explicitly rejecting the alternative version. This syntactical technique of literary disputation can be observed in the sceptical report concerning the cause of the traffic patterns of Nile fish (2.93.4) and in the contrasted Samian and Spartan accounts regarding the disappearance of Croesus' gift of a bowl (1.70.2), in the telling of which the Samians have an encouraging indicative, the Spartans a doubting and ironic optative.[10] Herodotus uses recognizable syntactical idioms to distance himself firmly but politely from a reported account.

Nescire quaedam magna pars sapientiae est. Herodotus avows uncertainty at times, and in such a situation he may tell available variants if he thinks they offer some useful or interesting information. When he knows no more than his audience, he leaves open the process and option of determining the truth, or admits that the evidence is insufficient even for a confident suggestion.[11] When the author does choose, results are unpredictable. His versions of the birth and death of Cyrus, supposedly chosen for their credibility from four and more stories, make one shudder to imagine how the rejected versions could have appeared even more patently biased and unlikely.

3 'Logical possibilities' concerning personal motives, are neither attributed to any particular source nor dwelled upon. Megacles' daughter, Pisistratus' newly wed wife, 'at first hid the fact [that her husband's sexual activity with her was not the usual sort], but afterwards, she tells her mother, whether she was snooping around (ἱστορεύσῃ!) about it *or* not ...' (1.61.2). No accessible version reported the mother's efforts one way or another, but Herodotus conveyed his ignorance and a guess about how the news reached Megacles. A possible motivation fills in a historical blank. Such logical alternatives, a limited analysis, create a space for historiographical mediation between probable fiction and actual history. Serving respectable historical ends, such conjectural motives are found in other narratives: eg, the motives of Sesostris' troops far from home, the motive of Amasis' Hellenic marriage, Arcesilaus' interpretation of an oracle, Demaratus' motives for writing to Sparta long before the battle of Thermopylae.[12]

Alternatives of a more important type can be found in accounts of political cause (see chapter 9). Herodotus, like Thucydides, sometimes distinguishes real political cause from pretext.[13] Although he has not 'freed' himself from non- and supra-political causation, there is hardly an important incident of the historical period, ie, from the time of Croesus, which does not have its political motive, whatever else in the way of causation he may add.[14] If the Trojan War finds no political explanation, it is because none was told him, and the event is too far in the past to reconstruct meaningfully. Thucydides ingeniously reconstructs Agamemnon's alliance (1.9.3) on the basis of *Realpolitik*, but, like Herodotus, he does not bother to rationalize this ancient war's cause. Herodotus absurdly rationalizes why the Trojans fought on: not for the sake of Helen, but rather because they had no choice, since she was not present in Troy to be given back (2.120.5). The Greeks, however, would not believe the Trojan statement and sacked the city! This may be an ironic comment on an earlier rationalizing or moralizing logographer's account of the Trojan War. In its context, Herodotus uses the Egyptian variant to contradict Homer and to support his view that something metaphysical restores balance when one nation wrongs another. The author here momentarily and unfortunately contradicts his own restriction of history to the recent human epoch.

Herodotus on occasion indulges in 'might have been's' and constructs scenarios describing how history might have been different had something contingent been otherwise. Here one discovers alternative histories, imaginative reconstructions. These include simple conjectures, eg, that Psammenitus would have lived out his life pleasantly at the Persian court had he not meddled in politics. They also encompass far-reaching historical reconstructions on contrary-to-fact suppositions such as the Corcyraeans' expectation in not sending their navy to join the Greek fleet, the likely result of Mardonius' potential combination of his forces with Athens' navy, and Masistes' probable success as a rebel, had he escaped.[15] The would-be decisive consequences of these thwarted historical hypotheses are stressed by a limiting phrase, τά περ ἂν καὶ ἦν, 'which indeed would have happened,' and the like. A few other examples may be cited. If only the Thracians could unite, no people would match them in strength. If the only two sick Spartans had both avoided battle or both had fought at Thermopylae, the fate of the one 'survivor' would have been different. If only the Abderites had been constrained to supply two meals rather than one to Xerxes' forces, they would have had to depart their city or suffer terribly.[16]

The most extended hypothetical consideration appears in Herodotus' praise of Athens.[17] The particle of hypothesis, ἄν, appears eleven times in fourteen lines that stress that the Greek cause would have been doomed, had Athens not remained loyal to the Greeks. 'If they had emigrated altogether, or if they had surrendered to Xerxes, there *would* have been no naval contest, and the following *would* have occurred ... And if there had been no sea-battle, no matter how many walls were built across the Isthmus, Sparta *would* have been betrayed because the allies of Sparta would have been compelled to join Xerxes by his navy, and the isolated Spartans *would* have nobly perished. They *would* have suffered this, or they too *would* have come to terms (ἄν, *bis*) with the Persians. Either way, Greece *would* have become another Persian vassal-state. No advantage *could* have come from the wall at the Isthmus. Therefore whoever *might* call the Athenians 'saviours of Hellas' *would* not miss the truth.' Such a varied and imaginative set of hypotheses and reconstructions suggests that Herodotus could recognize and flexibly handle central and complex historical questions. Here he is not reporter, mouthpiece, dupe, or chronicler, but an analyst considering military strategy, national morale, political expediency, and historical alternatives.

Which stories and variants will Herodotus incorporate and why? Far from being the victim of childish curiosity, he directs his narrative. Critics who believe that the story of the floating island of Chemmis 'is such an amazing story that [Herodotus] cannot resist telling it' misunderstand Herodotus' method of composition.[18] Although isolating Herodotus' motive for including each tale is impossible, here one can note his running polemic against his predecessor Hecataeus (1 *FGrHist* F 305); his intermittent, rationalizing scepticism about reported exceptions to natural law (cf 7.129.4); his amusement in reporting local, bizarre mythic aetiologies, here the birth of Apollo and Artemis on another floating island, not Delos; and his basic thesis in book 2 concerning the Greek debt to Egypt for myth and religion among other things. These conscious, dynamic influences on his narrative encourage him to report the story that he has heard, however emphatically he divorces himself from its veracity (for example, 2.156: λέγεται ... αὐτὸς μὲν ἔγωγε οὔτε ... εἶδον, τέθηπα δὲ ἀκούων εἰ ... ἀληθέως ... λόγον ... ἐπιλέγοντες οἱ Αἰγύπτιοί φασι ... ἐν τῇ νῦν πλωτῇ λεγομένῃ νήσῳ ... οὕτω λέγουσι). No lack of discipline but convergence of his various interests explain much that may seem eccentric to modern expectation.

Herodotus' self-imposed duty is to report stories as they are told, but hardly all stories.[19] He reports only one of the several variants of the story of Gyges known even today. In this case perhaps the structural importance of initial position and the thematic significance (happiness and minding one's own business) take precedence over the paltry historical value of the other versions, but a will to limit amorphous and infinite data informs even the proem, the conclusion of which directs the beginning of the historical narrative to Croesus, the first of a finite series of historical rulers who wronged the Greeks.[20] The existence of a dominant theme is confirmed by occasional reference to excursus, προσθήκη or παρενθήκη (4.30.1, 7.171.1). These indicate some implicit standard of relevance, exceptions to which require explanation like the 'addition' to Mardonius' speech on the desirability of conquering Greece, and the Delphic hierophant's 'addition' for the Milesians to an oracle for the Argives (7.5.3, 6.19.1). Herodotus calls these speech acts *parenthekai* in order to distinguish the central matter from the peripheral, the essential from the simply relevant and interesting. Alternative versions, however, are not *parenthekai* but necessary warnings against unjustified credulity.

Alternative versions result from one of two opposed motives, 'genuine inability to choose between the variants or a desire to stress the superiority' of one, 'especially when he was anxious to discredit a popular tradition of which he disapproved.'[21] Thus, for instance, Herodotus does not choose between the two accounts, Sybarite and Crotoniate, concerning whether Dorieus participated in their war, but he emphatically chooses between opinions concerning the innocence of the Alcmaeonidae at Marathon (5.44.2–45.2, especially *fin*; 6.121–4). Herodotus evaluates many historical narratives in terms of their supposed factuality. Some stories are trustworthy (πιστά, πιθανά); others are vain and silly (μάταια).[22] Those who hold differing opinions can be quantified (3.120–1: οἱ πλεῦνες, οἱ ἐλάσσονες), and their opinions can be qualified as most, more, less, or not credible (1.214.5, 3.9.2, 2.123.1 and 3.3.1; cf 3.56.2, 2.2.5, and 118.1). But probability or demonstrability alone is not decisive for Herodotus' decision to include data.

Herodotus reports even obvious errors in order to conserve knowledge about humans, their manners, beliefs, and institutions.[23] The report, however, does not constitute an endorsement. While Thucydides suppresses magisterially the entire process of inquiry and presents only his weighed results, Herodotus sometimes specifies the office (2.3.1, 28, 53.3, 54.2), the names (rarely: 2.55.3, 3.55.2, 4.76.6, 8.65 with 66.6, 9.16.1), or the ethnic provenance (frequently, eg, 1.20, 8.38–9) of his sources.[24] Such footnotes, so to speak, cannot now be verified, but they aid the student in estimating the probable credibility of the events reported and in glimpsing the nature of the sources for a given event, including living local tradition and the political disputes that gave rise to different interpretations of the past. Herodotus thus provides some control on the evidence, and often there is no other in his 'salvage operation.' He and Thucydides furnished different solutions to different problems of evidence. Thucydides' failure to mention the who, where, and when of his interrogations does not constitute a virtue. *Apodexis histories,* the demonstration of his investigations, for Herodotus means serving as a *histor*: to see, report, compare, and arbitrate among contending claims of truthfulness.[25] In terms of both source criticism and furnishing his readers with different perspectives, Herodotus' method seems at least as meritorious. His largesse in offering an organization of opinions invites the audience's active participation, intervention, even disbelief. In his distrust of revealed, eternal truths, he considers all issues discussable, his own version merely the best working hypothesis, and other accounts not merely prejudices to be reduced in presentation or dismissed.[26]

Inventory

1 Wherever the form 'Herodotus v someone else' appears, Herodotus himself presents a theory and a preference. (It is different from 'Herodotus chooses,' which appears when he is *not* one of the contending authorities.)
2 A final mark of interrogation indicates that Herodotus has found no version convincing to the extent of rejecting the alternative(s) given, although on occasion his preference can be ascertained (eg, 1.70.2–3; 7.191.2).
3 The specific authorities for the different versions are indicated when Herodotus mentions them. Frequently he only reports 'Some say this, while others say that.'
4 Passages marked 'Method' offer Herodotus' generalizations on alternative versions.
5 Wherever 'hypothesis' appears, Herodotus offers a 'might have been,' a hypothetical situation which did *not* in fact develop. It thus offers an unrealized alternative.

Alternative Versions

BOOK 1

2.1	Persians v Greeks: Io's seizure
5.2	Persians v Phoenicians: Io's seizure
5.3	Method: other versions: Io's seizure
19.2	Alyattes' Delphic query: his idea or another's?
51.3	Herodotus v the Lacedaemonians: Croesus' Delphic dedication, not Lacedaemonians'
61.2	Was Megacles' daughter asked about her sex-life with Pisistratus?
65.4	Some Greeks v the Lacedaemonians: Spartan constitution determined by Delphi or Lycurgus?

BOOK 3

120.1–121.1	Polycrates or Mitrobates insulted Oroetes?
121.2	Polycrates ignored messenger by plan or chance?
122.1	Method: Take your choice from stories of Polycrates' death

BOOK 4

1.1	(with 118.1) Darius' Scythian venture: revenge or expansion?
5.1	(cf 8.1, 11.1) Greeks v Scyths on Scyth origins
5.1	Herodotus v Scyths: Targitaeus' father was human, not divine
6.2	Greeks v Scyths: Scythians' name
11.1	Herodotus v Greeks of Pontus: Scyths originally from Asia
42.4	Herodotus v Phoenician sailors: Sun to north as they sailed around 'Libya'
45.2	Herodotus v Greek geographers: continental boundaries
77.1	Scyths v Peloponnesians: Anarcharsis' death. Herodotus chooses, terming the Greek version only a joke
81.1	Population of Scythia: estimates do not agree
95.1–96.2	Getae v Black Sea Greeks: was Salmoxis a man or god? Herodotus suspends judgment
103.2	Scythian sacrifice: bodies of sailors pushed over the cliff or not?
147.4	Cadmus' landing on Thera: pleased with country or otherwise
150.1	Theraeans and Lacedaemonians on Battus (some agreement)
150.1,154.1	Theraeans are the sole authority for the account of the founding of the African colony
154.1	Theraeans v Cyrenaeans: the tale of Battus (some agreement on his antecedents)
155.1	Herodotus v Theraeans and Cyrenaeans on origin of Battus' name
164.4	Arcesilaus' willy-nilly erroneous interpretation of oracle
167.3	Aryandes' Libyan expedition: not alleged revenge but expansion. Herodotus chooses (cf 7.138.1)
195.2	Method: (cf 2.123.1, 7.152.3) Girls dig for gold with feathers? Herodotus writes what he hears. Some such process is possible, and he has seen something like it in Zacynthus.

BOOK 5

3.1	If Thracians could unite, would be most powerful nation (hypothesis)
9.3	Herodotus v Sigynnae who assert that they are Median Colonists. Anything can happen over the long run, but

BOOK 6

BOOK 7

3.4	Did Xerxes become king through Atossa's influence or Demaratus' argument? Herodotus chooses
35.1	Did Xerxes brand as well as whip the Hellespont?
54.3	Did Xerxes throw the votive saucer into Hellespont as an offering or as repentance for having it whipped?
55.3	Did Xerxes cross Hellespont last or in the middle of his army?
120.2	If Abderites had had to supply two meals to Xerxes' army (hypothesis)
138.1	Did Xerxes march against Athens or all Greece? Herodotus chooses the real objective over the pretext
139.2	If Athens had been abandoned permanently or Medized (hypothesis)
139.2	If no navy had opposed Xerxes at sea (hypothesis)
139.3	If Lacedaemonians had blocked the Isthmus (hypothesis)
149.3–150	Argives v Greeks: did a Persian herald travel to Argos?
152.1	Argive v another version: did the Argives request Xerxes to invade Greece?
152	Method: Argives' position: Herodotus reports what he hears but does not necessarily believe it. Accounts are bound to be partial
153.3	Did Telines seize or did he purchase *sacra*? Herodotus has no other information
167.2	Phoenicians v others: how Hamilcar disappeared at Himera
168.3	The situation of Corcyra, if Xerxes had conquered the Greeks (hypothesis)
189.3	Did Boreas blow at Athenian request and prayer?
191.2	Did Boreas desist at Magi's sacrifice or otherwise?
214	Ephialtes, not Onetes, outlawed; Herodotus chooses
220.1–2	Why Leonidas sent some allies away at Thermopylae; Herodotus chooses
229.2	If two Spartan invalids had both stayed or both left (hypothesis)
230	Did Aristodemus survive because he was ill or because he was sent away as a messenger?
239.2	Was Demaratus friendly or hostile to Sparta? Herodotus chooses (*eikazein*)

BOOK 8

BOOK 9

4

Disputation: Herodotus' Use of Written Sources

Historians are always revisionists. They contest accepted views of the past. Even Herodotus, the inventor of history, disagrees with predecessors and contemporaries. He often disputes learned opinion, common belief, and the poets, despite his emphasis on 'preservation and respect as opposed to criticism.'[1]

Herodotus recognizes the need to apply critical tests where possible to the salvageable evidence (2.21, 45.1, 44.1: σαφές τι εἰδέναι ἐξ ὧν οἶόν τε ἦν). He stresses the limits and fallible nature of his method of collecting second-hand sources, later documents, and various versions. He transmits many of them faithfully, along with his best judgment as to what really happened, when he can form one. His logos is ἀληθής in that it does not distort available reports.[2] He acknowledges human fallibility (6.14.1, 8.87.1), and he often admits that he could not verify details. He doubts whether truth can be obtained on certain questions (1.5.3, 57.1; 2.2.2; 7.152, etc), even as he lays out the available evidence (1.1.5, 2.45.1). Verdicts of non liquet can constitute a historical virtue, in dealing with a poorly documented past. Herodotus, however, is never wholly at the mercy of his sources, as we shall see.

Herodotus frequently takes issue with other Greeks, rival logopoioi, common opinion, and mere polis partisanship. He is more suspicious of Greek than barbarian sources,[3] perhaps involuntarily, since the latter could not easily be cross-examined. It is not my purpose to settle any of these geographical or historical controversies and, in fact, sometimes Herodotus, sometimes his opponents, and often neither party, is correct. Rather, this brief discussion and the following list are meant to indicate the signs and frequency of polemic, especially against written sources, and the areas in which it is most commonly encountered.

Among early Greek writers, as Heidel notes, '"historical" facts, if accepted, were regarded as public property. Consider the thousands of (real or supposed) historical facts referred to by Aristotle in the *Politics*. His sources are practically never mentioned ...' Only when an assertion is to be controverted, do we find citation. To incorporate acceptable versions of history without credit was common practice in antiquity. Prose sources were often not identified even when the view was contradicted.[4] Examples of this literary practice and Herodotus' vehement disagreements with authorities include his laughter at the expense of Greeks who produce schematic, aprioristic maps; his scoffing at Greeks unwilling to believe that Persians could discuss forms of government; his curt dismissal of Greek claims to know the Nile's source.[5] He rightly considers the story of Anacharsis a Greek joke (πέπαισται, 4.77.2). He corrects common Greek errors in ethnographic and geographic matters and other views that he considers historically naive, such as the identity of Xerxes' guide at Thermopylae.[6]

The noun *histor* describes one who tries to develop a correct account when opinions differ and partisan passions interfere. Herodotus employs the verb from this root, 'to inquire or investigate,' and the abstract noun, 'inquiry or investigation,' to describe his own activities. We may divide his investigation of sources into four groups. He particularly likes to examine, judge, and correct his eminent predecessor in geographic and chronographic matters, Hecateus.[7] He solicitously preserves local accounts and identifies these sources (by ethnics), and refers to other Greek written versions, but often his purpose is to show their inadequacy. Poets, as a third group of sources for historical facts, generally meet contradiction and scorn; the most revered, Homer and Hesiod, are mentioned only to be condemned.[8] His other, final group of sources includes Oriental oral accounts, monumental inscriptions, and archival documents, but Herodotus' access to, and understanding of, these barbarian materials was extremely limited.

Polemic can be identified in several ways. Sometimes the disputant is identified. Often the phrase οἶδα αὐτός, 'I know because of my own research' (eg, 1.5.3; cf 1.131.1, 140.2; 2.17.1, 156.2)[9] implies disagreement. On occasion this and similar phrases such as οἶδα ἐγώ merely highlight Herodotus' first-hand knowledge or research (eg, 1.20, 7.224.1), or they can limit his claim to confidence (eg, 4.17.2, 18.3, 20.2; 7.111.1). More often they reject the views of others, as he tries to demonstrate superior *historie* (eg, 2.17.1; 7.214.2).[10] Other phrases marking polemic, at least some of the time, include various forms of δοκέω, κατὰ γνώμην τὴν ἐμήν (eg, 2.63.3, 4.53.5, 9.65.2; 2.26.1, 4.59.2, 5.3.1; cf 9.71.2). A first-person pronoun or verb need not mark a definite opposing view; it may signify by a rhetorical flourish his serious celebratory intent, as in the phrase τῶν ἡμεῖς ἴδμεν (eg, 1.6.2, 1.94.1, 9.64.1).

Hecataeus

Few relevant books were available when Herodotus wrote. He names as a
source only one rival prose-writer. Hecataeus is explicitly cited among
writers of prose, but his presence has been suspected in other polemical
contexts where no name appears.[11] The disputed views are generally
attributed to certain Greeks, or the Ionians, or certain men or cities,[12] or even
learned barbarians, especially Egyptians (see the categorized list of polemical
passages at the end of this chapter). In other cases, written as well as oral
sources can be cautiously surmised from the vague λέγεται, 'it is reported,'
and similar expressions. In not naming prose sources Herodotus conformed
to Greek practice.

Revisionism itself, the desire to set the record straight, may be regarded as
a motive force in the Ionian enlightenment. Xenophanes criticized Pythagoras, Heraclitus criticized Xenophanes (*Vors* 21 B 7; 22 B 40). Destructive
criticism also seems to be 'a symptom of history,'[13] descending from
Hecataeus' preface to all his successors in *historie*. Factual information and
explanatory hypotheses, to be sure, are always open to correction, argument,
and refutation. Only with Timaeus in the third century, however, did
extended polemic against named predecessors become part of Greek
historiography, for earlier writers could not expect, and did not desire, their
audience to have detailed knowledge of their predecessors' works.[14]

Herodotus most frequently contradicts Hecataeus[15] among named sources,
because he was the relevant authority to supersede and because their
differences transcend particular questions, for instance, about the nature of
an Egyptian island or an animal. So far as the fragments reveal, Hecataeus
was a questioner of traditional beliefs, a clever writer, a perceptive traveller,
and practical man of the world. His work, an 'amalgam of rationalism and
fantasy,' scaled down legend and travellers' tales to human dimensions.
Hecataeus schematized, aetiologized, and rationalized all tales, however
weird. When they met his common-sense criterion of probability or were
useful for moralizing, evidence was not necessary.[16]

Herodotus' journeys have been viewed by some as attempts to substantiate or disprove, by autopsy, the geographical, chronological, and ethnological statements of Hecataeus and others (see, eg, 2.16–19, 29, 43–5, especially
44.1).[17] Hecataeus' words ὡς μοι δοκεῖ ἀληθέα introduced critical
consciousness to history, and he extended by his method the heretofore
small realm of *logoi* susceptible to scientific investigation.[18] His thinking-
machine demolished some of the contradictory and preposterous tales of
Greek religion and epic (λόγοι πολλοί τε καὶ γελοῖοι), but could not yet
produce positive results. Hecataeus' empiricism had been arbitrary; he was

incapable of developing the instrument of historical knowledge that he had partially created.

Herodotus enjoys the impulse of his predecessors' theories, which give him the advantage of having ideas and explanations to object to. His rejection of over-regularity sometimes leads him to dismiss rashly a good idea (a round earth, in two dimensions, if not three). Similarly he scorns the *a priori* geographical constructs of Anaxagoras and Hecataeus (2.20–3; 4.36.2, 42.1).[19]

Herodotus marks an advance in empirical and historical argument. He dismisses generally the timelessness and the pseudo-precision of the mythographers (eg, 1.5.3) who would not or could not find new information (*historie*). He appreciates the fact that there are limits to what can be known, and he substitutes commemoration for scepticism, reasoned restraint for uncritical belief. Most importantly, he transcends Hecataeus' common-sense rationalizations of the impossible with the help of a recent and accessible historical event equal in magnitude to any tale of the distant heroes.[20]

Herodotus and Hecataeus, to be sure, shared many interests: both were travellers, geographers, conservators of native and foreign myths, and barbarophiles, at least by Greek standards.[21] Because, however, Herodotus presents his work as something new and superior, he explicitly criticizes his predecessor, and charges him with inaccuracy and 'sensationalism'[22] in his (and others') reports of moving islands, one-eyed griffins, and such.

Hecataeus is mentioned by name four times, twice as a literary authority (2.143.1, 6.137.1). But the list of probable other references to him is long, sometimes under the rubric of 'the Ionians,' sometimes more covertly. For example, Hecataeus F 305 (Stephanus of Byzantium) reads, in part, 'In Bouto, near the temple of Leto is an island, Chembis by name, sacred to Apollo. This island is floating, it sails about and moves (περιπλεῖ, κινέεται) over the water.'[23] No rationalization here, to be sure, just gullibility. Herodotus responds (2.156.1–2): 'Near the temple in Bouto is an island called Chemmis. This island is said by the Egyptians to float. Now I myself certainly (αὐτὸς μὲν ἔγωγε) did not see it sailing or moved (πλέουσαν, κινηθεῖσαν), and I wonder, hearing of it, whether an island truly can float.' He goes on to give the Egyptian 'explanation' which he clearly does not accept (2.156.4–6). These passages are as close to text and quotation as one may discover, although only chance preserves Hecataeus' credulous account of the phenomenon. The foolishness of Hecataeus, here nameless, is also asserted in the passage concerning his confutation by the Egyptian priests, to whom he had boasted that he was sixteenth in descent from a god (2.143.1). Their 'anti-genealogy' with 345 'proofs' confounded him.[24]

Herodotus' few explicit criticisms ought not to blind us to his frequent though unacknowledged dependence on the remarkable geographer-genealogist. His comments on the sources of the Ister, for example, are definite but not based on autopsy. He was so far from knowing western European geography that he did not accept the idea of the existence of the Atlantic, but he argues that the Ister rises in the Far West among the Celts of Pyrene, who dwell 'outside the Pillars of Heracles' (2.23, 33.3; cf 4.49.3). His confident knowledge and his numerous attacks on map-makers who had described the Atlantic (4.36.2, 2.23, 3.115, 4.8.2) suggest that he had read Hecataeus' *World Tour* on the subject of the Celts and their territory and somehow perverted the (probably correct) information found therein.[25] Herodotus' vehemence on the sources of the Nile and its relation to Ocean suggests that Hecataeus is here again his target, and we know the Milesian wrote on this question (2.20–2, 4.8.2; *FGrHist* 1 F 302). Here are two nearly certain instances of his unacknowledged use of Hecataeus, sufficient examples for positing others, where written sources may be assumed.

Hellenic Views

Local Patriots

We saw in chapter 3 that rival states often offered different versions of an event to the inquiring Herodotus. Such local partisanship is common in the *Histories*, and as often as not Herodotus takes sides, as when he defends the Corinthians at Salamis against Athenian charges of desertion. For this view he had the support of the rest of Greece (8.94.4). In several passages, however, Herodotus perceives himself as proceeding with an idea that hardly anyone would agree with, and consequently his tone becomes aggressively polemical.

The Hellenion precinct at Naucratis belongs to nine Greek cities that he lists: 'all the other cities that lay claim to it do so without any justification' (2.178.2). Here he seems to reject a number of other cities' claims to Amasis' privileges – perhaps those of Aegina, Samos, and Miletus. By his reasoning, a shield to signal to the Persians at Marathon cannot have been held up by the Alcmaeonidae. 'But a shield was shown; it is not possible to deny this; it happened! Who, however, did it, I cannot say more than I have already.' Here he concedes the evidence for the signal but contests the alleged identity of the agent. Concerning Xerxes' threat to Greek independence, he says: 'Here I am constrained to reveal an opinion distasteful to most men, but since it seems true to me, I will not hold back ... Whoever says that the Athenians were the saviours of Greece, would not miss the truth.' In this case, by the use of counter-factual arguments he defends the latterly unpopular Athenians. The logical analysis of the alternatives buttresses his argument. He analyses the neutrality of some Hellenic towns: 'The remaining cities of the seven nations of the Peloponnese, except for those I've mentioned, sat out the war as neutrals. But if one may speak freely, by sitting it out, they in fact Medized.' He insists, contrary to the position of certain Greeks (writers, perhaps), that the Persian conspirators against the Magus discussed the merits of various types of government.[26] Perhaps a literary strategy produced the rhetorical emphasis, but Herodotus marks as serious the hostility that these judgments evoke.[27] He assesses the evidence and takes sides on important historical issues.

Greek Geography

Herodotus uses geographical sources, but does not hesitate to apply to them a rudimentary but serviceable criticism. Here is a field in which he applies his argumentative skills. Herodotus was sometimes too credulous, more often too sceptical.[28] He seems to accept a story about Indian gold-digging ants (3.102.2–3), but he hypercritically rejects a garbled account of long polar nights (4.25), or the existence of the Tin Isles (Britain, 3.115.1), or even the Northern Ocean. The reason was a logical application of his autoptic method: no one that he had met had ever seen them (οὐδενὸς αὐτόπτεω γενομένου, 115.2).

He scoffs at the idea that, rounding the southern tip of Africa, Phoenician sailors had seen the sun to the North (4.42.2–4). He is inconsistently sceptical on matters of geography and ethnography, for reasons difficult to penetrate. He rejects geographers' statements on the circular nature of the earth (4.36), and a one-eyed race of men called the Arimaspians (3.116.2). By our standards he scores one out of two, but his empirical method is sound in both cases: historians incline to reject assertions that cannot be supported by observable data. For similar reasons he prefers to shunt aside myth from historical discourse, although not from local legends (1.5.3, 2.120.1–2, 3.122.2). He is also uncomfortable with miracles (eg, 5.86.3, 7.166–7), but he reports many that are integral to the living traditions about an event (*logos legomenos*, 2.47.2, 62.2, 81.2; 7.167.1). When evidence fails, Herodotus reserves judgment or subjects all the available reports to a rational critique (eg, 2.5–10.2, 3.115, 8.119–20), although he recognizes the limits of such criticisms (2.34.1).

The lengthiest exercise that Herodotus offers in criticism of geographical evidence and theory can be found in his account of Egypt's greatest marvel, the Nile river. It illustrates the historian's methods of verification and argument in geography, that is, when questions are open to empirical research.

Herodotus uses Egyptian geography to demonstrate general Greek ignorance and inadequate *historie*. Book 2 is by far the most polemical.[29] His autoptic account of the Nile is marked by extreme contentiousness, a result of the availability of other sources on this question. He employs the rhetorical question (11.4), arguments dependent on the *reductio ad absurdum* (15.1), an allegation of arithmetical ignorance (16.1), a dramatic rejection of further consideration (Ἰώνων γνώμην ἀπίεμεν, 17.1), and a condemnation *ad hominem* of motive (20.1): 'But some of the Greeks, wishing to become famous for their wisdom, say of the Nile's flood ...' All of this controversy proves the existence of influential previous accounts. A proper account (ὀρθὸς λόγος) of the geographical limits (οὔρισμα) of Egypt requires better evidence and argument than 'the Ionians' provide (2.17.1). An oracle relevant to this issue provides some feeble external corroboration of Herodotus' position (18.1). The nature of the Nile's flow is impossible to ascertain (πυθέσθαι) despite Herodotus' strenuous efforts (πρόθυμος, 19). When he presents three Greek theories about the source of its waters (20), he canvasses them on the basis of evidence and logical argument (eg, argument *a fortiori* and counter-factual hypothesis, 20.3). The second theory, Hecataeus', is rejected because it is 'too wonderful' and not the product of scientific observation (θωμασιωτέρη, ἀνεπιστημονεστέρη, 21). Any explanation (μῦθος) that depends solely on the invisible (τὸ ἀφανές) does not deserve credence, for no refutation is possible (ἔλεγχος, 23). This rejected explanation is worthy of Homer: it is fiction (εὑρόντα), not reality (ἐόντα, 2.23; cf 109.3); an embellished invention (ποιηθέν, as in 3.115.2), not scientific observation.

Anaxagoras' explanation, that snow to the south provides the Nile with water, Herodotus considers 'the most plausible [probably a nod to its contemporary popularity] but the least true' (22.1; cf Diodorus 1.38.4 = *FGrHist* 646 F 1 (4); *Vors* 59 A 42 (5), 91; this account is substantially correct). Herodotus legitimately tries to disprove this hypothesis through the use of evidence, logic, counter-factual hypotheses (μαρτύριον; three uses of ἄν in unreal conditional and potential clauses), but in the absence of adequate information, Herodotus is constrained to depend on likelihood (λογίζεσθαι, οἰκός, ὡς ἡ ἀνάγκη ἐλέγχει, 22.2,4). These are his methods of argument in geography when observation cannot be applied.

Other Hellenic Writers and Common Belief

More significant in the search for the usable past is Herodotus' critique of historical reports. The variety of tests to which he subjects information about past events includes comparisons, logical exercises, probabilities, and alternative hypotheses. Nor can one assume that Herodotus accepts a story just because he does not explicitly reject it – unlike Thucydides. His use of probability illustrates one way in which he tries to control the sources.

When reliable information fails, when a course of events ended long ago, the historian turns to probability or likelihood (τὸ οἰκός). The terms offer another name for what our senses and experience have taught us to expect in this world.

On the basis of experience and a consequent concept of historical probability, Herodotus rejects stories of sudden disappearances of generals from battlefields and the idea that inter-continental wars are caused by the theft of a woman (7.167.1; 1.1–5, 2.120.2–3). He nevertheless reports such stories, because probability cannot refute the possibility that bizarre reports can be true. At the least, such reports embody popular beliefs that deserve record (3.9.2). Contrary to the misreadings of historians who look only for textual support for their narrative and who do not heed the context of a tale, Herodotus distances himself from the improbable event or reported motive (θωμάζω: 8.8.2, 7.153.4, 4.30.1, 7.125; λέγω δὲ τὰ λέγουσι αὐτοὶ Λίβυες 4.187.3, 173.3; οὐκ οἰκότα: 5.10, 2.22.2, 27; οὐ πιστά: 5.86.3, 1.182.1, 7.214.1, 8.119, etc).

Τὸ οἰκός might supply a means to separate the real kernel from its false elaboration in historical sources, but often no decision is possible (eg, 6.14.1). In such cases, Herodotus abstains. *To oikos* might have led Herodotus to reject Delphic reports of miracles that occurred when the Persians appeared in Phocis, but, in this peculiar case, the existence of the boulders seemingly moved from their former position (8.39) prevents Herodotus from scotching the report on the basis of his knowledge of physics.[30] In other words, the privileged method of autopsy overwhelmed the fall-back method of generalized experience.

His demonstrable errors need to be noted but no less so his frequent struggle to reject unsupported assertions. More importantly, for Herodotus, *to reject is not to suppress*, so his historiography permits us to contradict him. It initiates an open-ended dialectical process.

The polemical aspect of book 2 can be illustrated further. Here he is most like Hecataeus. He is equally intolerant of 'thoughtless' tales and 'silly' stories of Heracles in Egypt (45.1). He seems to speak of a Hellenic *opinio communis*, which he derisively calls a 'myth.'[31] Similarly he scornfully attacks vulgar Greek opinion on the nature of the Nile Delta and its extent, the tale of Troy, and the history of Rhodopis.[32] The Greeks had no knowledge of the gods 'until the day before yesterday, to speak boldly' (53.1). The Greek version of the Trojan War he considers 'silly' (μάταιος, 2.118.1; cf 3.56.2). Their version of Psammetichus' anthropological experiment is likewise 'silly.' Some Greeks, who remain nameless, falsely claim credit for the Egyptian doctrine of metempsychosis (2.5; 123.3). Prevailing Greek misinformation about Egypt justifies Herodotus' inquiries and necessitates his polemics.

Not all references to Greek sources are derogatory. Knowledge of Egyptian history had only become certain since Psammetichus, when Greek commercial activities became frequent. Hellenic king-lists (composed by Greeks such as Hecataeus) find limited credence, and Herodotus at least once explicitly forbears to record tales and events which other writers have recorded sufficiently.[33] The very composition of the *Histories* attests to a limited confidence in the reliability and durability of ordinary testimony, as well as elicited oral accounts and even written ones.[34]

Hellenic Poets

Herodotus refers to poets, often by name, but never compliments the veracity of their facts. When Herodotus approaches the recent Greco-Oriental conflict, they disappear entirely. Twelve of the thirteen references to the poetry of Homer and Hesiod, and six of the eight references to 'poets' and 'poetry' occur in books 1 through 4 where Herodotus is more dependent on, and anxious for, literary sources. But even here references to poets as historical sources are rare. Not only does he state that the epic poets Homer and Hesiod created the Greek theogony out of whole cloth, but Homer also invented the idea of 'Ocean' and the Hyperboreans, and probably concocted the Trojan saga![35] Later Hellenic poets, Aeschylus for instance, freely borrowed Egyptian religious wisdom, or they fabricated, if that suited their purpose, the name of the river Eridanus or the supposed river 'Ocean.'[36]

They invent rather than research (εὑρόντα ἐσενείκασθαι). Herodotus here employs the satirical mode of Xenophanes (especially *Vors* 21 B 10–12), twitting the Greeks for considering poets to be purveyors of factual knowledge. The poets, he asserts, prefer the suitable or specious (εὐπρεπής) to the accurate (eg, 2.23, 2.116–17, 3.115.2). To trust epic poets for historical information shows a lack of common sense: no man would have been fool enough to keep Helen, if giving her back would have prevented war and genocide.[37] This contempt for the epic poets exceeds Thucydides', who distrusts the data of epic (1.9.4, 10.3; 6.2.1), but nevertheless uses it to construct 'probable' historical hypotheses. Both Thucydides and Herodotus believe in the existence of Minos (1.8.2; cf 10.3, 11.2, 12.3),[38] but Herodotus thinks it worthless to try to know anything about him, while Thucydides uses his story to bolster his essential theory of the influence of seapower on history. The approach of each is justifiable, given their methods. Herodotus once quotes Homer to agree with him; the instance concerns exotic zoology, where the poet is considered an expert on cattle. When the historian adds to his citation 'rightly said' (4.29.1), it seems condescending if not jocular.

When Herodotus declares that the Spartans contradict all the poets in their account of their nation's unique dual kingship, he asserts not the trustworthiness of poets, but the aberrancy of the Spartan legend (6.52.1). He has little confidence in the common genealogizing traditions (poetry and prose) as well. The argument against the Spartan tradition is *a fortiori*; not even a poor source, poetry, agrees with the Spartan aetiological legend (cf 6.53.1). He next mocks the genealogies of Perseus: is he Greek, Egyptian, or Assyrian? Finally he dismisses the entire matter (6.53–5), explicitly because others have canvassed it, implicitly because Heroic genealogy is not subject to his kind of critical investigation. Again, when the Athenians quote Homeric scripture to prove a point to Gelon (7.161.3; *Iliad* 2.552), the argument is feeble, and Gelon's laconic and humorous reply underlines that appropriate scornful reaction. In sum, poets aim to please, not to investigate historical truth. He mentions them frequently because they are esteemed Panhellenic authorities worthy of refutation, and they preserve interesting traditions (sometimes the only ones), but they cannot be quoted with confidence for historical facts. Herodotus' view, an advance over his predecessors', is further refined by Thucydides, who realizes that poetic evidence might be 'tortured' (1.20.1, 3; cf 6.53.2) in certain ways to yield useful data.

Barbarian Authorities

Herodotus constantly employs barbarian sources. Any comprehensive list of his sources – oral, written, monumental, and natural-geographical – impresses by its sheer number and diversity. When he names ethnic sources, 'the Chaldeans say,' 'the Arabs tell,' oral report may generally be assumed. He travelled to Egypt, Phoenicia, and the Black Sea, at least, to learn of alien civilizations, present activities, and past history. He reports what he saw and what he heard, and sometimes gives disputed accounts on the basis of conflicting visible evidence or probability. For instance, he rejects Egyptian accounts of the source of the Nile, the existence and reputed habits of the phoenix, and the floating island Chemmis,[39] all matters still available for investigation. He never asserts that he read barbarian documents for himself or that he could speak another language. This was fortunate for his reputation, given his linguistic gaffes (1.139; 6.98.3). He could not consult Persian or other written sources because he did not know the languages. The initial, trivial account attributed to Persian 'scholars' (oral informants?) is immediately and totally displaced for a non-mythic account of Greco-Oriental conflict. The purpose of the quintuple reference to sources certainly was not to persuade by authority, but to amuse by a parody of appeals to (bad) evidence.

Asiatic Written and Oral Sources

Aside from the Greeks, only the Persians and Egyptians seem able to have provided Herodotus with written sources. North of the Scythian tribes, no *sophie* or man learned in history is known to have existed (4.46.1). The same is true in other directions, as far as written sources are concerned. Even where written sources existed, *opsis* and *historie* of local, living tradition prevailed for his method, unless Herodotus is a liar.[40] For Libya, Scythia, and India, and elsewhere on the fringe, where generally written sources did not exist or were unintelligible to the Greek, Herodotus prefers to narrate current customs and characteristics, in part because these alone can to some extent be verified or falsified; they allow appeal to *opsis*, the first criterion of *historie*.[41]

Achaemenid Persian documents were produced for public and private consumption. Imperial propaganda was intended by autocratic publishers for subjects present and future and not for foreign historians.[42] Some innocent errors thus appear in otherwise valuable summaries. Herodotus' references to Persian experts, Περσέων ... οἱ λόγιοι (1.1.1–5.2), have suggested to some that he used Persian written historical sources. There is, however, no evidence for the existence of Persian literary chronicles. Persian inscriptions are surprisingly few.

The actual sources of Herodotus' knowledge of Median and Persian life and history are impossible to identify with precision.[43] He mentions personal observations (1.131.1, 140. 1–2) and Persian reports that he had himself heard (1.95.1, 133.2; 3.1.5, 105.2; 7.12.1); once he refers to a Persian inscription (4.87.1–2); he mentions the 'scholars' noted above; often, of course, no source at all is identified (eg, 3.1, 4.1, 5.1, 7.1, 9.84.1). Zopyrus, the Persian aristocrat who fled to Athens, may have supplied much of Herodotus' Persian history (3.160.2), especially the account of the names of the conspirators and their 'constitutional debate' (3.80–3, 87) and the story of the capture of Babylon (3.150–60) in which his grandfather is reported to have played the leading role. [44] Indeed he may alone represent all the 'Persian sources,' when they are noted. Many of Herodotus' reports about Near Eastern monuments (eg, a Babylonian temple, 1.181) and Egyptian and Persian religion (eg, polytheism, hostility to the 'lie,' willingness of kings to protect foreign gods, 1.131–8, 3.65; cf Ezra 1.2) have proved to be accurate.

Another class of evidence lies behind Herodotus' reliable accounts of Darius' twenty taxation-districts and their tributes (3.89.1–97.1) and the contingents of Xerxes' expeditionary force (7.61–99). Here a documentary source seems likely, for the information is substantially in agreement with extant Persian documents. [45] His description of the King's Highway (5.52–3), complete with distances between posting stations, would also seem to have a documentary basis. The current ethnography of the ancient Near East has no better literary source than Herodotus in these reports. One other set of detailed references to the Persians may be mentioned, the so-called parallel diaries that Herodotus compiled for Persian army and navy manoeuvres in the Thermopylae-Artemisium campaign. [46] Here, however, the source may have been Greek commanders in Xerxes' service. Herodotus never quarrels with these administrative and logistical sources, however obtained. He had no way to criticize them systematically, and no reason to want to. His thorough exploitation of them is commendable, although his failure to identify their provenance each time one appears reminds us of the different ancient principles of citation.

The Learned Egyptians

The Egyptians affected Herodotus' conception of history because of their society's demonstrable antiquity and their vast influence on Hellenic culture. They provided historical authority by which Herodotus could whip Greek chauvinism and Greek literary predecessors. No one exercised memory in a more systematic way than the Egyptians; the priests of Memphis were learned, those of Heliopolis even more so. [47] The care the Egyptians devoted to chronography (2.145.3) and their calendar (2.4.1) led Herodotus to trust them on ancient 'history' (Menelaus, 2.119.3; 'human' history, 2.143.1), but he did not accept all their stories uncritically.

The Egyptians' knowledge of their past so impressed Herodotus that he ascribed an Egyptian origin to any coincidence of Greek and Egyptian custom: 'I shall not say that the Egyptians took from the Greeks this or any other institution at all' (ἄλλο κού τι νόμαιον). [48]

He became convinced that much of Greek civilization was borrowed from the older culture. He argues on the basis of barbarian evidence that the Greeks must acknowledge the influence of others. Book 2 offers evidence of the wonderful deeds of certain barbarians in a way that places the particular Greek achievement in the Great War in a comparative perspective. The structural purpose of this *logos* for the entire *Histories* is to record another of Persia's imperial conquests, but equally important, it commemorates Egyptian achievements, offers a new chronology for world history, demonstrates Hellenic debt to a barbarian nation, and illustrates how Herodotus chooses to argue against the opinions of others.

Polemic is part of Herodotus' historical method. He often has to set the record straight. He wants his countrymen to realize how and why they had succeeded in the recent war against frightening odds. His book is a record of historical change and a contribution to it, by showing his contemporaries how to benefit by the dynamic forces present in their cities. The Greeks, he thought, adapted best to new situations and information. Their fitful awareness of cultural relativism could be encouraged (cf 3.38 and 7.152.2). In order to escape the limitations of self-reference and cultural parochialism, the Greeks must develop critical skills, must thoughtfully assimilate alien ideas. Therefore, although he never justifies inclusion of polemic except on the grounds of truth (ἀληθείη, eg, 2.106.5, 4.195.2, 7.139.1),[49] this source-critical method is one of his intended contributions to Greek political and intellectual independence in a world populated by imperial subjects and narrow perspectives, a way of thinking that will enable the Greeks to have some control of their political destiny by searching out useful truths.[50]

In his willingness to record fully those views he disputed, Herodotus seems to have been more protective, less destructive of the past than Hecataeus who opens his work with a sneer at Greek beliefs, or Thucydides who rarely reports popular traditions (eg, 1.20–2, 6.54–9) or alternative versions. The number of reported disagreements in Herodotus' text emphasizes the real and fundamental respect for his sources, written and oral, that his idiosyncratic type of history demands.

In arguments with other authors, then, Herodotus concentrates on historical issues, but literary and current political issues (such as Athens' past services) obtrude. Herodotus does not exhibit personal animosity; even Hecataeus, though pilloried for errors in his writings, is treated respectfully as a statesman.[51] The number and types of disagreement in his text can be gleaned from the following list tabulated according to opponents. Disputation enlivens the narrative and indicates the kinds of sources available to him. The rhetoric of his polemic provides evidence of his will to preserve rather than to suppress, to reveal and conserve the beliefs of others. In this author, historiography begins to embody an intellectual and impartial effort to understand the dynamics of politics rather to establish by superior power an official, partisan version of the past.

Inventory of Herodotean Polemic

The following pages list the passages where Herodotus clearly opposes the views of another author, document, or oral source. The list reveals Herodotus' willingness to take an independent position and the ubiquity of argument and revisionism in the *Histories*.

Hecataeus

Hecataeus is the most important single literary source of information. He is the only prose-writer quoted by name. * = passages that mention his name.

1.56–8	The races of Greece (cf *FGrHist* 1 F 119)
1.146.1	The purity of Ionian blood (?)
2.2.5	Psammetichus and the age of the Egyptian people
2.5.1	Egypt, 'the gift of the Nile' (cf F 301 = Arrian *Anabasis* 5.6.5)
2.16	Triple division of the world (cf 2.15.1, 3)
2.21	Ocean which flows around all lands (cf F 302b)
2.23	The *mythos* on Ocean cannot be disproved
2.69	The crocodile
2.70, 71, 73	Crocodile, hippopotamus, phoenix (cf Porphyry at T 22, F 324; Suidas, T 1; Hermogenes, T 18)
2.120	Trojan War (?)
*2.143.1, 4	*logopoios* Hecataeus was vain and ignorant; cf T 4, F 300; (*logographos* first appears at Thucydides 1.21).
2.156.2	Chemmis, the floating island (F 305)
4.36	Hyperboreans (F 36)
*5.36.2	Hecataeus, a prudent statesman (T 5)
*5.125	Hecataeus, a prudent statesman (T 6)
*6.137.1	Pelasgian controversy; Hecataeus doubted (F 127)

Hellenic Views

Local Patriots

Local patriots offered self-serving accounts of their role in past events, some of which require modification.

2.178.3	Certain cities falsely lay claim to a stake in Naucratis
6.14.1–2	Eleven Samian ships remained loyal to the Ionian cause
6.124.2	No Alcmaeonid showed a shield at Marathon

7.139.1,5	The services of Athens are praised (cf 8.3.1, confirmation of Athenian dedication to Hellenism)
8.73.3	Certain Peloponnesians Medized
8.94.1,4	Athenians and Corinthians dispute Corinthian role at Salamis
9.85.3	Aeginetan cenotaph at Plataea is unearned

Other Hellenic Writers

Other Hellenic writers and common beliefs demand notice for correction (* = geographical issue).

1.140.1–2	Certain Greeks doubt a Persian burial custom
2.2.5	Greeks have silly account of Psammetichus' experiment
2.10–14*	The origin of the land of Egypt
2.15.1, 3*	Ionians (= Hecataeus?) declare only Delta is Egypt, the rest is Arabia or Libya
2.16.1*	If Ionians correct about the division of continents, Greeks and Ionians cannot add; cf 2.17.1, Herodotus' opinion
2.17.1 & 2*	Ionians, and then Greeks: wrong on the territory of Egypt
2.20.1–27*	Some Greeks merely seek reputation (for explaining Nile floods)
2.45.1	Greeks speak thoughtlessly (ἀνεπισκέπτως) on Heracles in Egypt
2.53.1	Greeks learned just recently of their gods
2.118.1	Greeks on Ilion and the Trojan War (Menelaus)
2.123.3	Some Greeks falsely claim credit for doctrine of the transmigration of souls
2.134.1	Some ignorant Greeks assert Rhodopis built a pyramid
2.154.4	After the time of Psammetichus, Greeks are the best source for accurate knowledge of Egypt
2.156.6	Aeschylus' version of Artemis' birth is Egyptian in origin
3.38	Relativity and power of *nomos*: Protagoras?
3.80.1	Greeks doubt that there was a debate over the form of the Persian government (also 6.43.3)
4.8.2*	Greeks on Geryon and the nature of Ocean
4.36.2*	Scorn for Hellenic *a priori* map-makers (also 42.1)
4.44.1*	Scylax sent to explore the Indus and proved that Asia and Africa have similar shapes
4.52.5*	No Greek knows the Nile's source
4.77.2	Greeks made up an Anacharsis story as a joke (πέπαισται)
4.109.1*	Common Greek error: to think the Boudini are Geloni
5.54.1–2*	Aristagoras corrected on details of his map

6.53–54	Dorian king lists: Herodotus indicates their limitations (53.2)
6.55	Herodotus omits that which others (Greeks) have written
7.20.2–21.1	Xerxes' expedition was the greatest military venture ever
7.214.2	Some Greeks wrongly believe that Ephialtes was not the traitor at Thermopylae
8.77.1–2	Herodotus defends the veracity of some oracles
8.120	The Abderites incorrectly claim that Xerxes in retreat did not loosen his belt before reaching their city

Prose Sources Other Than Hecataeus

Prose sources other than Hecataeus are likely, but none are explicitly cited. The following are the most probable.

Charon (IIIA, *FGrHist* 262) 1.107; 6.37; cf *FGrHist* 4 T 12
Euagon (IIIB, 535) 4.58–61, 2.134(?)
Scylax (IIIC, 709) 4.44.1, 2.8.3, 2.17.3–7
Xanthus (IIIC, 765) 1.94.2; cf *FGrHist* 70 F 180; 1.107; *FGrHist* 765 T 5
Greek *opinio communis* specified (all from book 2): 2.5.1 (known from Hecataeus?); 2.17.2; 2.45.1; 2.118.1; 2.134; cf 2.23

Epic Poets

Epic poets can never be trusted for historical facts, but sometimes Herodotus presents their widely shared views.

2.23	Homer invented Ocean, or another poet
2.53.2	Homer and Hesiod created Greek mythology; there were no earlier poets (2.53.3)
2.82.1	Homer and Hesiod appropriated for themselves Egyptian religious discoveries
2.116–17	Homer preferred something 'suitable,' εὐπρεπής, about Helen for his epic to an Egyptian version
2.117	Homer did not write the *Cypria*, but let both topics go!
2.118.1	Herodotus expectantly inquired in Egypt if Greek accounts of the tale of Ilion (= epic) were silly
2.120.3	Can and must one trust epic poets? No
3.115.2	Eridanus river: a Greek name, made up by a poet
4.13.1	Aristeas claimed divine inspiration (φοιβόλαμπτος)
4.29	Homer on cattle, for once ὀρθῶς εἰρημένον
4.32	Hesiod and Homer (if it be Homer) speak of Hyperboreans, but hardly anyone else does (cf 4.36.1)

6.52.1	Spartans have no poetic authority on their side (concerning the Kings)
7.161.3*	Athenians use Homer to prove a point (cf *Iliad* 2.552), but the point is feeble (cf the myths assembled in 9.26ff)

Other Poets

Other poets are rarely mentioned. They appear more often as participants in some story or action than as historical authorities. Archilochus, 1.12.2; Arion, 1.23–4; Sappho, 2.135.6; Aeschylus, 2.156.6; Pindar, 3.38.4; Anacreon, 3.121.1; Olen, 4.35.3; Homeric poems and tragic choruses, 5.67; Alcaeus, 5.95.1–2; Simonides, 5.102.3, 7.228.4; Solon, 5.113.2; Phrynichus, 6.21.2; Lasus, 7.6.3

Barbarian Learned Men

Barbarian learned men (λόγιοι) provide a foil to Greek complacency or error. Herodotus once invokes Near Eastern, and Egyptian 'authorities' many times to support his heterodox chronologies or explanations.

Asiatic Sources Explicitly Cited

1.1.1, 2.1, 4.3 and 5.1–3	Persian and Phoenician 'authorities' on origins of East-West hostility
4.46.1	No learned man has ever existed in the Black Sea region except Anacharsis

Learned Egyptians

The learned Egyptians provide a foil to Greek pretensions to knowledge of the past.

2.2.5	Memphis priests had many historical facts to report to Herodotus
2.3.1	Heliopolitans are the most learned men of Egypt (*logiotatoi*)
2.4.1	Egyptians know more of calendar than Greeks
2.4.2	Egyptians claim priority on naming gods, altars, statues, temples, sculpture (cf 2.52.2–3)
2.49.2	Melampus took much from the Egyptians and only slightly altered it
2.49.2	No coincidence: Similarity of Egyptian and Greek worship of Dionysus

2.49.3	The Egyptians did not borrow any *nomos* from the Greeks
2.73	Herodotus disbelieves Heliopolitans' elaborate account of the phoenix (§§1,3,4)
2.77.1	Egyptians keep the best records and are by far the most knowledgeable of all men about human history
2.118.1	Egyptians are superior to Greeks as authorities on the Trojan War
2.119.3	Herodotus accepts the Egyptian story of Menelaus
2.123.2	Egyptians developed the doctrine of metempsychosis, not the Greeks
2.145.3	Egyptians are careful chronographers
4.180.4	Egyptians showed the Greeks their inventions of the shield and helmet

Poiesis:
How Herodotus Makes Sense
of Historical Facts

INTRODUCTION TO PART THREE

The past contains more discrete facts than anyone has use for. Every report selects and organizes according to its author's concerns, beliefs, and limitations. To invent history requires Herodotus to craft a shape for the past and to provide an internal structure to support that constructed reality. *Poiesis* is the Greek word for something created and it applies to written histories as well as to dramas, epics, statues, and vases.[1] This part of the essay considers four systems that articulate and support the image of the past owed to Herodotus. They are not the only four that can be found, but I believe they are the most important. They transmuted Herodotus' epistemic isolation into an intellectual tool available to other researchers. The problem addressed is the following: What concepts glue the elements of the *Histories* together? Time, limit, ethnography, and an abstracted pattern of political behaviour structure and unify the data, the raw materials of the *Histories* into a remarkably comprehensive and comprehensible narrative form. They are the subject of the next four chapters.

The importance of chronology is self-evident in a work of history, but we shall underline in chapter 5 the attention Herodotus paid to correct dates (in a world without encyclopedias, a universal calendar, or almanacs). We shall consider his awareness of the limitations of his chronological results as well as the inherent limitations of his chronological method.

Less obviously than with the use of relative and absolute dates, historians unify their narratives with particular words, themes, symbols, metaphors, seemingly peripheral subjects, and recurrent metaphysical ideas (including the presence or absence of a transcendent being, natural force, or moral nexus implicated in men's activities). No writer of non-fiction prose before Herodotus seems to have employed such elements to structure a lengthy exposition; his manipulation of these potent unifiers owes much to Homeric epic. We may call such elements poetic or metaphysical, but no historian since has succeeded in dispensing entirely with them. Chapter 6 explores the concept of limit in nature and human affairs.

Ethnography existed prior to history as a literary genre, and therefore it is not surprising to find it incorporated into the *Histories*, but there it has meaning beyond the simple fascination with everyday life 'elsewhere' that Greek literature had already recognized and catered to. The doctrine of environmental determinism found in some medical writers, the doctrine of essential ethnic differences adumbrated by some Sophists, the economic, social, and political data gathered by logographers and associated researchers, all these impinged on Herodotus' concept of historical action. Environment, geography, economic status, and political structure were seen to affect national development and thought. Patterns of behaviour within a culture and in conflict with others might account for the course of the war between Hellenes and barbarians. Ethnography, in short, might help to explain historical outcomes, and therefore its role is examined in chapter 7.

Patterns emerge in the behaviour of individuals, institutions, and nations. Herodotus observed certain similarities in the behaviour of autocrats in the nations of the East and West. His 'reading' of past history resulted in one of his most widely recognized techniques for structuring narratives in his work, the pattern of the rise and fall of despots and despotisms. Less well appreciated is the way the 'Constitutional Debate' in book 3 provides an abstract of the faults and virtues of three types of governments classified by the holders of legislative authority – democracy, oligarchy, and monarchy (see chapter 8).

As with many other dramatized incidents in the *Histories*, Herodotus firmly believes in an historical substrate for the Persian debate that preceded the elevation of Darius. The limited historicity of that discussion, however, has been elaborated in a dramatic set of speeches that describe possible polities. These descriptions structure the historical narratives that appear before and after the 'privileged' scene. His own beliefs in the value of national independence, the rule of law, and self-determination led him to report frequently the many ways in which historical communities had developed and maintained these values for themselves, and to argue more forcefully in this privileged scene the political advantages of *isonomia*. In fact, he regards these last two criteria as more significant than the percentage of the community that legislates.

An examination of these structuring techniques demonstrates how Herodotus made a puzzling array of sources and information meaningful. Such micro-level studies prepare the way for part 4, which contains chapter 9 on explanations in the *Histories* and on the meanings that Herodotus found in historical events. The final chapter 10 summarizes his achievement and the reasons for his historiographical isolation. In the last part, his uniqueness is described from the inside as a new kind of causality that he invented for explaining historical events and from the outside showing how his explanations offer a wider vision than most subsequent historians could, or chose to, give. Nevertheless his historical achievement provides the basis for any subsequent argument or consensus on the rules of the historiographical game.

5

The Place of Chronology

It was not till after many designs, and many trials that I preferred, as I still prefer, the method of grouping my picture by nations: and the seeming neglect of chronological order is surely compensated by the superior merits of interest and perspicuity.

Gibbon *Memoirs*

Chronological order provides the obvious principle of organization for most historians, but not for Herodotus. Chronological research is as necessary for him as for any other historian, but not for the structure of his historical study. This chapter discusses types of dates, the purposes that relative and absolute chronologies serve in the *Histories*, and how they are subordinate to other more significant and signifying principles of structure. It then considers the pace of the narrative, certain gaps in his chronologically arranged accounts of men and nations, a division of past history into periods determined by their differing availability to research, and the accurate chronology of his critical event, Xerxes' attack on the Greek peninsula.

To Greeks, earlier and later than Herodotus, writing in all genres, past events chiefly provided a convenient source of moral examples and parallels. So it is with Homer's Trojan War, Thucydides' 'Archaeology,' the speeches of Demosthenes and the *Rhetoric* of Aristotle (1.4.9, 12–13 = 1359b–60a). The specific events of the past were perceived as less true to the constants in life than poetry (*Poetics* 9 = 1451a37ff), especially epic poetry set in a long-distant, mythical time despite its pseudo-precision with dates. Achilles and Theseus seemed to illuminate the present better than the 'facts' of the past. Greek communities in the fifth century still functioned without state archives or even lists of magistrates that would be needed by an historian, if one had existed, to construct a chronology.[1] Even the more useful artifice and convention of universal dating by years from a fixed point had not yet been invented. Hellenes knew only local and panhellenic legends and recent past acts. This relatively recordless state of affairs did not prevent the ruling class in each city from creating – more than reliably transmitting – the historical facts 'worthy of memory,' the so-called Tradition. Oral tradition in Egypt, Greece, and elsewhere depended on those who had the interest (cult, hereditary office, etc) and the status (social, economic, and political) to shape it. Thucydides understood this situation and faulted local traditions as inherently unsound (1.20.1, 3; 6.2; 6.54.1). He questioned the reliability of detailed historical accounts of any event before his war (τὰ γὰρ πρὸ αὐτῶν ... εὑρεῖν ... ἀδύνατα, 1.1.3), especially those more than a century earlier (1.20.2), but also those of the Persian Wars and the Fifty Years following (1.21.1, 97.2).[2]

The concept of time as a means of distinguishing what is from what was and what will be, was familiar to Hellenic consciousness.[3] Homer's Calchas 'knew the things that are and those that will be and those of former time' (Iliad 1.70; cf Hesiod Theogony 38). The epic was set in the past, but a past clearly separated, in truth isolated, from the singer's present. Poets celebrated heroic men's great deeds (Odyssey 1.338; Theogony 99–101). Hesiod needed the Muses' inspiration to celebrate actions of the distant past (Theogony 32; Erga 1). Homer likewise emphasized the Muses' divine knowledge and his own ignorance: ... ἴστε τε πάντα / ἡμεῖς δὲ κλέος οἶον ἀκούομεν οὐδέ τι ἴδμεν (Iliad 2.485–6).[4] The invocation of the Muses may be a formulaic cliché or a necessary refreshment before a catalogue, but such explanations do not exhaust the meaning or seriousness of the process of invocation. The heroic past cannot be recovered by merely human investigation. It is beyond human power to report with certainty the names of the men who went to Troy, and even the poet disclaimed responsibility for the list.

Herodotus' proem announces an anxiety that recent human events and accomplishments worthy of commemoration might soon be forgotten (exitela, aklea);[5] his own dead-ends in inquiry probably underlie this concern. In a modern idiom, 'unless a generation is captured on paper ...,' either contemporaneously or soon after, the future historian is forever blocked.'[6] As Herodotus' choice of prose as his literary medium immediately distinguished him from his predecessors the poets, so his subject and purpose distanced him from his immediate successor in history. Thucydides denied the possibility of accurate knowledge of events not studied as they unfold (1.1.3; 20.1,3; 21), but Herodotus had not the fortune of having been born early enough, say in 520 BCE, to live through all the major events that he chose to commemorate while his understanding was fully developed. The nature of the evidence forced the historian to employ several different degrees of historical credence and kinds of temporal measurement, depending on the types of sources available and length of time elapsed before his inquiries. Although the consequent mixture of annalistic Eastern king-lists, physical monuments and inscriptions, and local Greek traditions produced chronological indications that are open to many questions of detail, the totality proves to be more coherent and reasonable than would have been expected.[7]

Until the end of the fifth century, the Hellenic world had few dated records and only inefficient methods for preserving, much less retrieving, its past. Athens, remarkable for its concern for commemoration and publication, had no central archive until the very end of the century, and even its public list of eponymous magistrates does not go back before c 425 BCE,[8] the most likely period for Herodotus' publication. Before Herodotus, in the prehistoriographic age, one finds little evidence of attitudes towards the past conducive to, or capable of, preserving knowledge of the motives and causes of recent events. The poet Xenophanes had asked 'What age were you when the Mede came?' to recall the great catastrophe in terms of an individual's experience. The biographical phrase is best used as evidence for the lack of a universal Greek chronological system or concern with chronology.[9] Similarly, the not so distant demise of Croesus, a popular subject in contemporary and subsequent literature and art, served as a paradigm of human instability and sudden disaster – one of Herodotus' themes – and not as a matter that required an exact date, much less an explication of causes and results. The actual date of his fall had been forgotten less than one hundred years later.[10]

Shreds of works entitled *Persica* or *Hellenica* are hard to interpret.[11] The very existence of Dionysius of Miletus is disputed; Xanthus the Lydian probably published his *Lydiaca* after Herodotus; the Lampsacene Charon and the Carian Scylax probably wrote about people, places, and events up to and including the Persian Wars, but their once well-known descriptive works offered Herodotus' many critics very little help in challenging his thematically unified account, to judge by their fragments and Plutarch's malignant essay on Herodotus.[12]

As many myths as historical relationships and descriptions of places and peoples were recorded by genealogy, geography, horography, and ethnography. These genres did not attempt to explain how forces in the recent past interacted; they were antiquarian at best, and their mythical component, however paradoxical it may seem to the modern student, was often more important than recent history. When they embodied non-mythical, non-fictional material, they recorded contemporary peoples and places with occasional historical notes.

Herodotus offers no exact dates. When he for once notes the Athenian official archon year, he does not specify, at that time, the season, month, or day for the event. Furthermore, this formal date on an epichoric system governs only two events explicitly (Xerxes' crossing, 8.51.1; Mardonius' invasion of Attica, 9.3.2), so he does not treat it as a fixed point for an array of other dates (although many can be roughly extrapolated from it), as Thucydides was to do for his chronological fixed point of reference (2.2.1: Argive priestess, Spartan ephor, month of the Athenian archon; further, dates relative to the Thirty Years Peace and the battle at Potidaea, as well as the season of the year).[13] The difficulties posed by the numerous Greek epichoric calendrical systems are sketched by Thucydides (5.20.2) whose concern with an absolute and precise chronology is well known. Herodotus and Thucydides may well have avoided existing formal systems in part because their parochial nature rendered them meaningless in the next city, but an equally persuasive explanation is the paucity of dated records available to the first historians. It seems anachronistic to allege that the Athenian archon's name, Calliades, is inserted in the account of Xerxes' capture of Athens (8.51.1), Athens' darkest hour, to provide chronological accuracy.[14] More probably, participants repeated it often, a folkloric formula dating a communal experience, to Herodotus, the preserver of oral tradition. The presence of the unique date, not the absence of others, requires explanation.

For the period before 550 BCE, Herodotus stood at the mercy of unreliable Greek traditions and knew it (eg, 2.53.1, 2.143.4: 3.122.2; 7.20.2). Heroes, poets, and events may be placed and dated but only approximately. For the sixth century, an occasional number (Pisistratid traditions at 1.62.1, 5.65.3) or a vague indication does not clarify the general scheme which is unsynchronized and often completely undated (eg, the first war between Athens and Aegina, 5.82–7) or confused (eg, Periander's relations with Samos, 3.48). Herodotus recognized that he could not evaluate or rectify the reconstructive work of predecessors on chronology, or he did not regard it as the most pressing aspect of his work, or both. He follows the genealogical logographers but precedes the chronographers. Thus he confronts historical time with various but unsystematic indications that include traditional genealogies, reported intervals, synchronisms in reported tales, constructed king lists (as for the Lydians), and statements that certain events took place a generation or two before others.[15]

The narrative of the Ionian revolt divides the *Histories* with respect to chronological precision. After this event, Herodotus overcomes the substantial difficulties involved in establishing an accurate chronology of important events. He now offers more specific, though still sporadic and perplexing, indications of a relative chronology; for instance, the capture of Miletus is dated to the sixth year of the undated revolt (6.18).[16] The accounts of the Marathon campaign and Xerxes' invasion provide more markers.[17]

Pervasive chronological inexactness is not a fault in Herodotus but a result of primitive technology and the lack of an interest in recent history and secular chronology in the Aegean world. Herodotus made the past important and recorded it in a comprehensible way. He created a concern for preserving human memory and made possible the progress of his successors.[18]

Generally he is inexact about dates and time: 'at this time,' 'at the same time,' 'after this,' 'up to my day,' or 'still now'. Occasionally he gives no temporal indication at all, or merely marks sequence, or employs a phrase that encompasses an indeterminate period, such as 'at this time and before also' (τοῦτον δ' ἔτι τὸν χρόνον καὶ πρὸ τοῦ, 5.83.1).[19]

On thirty-one occasions Herodotus asserts that someone (or something) was 'the first of whom (or which) we know.'[20] The phrase πρῶτος τῶν ἡμεῖς ἴδμεν suggests his sense of achievement in chronological research and justifies the inclusion of material that might otherwise seem inappropriate. The celebratory words mark an end-point of effort at chronological knowledge and the beginning of a historical development that deserves commemoration. On the positive side, the phrase intimates that Herodotus believes historical evidence (not poetic inspiration or miraculous legend) supports his statement (apodexis), and he therefore expresses his personal assurance in reproducing one or another particular bit of oral tradition that he has examined. Negatively, the modification reminds the reader of the author's great separation from his data, the increasing inadequacy of sources as inquiry is pushed back to the limits of known time.[21] A note inserted towards the end of the story of Polycrates clarifies the deployment of the phrase (3.122.2):

Polycrates was *the first* Greek *we know of* to plan the dominion of the sea, unless we count Minos of Cnossus and any other who may possibly have ruled the sea at an earlier date. In *ordinary human history* at any rate, Polycrates was the first ...[22]

Polycrates' priority among historical Greek thalassocrats is contrasted to super-human, 'pre-historic' Minos and to other possible rulers of the sea, pre-Minoan or (the phrase is ambiguous) post-Minoan but unknown to Herodotus' research. With a similar emphasis at 6.53.2 Herodotus will not go beyond the mortal progenitors of Perseus in his inquiry into that man's ancestry. He will mention tales of gods and heroes, generally to disprove a Greek belief (2.120, 43.2, 45), but he prefers to avoid such stories (2.3.2, 117 fin). He scorns, for the most part, chronologies that date them (2. 53, 143.1) because he appreciated the absence of controls on the information available.

For the legendary period, 'Herodotus himself was completely uncon-cerned with a thoroughgoing, consistent chronology,' and this seems quite sensible given his resources. Thucydides seems to have employed an already established genealogical chronology for the mythical period, some standard work of reference, perhaps the one composed by Hellanicus, which was not yet available when Herodotus wrote.[23] Herodotus, whose interest in mythical chronology was slight (for good historical reasons adumbrated in 2.45, 141–6, 6.53.2) and whose tales from myth are disconnected one from another, records mythological stories merely with such temporal indications as they were presented to him. He rarely checks their irreconcilable and irresponsible chronological arithmetic. He had no personal or borrowed comprehensive system for reckoning pre-historic and historical time, and sixteen times sensibly satisfies himself with a vague reckoning by genera-tions, when many generations were involved.[24] In these situations no precise information was available, and an 'honest indefiniteness' reflects what was possible for him and, indeed, for subsequent historians.

The contrast between the 'well-wrought chronology of the Persian Wars and the schemeless inconsistent chronology of the mythical period' exhibits Herodotus' sensitivity to what is historically open to chronological research and what can best be handled by a light literary touch without wasting time in an attempt to reduce myth, legend, and folktale to a meaningless, pedantic, and impossible precision sometimes attained by his successors.[25]

Precise and frequent chronological markers seemed necessary to Thu-cydides, chronicler of the contemporary event, but such a systematic concern was not possible for his predecessor.[26] He was not 'unaware of the relevance of such [contemporary] chronological research,'[27] but he devoted his main energies to extracting historical events from a farrago of myth, saga, legend, folktale, monuments, and historical tradition.[28] Herodotus conveys 'a feeling of time but no scheme.'[29] He labels major events in his grand design by relative time, such as the first, second, and third conquests of Ionia (1.28, 169.2; 6.32); the two conquests of Babylon (1.191.6; 3.159.1, cf 3.56.2, 138.4), and so on. There are traces of a systematic chronology in the accounts of the regnal duration of the Mermnad and Achaemenid dynasties, and the penultimate chapter 9.121 oddly presages the later annalistic framework (perhaps borrowed from, or added by, a chronicler): καὶ κατὰ τὸ ἔτος τοῦτο οὐδὲν ἔτι πλέον τούτων ἐγένετο 'and in this year nothing further happened.'[30] The absence of other annalistic traces in Herodotus' *Histories* casts further doubt on the availability of public documentary or literary chronicles to the historian. 'Annalism' employs chronology as a *formal* framework; it organizes the works of Hellanicus, Thucydides, and his most notable continuators (the so-called Oxyrhynchus historian and the first section of Xenophon's *Hellenica*). Herodotus, then, conceived that some history of the recent and more distant past, on the basis of diligent inquiry (*historie*) and containing not merely ethnographic description or local chronicles, was desirable and possible. He constructed what had never before existed – a history of the peoples who had become subject to the power of Persia; he preserved what could be known of the recent past of the Greek states in their relations to one another and to the Eastern kingdoms; and based on his Egyptian experience, he developed Hecataeus' discovery (for the Greeks) of the scope of human time, a span that dwarfed previous Hellenic concepts of time. Thus he not only acquainted his countrymen with a more correct chronological context for their past than his predecessors had been able or cared to provide, but he made it more usable and useful with his 'synchronistic relativism.'[31]

When any extraordinary scene presents itself ... we shall spare no pains nor paper to open it at large to our readers; but if whole years should pass without producing anything worthy his notice, we shall not be afraid of a chasm in our history, but shall hasten on to matters of consequence, and leave such periods of time totally unobserved ... My reader then is not to be surprised, if ... he shall find some chapters very short, and others altogether as long; some that contain only the time of a single day, and others that comprise years; in a word, if my history sometimes seems to stand still, and sometimes to fly ... As I am, in reality, the founder of a new province of writing, so I am at liberty to make what laws I please therein. And these laws, my readers, whom I consider as my subjects, are bound to believe in and obey ...

Henry Fielding *Tom Jones* II, 1

The historian, like the novelist – and unlike the newsman or chronicler who must allot time and detail to days, months, and sometimes epochs of insignificance – both selects material for exposition and determines which scenes and incidents will receive detailed treatment. Furthermore, he chooses a pace of temporal progress, depending on whether his study covers a day or a century. In this respect, Thucydides' troublesome framework of summers and winters constitutes a literary regress, as Dionysius remarks (*De Thucydide* 9, U-R 335–8), for he uses relatively rigid topographical and chronological subdivisions that are hard to follow.[32] His scientific innovation preserves temporal precision at the cost of ease of comprehension. Exceptions (eg, 3.68.3 on a Plataean temple) to the rule of relating everything in its proper season are remarkably rare. They are either trivial in substance or furnish comprehensive evaluations.[33] Thucydides' third book furnishes Dionysius with an outstanding example of the process that butchers the linear sequence of historical events. Herodotus sometimes interrupts himself, but not systematically and only in order to explain what has just been narrated, as the narrative of Periander and his son Lycophron interrupts the Peloponnesian attack on Samos in order to explain Corinthian participation.[34]

The question of pace concerns the speed at which the central theme unfolds and the progress of intermediate incidents. It sometimes requires going backward to explain or forward to anticipate events later than his war (rare in Herodotus, but eg, the Decelean War, 9.73.3).[35] In the account of Egypt, 10,000 years and 300 kings are magisterially dismissed in a paragraph (2.100–1), for they left no memorials and nothing noteworthy occurred. Xerxes' reconquest of Egypt was potentially as interesting as Cambyses' original conquest or Darius' conquest of Babylon, but Herodotus scarcely mentions it in passing (7.5.1, 7). His accounts of the reigns of Gyges, Ardys (forty-nine years), and even Croesus (fourteen years) concentrate on one, two, or at most a few events. It is likely that he knew more,[36] but he limits his narrative to effect his original purpose: to commemorate and to explain at necessary length the decisive events in recent Greek history. 'The new subject required a new method ... [Herodotus] pursue[s] a subject of his own definition.' His thematic conception for presenting the meaningful recent past differentiates him from the chroniclers and ethnographers who were at the mercy of schematic genres articulated by years, reigns, and itineraries. Herodotus' larger purpose led him to enlarge or diminish narratives. The reader may often be more conscious of missing information than of generous detail, but in the last three books especially, extensive detail often slows the race of events to a standstill.[37]

One should not misunderstand the gaps in Herodotus' record of early or more recent history. The nearly blank history of Athens between the battles of Marathon and Thermopylae is a good example for the later period. Herodotus' account lacks detail after Miltiades' fall because he does not intend to furnish a continuous history of the Athenian state.[38] Furthermore, modern epigraphy, archaeology, and the other extant ancient literary sources can provide in this period no Athenian event of international significance, other than the development of the Laureion silver vein and the dispensation of the proceeds. These last two events he does narrate at the dramatic moment, when Themistocles 'first' appears and guides through the assembly the legislation that indirectly 'saved Greece' (7.143–4).[39] It would be absurd to imagine that he heard nothing else; rather, he relates what was essential for his *apodexis*, when it was essential. The choice of significant moment also explains the delay in presenting other important narratives. Thus the brutal murder of Darius' envoys sent to Sparta and Athens for 'earth and water' is not mentioned at its proper time in the narrative (6.48–9), but is narrated during the similar later mission of Xerxes' envoys (7.133–7).[40]

Another feature of non-chronological method is the way Herodotus frequently brings back on stage minor personages of symbolic importance. A glance at Hude's *Index Nominum* will show how, for instance, King Cleomenes,[41] the tyrants Cypselus and Polycrates, and the viziers Artabanus and Artabazus,[42] weave in and out as wanted. They do not receive one continuous exposition for either their historical or aesthetic significance, as do Pythius (7.27–39), Leonidas (7.204–39), and Tomyris (1.205–14). Flexible treatment of chronology, always serving his comprehensive thematic purpose, enables Herodotus to control material disparate in time, space, and significance.

'In organizing the parts of his *Histories*, Herodotus was forced to find a principle of connection other than mere chronology (for chronology does not explain anything).'[43] Herodotus sometimes presents events as links on a chain, but, just as often, for the subordinate narratives, he creates a cluster of events that attach themselves at many points to the central event's circumference. The historical logic must be deduced. An example of this 'globular,' non-linear chronological technique appears in the various stories that attach themselves to the first Polycrates-narrative (3.39–60): the tyrant's ring; the despatch of Polycrates' domestic enemies to Egypt; the Spartan alliance with the exiles; an Egyptian corselet; Corinthian enmity to Samos; the long narrative of Periander, his son, and Corcyra; the unsuccessful Spartan siege; Polycrates' alleged pay-off to the Spartans; the Samian exiles' later siege of Siphnos (with another excursus on Siphnian wealth and dealings with Delphi); Samian settlement of Cydonia in Crete and their subsequent enslavement; and finally the world-famous Samian wonders. These events are connected by the Samian theme. Chronology, except for the vaguest indications, is ignored because the focus is on the outlaw nature of Samos.[44]

Aside from the dramatic placement of the history of Lydia, a generally chronological scheme of the major units obtains, articulated by the progressive growth of the Persian empire. Croesus' story was perhaps (even though one cannot prove it) the last written, like a modern writer's explicit introduction that illustrates the leading ideas of his approach to the past.[45] It also introduces the major powers (Persia, Sparta, and Athens) by means of the geographically and culturally mediating state, Lydia, and the politically mediating individual who brought them to one another's notice, Croesus. Croesus was familiar to the Greeks as Cyrus was not, and thus made entry into the *Histories* easier. From the time of Croesus on the frequency of interconnected events increases. As soon as Herodotus resumes the narrative of Cyrus' conquests after Croesus' defeat (1.141.1 picks up 92.1), the endangered Ionians plead for Spartan help (141.4, resumed 152.1). The Spartans refused but sent spies to determine Cyrus' plans and the situation of Ionia (152.2). The Spartans are ignorant of Persia and its policy, but less so than King Cyrus is of them. The monarch is made to ask some of his Greek chamberlains, after the Spartan envoy had warned him against attacking Ionia, who on earth were these Lacedaemonians, and how many were they that they issued such commands to him (153.1)? Again chronological logic yields to the opportunity for dramatic confrontation and contemptuous rhetoric (1.153.1, as with Croesus and Solon, or Hydarnes and the Spartan heralds). At this time no further mediators between the principal combatants exist, but Herodotus reverses direction to introduce the chronological series of Persian conquests. Dramatic logic supplants chronological order when it does not interfere with the main historical thread.[46] The thematic weight of such interludes grants an exemption from linear order. The violation of chronological order highlights *exempla* of leading themes, and Herodotus marks commencement and closure of most injected non-historical anecdotes.[47] His complex movements back and forth and within time should not be scorned because he does not conform to modern historiographical conventions.[48]

Herodotus seems to divide the history of Helleno-Anatolian affairs into three zones. The division follows from the way he treats stories of different epochs and from certain methodological statements. Dependable knowledge exists for only the immediately past three generations that begin with Croesus about one hundred years before his own day (c 545–425). This epochal point of departure and its sequel often are characterized by a verb of knowing (*oida, idmen*: 1.5.3., 1.6.2, 3.122.2, 7.20.2, etc). Some reliable information based on monuments or events reported from several sides exists for the previous one hundred or one hundred and fifty years, but there is no sufficient control or method of verification for this history. This epoch includes, for instance, Gyges, the early career of Cyrus, and Solon. The earliest epoch provides Herodotus with many stories (*legomena*), some credible and many less so, but all unworthy of historical confidence (*pace* Hecataeus).[49] This distant past – mythic, heroic, prehistoric – includes Heracles, Minos, and Theras (4.147–8). He may be specifying these three periods at 7.20.2, where Herodotus claims that Xerxes' expedition is the largest of which we know (ἴδμεν), greater than Darius' against the Scyths, c 510 (within the dependable *spatium historicum*, cf 3.122.2), greater than the Scyths' pursuit of the Cimmerians, c 600 (ie, during the reign of the earlier Lydian Mermnads [cf 1.15], a period about which some dependable information exists), and greater than both the Greek expedition against Troy, c 1240 (see 2.145.4), and the even earlier Mysian and Teucrian invasion of Europe (κατὰ τὰ λεγόμενα), the prehistoric period for which traditions can only be reported, never accepted as factual.

This gradation of past periods allows differentiation among degrees of confidence in historical reports; it naturally varies nation by nation. Thus Croesus is the first certainly *known* (οἶδα, ἴδμεν) Eastern aggressor against the Hellenes, known that is by dependable reporters, eye-witnesses or their sons, and by *erga*. Gyges' capture of three Greek cities belongs to the second, less verifiable stage (1.5.3 and 1.6.2; 1.14.4).[50] However, Gyges' Delphic dedications, objects still visible and open to autopsy (cf 2.99.1) can be qualified as the first *known* (ἴδμεν) monuments there given by a barbarian, Midas aside (1.14.2).[51] Herodotus' awareness of the historical significance of physical objects furnishes some control for knowledge of past events when oral tradition does not.

This distinction among epochs helps to explain the cursory treatment that Herodotus affords most Anatolian events before Croesus, for instance the earlier Mermnad kings of Lydia. The account of Gyges' campaigns may be insufficient,[52] but a longer one probably would have required the invention of 'facts' or the acceptance of unreliable information. Since the history of the earlier Mermnads serves chiefly as a Homeric genealogy for Croesus, Herodotus has already given the reader much more than he promises, because he believes that reliable historical knowledge concerns humans only (τὰ λεγόμενα ἐξ ἀνθρώπων, τῆς ἀνθρωπηίης γενεῆς), and goes back no further than one man can report to another from personal knowledge or from an eye-witness.[53] In the absence of written records an investigator thus can know the particulars of the past only as far as his grandfather's generation remembers from personal experience.

Chronology like aetiology varies in technique and assurance, to adapt itself to epochs more or less distant in time.[54] Thus for the prehistoric Trojans and Astyages, and proto-historic Croesus, one encounters primarily the motives of *tisis*, *phthonos*, and *nemesis*, with little political analysis, while imperialism and strategic necessity receive more emphasis for the historical Darius and Xerxes. The bipartite periodization found in the Egyptian *logos* divides that land's history into more and less reliable sections at the time of Psammetichus (2.154.4). The principle of partition is the same – the reliability of evidence – but both the dates and the cause of the division differ from those for Hellenic history. In Egypt, the presence of older visible, datable monuments and the arrival of Greek settlers is decisive for the research of a Greek inquirer (cf 2.147.1).

Herodotus' chronology of Xerxes' invasion is sufficiently accurate to encourage historians to posit 'a diary of the Persian fleet which dated its movements from day to day' and another diary for the battle of Plataea.[55] A careful and substantially correct time-sequence obtains. Given his own contemporaries' – not to mention the earlier generation's combatants' – rudimentary calendars and lack of calendrical uniformity, his overall accuracy is remarkable. The chronological cross-references indicate extensive research. The resulting narrative and its chronology are defensible and plausible. The accuracy of attempted synchronisms (7.206.1; 8.26.2; 9.3.2, 100.2)[56] matters less for the present purpose than the implication of their explicit presence. Even when Herodotus' chronology needs modification, his semi-systematized data usually offer the best basis for a modern improved scheme of time. For the climactic and decisive series of events, he sought out more eye-witnesses, consulted more documentary sources, visited the battle-sites, and was least hampered by the (briefer) gap in time.[57] Thus the account of the campaigns of 480–79 represents his most sustained and most successful chronological study. The greater concern with time here (sequence, intervals, total elapsed months) requires him, however, to reduce the scope of events to relate.

Among the Greeks, where 'everything was against the idea of history,' Herodotus trapped the transitory in order to attain a knowledge of past events in their order that his contemporaries had thought impossible or hardly worth the effort (cf again Thucydides 1.1.3, 20–1).[58] Chronological inquiry has several fruitful functions for Herodotus. It disproves the ideas that others hold of time, it connects previously unrelated periods of Greek and barbarian histories, and it articulates the steps of an account of the past. Before fragile living memory perished, Herodotus investigated. His new method of mapping the past and his diachronic approaches to a vast and unwieldy body of material constitute his unique contribution to intellectual history. These tools, rarely explicit and therefore frequently misunderstood, must be deduced from his practice, and they necessarily vary from epoch to epoch within his text. The various metaphysical assumptions underlying many assertions about cities, empires, gods, wars, and human wisdom, and his inconsistently independent philosophy of history, inform the *Histories* but do not constitute his originality. Many of these views were his legacy from a preliterate if not prerational culture. A newly perceived need to explain why, when, and how the crucial conflict of Greeks and barbarians had happened provoked the new intellectual endeavour. Whether the resulting literary genre takes the momentary shape of a cautionary lesson, an alternative view of the world, a dramatic entertainment, a study in political psychology, or a geographical survey, Herodotus always returns his account to the main themes, the memorable deeds of the Greeks and barbarians, and the reason why they fought the recent war against one another. The next three chapters explore how he made sense of those events.

6

Limit, Propriety, and Transgression: A Structuring Concept in the *Histories*

The *Histories* exhibit the usual problems of experimental literature; they lack obvious consistency, intelligibility, and coherence. The elucidation of Herodotus' ideas and attitudes has been hindered by the unparalleled bulk of his *Histories* and by the absence of an explicit program of method and purpose. Herodotus' report on distant places and bygone times was constructed both to combat his Hellenic contemporaries' ethnic prejudices and conceptual limitations, and to create a lasting record of Greek and barbarian achievements. This dual, and somewhat conflicting, purpose obscures the progress of his account and his leading ideas. The text contains discernible patterns of thought, habitual standards of comparison, concepts of relevance and significance, historiographical notions, and ideas about morality and causality, as we shall now show, but his work lacks a covering theory, a regulating ideology, or even a controlling metaphor. Such 'laws' and such language can aid, yet often hinder, historical research, which by nature often deals with 'unpredictable' events.

Only recently have historians escaped from the persuasive yet inhibiting metaphor of 'decline and fall' for the Roman Empire. They now happily speak of 'organic transformation' and even a 'salutary dislocation.'[1] 'Manifest Destiny' and similar catchwords, often metaphoric as well as metaphysical, have produced national policy and works of history. The image of the state as a living organism, the 'body politic,' perhaps an animal or a man-shaped monster (for instance, Hobbes' leviathan), can aid or derail discourse in politics and history. Aristotle described Attic tragedy as experiencing a biological evolution that reached maturity. Polybius mechanically posited a necessary old age and decay to the 'natural growth' of the Roman state.[2] Ancient critics did not comment on the hidden authority of these literary devices. We cannot escape metaphor in any discourse, but modern critics of philosophy and literature have sensitized readers to their power. Historical discourse from the start employed metaphors in many contexts.

Herodotus has no one governing image or idea that articulates or controls his entire work, for different types of phenomena require different kinds of accounts and explanations. Nevertheless, one constantly recurring image concerns boundaries and proper limits, physical, social, and moral. This loose set of ideas, all connected to the polyvalent word *nomos*, helps to define historical forces in the *Histories*.

Here we examine three ways limits are set in Herodotus' text: first, by geographical boundaries, their trangression, and related metaphors; second, by the subject of women who provide the ethnographic background for the extraordinary events, a relevant social and cultural horizon of 'normality,' and a contrast of the private realm to the main thread of historical actions, war, revolution, and political coups (1.5.3, 140.3; 4.82; 5.62.1; 7.137.3, 171); and, third, by the moral principle related to limit, the rule to 'mind your own business,' an adage of propriety whose neglect leads to the extermination of families and the debilitation of nations. These three different notions illustrate the *nomoi* of various peoples, proving their variety but also, and more importantly, confirming the author's belief that certain constants transcend ethnic differences.

I. 'Limit,' 'Transgression,' and Related Metaphors

Herodotus employs no single idea or metaphor to shape his entire narrative in a simple pattern or to subordinate it to an epic model. Recurrent concepts and metaphors, however, of the proper realm and its limits, the transgression of which leads to failure, have analogues throughout the work. The conceptual nexus of rightful boundary and transgression can also be found explicitly in earlier literature, for instance in the Presocratic philosophers (eg, Anaximander F 1; Heraclitus FF 94, 120; Parmenides F 8) and Aeschylus' *Persians*.

There are delimited geographical spheres in every realm. Territorial limit exists in the animal kingdom for lions, adders, birds, ants, and other creatures. The ibis is said to keep Arabian flying snakes out of Egypt (2.75.3; also 5.10 and 7.126). Many vegetable species such as myrrh, cinnamon, cotton, and frankincense have their own very restricted habitats in exotic lands (3.106–7); other, more humble *flora* have a much wider range: the olive, wheat, barley, and grapes, for instance (1.193, etc). Anything that exceeds limit, or has an unusual nature, constitutes a marvel, *thoma*, and deserves description, such as the camel's amusing peculiarities (3.109).[3]

Similarly, in the human realm, all men and nations must remain within their proper nature and territory and look to their own families and property.

Distinct and separate land masses and continents must not be joined or otherwise confused. Thus, the Persians are reported to believe, at the beginning of the *Histories*, that Asia is the property of the Persians, Europe of the Greeks (1.4.4); near the end of his work, in counterpoise, Herodotus mentions once more Persia's claim to Asia, separate from the Greeks (9.116.3). The tale of Xerxes' attempt to bring together the two separate realms is concluded – it is the last recorded historical event in the book – with the Greek dedication of the broken cables that once briefly and disastrously linked Europe and Asia (9.121).[4] Europe and Asia were intended to be separate, a truth central also to Aeschylus' *Persai*. Herodotus certainly was familiar with the historical tragedy; the two accounts agree in many points but also differ in details. Our concern is with their shared concept of distinct territories and the ill-fated attempt to join them.[5]

Aeschylus (whom Herodotus often echoes) has the Persian queen-mother report a dream in which two daughters are to divide the world under the direction and control (ζευγνύω, 190) of the Persian King: 'one was allotted Greek land and the other that of the barbarians.' The women quarrel and Xerxes forces them to pull chariots, like horses. The Persian proudly carries the bit in her mouth but the Doric female struggles against it, destroys the chariot and the yoke (ζυγόν, 196). Xerxes the charioteer falls to the ground. The dream foreshadows the play's historical action; the symbolism of the yoke and reins has obvious reference to external sexual and imperial constraints. Aeschylus also refers to an inherent hostility between the two women or races (188). The attempt to bring under one master what nature has made separate fails in the play, as it does also in Herodotus, where Xerxes pretends that Greece is part of his patrimony, settled once by Pelops the Phrygian, ancestor of his present vassals (7.8γ1*; cf Croesus' and the Persians' distinct *moirai*: 1.73.1, 75.2).[6]

Aeschylus speaks not only in the images of restraining yokes and reins but also of repressive blocking up: to bridge the Bosporus (72, 130, 191, 722, 736, etc) was to block up free-flowing waters, to treat or maltreat a god as if he were a slave (723, 745–6, 749–50) or even an animal (the metaphor is from the farmer's world). Although the verb ζευγνύω ordinarily expresses bridging, Herodotus' presentation of this word, in marked contexts such as 7.8β1* and γ3* where Xerxes' disdain for boundaries is most pointedly expressed, suggests that the verb is part of his systematic attention to proper realms. Xerxes is portrayed as threatening divine as well as human prerogatives when he says: 'If and when we subdue the Athenians and their neighbours ..., we shall demonstrate [ἀποδέξομεν is the king's verb] that

Persian territory is coterminous with the *aether* of Zeus. For the [divine] sun will look down on no land that borders ours, because I shall make all their lands our one country, with your help, passing through European communities one by one' (7.8γ2*).

Xerxes here managed to show insolence towards Zeus, the sun, the sky above, and land and sea, as well as towards his fellow men. From Cyrus who went beyond his own (1.206.1*), to Darius, who first 'planned to bridge [ζεύξας] this continent here [Asia] to the other one, for the conquest of Scythia' (3.134.4*), to Xerxes who did it again, the Persians try to 'render Persian territory coterminous with Zeus' heaven' (7.8*).[7] They failed, Herodotus believes, in part because their attempt disregarded proper realms and boundaries.

Herodotus has oracular testimony to argue against interfering with nature, making land into sea (1.174.3–6). The Pythia declared that 'Zeus would have made [Cnidus] an island, if he so desired.' Thus, the later preparations for Xerxes' Athos canal, or *a fortiori* for Xerxes' bridge on the Hellespont, suggest to the attentive that these efforts will have unhappy consequences (7.22.1, etc; 7.34–6). Xerxes had the delimiting waters whipped because they demolished his first bridge. 'Rivers ... are boundaries not only in the geographic sense,'[8] but they also have a moral significance. They present a choice, a point of no return, and 'the crossing of rivers ... is always used to prove the *hybris* of the aggressor.'[9] The Halys was Croesus' limit of success, the Danube Darius' (4.99.1–2, 134.3*). Xerxes' moral transgression is compounded by the whipping of what he chooses to call a 'foul and salty river,' since Herodotus reports that the Persians, more than any other people, worshipped rivers (7.35.2*, 1.138.2).[10]

Everything on earth has its limits; nothing is boundless, ἄπειρον. The only apparent exceptions occur in momentarily hyperbolical descriptions of unexplored lands beyond the Danube and the Plain of the Caucasus (5.9.1 [Bekker: ἄπορος]; 1.204.1). Every 'realm' is defined by 'boundary,' οὖρος. Sometimes the boundary is an inescapable, inviolable natural law, such as the limit to a man's life (1.32.2*, 216.2), or the range and territory of European lions (7.126), or an eclipse (1.74.3). Man simply cannot transgress these. More often, Herodotus' 'boundaries' are the apparently more fragile product of political geography, such as the employment of natural features to serve as political divisions, for instance the Halys river dividing the Persian from the Lydian empire, or the Euphrates dividing Cilicia from Armenia (1.72.2; 5.52.3). He pauses to demarcate 'natural' boundaries of, for instance, Egypt, of Europe, of the Cnidians and the Mygdonians (2.17.1–2; 4.45; 1.174; 7.123.1, etc). An oracle from Ammon decided a dispute over the boundaries of Egypt (2.18). Herodotus quotes the oracle to suggest that limits are more than a human convenience. When he describes the man-made, 'artificial' boundaries of Thebes and Plataea (6.108.5–6), not the natural product of geography, they seem less likely to provide a secure basis for lasting, peaceful intercourse. The first chapters of the *Histories* (1.1.1–5.2, especially 1.4.4) proffer an aetiology for Hellenic-Asiatic enmity and division based in part on geography, and the last, epilogic chapter distinguishes a geographic realm proper for hardy, free Persians that is far separated from the fertile territories of docile slaves, ripe for conquest. Both framing chapters, whatever other meanings they carry, deal with the problem of natural boundaries whose transgression carries undesirable consequences.

The Persians, Herodotus reports, hypostatize distance into a political value. They themselves rule the nations closest to them and allow these neighbouring subjects to rule those more distant. This is only to be expected of a people that 'honours and respects – after themselves – those who dwell nearest them, honour thirdly the next farthest and thereafter in order of proximity' (3.89.1; 1.134.2).

Herodotus employs various forms of ἕκας, 'far,' to mark the monitory concept of a liminal area, when men stray dangerously far beyond their own territory and beyond their capacities. Herodotus solemnly commemorates the furthest points west, ἑκαστάτω τῆς Λιβύης / τῆς Εὐρώπης, that were reached by Aryandes' army invading Libya and Mardonius' army attacking Europe (4.204; 9.14). The phrases celebrate the accomplishment but also mark the 'catastrophe,' the necessity of turning back. The formulaic statements record a limit that ought not to be forgotten, a limit of both geography and human achievement.

Artabanus advises Xerxes: 'The land [of Greece] itself will be your enemy. If nothing stands up to you, the *farther* you get, the more opposed to you distance becomes. You will always be cheated by what lies just beyond ... The more land you cover and the more time you spend there, the more you will starve' (7.49.4–5*; cf Aeschylus *Persai* 792). Cambyses foolishly sets out with his army but few supplies 'for the ends of the earth' (ἔσχατα γῆς, 3.25.1). He cannot conceive of a limit to his power, megalomaniac that he is.

Limits ought not to be trangressed, yet they are, and their transgression functions as a cause, necessary and sometimes sufficient, of historically significant events. Xerxes' crossing of the Hellespont (especially 7.34–6, 53.2–57.1) presents the most fully articulated and best-known example of human transgression in the *Histories*, in which moral and physical transgression run parallel.[11] Darius at the Danube offers an earlier example, where water and the bridge that briefly connects the Persians to their intended victims, the Scyths, again mark the dangerous violation of a boundary (4.99.1–2, 118.1, 140.4).

At Plataea, the crossing of the Asopus constitutes another symbolic transgression. The Greeks are told by their seer that they will conquer if they remain in place, but they will lose the battle if they cross the stream (9.36). Mardonius obtained the same message from heaven, so for allegedly thirteen days neither side crossed (37.1, 40). Then, Mardonius, grown impatient with stalemate or unable to delay longer, led his troops across the Asopus and, as predicted, lost the battle (59.1). The religious rigamarole about the omens, recorded in full detail, in fact crystallizes the secular, strategic dilemma on each side. In addition to the oracles, Herodotus records at length the elaborate tactical manoeuvres of the Persian and the Hellenic armies. Although his rank-and-file informants ill understood the high command's attempt to draw Mardonius into battle on favourable ground for Greek hoplites, the detailed account of omens and armies well represents the various gambits and the psychological tension, a duel of wits and discipline. The *Histories* are held together by this juxtaposition and assemblage of events and explanations on different levels.

Herodotus saw transgression of limits on both sides. The Greeks share responsibility in the tongue-in-cheek mythical *logos* (1.1–5) and the non-mythical historical proem exculpates neither side: Herodotus speaks of the war which the Greeks and Persians 'began to fight against each other.' Although Croesus began and the Persians continued the series of injustices, some Greeks shared blame for bringing the Persian Wars on themselves (1.5.3; 6.98.2; 5.28, 97.3). The hostile epithet φιλοβάρβαρος would have puzzled but not entirely displeased an author fully cognizant of Hellenic weaknesses and barbarian strengths.

'To cross,' διαβαίνειν, a verb that has ominously marked unwise imperial ventures, appears last (9.114.2) when the Greeks sail north to Abydos. From there the Spartans return home while the Athenians 'cross over' to Sestos and besiege it. At this point the Greeks commence a series of aggressive acts. Sestos, to be sure, is in Europe, but the crossing marks a change from a Hellenic defensive to an Athenian offensive campaign, a moment not meaningless to an Ionian, Athenian, or any other Greek audience in 430, 420, or 410 BCE.

Neither διάβατος nor διάβασις has been found in any earlier author. Their use by Herodotus, therefore, must be examined carefully. Powell in his *Lexicon* translates them neutrally as 'fordable' and 'crossing,' but the contexts justify a more pointed interpretation. Three of the former word's four appearances pertain to military attack or invasion (1.75.5, 191.2, 3); six of the latter word's seven occurrences pertain to the same, three of them to Xerxes' disastrous invasion across the Hellespont, the greatest of all symbolic barriers between mainland Greeks and the barbarians (1.205.2, 208; 4.7.1; 7.54.1; 8.51.1, 115.1). Thus, nine of eleven instances refer to imperial aggression, against Persians, Babylonians, Massagetae, Scyths, and Greeks. The words are sometimes joined with ἐπί (eg, 1.208) to emphasize the hostile, transgressive connotation. The verb διαβαίνειν, which long predates Herodotus, occurs 89 times. Not only are almost all instances military and aggressive (with ἐπί: 1.208; 6.64; 7.10γ1*), but several mark critical military offensives (1.208 *ter*; 4.118.1; 7.35.2*; 9.36). Like the similarly innocent ζευγνύειν, repetition in contexts of imperialist adventurism suggests the author's attitude. The verb and its derivatives generally mark an action as unwise. Aeschylus also spoke of the many victories that Darius and the Persians achieved without crossing the watery divide (πόρον οὐ διαβάς, 865). Even if διαβάντες in 9.114.2 recalls earlier instances of imperialism, this alone does not suffice to prove that Herodotus condemned Athenian strategic policy in the decades after Mycale.

Herodotus' attitude towards Athenian policy following the successful attack on Sestos, the last Persian foothold in Europe, has been hotly disputed (9.114.2). He could be expected to approve of the recovery of European soil, the punishment of Artaÿctes, the vengeance for the Persians' desecration of all Athenian and many other temples and Protesilaus' shrine, the liberation of the Chersonese Greeks, the freeing of the Euxine supply line from Persian power, and the Athenian capture of the cables from Xerxes' bridge which were subsequently dedicated to the god at Delphi. Did he think, however, that the Athenians were justified in taking the offensive, in continuing the war on Asian soil, and in organizing an empire of their own?

The passages in the *Histories* that look beyond the year 479 and that therefore might indicate the historian's political affinities as well as historical perspective[12] suggest that he wrote for future generations as well as for a contemporary audience. Certain remarks were meant for those who had already lived through and still were experiencing the conflicts of the fifty or sixty years after the battle at Mycale.

The difficult topic exceeds his (and our) chosen limits, but his attention at the end of his monumental narrative to the wretched fate of the Persian Oeobazus (Thracian human sacrifice, 9.119.1) and to the Greek crucifixion of the Persian Artaÿctes oddly echoes earlier reports of inhuman conduct, mostly the work of barbarians.[13] The cruel and unusual punishment meted out by Athenians to Artaÿctes, similar to that suffered by Polycrates and condemned by Herodotus (3.120.1, 125.2), resembles other activity that draws the author's censure.

This point of closure for the *Histories'* narrative is not irrelevant to Herodotus' politics. This end for the continuous narrative is not self-evident, even after the fact, and the choice of the Artaÿctes incident ought to be justified on several levels – chronological, symbolic, and thematic. The battle-narrative could have ended with the victory at Mycale, at 9.106.4,[14] but Herodotus chooses a later moment, clearly pointing to subsequent problems. Such superhuman silences about future events can be proved for several persons and actions, most saliently for the later notorious Pausanias of Sparta.

Transgression of *nomos* again shifts to the Greek side with the report of the horrible punishment inflicted on Artaÿctes and his son (cf 9.78.3*). Self-defence and piety become useful pretexts for aggression and behaviour characterized just a few pages before by Pausanias as a violation of *nomos* (9.79.1*). The 'Janus' incident of Artaÿctes' death sheds light on Athens' future as well as on Greece's past and echoes other discussions of West-East outrage and conflicts that took place in much the same locale (Medea and Helen: 1.2–5; 2.118–20). The forward historical sequence ends with an ugly moment that portends a similarly disastrous future (cf 6.98.2). Continental 'to and fro,' marked here by the verb *diabainein*, suggests the beginning of yet another destructive *kyklos*.[15]

Herodotus' sympathy and admiration for the Athenian achievements of 490 and 480 are considerable, and the league and empire that developed from that time are never condemned. Herodotus the East Aegean Greek knew better than we that if Athens had not established a navy with a secure financial base after Mycale, Asia Minor and the offshore islands would never have been freed or secured from barbarian control and a third Persian offensive against a fragmented Greece could have been anticipated. He states, in one of his more speculative paragraphs, that total subjugation of the Hellenic nation would have been inevitable (7.139). The colonization of Thurii seems to have been acceptable to him;[16] even the expansion of Persian power is not portrayed as an unmitigated disaster for the Greeks (eg, the end of the tyrants and the establishment of democracies in Ionia at 6.43.3). Nevertheless, it is unjustified to assert that Herodotus was a propagandizing partisan of Pericles, the Alcmaeonidae, or the Athenian empire.[17]

Allegations of the historian's Dorian preferences and supreme admiration for the Spartans and their system[18] are shaken by his willingness to imagine the Spartans joining forces with the Persians (7.139.4), the distressing frequency with which Sparta lets down Greek allies as well as Croesus,[19] and the number of times that he shows the Spartan system, especially the kingship, stretched to the breaking point, with these magistrates being described as deranged or bought. Neither Sparta nor Athens lacks its proper measure of glory, precisely because Herodotus never chooses sides in the later debates, having understood that neither Greek power could have survived in 480 without the other and the rest of the allies. The political thrust of his work argues for – if anything – the continuation of the dual hegemony. The moral point is that Greeks should treat each other with justice, observe proper limits as communities.

The *Histories* are more likely to explore the tragic consequences of Greek and Athenian success, providing evidence that the author 'considered the events of his own time an unmitigated but thoroughly unavoidable disaster.' Certainly the Peloponnesian War witnessed new levels of horror during intercity warfare in Greece (cf 6.98.2, 8.3.1), although Herodotus cannot be held to have argued or clearly believed that the Peloponnesian War was the result of 'the cancerous nature of imperialism,' Athenian or otherwise. It should be obvious that he celebrates the past rather than condemns the present with a 'tract for the times.'[20]

After the battle near Cape Mycale had been won, several opportunities to end the book are not taken. There is the Panhellenic debate about the future home of the Ionians in which the Peloponnesians favour emigration from Asiatic territory (106.2–4, echoing the continental divide of 1.4.3–4). There follows the discovery by the Hellenic fleet that the Hellespont bridges, which they had come to destroy, were already down (114.1). Once the Persians' threatening bridges had been eliminated, the Peloponnesians and their allies departed in a manner that made clear that they, at least, thought that the war was over (9.114.1–2). Except for some mopping-up operations, Europe was now free, both symbolically and in fact, from the threat of Persian armies. Still, the narrative continues to the moment when the Athenians embarked alone on an aggressive policy that soon led to small states' dissatisfaction (117), Athenian attacks on other Hellenes, and imperial revenues for Athens, in short, to the Athenian empire. All these developments of *Machtpolitik* are compatible with, or even suggest, the cycle of power and overextension adumbrated at the end of the preface (1.5.4).

Herodotus' use of the concept of boundary and transgression carries a moral criticism of aggressive war and imperialism. Herodotus considers war a calamity. The Athenian and Eretrian ships dispatched to Ionia are described Homerically as the 'beginning of evils for both Greeks and barbarians.' For Herodotus the Delian earthquake signifies somehow (κου) three generations of war with more calamities than the previous twenty (approximately seven hundred years) had witnessed. When Herodotus praises the Athenians for yielding hegemony of the Greek forces before the battle of Salamis, he asserts that the evil of 'discord within a nation is much worse than war fought with a united front, just as war itself is worse than peace.'[21] To be sure, a defensive war fought by a self-conscious nation, such as the Panhellenic alliance against the Persian invaders, can be justified and necessary.

The Athenians had few opportunities for inappropriate national enter-prises (the Sardis folly and the Parian failure excepted; cf 5.106.1; 6.135.1), at least until after the battle of Mycale. The Spartans drew too narrow a limit to Greece, first abandoning Thessaly early and weakly defending Thermopylae, then thinking to cut Greece off at the Isthmus (7.173, 220.1, 235*; 8.71–2), but later they were persuaded to defend not merely their own land and league, but – at least briefly – all mainland Greece, and Leutychides went even beyond (9.90–2). The Greeks' awareness of their own proper limits, in the face of Datis' and Xerxes' forces, and the justified defence of their own families and land, promoted the successful repulse of Persian expansionism in 490 and 480 (5.97.2; 6.109.3, 6*; 7.139.5; 8.109.3*; cf 1.152.3). The failure of first the Spartans and then the Athenians to maintain a principled policy of territorial limit after 479 produced continual friction and conflict with their powerful imperial Eastern neighbour. Herodotus never expresses any hope that the Greeks could expel the Persians from Asia Minor.

Herodotus' reasoning may sometimes be metaphysical, but he supplies historical causes sufficient to explain the historical failures.[22] The metaphoric complex of limit and transgression, at once biological, strategic, political, and moral, never exhausts his attempt to understand major events, but suggests certain underlying principles of action in man and nature. Herodotus offers *apodexis*, *memoranda* and *comparanda*, not abstract explanation or instruction. The reader is often shown and affected rather than overtly taught.[23] Historical events that reflect on each other by Herodotus' verbal and structural 'coincidences' help explain each other, because Herodotus' method is not to offer an explanation of why they happened, but to suggest appropriate historical comparisons.

The Subject of Women

But history, real solemn history ... the quarrels of ... kings, with wars and pestilences, in every page ... and hardly any women at all – it is very tiresome ...

Jane Austen *Northanger Abbey* Book I, chapter xiv

The representation of the private and public acts of women bears two roles in the *Histories*. Women are symbolic of the family, the household, the private realm that generally has played little part in Western historiography, but they also have a special function in the *Histories* of the first historian as indicators of the health of the commonweal. He starts with Io and the wife of Candaules, two women who seem to influence the course of history. Women are mentioned in Herodotus with unusual frequency, sometimes because they committed extraordinary deeds, good or bad, as ruling queens, tyrants, or monarchs' wives,[24] but generally because of their ordinary role in family and social life, their normative function. Herodotus presents no separate and systematic study of females,[25] but he does mention the habits and practices by which women from exotic climes differ from Greek social practice and expectation. Marriage *nomoi* can be admired or castigated (eg, 1.196.1, 199.1; 4.180.5), or recorded without comment. Because the concerns of women are prior to, and usually outside, the realm of politics, they provide useful glimpses of social structure and custom. Like the gestures examined in chapter 1, they appear both in ethnographic reports that describe the norms of alien cultures and in dramatic narratives where their violations of *nomos* reflect on the main historical story. Herodotus combines normal patterns and extraordinary breaches to make up an amalgam of the disciplines that we call sociology, anthropology, and history.

Herodotus portrays oriental women less stereotypically and more generously than any other Greek historiographer. They have dignity, personality, and sometimes they decide the course of history. There were almost no sources, Egyptian, Babylonian, Persian, or Greek, beyond oral and written story-telling traditions and limited personal observation, for the life and history of oriental women. They do not appear on the Persepolis reliefs; there is no Achaemenid Persian literature; and they rarely occur in the inscriptions. The little that one can safely deduce from the sources suggests that unintentional distortion of palace life and harem politics should be found in the *Histories*: the popular legend of Intaphrenes' wife perhaps provided a model for traditional Iranian female behaviour before it was appropriated by Herodotus; the legend of Masistes' wife in our text probably obscures some Persian oral account of his rebellion. An historical core of Persian information has been adapted to the structural needs of the *Histories*.[26]

Most of the references to women, as individuals or as a group, are in the earlier books, especially 1, 2, and 4, where anthropological curiosity is at its acme. Herodotus often seems to assume that his audience subscribes to conventional Greek (Athenian?) male attitudes towards women, that they should be submissive and usually remain secluded. Generally, women appear as sexual objects, either bluntly equated with property or reported as helpless victims of men's lust, or they are considered to be necessary machines for producing children.[27] Euelthon of Salamis well expresses the conventional, condescending attitude towards women when he grants ferocious Pheretime not the army that she wants but a golden spindle, a distaff, and some wool (4.162.5).

The *nomoi* of each society differ (3.38), and Herodotus, like the tragedians, sometimes exhibits an independent, very positive judgment of women in ways that undercut Greek commonplaces about their abilities and status. Women and children sometimes appear as active protectors of the values and customs of society, for instance, Candaules' wife, the child Gorgo, the abducted Carian women (at 1.146). Thus they can reaffirm the existence of particular *nomoi*, in and out of ethnographic contexts. *Nomos* neutrally embraces custom, culture, and law; it also defines various moral limits, acceptable and unacceptable behaviours. *Nomos* defines the activities both within and outside a boundary, a limit that is clarified by depicted transgressions.[28]

Women and another category of distanced observers, children, not only represent or affirm healthy norms; they are also sometimes portrayed sympathetically as historical agents or – more often – as dramatic *personae* in embedded stories. Humble Cyno shows a life-nurturing cleverness, regal Nitocris and Tomyris appear to be wise and skilful rulers, Masistes' silent wife resisted Xerxes' attempts on her honour, Artemisia is a compendium of political, strategic, and intellectual excellence, both conventional and unconventional. Tomyris, Cambyses' younger sister, Intaphrenes' wife, Phaidymie, Polycrates' daughter, and Demaratus' mother, *inter alias*, are courageous, rational, and patriotic women who defend, or try to sustain their families and peoples. Further, looking at the rare but consistently positive presentations of children, we recall the life-saving aid of Croesus' long-mute, dependent son, the valour of Atys, the sage advice of Cleomenes' daughter Gorgo to her father and King, and the infant Cypselus' benign and timely smile that forestalled his own murder.[29]

Herodotus, like Homer and his own contemporary Euripides, also employs women in dramatic tales as a foil to highlight destructive aspects of the patriarchal *oikos* and of male political values. Powerless women and children convey human fragility, loss, the situation of the victim, the demands of *nomos* in preserving the *oikos* or family, and social values under siege. They thus bear witness to positive values in the private sphere.[30] In the public realm, a few heroic women oppose Persian imperialism or maintain their precarious position before the Persians' established, male-centred power: Tomyris, Nitocris, and Artemisia. Individual women and children in the *Histories* surface at moments of crisis; they may aid or harm the male protagonists. Like the oracles, they provide an extra-political, reflective comment or control on the nearly all-male narrative.[31]

Herodotus collected data on the dress, marriage customs, and sexual mores of foreign women. Their ordinary behaviour often broke Greek rules for women. Herodotus' openness to alien customs is not, however, unlimited; while he generally refrains from making judgments, he never completely disavows Hellenic standards. His relativism is not absolute. He disapproves of sexual promiscuity and especially sexual activity in sacred precincts.[32] He notes that almost all peoples except the Greeks and Egyptians permit such practices, and was a consistent enough relativist to report their argument that the gods would prevent beasts and birds from copulating openly and on holy ground, if such acts offended them. He strongly disliked (αἴσχιστος) the Babylonian and Cypriot custom of sacred prostitution and the unhallowed, animal-like (κτηνηδόν) copulations of the Auses and others (1.199.1, 5; 4.180.5; 1.203.2; 3.101.1). He acknowledges or shares Greek prudery, when he remarks on the naked breasts of Egyptian women in mourning and Egyptian statues of naked women (2.85.1, 130.2). He does not condemn the sexual components in foreign religious rituals, but his Greek speaker is distressed at Periander's necrophily with his wife and the way he stripped the clothes off the women of Corinth (5.92η3*, cf 1.61.1). The difference lies in the latter instance's gross violation of Greek *nomos* for women.

Herodotus has a Hellenic bias when he writes about women in politics. Women who assert themselves in public appear monstrous, as they do in comtemporary fifth-century Athenian drama as well. Examples in the *Histories* include the Egyptian Nitocris, Pheretime, Atossa, and Amestris. Female chariot-drivers among the Zaueces (4.193), Egyptian women parading with ithyphallic puppets (2.48.2), and women in politics are all presented as odd, at least by Greek standards.

When kingship is in the hands of scheming women, disruption, injustice, or both follow. Candaules' wife rights one wrong with another in the *Histories'* first story (1.7–12). Atossa – daughter of Cyrus, sister and wife of Cambyses and the false Smerdis, chief wife of Darius, and mother of Xerxes (3.31, 68.4*, 88.2, 133.1) – manipulates election to the Persian throne. 'I think Xerxes would have become king even without Demaratus' suggestion, for Atossa held all authority (τὸ πᾶν κράτος)' (7.3.4) even while Darius lived.

Women can apply or imply compulsion (ἀνάγκη). Candaules' wife demands a hasty decision; Xerxes' promised generosity forces him to concede to his mistress, Artaÿnte, against his judgment.[33] This last sexual imbroglio of an Eastern despot offers a typically indirect Herodotean way of showing 'men unmanned' or 'the ruler enslaved,' a motif of 'norms violated' also present in the epilogue's last words where the ubiquitous dichotomy of freedom and slavery has its final reprise. The power of women signifies disruption.

Particularly savage acts of violence by females meet unusual censure (eg, 2.100.2–3, 131.2; 4.160.4). Two of the most violent people in Herodotus, sadists not motivated by a reasonable desire for revenge, are Pheretime of Cyrene and Amestris, wife of Xerxes. The former impales her male enemies, cuts off the breasts of their wives, and 'adorns the city wall at intervals with the victims' (4.202.1). Her excesses were punished by a correspondingly dreadful death after she contracted a disease of worms (4.205). Queen Amestris had fourteen noble Persian youths buried alive as a sacrifice to the god of the underworld in place of herself (7.114.2). When Persian autocrats practise human sacrifice, they are presented as the paradigm of human brutality. When women imitate them, the results are even more horrifying. In a jealous but misdirected rage, Xerxes' wife Amestris chopped off the breasts, nose, ears, lips and tongue of the innocent wife of Masistes (9.112). This outrage beyond all others is part of the final indictment of despotism in Herodotus' *Histories*. These two women violate *nomos*; they are clearly monsters in Herodotus' opinion. They illustrate the historian's thesis that outrage and anomaly flourish in despotisms.

But it is a structural defect in all despotisms, including the Persian, not the sadism of one or two women, that condemns autocratic society. Family history there, including sexual irregularities, determines the nation's fate, and palace politics direct national policy. The despot is destined by his unbalanced power to interfere with the private lives (here: the women) of his subjects (3.80.4–5*). But the fault permeates autocratic societies, not only royal families. Persian ambassadors impudently referred to beautiful Macedonian women kept at a distance as 'vexations of the eye.' They then tried to enjoy these women's bodies despite their hosts' objections on the basis of *nomos* (5.18.3–4*). For Herodotus, women in autocracies too easily become dangerous sexual objects; men and women are both better off in nations ruled by laws where women are better insulated from public life. Their presence interferes with rational policies.

The woman Atossa is ironically made to say that Darius should prove himself to be a man, the only sex fit to rule Persians (3.134.2*; cf 8.88.3*). Barbarian women, other than royalty, are sometimes portrayed as having no personal honour (eg, 1.94.1, 4.172.2, 5.6.1). Their supposed subjection – or even liberation (5.6.1 or 4.172.2, 176) – points a contrast to Greek 'respect' for women, the implicit standard by which Candaules, Rhampsinitus, Mycerinus, Xerxes, and other named barbarians are judged as wanting (1.8.3*, 2.121ε1–2, 2.131, 9.110.3). Besides indicating either normal and normative behaviours in a society, or monstrous deviation, women in the *Histories* suggest the vulnerability of a culture to external enemies or internal stress. So the capture of Lemnian or Carian females and their subjugation to conquering males marks the end of their group's ethnic identity, and the rapid success of the Persians leads to various abuses to (and sometimes by) the women of their élite.

Women, according to the general male chauvinism of the Greeks, are by nature and proverbially weaker in mind and body and subservient to men (2.102.5; 6.77.2 [oracle]; 7.57.2 [?], 8.88.3*). Even so, any one woman might somehow confound *nomos*, expected standards, and surpass her sex. Artemisia, tyrant of Halicarnassus, reported to have provided the second-best fleet and the best advice to Xerxes (7.99.1), is characterized as serving with manly courage (λήματός τε καὶ ἀνδρηίης). The exception proves the rule. She combines feminine gender with a conspicuous masculine role. The Persians' most serious reproach was to call someone 'worse than a woman,' yet 'women' is the insult that Artemisia hurls at the Persian forces at Salamis, comparing them to the Greeks in naval skills (8.68α1*; cf 88.3*; 3.120.3*, 9.20). She foresees and explains Xerxes' defeat. Women are ubiquitous in Herodotus' *Histories*, but rarely do they have Artemisia's insight and historical significance, a place in the record separate from a generalized moral point about inverted or perverted values.

By contrast with Herodotus, Thucydides briefly mentions only six women.[34] In general, they are relevant to Thucydides chiefly as examples of helpless pawns in warfare. Often a grim and savage tale tells of their exile (Potidaea, 2.70.3), massacre, or enslavement (Plataea and Corcyra, 3.68.2 and 4.48.4). Speakers mention the dreadful fate of wives and children following defeat when they conventionally exhort their soldiers to bravery (Gylippus, 7.68.2*; Nicias, 69.2*). Unparalleled female wall-builders or bread-makers for a besieged skeleton force require Thucydides' comment (5.82.6; 2.78.3) and at Plataea and Corcyra, the ferocity and strangeness of the warfare is emphasized by the womenfolk's throwing of stones and roof-tiles.[35] For Thucydides, women almost never make history or play in it any significant role. They have only a limited and largely symbolic significance, to indicate unprecedented and distressing situations when normal limits of civil behaviour and military practice are broken (see the generalizations of 3.82–3).[36]

Women provide Herodotus with a horizon. Ordinary mothers, wives, or female progeny are indicators of normality; they furnish the reader with a standard of private behaviour by which to gauge political irregularities and international upheavals. When, however, women rise to prominence, there are usually difficulties ahead for the immediate male protagonist. Remarkable women violate some *nomos* – if only to protect another – or, like Candaules' wife, stand seductively at a threshold of decisive action, an entrance to a dangerous world.

 Moral Principles in History

The third category of limit in Herodotus illustrates a moral principle. His morality is largely cautionary. He does not preach dogma, he re-presents the past, the results of his careful collecting, selecting, and ordering of historical data.[37] He apprehends a set of delicate and easily disturbed balances in the world (1.207.2*; 3.106.1), violations of which entail a cosmic restoration of balance or revenge by τίσις, aggressive acts of a self-interested party that seem to serve larger purposes (5.56.1 [oracle]). For his audience, such *tisis* was a more convenient and familiar way of linking events than the original historiographical analysis of cause that Herodotus invented. The balance sometimes seems to result, in the realm of nature especially, from 'divine foresight' (3.108.2). On the human and historical level, the *nomoi* of each society furnishes a more useful norm by which it can and ought to be judged.[38] Those who exceed their own *nomoi* or violate others' are either mad or foolish – or philosophical like Herodotus when he invites the Hellenes to question their own values, as he has.

A cultural relativist, Herodotus explicitly recognizes the legitimacy of each society's peculiar habits (3.38; 7.152.2). Cambyses' disregard of 'Nomos King of all' in both his own family and his foreign policy is described as insanity. Some principles he finds universal, never to be transgressed without recoil. One such universal prescriptive postulate is *suum cuique*, 'to each his own' (1.8.4*), or 'mind your own business.' Gyges' piety has its self-serving aspect, but Herodotus here as elsewhere momentarily employs an all-too-human dramatic character to voice a general truth. Violations of this fundamental rule disturb the natural, social, and political order. Transgressors are often severely punished by the extermination of their families. When men exceed their limits, perpetuation of the *oikos*, the family, fails and therewith the orderly descent of property (παῖς παρὰ πατρός, 1.7.4; 2.65.3, 166.2; cf 4.26.2). This folkloristic warning is embodied in many dramatic examples of retribution, τίσις, a most pervasive Herodotean theme. Limiting cases of human behaviour define and establish acceptable patterns in the personal and the public realms.

Disregard for that nearly universal rule of private property, the exclusive enjoyment of a wife by her husband, opens and closes the *Histories*.[39] Initially, Candaules' love for his own wife led him to transgress custom and urge his loyal minister Gyges to do what he should not: see his master's wife naked. It is at once stated that 'every man ought to look to his own' only: σκοπέειν τινὰ τὰ ἑωυτοῦ. Nearly the first aphorism in the *Histories*, the personal warning will find extensive application to international war and imperialism. Candaules soon lost his kingdom, dynasty, wife, family, and life.[40]

At the end of the *Histories*, the despot Xerxes violated Persian law and custom on incest. After seducing Artaÿnte, his daughter-in-law, he ordered his brother Masistes to give up his wife. Masistes politely at first requested that he be allowed to keep her but finally refused to comply. For his insubordination, defending his own *oikos*, Masistes and his family were destroyed.[41] Xerxes' incestuous infatuation eventually led to his assassination at the hands of his own son, Artaÿnte's husband. Lust for another's property violates established social and political structure, whether the object be another's wife or all Europe and often leads to disaster.

Cyrus and Darius won empires, established law and order, and prospered. They were strategists and statesmen. Cambyses and Xerxes, who inherited their power, were less secure and often less wise about preserving it. They did not look to their own at home and abroad; they did not know their own and wrongly thought indefinite appropriation of nearby women and indefinite expansion abroad to be their manifest destiny (3.17.1; 7.8*, especially α1*). Their violations of sexual morality and religious custom are analogous to their international aggression and failures.[42]

The extirpation of the house of the aggrandizing wrongdoer is a consequence (τίσις) that Herodotus is fond of noting. Seven violators of supra-national *nomoi* are said to be *childless*, at least in the male line: Astyages, Cambyses, Cleomenes, the elder Miltiades, son of Cypselus, Stesagoras, son of Cimon, and the legendary Polybus and Cepheus. Solon calls Tellus the happiest man he had ever seen, in part because he had sons and grandsons (1.30.4*). This pointed reflection of Greek anxiety for continuity of the family marks Tellus' blessedness and wicked men's deserved *tisis*. The five historical figures who die childless are strongly condemned for such actions as religious impiety or murder of kin, outlaw behaviour condemned by universal *nomos*, not local *nomoi*. King Astyages who tried to kill his grandson Cyrus, against the universal custom of respect for blood-ties and inheritance, was overthrown and incarcerated.[43] Cambyses' crimes were legion: incest with two sisters,[44] murder of one of them, and his senseless imperial aggression appear as outrages that seem to cause him to die ἄπαις, childless.[45] Cleomenes, a victim of Herodotus' hostile sources, is falsely said to have reigned briefly, but he is correctly reported as childless in the male line.[46] Both misfortunes serve presumably as retribution for his moral and political 'crimes.' The elder Miltiades and his nephew Stesagoras both die without children (6.38.1–2, 134.2, 135.3). Some curse afflicted the family, or at least Herodotus' informants wished to think so.

Artaÿctes and his only son meet violent torture and barbaric death (9.120.4), fit for one guilty of monstrous crimes.[47] Herodotus confirms the principle of *tisis* and employs little subtlety in connecting problems of family perpetuation with deeds of extraordinary wickedness. The childlessness of Phoenix, a punishment sent by the gods, provided Homeric precedent (*Iliad* 9.453–7, 492–5).

Children comprise the future of one's house (7.224.2); 'oikocide' is obviously the worst fate imaginable, short of genocide.[48] The dreadful baking and stewing of Harpagus' son by Astyages, incidentally ending the former's family line, justified his subsequent treason, his betrayal of the entire Median empire to the Persians. Phanes had to watch all his sons be executed and cannibalized; Leutychides, cursed by Demaratus' mother for destroying her son's position as Spartan king, had no sons afterwards and subsequently suffered exile, the latter explicitly described as *tisis* (3.11; 6.69.5* [the curse on children], 71.2, 72.1).

Tisis tends to level human fortunes. Many readers have remarked on the nemesis that strikes the houses of the wealthy and powerful in the *Histories*, at least through the words of Solon, Amasis, and Artabanus (1.32.9*, 3.40.2–3*, 7.10ε*). The Spartan Talthybiad heralds, the Mermnads, and the Achaemenids are called to suffering in order to expiate crimes; important Spartan and Athenian clans (the *oikoi* of Cleomenes, Leutychides, Miltiades, Pisistratus) fall for offences large or small. Herodotus or his Solon twice suggest that the dispensation has no other ascertainable morality than the restoration of a *status quo ante* (1.5.4, 207.2*). As an observation on the nature of historical events in his time, this considered agreement with folk wisdom is certainly defensible, not a mindless aping of archaic platitudes. Themistocles opined to Eurybiades before Salamis: 'Human plans that are well thought out generally succeed, but divinity is not accustomed to assist foolish human projects' (8.60γ*). Here the workings of providence are not disallowed but they are distanced from the choices that men are forced to make. It is no discredit to Herodotus that he has not finally solved the historical problems of free-will and the role of non-human powers in human events.

Two mini-dramas even more explicitly show that οὐδεὶς ἀνθρώπων ἀδικῶν τίσιν οὐκ ἀποτίσει ('Every man will pay back the debt for his wrongs,' 5.56.1 [oracle]). Panionius made his fortune by castrating young men and selling them as eunuchs. A certain Hermotimus, one of his victims, eventually became the most trusted eunuch of Xerxes. One day he lured his Greek mutilator into bringing his whole family into his power.[49] Thereupon accusing him of 'deeds most unholy' and asserting that his capture and now his punishment were by divine dispensation, he forced Panionius to castrate all four of his sons, and then compelled the sons to castrate their father. Herodotus characterizes this action (8.105.1, cf 106.4) as 'the greatest vengenance (*tisis*) indeed of all we know that ever befell someone who had been wronged.' The deed may be monstrous, but Herodotus does not disapprove. He records it as a warning.

Herodotus (like Anaximander 12 *Vors* F 1) believes that *Dike*, or Justice, exists to restore balance, to right wrongs. 'To pay back the debt that is due' quantitatively states the idea of keeping your own and not appropriating what belongs to another.[50] King Leutychides retells at Athens a traditional tale concerning Glaucus, a fellow Spartan (6.86α–δ*).[51] Glaucus was universally esteemed for his just dealing (δικαιοσύνη). A Milesian entrusted to him a large sum of money (παραθήκη), because of his good reputation and because Sparta was stable whereas Ionia was always exposed to danger and financial uncertainty. Glaucus did not pay back the owed sum as agreed. When he asked for Delphic advice about his perjury, the Pythia rebuked him saying (in paraphrase) that 'Oath has an anonymous child who destroys perjurers and their progeny. He who profits by theft and false oaths will have no offspring, no family (οἶκος) at all, for Oath's son will blot them out, while the man who abides by his oath will have blessed progeny (γενεή).' Glaucus then gave back the money, but to no avail. The historian's character Leutychides here offers what the author Herodotus shrinks from; he tells us what to make of his fable: 'Why I've told you this story will now be stated: Of Glaucus now there is no descendant (ἀπόγονον) whatsoever, nor is there any family thought to be related to Glaucus. Indeed he has been wiped out root and branch (πρόρριζος).'

Only thrice, in exceptionally significant narratives, does Herodotus employ the poetic word *prorrhizos*: Solon's warning to Croesus, Amasis' warning to Polycrates,[52] and here. In all these cases, great good fortune is dangerous; it leads men to greed and other acts that destroy them and their hope of progeny. Glaucus' gratuitous misdeed and its penalty points the moral: the norm, the moral principle of 'from father to son,'[53] the perpetuation of family and family property, fails when respect for obligations is ignored.

To conclude: privileged vocabulary ('boundary' words, images, and metaphors), the subject of women, and a repeated pattern of historical action articulate a ubiquitous notion of boundaries and their violation in the *Histories*. The process of Herodotus investigating the past finds connections as often in parallel events as in sequential ones: actions attract comparison with other actions, repercussions of a minor event lead to major collisions. Herodotus identifies customs and patterns of thought and action within a culture and across societies. The report of their observance and violation becomes a mode of explanation. Historical explanations surface in analogous events narrated with recurrent images, subjects, and principles.[54]

7

Ethnography as Access
to History

The Kwakiutl Indian ... was quite indifferent to the panorama of skyscrapers and of
streets ploughed and furrowed by cars. He reserved all his intellectual curiosity for
the dwarfs, giants and bearded ladies who were exhibited in Times Square ..., for
automats and for the brass balls decorating staircase banisters ... All these things
challenged his own culture, and it was that culture alone which he was seeking to
recognize in certain aspects of ours.

Claude Lévi-Strauss, *The Scope of Anthropology*

Herodotus' ethnological research assisted him in defining the virtues and
deficiencies of the Greeks themselves. The first four books define Greekness
negatively by pointing out how others are different, while the story of their
conduct during the war and the summation of Hellenism found in the
Athenian speech at 8.144.2* establish this essence positively. Similarly, on
an Attic vase the establishment of the outline of a figure precedes the inner
articulation and the colouring of the individual. Herodotus' ethnographic
comprehensiveness adds weight to his historical judgments. Among his
Hellenic contemporaries, confident in the superiority of their civilization, he
shows a unique generosity towards alien cultures and wisdom. Only a
madman laughs at the apparently arbitrary νόμοι, customs and habits, of
others (3.38.2), he argues, but even the relativist cultural anthropologist or
historian can define and judge otherness only from the standpoint of his own
education and culture. Such evaluations have little worth if they are reached
in a manner either condescending or unaware of a functional approach to
human institutions. Yet a conscientious investigator using his own heritage
as a standard by which to discuss others' success and failure, efficiency,
sophistication, science, and so on, can transcend parochialism.

Herodotus had no time-tested method for evaluating native informants, and he sometimes misunderstood accurate information in his passion for the unusual, the opposite, and the symmetrical. Correspondences between cultures stimulated his interrogations. The startling growth of the Persian empire provided an impetus for Herodotus to discover what made Greek resistance uniquely successful. The ethnologist, unlike the Kwakiutl tourist, tries to extend sympathetic observation to objects and events that find no parallel in his own, but, like the Indian, he will find himself exploring those aspects of a foreign culture that respond to his curiosity about his own. This chapter examines why Herodotus thought extended accounts of other peoples, not least ones unimportant for his history (the Indians) or politically feeble (the Egyptians), could advance his central historical purpose. Herodotus' motive, we argue, was to suggest explanatory hypotheses for the conflict and for the unexpected Greek victory in the Persian Wars. *Nomos* and *nomoi* are at the root of both. Herodotus approaches historical explanation not by presenting his material as cause-and-effect reasoning, but by high-lighting polarities between cultures. As a Greek, he sometimes is more interested in explaining differences than in the events themselves.

Herodotus' own θεωρίη, autopsy, and intelligent questions invited the suggestive comparisons in books 1 through 5, chapter 17, more ethnography and geography than an account of major rulers and battles. From his point of view, these contemporary phenomena permitted his own autopsy, whereas historical accounts depended on the reports and memories of others (ἀκοή, cf 2.99.1), the day-to-day perspectives of the combatants that were only open to the test of comparison with other, equally limited informants. His sources were more likely to have been ordinary folks than the δόκιμοι, Alcmaeonid nobles, Spartan kings, and the like. Because in historical accounts Herodotus could not see for himself but only compare the recollections of his sources, the war narrative of the later books is more derivative, more distant from ascertainable facts than the anthropological, ethnological, and even geographical sections. Therefore and paradoxically, what we prize as the most important historiographical section of the *Histories* may have seemed inferior to him.[1]

The phrase 'as far as we know' appears in books 1 through 4 twenty-four times, but only nine times in books 6 through 9,[2] not because the history of the war was more perfectly ascertained, but for two other, widely divergent reasons. First, the earlier books explore many matters where there was a clear line between what could be directly observed (eg, a pyramid) and what could not (eg, source of the Nile), whereas the later books detail matters where little empirical control was conceivable. Second, on some ethnographic and geographic questions no answers at all were proffered to the investigator, and Herodotus likes to mark utter absence of human knowledge. Therefore, when the phrase contains more than rhetorical emphasis, it underlines the possibility and limits of knowledge of ethnographic and geographic *historie*, which differ from those for historical, or temporal, *historie*.

Books 2 and 4 especially, by the choice of subjects selected for mention, indicate what Herodotus thought most un-Greek and most noteworthy. Babylonians use no olive oil but sesame oil, no grape wine but palm wine, grow no figs but produce large and plentiful grain crops; they do not rely on rainfall but create their own irrigation networks. They have round rather than pointed water-craft. The Red Sea (ie, the northeast part of the Indian Ocean), unlike the Mediterranean, has daily tides. The land of Egypt is irrigated and grows its crops with little labour; bread there is made from spelt, not ordinary wheat; they too have no grapes. The Egyptian climate is constant. They have a specialist for every disease. Scythian farmers 'plant grain not to eat but to sell,' an impossible feat in the agricultural poverty of old Greece. The Northern cold turns the ground to rock and the water into ice, and it rains in summer not winter, 'unlike anywhere else.' The rivers never fail and the Ister never even varies its flow. There are no pigs in Scythia, but so much wood that houses and even temples are made from it. The Scyths shun Greek customs; just as peculiar are the African Asbystae who imitate these customs (4.76.1, 170). Circumcision, more repugnant and alien to the Greeks than castration, is regularly mentioned,[3] a self-evident proof of a group's un-Greekness.

Egyptians

Herodotus in Egypt provides more ethnography than history;[4] he had little choice since the only men knowledgeable in past Egyptian traditions and available to him possessed a complete list of the names of Kings but knew little of noteworthy historical achievements (2.143.4; 100.1, 101.1–2). They provided a kind of annals but no history. Yet Herodotus was not seeking battles, kings, and revolutions for his narrative, but a *prolegomenon* to understanding the war he was to record.

The principal method of his ethnological investigations, especially in 2.1–99, is polarity.[5] All Herodotean *logoi* are ethnocentric, with the Greeks at the centre, from 1.1.1 (ἐπὶ τήνδε τὴν θάλασσαν). This is even true of his account of the Egyptians. The Greeks provide one familiar standard, the Egyptians a counter-standard among the civilized peoples, the Scyths another standard among the uncivilized. The peculiar Egyptians furnish data by which to contrast and measure other settled societies, particularly the Greeks. Croesus the Hellenized Lydian serves as a bridge between Greeks and barbarians, but the Egyptians appear to be a civilized people as opposite to the Greeks as he can discover. 'In almost all cases they established customs and laws opposite (ἔμπαλιν) to those of the rest of mankind' (35.2; so too the Ethiopians, 3.20.2). This ethnographic assertion introduces a long list of substantiating antithetical customs and actions. Similarly Herodotus himself explicitly raises the topic of opposites at the end of a geographical discussion of the unique Nile and Egypt's unique climate: 'Egypt has a different climate and a river contrary in nature to all other rivers' (35.2; also 19.3). These 'contrary' characteristics are θωμάσια, marvels: 'I shall go on with my account of Egypt because it has the most *thomasia*' and 'because of the fact that more monuments which beggar description (ἔργα λόγου μέζω) are to be found there than anywhere else in the world.'[6]

Bigger often means better for the logographer who intends to 'one-up' Greek beliefs of greatness and challenge common assumptions (cf 2.10).[7] The large, the opposite, the peculiar, the paradoxical, all were marvellous to Greeks and possessed, we believe, explanatory power for Herodotus. Cambyses' threat to turn everything in Egypt topsy-turvy[8] would amuse Herodotus' audience because, to the Greeks, everything was upside-down to begin with. In the lengthy list of about twenty-six peculiarities found in chapters 35 and 36, Herodotus indicates on eleven occasions that Egyptians differ from the Greeks or from all men: the nature of their climate and their river, their customs in general, the direction of their weaver's weft, their priests' shaven heads, their growing of hair in mourning, their cohabitation with animals, their scorn for a diet of wheat and barley (one of Herodotus' most preposterous errors), their practice of cicumcision, their fastening of ships' sails in-board, and their writing from right to left. Later he offers more of the same (eg, 37.1, 80.2, 82.2, and especially 91.1). One must not chastise Herodotus' frequent mistakes in isolating the Egyptians. The fact that he fastens on the exceptions and 'struck by the contrasts to Greece, forgets to notice that they are only occasional in Egypt,'[9] only strengthens our point, namely that Herodotus sought the surprising in order to demonstrate a thesis, Egyptian polarity to the rest of mankind, especially to the Greeks (35.1–2). Here and in modern ethnography, the researcher often implicitly feeds a model to his informants, who, unconsciously, feed it back to him: seek polarities and you will find them. Herodotus was not attempting a full-scale history of Egypt or an ethnographic survey for its own sake. Just as success in the Persian Wars helped the Greeks define themselves, so Herodotus wishes to understand the implications of the war's result, by defining Hellas' unique qualities. Therefore it is wrong to argue that his only aim in book 2 is entertainment.[10] The 'new and different' helps explain the 'old and familiar.'

Definition demands description, measurement, comparison, and contrast. Although Herodotus may be interested in Egypt for itself, his descriptions of Egyptians and other non-Greek peoples describe humanity as it was known, and demarcate both those facets unique to the Greeks and those which the Greeks shared or borrowed. Books 1 through 4 range over the known peoples to the South, East, and North, all different from each other but all contributing something to the human totality. Discussion of earthly extremes indicates and demarcates the temperate and the moderate, the concept of limit in climate, products, human customs, and societies. Herodotus has an anthropocentric geography. Geography concerns him insofar as it reveals human custom and history. What is not 'home' is 'away,' alternatives in space and time. [11]

The prominent role of women in Egypt can serve as an example of Egyptian anti-Greekness. In Egypt, women are the merchants while men weave at home; they carry burdens on their shoulders whereas men carry them on their heads; they urinate standing while men squat; daughters, not sons, have the responsibility of maintaining aged parents; women wear fewer garments than men; women, not men, lead phallic processions. [12] Even female fish in Egypt lead the males on the trip upstream (93.2).

Herodotus particularly emphasizes the Greeks' debt to Egyptian religion. He regards the Egyptians as the most religious of all men, and much attention is devoted to cult organization including rituals and convocations (4.2, 37.1–5, 58 et alibi). Egyptians instructed the Greeks about the gods, their names, their myths, and how and where to worship and depict them. [13] They taught the Greeks nearly all they believed about divine history and cult. [14] These two nations alone (he alleges) are alike in prohibiting sexual intercourse in religious precincts. [15] Herodotus, however, examines Egyptian religion primarily for the differences between the myths and the cults of the two nations, because these will reveal how the two cultures have diverged. The Egyptians have no heroic myths, no demigods (50.3). They are excessively god-fearing, but their gods and god-images are sub-human, animal in fact (65.2–67). They will grieve more for a dead dog or cat than for a family's house burned to the ground (66.3). When a Mendesian goat dies, the entire Egyptian district goes into mourning (46.3). These nomoi interest him just because they are foreign to Greek thought. [16]

This focus on religion introduces a less obvious point – Herodotus does not admire many aspects of Egyptian life and history. Although the Egyptians have the longest history and the most numerous extra-ordinary monuments, [17] only one Egyptian law and one custom are specifically praised (177.2; 64.1). The Egyptians are not able to adapt to changed circumstances or to change itself. Quite the contrary, they convert even the flowing river into stationary land, symbolic of their society frozen in past ways and glories.

Herodotus learned much in Egypt. The architectural marvels and the endless oddities, from humble greetings to the frequency of omens and the reported ages of the gods (80.2, 82.2, 145.1), are detailed. Sometimes he overgeneralizes his sketchy information (eg, on women, diet, clothing), but this results from his real concern, to portray a *civilized* society that was as different from the Greek as he could find, in order to transform his predecessors' ethnography from discrete, item-by-item description into a form of historical explanation.

His impulse towards discovering polarities led him to express surprise sometimes over the unexceptional. He marvels at the Egyptians' defecating inside and eating outside, at their kneading dough with their feet and clay with their hands (35.3, 36.3). His appetite for pricking the pride of the Greeks leads him to insist on barbarian priority, the antiquity of Egyptian civilization, its role as legal and religious example for the Athenians (177.2, 171.2–3), the way it has instructed the Greeks (58) and other peoples such as the Ethiopians (30.5).

He was particularly affected by Egyptian knowledge of things temporal. The civilization was old; Egyptians 'exercised' ancestral memory and attended to the calendar in a way that made knowledge of the past possible (2.1, 4.1, 142). Their unparalleled knowledge and respect for the past developed Herodotus' own scale of earthly time (11.4) and prepared the ground for *historie*, investigation of the human past. The temporal and cultural perspective that Herodotus gained from the Egyptians allows him to criticize more limited views, and this partly explains why book 2 is the most polemical of the *Histories*, richest in first-person singular pronouns, most different from its fellows.[18] Book 4 comes closest to book 2's disregard of events in the Greek world, but there the *uncivilized* societies of Europe and Africa provide the polarities to the Greeks.

Egyptian wonders and virtues do not shield that culture from the historian's critique of their political life. Their institutions are largely determined by geography, which we discuss below. The Egyptians are civilized but not free or even capable of enjoying the rights and obligations of citizens (147.2). Their material and spiritual culture, like that of most nations, precludes political freedom. They are trapped in their *nomoi*. Like the otherwise completely different Scyths, they shun the ideas of others, they cannot flexibly adapt to foreign ways or technological innovation (4.76.1 and 2.77.1, 80.1, 91.1, 79.1: 'they use their ancestral customs (νόμοι) and acquire none other'). Their *nomoi* promote internal cohesion but determine their political fate, political subjection, internal for millennia and now external as well. Their last independent rulers and subsequent pretenders had to rely on foreign mercenaries for military initiatives and protection (152.5, 154.3–4; 163.1; 3.4.1, 11.1, etc). Their servile destiny is a result not of accident but of geography, agricultural wealth and its consequences, and of a rigid and unchanging national character.

This point is underlined by a chance observation: 'Barbarians all, the Egyptians call those who do not share their language' (158.5). The attitude ironically reflects on the parallel Greek attitude and on the Persians' exalted opinion of themselves (1.134.2), but, more important, Herodotus attributes the successes of the Greeks and Persians to their adaptive capacities (1.135.1). He observes that these two nations above all others readily learn from others, welcome innovation and enterprise, are not trapped unreflectingly in their *nomoi*, like the Egyptians who are isolated from present reality by their reverence for the past. The successful Persians alone get explicit credit for adaptability (1.135), at least in superficial matters such as clothing and armour, but the Greeks borrow more customs and institutions than anyone else in the *Histories*, and a willingness to deviate from custom and pattern marks their successful figures (such as Pisistratus, Democedes, Miltiades, and Themistocles).

Nomos isolates every society from all others by creating a horizon of attitudes and expectations. Furthermore, it creates a basis from which each society judges other societies' acts. *Nomos* 'king of all' is yet a fragile monarch: to compare one *nomos* to another calls the basis of this kingship into question. To recognize the power of *nomos* is to be at one remove from it, and to possess the attitude necessary for studying it.[19] The historian's virtue, and surprisingly, that of Greek civilization in general according to Herodotus, is receptivity to foreign wisdom. He explodes the idea that the Greeks invented everything,[20] and his exposition proves that the Greeks were less unusual than some of them liked to think. He viewed the Greeks as latecomers in intellectual and religious matters (2.53.1), but their very dependence on others, their ability to adapt and adopt, turns out to be a decisive advantage.

The significant Greek discovery of the relativity of *nomos* may have been the result of the sudden intrusion of the Persians and their peoples into the narrow Aegean orbit. Hecataeus and Herodotus, following the lead of Xenophanes (21 *Vors* B 16), first substantiated the idea that *nomos* is geographically conditioned and Herodotus elevated it into a principle of historical explanation. Foreign *nomoi*, at first glance inexplicable and merely curious in themselves, become a kind of answer, a way to account for historical events. The interrelated use of polarities, environmental factors, and the idea that *nomoi* limit historical action involves, like any system of historical explanation, drastic simplification of intricate processes, but the innovative attempt to make sense of the disparate facts of the past marks the first step for Western historiography.

Persians

The virtues and vices of the Greeks are defined not only by the Egyptians. The function of Herodotus' lengthy ethnography is to give historical meaning to the dichotomy 'Greek versus Barbarian.' This comparative function sharply distinguishes it from Egyptian or Greek parochialism. He often praises barbarian habits (such as the separation of male Persians from infant sons), certain Persian penal practices (1.136.2–137.1), Babylonian and Venetic wisdom in selecting spouses (1.196), the Babylonian custom for curing the ill (1.197), Egyptian sexual abstinence in temple-precincts (2.64–65.1), Egyptian law requiring a declaration of assets (2.177.2), Scythian cannabis-vapour baths (4.75.1 *fin*), and the Scythian method of avoiding subjection, which he calls 'the one greatest thing of all human contrivance, more clever than anything else we know' (4.46.2).[21] Herodotus liked to acknowledge barbarian superiority and to cast aspersions on Hellenic claims to originality and wisdom. Even though he was not recommending that the Hellenes adopt these *nomoi*, they allowed him to criticize Greek practices.[22]

He admires the Persians more than any other foreign folk. For example, he generously records the Persians' deep respect for brave fallen foes (7.238.2) and the noteworthy deeds and characters of their great men (eg, Mascames, 7.106; Boges, 7.107.2). The picture of even the contemporary Persians conveyed by 1.131–41 presents a people simpler, tougher, and more generous than the Greeks, not merely noble savages but valiant and forthright truth-tellers, straight-shooters, sober and hard-riding conquerors nourished in a barren land (especially 1.71.2–3*, 136.2, 3.15.2–3, and 9.122). Even the portrait of the overly bold Xerxes is sometimes favourable. The handsome and stately autocrat (7.187.2) asserts in an existential moment that men must take courage and act, otherwise 'you will never do anything at all.' Fortune favours the bold, he declares, great deeds require great risks, and that is how the Persians reached their acme of power and wealth (7.50.1–3*). Mardonius had earlier appealed to Xerxes' ambitious nature (7.5.2, 7.9γ*), and Herodotus himself subscribes to the view that Xerxes was driven by a desire for historical achievement: 'As I believe after reflection, Xerxes ordered his men to dig [the unnecessary Athos canal] because of pride (μεγαλοφροσύνη), wishing to demonstrate his power and leave behind memorials (μνημόσυνα) of it' (7.24). The Persians turn out to be, in fact, most similar to the Greeks in their devotion to national freedom, in their courage and adaptiveness, and in their remarkable record of military achievement.

The generous praise, nevertheless, of Persian national character is modulated by the less favourable portraits of individual Persian autocrats. Each one, whatever his virtues, eventually chooses to attack, without a provocation convincing to the reader, a relatively poor, distant, often primitive, and always unyielding foe: for Cyrus the Massagetae, for Cambyses the Ethiopians and the Ammonians (3.26), for Darius the Scyths (see 4.83.1) and later the Athenians, for Xerxes the Greeks. Each meets his downfall – sometimes humiliation, disaster, and death – for mounting what seems a politically senseless and morally objectionable campaign. Without arguing here this hypothesis,[23] it is clear that Herodotus' respect for the Persian Empire and his presentation of their argument that Persian imperial *nomoi* encouraged, or demanded, constant expansion (7.8α1–2*, Xerxes; 7.11.2*; cf the words in Thucydides of Pericles, 2.62.3*, 63.2–3*; and of Alcibiades, 6.18.3*) did not justify for him the economic expoitation, the lack of political liberty, and the frequency of social indignity, that Persian despotism permitted and perhaps required. Despotism is always based on fear and compulsion (cf 7.103*), a vital point quietly reinforced by many details. One instance: orders for lashing in Herodotus invariably are given by despots (16 occurrences).[24] Twelve of these commands come from Persian rulers, seven from Xerxes himself. They are especially crowded in book 7 (22.1, 35.1, 54.3, 56.1, 103.4*, 223.3), where the contrast to Spartan 'freedom' and self-motivation is most dramatic. Xerxes may argue that one must attack or be attacked (7.11.2*), but, as presented by Herodotus, his and Mardonius' justifications based on 'revenge' and 'self-defence' are only a facade for imperialist aggression. In the end, the Persians are largely defeated by their own errors (as a Thucydidean speaker notes, 1.69.5*), not mere accidents but defects of their system.

Herodotus' admiration for the Persian *nomos* that forbids the King to execute anyone for only one offence (1.137.1) is seriously offset by its lack of illustration in the *Histories*. In fact admirable Persian *nomoi* are frequently conspicuous for the Kings' unpunished and unpunishable failures to observe them. Furthermore, the Persians' lauded devotion to the truth (1.136.2, 138.1) seems ludicrous when subject to such self-serving, casuistical interpretations as the Persian Amasis' fraudulent (δόλῳ) covenant of security when the attack on Barca failed to capture it (4.201). More unsettling than Persian disregard of reason and justice are the frightening caricatures of justice that the kings perpetrate. Cambyses, wishing to marry his sister, contrary to custom (οὐκ ἐωθότα; θεσμοί [only here]), called his supreme judicial council into session and asked whether a law, *nomos*, permitted a Persian to marry his sister. 'No,' they answered but then discovered another *nomos* which held that 'the King of the Persians might do whatever he wishes' (3.31*; *nomos* appears six times in this paragraph). Cambyses in a fit once wished to kill Croesus, the adviser that he had inherited, but Cambyses' servants saved him, since they knew their master's mercurial temper; soon after he indeed did call for his adviser, and although he was glad to find Croesus alive, he executed the servants for disobeying orders (3.36.5–6).

Herodotus believed that Cambyses was insane (3.29.1, 30.1, 37.1) and Xerxes over-ambitious. Yet even the generally sober Darius grotesquely rewards the imprisoned physician Democedes, who saved his life, with new chains, now of gold (3.130.4). Xerxes' justice was equally bizarre. Pythius the Lydian was generous to the Persian army and for this was befriended by Xerxes and was by him vastly enriched. When Pythius subsequently asked whether just one of his five sons might be excused from military service in order to care for him in his old age, the unpredictably enraged Xerxes had this eldest and beloved son cut in half and ordered the army to march between the halves to punish the shamelessness of this 'slave.' He spared the father because of his former good deeds and their *xeinia* (7.27–8, 38–9; cf a similar caprice of Darius, 4.84). Xerxes, fleeing Greece by ship after his naval defeat (in an alternative version of events that Herodotus rejects), is informed by the captain that his life can be saved only if his grandees will leap overboard to lighten the storm-tossed vessel. They grovel and jump off, and Xerxes is saved. On reaching shore Xerxes grants the captain a gold crown for saving the king's life, then immediately has his head cut off for destroying so many Persian nobles (8.118–19). This tale, though known by Herodotus to be historically false, nevertheless embodies Herodotus' concept of autocratic 'justice.'[25] The anecdote's ideological significance outweighs the historical falsehood.

Autocracy dominates civilized as well as most uncivilized, barbarian societies; it is both congenial to their *nomoi* and a reflex of greater centralization. Autocracy as a polarity to self-rule violates the norm developed in Hellenic communities; the age of kings is long past and tyrants are seen as anachronisms or imposed eccentricities. Egyptians cannot live without a monarch; the Medes and later the Persian conspirators freely choose to obey one, and the latter are tricked at once into accepting Darius the Huckster; but Greeks only unwillingly endure the coercion of despots (2.147.2; 1.96–8, 3.83.1, 85–8; 5.92.η5*, 1.164.2, 5.49.2*). The arbitrary rule of an individual is equated with slavery (eg, 2.1.2, 172.5; 3.83.3, 155.2*; 5.66.1; 7.102.2*, 135.3*; 156.2), and exemplary Greeks prefer autonomy with poverty to the material wealth of slaves (eg, 7.102.1*, 135.2–3*, 8.144.1*). The relentlessly negative portraits of despots are set in yet higher relief by the uniquely positive impact of the word 'despot' in the climactic speech to Xerxes at Thermopylae of the unkinged king, the 'apolitical' (ἄπολις) Demaratus: 'an unfettered autocrat (δεσπότης), Law (νόμος), rules the Spartans, and they tremble at and fear this ruler much more by far than your subjects fear you' (7.104.4*). The ex-monarch here underlines the difference between the fear of a man that motivates Persia's subjects and the obedience to *nomos* that will keep the Spartans at their battle-stations.

Nomos and justice are dear to every people in the *Histories* (the Median legend at 1.96–7 illustrates this observation), but despots manipulate customs and institutions for their own ends, regularly disturbing them, as Otanes warns, and Cambyses and Xerxes, Candaules and Croesus, Periander and Sicyonian Cleisthenes illustrate (3.80.5*; 3.3.3*, 31.2; 7.238.1–2; 8.109.3*; 1.8.4*, 10.3; 1.76.1–2, 92.4; 5.92η; 5.67–8). Pisistratus, the most remarkable exception, requires Herodotus to note his good behaviour (1.59.6; but cf 61.1), but the essential point remains: autocrats breach rather than observe custom, law, and justice, the foundations of society.

Scythians

Herodotus enlarges his account of the Scyths because they are very different both from the Greeks and from the Egyptians and from almost all other peoples as well. Although they share with the Egyptians an aversion to foreign customs (4.76.1, 80.5), in most other respects they present a diametrically opposed geography and organization of their people (4.29, 59.2, etc): they inhabit the cold and barren North; they call themselves the youngest of earth's peoples; they have no images of their gods and in fact do not generally distinguish among them; they are always in motion and even convert what is usually stationary – the community – into a transitory mode; they are nomadic pastoralists (φερέοικοι) who have no monuments, no cities, no walls or temples, few gods, no wise men, no wonders.[26] In short, these barbarians have no history, no record of their past for Herodotus to report, except when other men's policies or travels have impinged on them. Other than the rivers, there are no wonders, θωμάσια (4.82), natural or man-made.[27] Their very unremarkableness is remarkable. They provide a set of opposites for other communities, especially the Greek *polis*, in their locale, diet, sex habits, burial customs, and so on.

The Ister (or Danube), however, alone of rivers, can compare with the Nile in length, volume, and number of mouths. It is even larger, he says

(2.33.2–34.2; 2.10.2 with 4.47.2–48). Here is a start for a comparison of the Scyths with other nations. The courses of the rivers mirror each other, Herodotus believed (2.33.2–34.2), and, in several respects, the Scythian *logos* mirrors the Egyptian.

In general, his description of Scythian culture shows a more nuanced and consequential connection between habitat and habits than the Egyptian *logos* suggests (4.16–24). Here climate and topography provide checks and stimuli for human ingenuity. The Scyths employ unusual natural conditions to their advantage when the Persians attack, and receive due credit for their intelligent and effective response to danger (4.46.2–47.1; cf 7.49.1–2*, 7.102*). Civilized, hot, fertile, and rich Egypt fell victim to Persian aggression while savage, chill, infertile, and poor Scythia successfully resisted the Persians (cf 7.50.4*).[28] The unpredictable and incalculable behaviour of the Scythians made them unconquerable. Their particular *nomoi* 'explain' their historical actions; they describe what is characteristic and predictable about them. The reports of their *nomoi* have been reformulated into an explanation of their adaptive successes and failures.

The account of Darius' invasion of Scythia, difficult to date or explain, hardly squares with eastern European geography and the exigencies of time, and sometimes Herodotus' geography is even self-contradictory. Once, however, the reader accepts the extremely limited availability of trustworthy information (4.18, 88) or the limits to what the traveller might have seen for himself (4.76.6, 81.2), the errors are explicable. The narrative supplies a key to Xerxes' invasion, and the Scythian account is shaped to make the later invasion of Greece intelligible. Their nomadism is their essential strategy, and by it they defeat Darius' attempt on their liberty. Just so, but with the difference that they consciously select among alternatives, the Athenians' rational decision and willingness to abandon their city (cf 8.62* as well as 7.143.3), send away their families, become inaccessible to the Persian army, stymie the greater military machine's strategy and tactics.[29]

The great imperialistic failure of Darius serves to foreshadow Xerxes' failure and to illustrate the only example of Scythian political wisdom: in order to stay free and avoid subjection, men should never settle in one place (4.46.3 with 133.2, 136.4, 137.1, 139.2, on Ionian enslavement).

Herodotus also censured other aliens. In addition to Egyptian, Persian, and Scythian habits already noted, he deflated the origins of Median court etiquette (1.99); he objects to temple-prostitution (1.199); he criticizes the neighbours of the Scyths for their lack of civilized arts and for failing to educate themselves or produce any men learned in local lore (4.46.1–2, reading λόγιον). He seems to disdain the ignorance of the Garamantes who cannot even defend themselves (4.174); and he condemns the community of women and promiscuity found among the Auses (4.180.5). He is the first extant Greek writer to employ the word *barbaros* frequently (245 occurrences against Aeschylus' fourteen,[30] Pindar's one [*Isthmians* 6.24]; never in Homer), generally in a neutral mode, but at least twice with the later sense of 'barbarous' (7.35.2, 9.79*).

It would be too much to say 'he was free from national prejudice,'[31] for the contrast of Greek and barbarian is the basic polarity and principal theme of the *Histories*, and, certainly, in speeches delivered at climactic moments, his admiration for the Hellenes is evident (eg, 7.102*, 8.144*, 9.79*). Yet his judgments are *ad hoc*, and do not damage his cool presentation of important characters and peoples representing all sides. Croesus is foolish and later wise; Darius cheats when he is just a nobleman but he becomes a fair monarch; Themistocles is the Athenian hero of Salamis but also a greedy, self-seeking individual. Unadmirable qualities are attributed, in fact, to all the Greeks at Salamis. Because he was not searching for heroes and villains, because he had no *idée fixe* to skew his collection of data, he wins admiration for intellectual generosity and impartiality. Of course he expresses strong opinions on behaviours and policies of individuals and nations, but no party had a monopoly of good or bad qualities. Without a doubt, the Greeks furnish an absent model, a set of expectations. Yet other peoples are named, described, classified, and compared, but for a specific purpose, so that ethnology can supply more than exotic details. With Herodotus it supplies a new method for discovering the Greeks' differences and for appreciating their unique achievement.

Greeks

Two questions required a much wider scope than the history of Xerxes' invasion itself. What made the Greeks different from all their neighbours near and far? How could a small and disunited but civilized people have repelled the united might of vast Asia? Books 1 through 5 suggest answers. The thread for these *logoi* is the concentration of oriental might in Persian hands and the increasing contacts between Greeks and Persians, but the amount of space given here to the military campaigns and the activities of monarchs is negligible compared with the attention given to national customs and beliefs as well as with the history of institutions and political structure when there was one to be salvaged, as in the cases of Egypt and Persia. If we acknowledge an intent deeper than 'entertainment,' that purpose is to provide comparisons and contrasts, polarities and analogies, that isolate Greek uniqueness, defects and virtues. Greek parochialism, for instance, has good and bad consequences. It makes it harder for the Greeks to unite, but it also makes it harder for the Persian military forces to conquer them. Old Greece's poor soil makes life hard but (in Herodotus' view) makes hardier civilians and more intransigent soldiers. The exploration of alien nations in books 1 through 5 does not provide post-Aristotelian cause and effect explanation, of course, but offers polarities and analogies, empirical data that encourage the reader to consider how human events came to happen as they did. Indirect historical explanation, one might call this. Immerwahr formulates the distinction thus:[32] 'Herodotus' conception of history shows it to be an analogue (as well as part) of nature ...' And elsewhere he applies this observation to the Egyptian *logos*: 'Egyptian customs differ from those of the rest of mankind *not because* Egypt's geographical situation differs from the rest of the world, but *just as* it is different.'

Herodotus may be considered to some extent to be an 'environmental determinist.' Like the author of the Hippocratic *Airs, Waters, Places* (chapter 24), he believes that climate affects national character, just as climate affects appearance and physiology. The climate of Egypt differs completely (35.1) from that of Greece and anywhere else. It never varies, and this, he asserts, makes the Egyptians and the Libyans the healthiest of men (77.3), for disease arises from the changes of season which most men experience. Herodotus' interest in nature is conditioned by its relevance to cultural modes and historical action. Therefore, his purpose in commenting on the singularity of a river, an animal, human semen, cranial thickness, or a land's productivity in plants or animals (eg, 92–8, 68–74; 3.101.2, 12, 106–9) is generally to illustrate an ethnological consequence.

Herodotus on occasion 'explains' a national characteristic, character, or custom by climate or topography (1.71.2*, 1.142.1–2, 2.35.2, 4.29, 7.102.1*, 9.122.3), as the medical author regularly does (see especially *De aere* 12, 23–4), but neither regards climate as the sole or sufficient cause of human events, a position that is unarguable for Herodotus and can be observed in the Hippocratic writer's recognition of the significant role of human institutions (*nomos*, *De aere* 14.1–3; cf *Epidemica* 1.23.8). When Herodotus simplistically relates the uniqueness of the Egyptian people to the uniqueness of their river and climate (2.35.2), this solitary example may reflect a particular debt to Hecateus or another ethnological writer on a popular subject, but more probably the comparison was attractive because it furnished a transition from geography to anthropology.

Geography does not determine history in Herodotus; it can only condition human existence and action. Climate may influence devotion to liberty, but national spirit is no predictable product of natural forces. This discussion of factors pertinent to the character of political institutions and peoples is clearer in Herodotus than in the Hippocratic's account of environmental influences on national character and willingness to defend autonomy.

Although Herodotus does not say outright that the Egyptians' acceptance of despotism and unchanging institutions is the result of Egypt's stable climate, such a hypothesis concerning his attitude seems legitimate when one recollects his parallel reflections on the effect of climate and geography on the character and abilities of the Ionians, the Scythians, the Persians, the mainland Greeks, and the other peoples of the world.[33] The ecology of Egypt even defines the nation's boundaries. Where the Nile's water does not reach, there no Egyptians will be found. No land except Babylonia was richer (Babylon, 1.193.2; cf Libya, 4.199.2), no people less warlike. If any one thing was responsible for Egyptian peculiarity, it was geography. The edifices far surpassing anything Greek (2.124–34, 148.2–3, 149.1, 175, 176);[34] the 'infinite' extent of the land itself (ἄφθονος) and the huge population which it supported (6.2–3; 61.1, 124.3, 158.5, 165–6, 177.1); and, of course, the wonder of wonders for a Greek, the vast river that extends the very meaning of the term (4.3, 10, 31), the Nile, which in flood can only be compared to the Aegean sea (97); finally the fact that the folk of the Delta gain their generous agricultural produce almost without effort (14.2, ἀπονητότατα)[35] – all these geographical indices support Herodotus' belief that environment shapes national character and history. The scope of the accomplishments of the human race is thus expanded for a Greek audience. Ethnography provides a counter-movement, the background, to the forward thrust of historical events. Explanation, αἰτίη, sends the audience back frequently, while the historical apodexis idles for a moment.

Book 1 through chapter 27 of book 5 explores this non-Greek world, especially the extremes, and provides comparisons to Greek culture and the leading states of archaic Greece. Chapter 28 of book 5 through book 6 examines the territory of common interest to Persia and Hellas and, in the process, reveals the unique nature of Greek politics which will be decisive in books 7 through 9. It is originally unclear whether the Greeks can choose to face the Asian threat in their disunited state. Will the delicate balance between divisive forces and communal interests permit effective opposition?[36] The strengths and weaknesses of the Persian empire and its constituent peoples have been detailed, but only with books 6 and 7 does Herodotus focus on those Hellenic characteristics responsible for victory in the great war. Their unique combination of intelligence, independence, and adaptive organization, their sense of human limit and recognition of the need for moderation, their dedication to self-rule will be decisive. The Hellenes enjoy a variety of seasons and a temperate climate that stimulates rather than enervates them (3.106.1, 7.5.3; cf 1.142.1, 7.10α3* and De aere 12). They value and possess mental ability, σοφίη, in all its moral, scientific, and technical varieties (eg, Democedes, 3.130.3).[37] The laws and customs of the rest of the world, even in Persia and learned Egypt, rarely surpass Greek counterparts in intelligence (4.95.2 generalizes about the Thracians) and effectiveness (Greek medicine is gentler and more successful than Egyptian, and, by implication, Persian, 3.130.3). In sum, barbarian ingenuity and diversity do not obscure Herodotus' reasoned belief in Greek mental and moral superiority, a result of climate, poverty,[38] political institutions,[39] and competitiveness.[40]

Their bravery (τόλμα) at times can be a marvel (θῶμα, 7.135.1), nurtured by freedom (7.135.3*, 102.1–2*) and by poverty (7.102.1*, 8.111.3*). At their best, they value excellence, liberty, law, and human dignity and disdain brutal violence, the despotism of a single ruler, and luxury. From a run-away Spartan traitor comes the decisive distinction. Demaratus sums up for Herodotus what is quintessentially Greek and not oriental: 'Poverty is native, but valour (arete) must be acquired; we attain it from wisdom and mighty law. By arete Greece wards off poverty and despotism. The Lacedaemonians will never accept an offer involving slavery (δουλοσύνη) for Greece, even if all the other Greeks should assent. Numbers don't matter for them' (7.102*, paraphrased). Xerxes laughed at what he imagined to be the rodomontade of the refugee, fugitive from a nation of liars (cf 1.153.1). Yet he had earlier acknowledged that the courageous Greeks alone stood between him and universal dominion (7.53.2*), and soon he will perceive how true this is. Direct speech does not here distance Herodotus from his character Demaratus; the narrative endorses the dramatic rhetoric. The frequent insistence of Herodotus on Hellenic failures of nerve, mistakes, and fault[41] ought not to be overlooked, but his criticisms form part of the matrix that will explain the greatest and most wonderful achievements (ἔργα) of all, the survival and victory of the Hellenes.

The history of Sperthias and Boulis (7.133–7) recapitulates both Herodotus' generous presentation of barbarians and his Hellenic preferences. The Athenians and Spartans before the war of 480 had broken universal custom (τὰ νόμιμα) by killing Persian heralds. These two Talthybiad heralds volunteered to expiate by self-sacrifice the Spartans' crime. Their courage and the words that explain it are themselves thomata (135.1). When they arrived at the headquarters of General Hydarnes, they explained that the gifts and generous friendship of the Persian king were inferior to freedom, and that he could not judge the issue because he knew only slavery (135.3*). Sent on to the royal palace at Susa, they there refused to prostrate themselves before the king of kings since it was not acceptable (ἐν νόμῳ) in Sparta to worship mortals.[42] Their sole obligation was to pay with their lives the penalty for Spartan impiety (136.2*). Xerxes magnanimously allowed them to return home, refusing to match their countrymen's crime and thereby to free the Greeks from divine blame.

Thus Herodotus has enclosed – in a gloomy frame of Greek, indeed Spartan, sacrilegious rashness and political crime, and within an inner frame of Persian hospitality and moral dignity – a dramatic endorsement of Greek freedom, Greek ability to distinguish human from divine honours, and Greek political values. The insertion provides another incident in Herodotus' continuing contrast of freedom to slavery, Greek to barbarian values. Hydarnes could offer only material wealth, and at a cost of accepting tyrannical power and slavery (135.2*). Sweet (γλυκύ) freedom will be defended to the death by those who have enjoyed it (135.3*; cf 7.225.3). The hierarchy that exalts liberty and autonomy, highlighted throughout book 7, appears again. As the Spartans realize, the Persians cannot understand it. Hence, the latter's inferiority in spiritual power and, eventually, military combat.

Similarly, but in a purely barbarian context, the epilogue has Cyrus exalt the honourable poverty that encouraged Persian excellence, independence, and military power, and discouraged physical and political enervation (9.122). The monarch Cyrus, however, does not reject autocratic empire; by ignoring the issue of political institutions, the critical importance of which the reader has often seen, he fails to recognize the factors that produce a stable political entity. The theme, that poor lands produce good warriors, can be traced back to the *Odyssey* (9.27 and 13.243), but here it lacks the crucial other half of Demaratus' argument (7.102.1*): poverty is necessary, but not sufficient. *Arete*, moral, military, and indeed all significant excellence, is acquired (ἔπακτος) only when human wisdom and the strength of settled law (σοφίη and νόμος ἰσχυρός) are also present. Greek courage is based on Greek freedom, but Greek freedom acknowledges the law as master (7.104.4*). The author expects the reader to make such comparisons and to observe the meaningful omission of *arete*, the decisive factor favouring Greek success in the Great War.[43]

Comparisons with other cultures and their traditions helped Herodotus to describe the Hellenic past. Herodotus might not have written at all, had he not admired barbarian as well as Greek deeds (proem) and been able to see what Greeks and barbarians shared, their vulnerable humanity and political ambition at least. Respect for non-Greeks, their political organization and achievements, was one important stimulus for the origins of historiography.[44] His objectivity itself leads him to prefer the Greek way of life. Only Greek autonomy and competitiveness were able to halt the Persian juggernaut launched against Europe. Herodotus' larger historical purpose was to exhibit the power that the unique combination of national autonomy and freely accepted institutions released in the Greeks. Greeks, even or especially Spartans and Athenians, committed immoral acts and believed foolish claims (eg, Pisistratus' duping of the Athenians, 1.60.3), but their mistakes did not fundamentally damage their social and political structure. The proof for Herodotus was in the ultimate test of polity: war itself. His comparative ethnography drives home this point. A detailed survey of differences between the Greeks and the barbarian peoples dominated by the Achaemenids aids in explaining the deadly conflicts between 570 and 479 BCE: where, when, and how it happened, and why it ended with Greek victory. *Historie*, Herodotus' new mode of understanding past and present human reality provided the Greeks with a new and unique advantage, an autonomous and coherent method of investigating their past experience and making sense of it.

8

Historiographical Patterning: 'The Constitutional Debate'

But we must admit that if we had to give an *a priori* estimate of the chances of success in writing history by Herodotus' method, we should probably shake our heads in sheer despondency. Herodotus' success in touring the world and handling oral traditions is something exceptional by any standard – something that we are not yet in a position to explain fully. The secrets of his workshop are not yet all out.

Arnaldo Momigliano 'The place of Herodotus
in the history of historiography'

History, from the beginning, has been a peculiar mode of thought, a science or an art peculiarly distinguished for its mixture of methodologies. Unlike lyric poetry or technical writing that explains how to do something, it has no self-evident pleasure or utility.[1] The facts of human life are untidy and are tangled in a web of experience; particular events can only find meaning in context. Any historical account requires ruthless selection of data, and selection presupposes a conception, that is, an interpretation. Any coherent vision of the past requires a literary organization, a unity of parts, actions that display an internal logic. Aristotle's definition of a 'fiction' demands a minimum of conditions, causes, events, and consequences, a series of actions which lead to a result implicit in the original situation.[2] Herodotus' *Histories* provide this, and every ancient historian strove to meet the expectation.

Reported events, their literary presentation, and their meaning in an historiographical text are three areas of analysis that can only momentarily be separated by the critic. Ancient literary critics recognized Herodotus' literary ability to mimic passion, confusion, and emotion. For instance, *On the Sublime* praises Herodotus' naturalism: 'The best prose writers imitate nature ... They arrange words and ideas in an unnatural way to convey the character of vehement emotion ...' (22.1–2, citing *Histories* 6.11). Dionysius of Halicarnassus praises the historian's ability to integrate disparate subjects and themes: 'Choosing topics both numerous and nothing similar to each other, he has made one harmonious whole' (*Epistula ad Pompeium* § 3, 774U-R = Roberts 112). These basically literary judgments ignore, we might say, the scientific search for truth by the historian and his desire to fashion a new kind of understanding for a culture that had previously found its lessons in unreal or unverifiable events. Herodotus accepts the limitations and contradictions inherent in studying the recent as well as the distant past, as he records and preserves (more often than he explains) strange and even unique events and their connections. His solution to the 'problem basic to all historiography, of how to make a bare account carry an interpretation' led him to an inclusiveness that 'radically expanded the range of subject matter deemed worthy of literary treatment.'[3] In other words, the range of his reports finds a paradoxical explanation in his ceaseless search for the meaning of seemingly unrelated events. Striving for intelligibility, he suggests connections among phenomena that have perplexed later readers who have different categories of relevance.

Questions about the structure, argument, and meaning of the *Histories* have no single satisfactory answer, but selective studies can uncover explanatory systems latent in the text. Without a comprehensive abstract explanatory language, jettisoning his predecessors' mythology, often with no more than Homer's methods of comparison (Circe, Calypso, and Penelope) and contrast (the Phaeacians, the Cyclops, and the Ithacans), Herodotus suggests the meaning of one story by telling another or by presenting a speech. Explicit, authorial evaluation and analysis are subordinated to the presentation of additional stories with similar issues. Multiple examples and recurring descriptive terms generally explain as much as he thinks appropriate. One example of latent but demonstrable systematization will be examined here: Herodotus' implied comparisons of tyrants, of empires, and of dynamic factors in domestic and international politics.

The most explicit programmatic passages are the statement of purpose in the proem, the statement of subject at 1.5.3, and a few statements of method such as those on sources (6.14.1, 7.152.3). The mutability of political (as well as personal) fortunes is one of his constants. Failure and (especially) success for states are revealed to be relative and temporary; human ignorance is discovered to be a dynamic and constant principle of political history, not a curable mistake; the circumstances that promote political freedom appear to be culturally and historically limited, while the urge towards imperial expansion transcends particular forms of domestic organization with results dangerous to ruler and ruled. The instability of personal and national power provides the motor of historical action, and the catalogues of possible permutations of events engendered by power and empire sketch out the map of possible outcomes. Herodotus, however, 'does not discuss his interests; he pursues them.' The resulting account provides not scientific laws but 'casebook studies' that delimit the choices of 'civilized' man in politics and war.[4]

The exceptional 'Constitutional Debate' affords a uniquely analytical exposition of the historian's political beliefs. This *logos* is the most theoretical in the entire text. Its suggestive generalizations about politics confer a privileged position in a political history. It accounts for a very large number of phenomena by reducing them to their essential terms. Elsewhere Herodotus declines to separate narrative of actions from analysis of past events and political systems. The many accounts of various types of autocracies and constitutional governments will be found to illustrate and support the theoretical statements espoused here. That is, the author's perception of actual régimes shaped the arguments imaginatively presented here about various systems of government. The views presented by the Persians, historical or not, are inductions supported in various ways, positive and negative, by his data. The calm and rational discussion seems free from both the ubiquitous depotism of *nomos* (3.38) and the subsequent folktale roguery describing Darius' accession to, and consolidation of, power. The conspirators' debate clarifies significant differences among forms of government; the logic and clarity of the debate has brought its historicity into question but that schematic aspect of the event supports the hypothesis that the debate has interpretive significance.

Structure and Patterns

Since H.R. Immerwahr, following the lead of Bischoff and Hellman, published *Form and Thought in Herodotus*, most scholars have accepted the idea that Herodotus marshals and focuses his disparate material by patterning, by repeating or echoing key words, themes, motifs, and even series of events. Few would now dispute that 'preceding kings ... are in a sense the preparation for the full development of the figure of this last Persian king discussed by Herodotus. Hence Xerxes exhibits traits common to all other royal portraits.' He possesses many 'generic features that are characteristic of royalty as a whole. Xerxes ... is for Herodotus the typical Persian ... the typical tyrant ... motivated by passion rather than by reason.' Croesus, Cyrus, Cambyses, Darius and Xerxes are 'typical manifestations of royal power as such,' examples 'of a pattern that represents the typical and recurrent aspects of events.'[5] This structural approach to understanding a pluriform narrative can encompass all the modes of unification previously discussed. Here we apply it to an incident whose importance Herodotus himself underlines, in order to demonstrate the pervasiveness of this technique of marking recursive elements in human behaviour despite the multiplicity of particular events recorded by the *Histories*.

K.H. Waters argues, in the most thorough denial of the imposition of patterning in Herodotus, that the careers of monarchs and tyrants are naturally repetitious; that the autocrats are not 'mere representatives of a type,' and that 'Herodotus had no political or moral axe to grind when dealing with tyranny.' Furthermore he believes that no theme or pattern guides the *Histories* or influences the selection or arrangement of facts, and that the discovery of patterns in history amounts to a historiographical crime. References, moreover, in Herodotus' text to *hybris*, φθόνος, the jealousy of the gods, and the κύκλος, the cyclical nature of human (and other) affairs, could easily be excised without loss, since we encounter just the facts, without reflection on the morality of Xerxes and his invasion. While Waters rightly asserts that 'we should not expect sermons from Herodotus,' for historians need not preach, his denial that Herodotus prefers a government of institutions to the tyranny of an individual flatly contradicts the impression of casual readers and many other studies.[6] Waters never adequately defines his own or Herodotus' concept of historical 'objectivity.' Moral and political judgments and unifying themes do not in themselves preclude objectivity. Further, a history 'purified' of all moral judgment cannot be written. The desire to report facts while rigorously excluding interpretation and judgment is a relatively recent obsession, one which Waters himself had earlier criticized,[7] and his study cures one evil by a worse.

Such an awkward and dogmatically aschematic approach is, in the end, impossible of disproof, for it must be granted that human beings and governments, if capable of categorization at all, do share many characteristics prior to, and regardless of, any literary treatment of them. Reviewers have disposed of Waters' central thesis[8] while supporting efforts to save Herodotus from those who consider him too poetic or too theological to be usefully historical. Kitto said that fourth-century historians 'were inquiring into what would never happen again, Thucydides into what he rightly thought would.'[9] Herodotus establishes some intermediate level of generality. His method and original purpose encourages him to describe the events themselves and not to reach *exempla* of a high generality in Thucydides' manner. Nevertheless, he certainly believed in constants in human nature, although not in human fortunes. Successive events appear in linear order, each one told for itself and as if nothing like it was known.

Yet in this setting forth of facts, Herodotus embeds patterns and even predictions that shape the data of human experience.[10] Instead of 'causal' historiography in the modern mode, one encounters a 'symptomatic' variety, a method that connects more than it explains, analogizes more than it analyses. Patterns, numerous and of varied origins (from, eg, folktales, legends, epic, and popular philosophy), occur and recur in order to guide the reader through the maze of historical data and to lead him to an interpretation lurking in the text, the intellectual result of a vast and obscure sorting process on the author's part. The so-called Constitutional Debate (3.80–2) provides a neglected opportunity to inspect a master-pattern, an analysis of the effects of different régimes on political communities.[11]

The substance of the positions espoused by the Persian debaters and the sources for the antilogies have been thoroughly canvassed without final agreement.[12] Protagoras the Sophist has been frequently proposed as the original analyst, and Herodotus' interest here in the role of *nomos* as norm and positive law has been reasonably attributed to Sophistic influences in general. A Persian basis for the tale has been defended.[13]

Were we to ask if Herodotus invented the scene in order to propagate his personal views, or fashioned a report of something that he had heard or read of in such a way as to give the story a more universal meaning and pertinence to this text, the answer would be obvious. Herodotus had no more need here than elsewhere to insist on the veracity of his report, yet here he uniquely emphasizes the historicity of an event. Of course, that he believed that the debate was historical does not mean that it happened the way he describes it or even at all. With what we know today about Near Eastern contributions to Greek myth, philosophy, and fiction, a general discussion of the merits of monarchy in the Ancient Near East was certainly possible.[14] Here we explore the programmatic significance of the political arguments for the larger historical narrative.

The Hypotheses of the Participants

Otanes speaks first among the conspirators (3.80). He criticizes monarchy and praises popular government. His condemnation musters both historical and theoretical arguments. 'Monarch' and 'tyrant' are used by Otanes (80.2, 4) of a man who can do what he wishes without institutional control or recourse by his subjects (3, ἀνεύθυνος, only here, a word which suggests a contrast to democratic Athens). Such a situation is neither good nor pleasant (2), for it encourages self-indulgence, ὕβρις (four times in this speech alone), as it did in the frightful cases of Cambyses and the Magus. The autocrat's position in and of itself leads him to frequent vexation, envy, and presumption (3), for the possession of unlimited goods engenders *hybris* (3), and permanent superior status renders illicit temptations irresistible. Envy, φθόνος (3–4, four times in this speech alone), unavoidable for the autocrat, and *hybris* produce all the immorality, confusion, and harm that power is capable of (3). With wealth the tyrant ought to be superior to jealousy, but he never is. He envies good men their very existence (4); their lives reproach his habits. At the same time, he rejoices in the deeds of the basest citizens, especially when they slander the good (4). A most illogical and distressing bundle of contradictions results (5, ἀναρμοστότατον, only here): a being who demands undeserved adulation and who grows angry if he receives it. His acts are outrageous and impious, ἀτάσθαλα (4, like those of the *Odyssey*'s suitors and Aegisthus). The worst of an autocrat's defects can be summarized under three heads: he disturbs ancestral laws, he assaults other men's women, and he executes men without trial.[15]

These objections are set in higher relief by the contrasted virtues of popular government, government ἐς μέσον, ἐς τὸ κοινόν (2, 6). When the people (τὸ πλῆθος) rules, that noblest principle of government, equality before the law and equality of political rights, ἰσονομίη, obtains. It is declared free of the great faults of monarchy because its three essential features – sortition, accountability for offices held, and popular control of legislative assemblies[16] – effectively discourage concentrations of power and consequent intimidating violence and disturbance of established customs and institutions. Sortition implies frequent rotation and the right of all to hold office, the rendering of accounts at trial implies responsibility for all official acts, and popular sovereignty implies a regular supervision of men in office and the ultimate authority of the entire citizenry in assembly. Thus justice, equity, and responsible government are best promoted by a participatory political system, self-government under law.

Megabyzus' short speech for oligarchy endorses all Otanes' reasoning against autocracy (here, kingship), but condemns government by the people as uninformed, unable to judge what is good for itself, brainless, impetuous, and altogether useless.[17] Without judgment or wisdom, the people's government is bound to be unruly and to display a *hybris* (three more times in this speech) not much different from the tyrant's. It is preferable to select the best men to govern, for the best counsels and government will result from their thinking (81.3).

The surprising brevity of this paragraph promoting oligarchy, the type of government most commonly favoured in Greek intellectual circles, results not from a dearth of arguments, but from the unimportance of oligarchies in Herodotus' narrative. Monarchies, tyrannies, the unique Spartan system, and the Athenian democracy have important roles, but one hears very little of the important régimes which were structured as traditional oligarchies.[18] Corinth provides the notable exception, but even there tyranny receives more attention in the narrative than oligarchy (eg, 5.92β1) as a *form of government*.

Otanes' comments are longer and more detailed than Megabyzus' which follow (24 lines compared to 14), but Darius' third and decisive speech equals it in length (25 lines). He agreed with Megabyzus' criticisms of democracy, just as the latter had agreed with Otanes' criticisms of autocracy (82.1). But he proceeds to discuss the theoretically best (τῷ λόγῳ ἀρίστων) forms of the three constitutions, maintaining that monarchy is best, because nothing could be better than the careful and wise administration and quiet security against enemies that the one best man can devise by himself in secret. He, unlike his two comrades, eschews the word 'tyrant.' In oligarchies, the best men are excessively competitive with each other. This leads to faction, assassination, and, eventually, one-man rule (82.3). In democracies, trouble arises from the conspiracies for private profit among the wicked rather than from the competition of the good, until a leader from the people comes forward to meet the crisis. He gains adulation sufficient to achieve that same disliked autocratic power (4). Therefore in theory *and* actual practice, monarchy is the best and *inevitable* form of government, the result of natural political processes. Monarchy once gained the Persians their freedom from external oppression, and Darius concludes, 'leave our ancestral laws (πάτριοι νόμοι) alone; they have served us well and change will not bring improvement' (5).

Darius' brittle argument is as notable for what it omits as for what it includes.[19] He pointedly equates monarchy with ancestral customs (*nomoi*), while Otanes had claimed that the monarch violates ancestral customs (*nomaia*). He generally avoids questions of domestic administration, the substance of Otanes' criticism of autocracy. He is more interested in external aggression, by which means the Persians had achieved 'freedom' and power. He criticizes the degenerate forms of other constitutions while maintaining a discreet silence on tyranny.[20] Freedom in his speech refers only to the nation's freedom to dominate aliens.[21] The king is an efficient manager (ἐπιτροπεύοι).

In the subsequent vote Darius triumphed. Otanes then withdrew from the contest in which the other six competed for kingship, 'whether he be chosen by lot, popular election, or by some other mechanism,' on condition that he and his descendants not be ruled by the kings so long as they not overstep Persian *nomoi*. *Nomos* would be his only shield against power, a weak one as he realized. Herodotus comments that in Persia only Otanes' house has been free from then until his own day, before he retells the fraud by which Darius was selected to rule (3.83–4).

Otanes and Darius present parallel but opposite arguments. The former deliberately focuses on the reality of autocracy and the ideal democracy; the latter on the ideal autocracy and the reality of democracy. Their arguments complement rather than refute each other. But the narrative of Herodotus records the internal strains and external errors of policy of autocratic governments much more often than of governments structured by institutions. Granted, more examples of the former régime existed, but the advantages that Athens reaped from her change of régime from tyranny to self-government receive special stress, and Sparta's institutionalization of νόμος is directly compared to Xerxes' one-man rule. Ἰσοκρατίη and ἰσονομίη underline a participatory egalitarianism that most sharply differentiates the governments that Herodotus admired from despotic alternatives (5.92.α1*; 3.83.1, 142.3*; 5.37.2). The same may be claimed for the terms ἰσηγορίη and δημοκρατίη, specifically applied to Athens (5.78; 6.131.1)

When we turn to accounts of autocratic states, more than fifty traditional kingdoms and tyrannies with usurped power find significant mention in Herodotus.[22] The table below summarizes the historical record that supports the chief criticisms of tyrants and despots, as they are expounded at length in the speech of Otanes the Persian, and later in that of Socles the Corinthian. Modern historians have been able to say much that is positive about the Greek tyrants.[23] They advanced the general level of Greek civilization by their patronage of literature, the arts, and religion; they raised the standard of living by their encouragement of agriculture and trade, by schemes of colonization, by socially progressive measures, extension of overseas commercial contacts, and so on. Their military and naval policies indirectly aided Hellas' later repulse of the Persian invasions. Herodotus however does not stress these contributions, nor does he ever assemble them so as to present tyranny as an attractive or progressive form of government. Although the magnificence of Cleisthenes of Sicyon, the power of Gelon of Syracuse, and the courage of Artemisia of Halicarnassus are acknowledged, their political policies are ignored or disparaged and their wilfulness emphasized. In the crisis of war, Gelon was ready to join forces with the Persians and Artemisia betrayed her allies and compatriots (7.163.2, 8.87.2–3). Polycrates of Samos and Cypselus and Periander of Corinth are extensively portrayed in a sinister light with emphasis on banishments, confiscations, vicious mutilations, executions, and sexual outrage. When Herodotus speaks of Samos' three man-made wonders (3.60), two architects but no ruler or financier is mentioned. Polycrates was responsible,[24] but Herodotus would rather couple his name with fratricide (3.39.2), foreign aggression (39.3), piracy (ibid), deceitful execution (44.2), threatened incineration of his citizens' women and children (45.4), and so on. Pisistratus also is presented as repeatedly dishonest and duplicitous; Herodotus' generous but brief praise of the Pisistratid government (1.59.6) is overshadowed by tales of deceit, murder, constriction, and oppression (1.59.1,3–5, 60.3, 64.1, 66.1, 78, 91.1; 6.103.3, 109.3*).[25] Periander's benefactions to Corinth are ignored in order to emblazon his suspicious and bloodthirsty nature. His selection as an international arbitrator is mentioned in passing, but not explained, nor is the contradiction admitted. Herodotus endorses the thesis of Otanes, in others' speeches or on his own authority, namely that tyranny is incompatible with good government or justice (δικαιοσύνη) (3.142.3*, 7.164.1).[26]

The theoretical views of Otanes are reinforced by the historical lesson that the Corinthian Socles inflicts on the Spartans; ironically enough, since tyranny contradicts Spartan principles. A Corinthian knows full well that tyrannical régimes are blood-stained, unjust, and amount to a negation of freedom (5.92.α1*, η5*, ζ1*; cf 1.62.1). The tyrannies of book 5 continually subvert *nomos* and peace, and are inherently unstable, σφαλερόν (3.53.4*).[27] Even the often criticized Ionians endeavour to escape despotism, when given a chance (1.164.2; 5.49.2*; 9.90.2).

Herodotus does not categorically condemn one-man rule.[28] The Egyptians, he condescendingly comments, could not get along without it (2.147.1), and perhaps none but the Greeks could. Croesus, Cyrus, Pisistratus, and Darius receive credit for their achievements (eg, 1.29.1; 1.191; 3.88–9), but autocracy at best depends on the character of a talented individual, as the sons of Cyrus, Pisistratus, and Darius demonstrated.

Cambyses' reign was short but memorable. Herodotus' portrait of him is grotesque.[29] The account concentrates on his sadistic, sacrilegious behaviour and his military failures. Herodotus minimizes the great importance of the conquest of Egypt and the extension of Persian influence in Africa to the south and west (Xerxes' reconquest of Egypt similarly receives a bare sentence [7.7]). Cambyses' mustering of the amphibious invasionary force, and his engineering triumphs are treated primarily as symptoms of megalomania. His administrative and architectural achievements are ignored.[30]

Even when the offences of an autocrat in power are barely mentioned, as in the cautionary tale of the rise of Deioces to a tyrant's state, the aspects of deception,[31] ambition for power, and oppression are highlighted. Among the free and hitherto autonomous Medes, Deioces came to power because of his strict dispensation of justice, but once his power was secured, hierarchical ceremonies, centralization of authority, and bizarre uses of compulsion revealed his tyrannous intent and consolidated his autocratic government and exalted position (1.98.3–99.2).[32] For Herodotus, oriental kingship was

THE CHARACTERISTICS OF AUTOCRATS AND THEIR ILLUSTRATION IN THE *HISTORIES* OF HERODOTUS

(# = *contra*)

I	Cyrus	Cambyses	Darius	Xerxes	Persians in General
A THE PERSONALITY OF THE AUTOCRAT					
1 He is ruled by arrogant pride: *hybris* & *megalophrosyne* (3.80.2–3)		3.29.1–2, 37.1–3, 38.1, 80.2*		7.16α2*,7.8γ1*, 24, 136.2; 8.77.1 [or.]	3.80.2*, 127.3*
2 He equates his will or fancy with the law (80.3)	2.1.1.	3.1.5, 14.1, 36.1 & 6	3.119.7, 134.6	7.41.1, 43.1, 128.2; 9.109.2	1.132.3
His acts are impulsive, unpredictable		3.14.11, 25.1, 64.2, 65.3*	3.130.4, 133.2; 6.119.1	7.27.1 & 38.1, 45; 8.118.4; 9.109.2–3	
3 He exhibits rapacious greed and unchecked aggression (80.4)	1.177, 201; 7.8α1*	3.21.3*, 25.1, 26.1; 7.8α1*	3.134.1–3; 4.1.1, 167.2–3; 5.31.2*; 6.44.1, 94.1; 7.8α1*	7.5.2–3, 16α2, 8α1–2*, 8γ1–3*, 50.3–4*, 54.2;	3.117.6; 7.16α2* #
4 He fears for his own life and shows jealousy of others' (80.4–5)			3.119.1–2	8.97.1, 100.1	
His delicate honour always seems threatened (need for revenge)	1.124.2	3.1, 21.2	4.1.1, 118.1; 6.94.1	7.5.2*, 8α2*, β2*, 11.2; 9.116.3	

I	Cyrus	Cambyses	Darius	Xerxes	Persians in General
B THE UNJUST AND VIOLENT ACTS OF THE AUTOCRAT					
1 He commits atrocities: *atasthala* & *anarsia* (80.4: thematic words)	1.114.5	3.74.1		7.35.2; 8.109.3*; 9.78.2*–79.1*, 110.3 (Amestris)	9.116 & 7.33
2 And he perpetrates other outrages		3.14.5, 16.1–2, 27.3, 29.2, 31.6, 32.4, 33, 35–38; 5.25.1–2	3.155.2, 159.1; 6.32	7.39, 114.2 (Amestris); 8.90.3; 9.112	3.69.2 & 4, 92.1, 125.2, 126.2; 5.18.5
3 He forces his will on women (80.5)		3.14.2, 31.1 & 6		9.108.1–2, 111.4* & 112	9.116 & 7.33
He confuses sex and politics			3.118.1	7.39.1; 9.108–13;	
4 He executes subjects without trial (80.5)		3.15.1, 32.4, 35.3 & 5, 36.1* & 4, 64.2, 65.3*, 67.1	3.118–20, 4.84.1–2	7.35.3, 39, 146.3#; 8.90.3	1.137.1#

I	Cyrus	Cambyses	Darius	Xerxes	Persians in General
C THE AUTOCRAT SUFFERS SERIOUS LIABILITIES IN POLITICAL DECISIONS					
1 He is not accountable: *aneuthynos* (80.3)		3.31.4		9.109.2–3	
2 He is hard to suit: *anarmostos* (80.5)		3.34–5, 36.5–6		7.8δ2; 9.109.3,	
3 He shows hostility to virtue and pleasure in wicked subjects: *phthonos* & *charis* (80.3–4)		3.30.1, 74.1			
4 He is gullible and prone to believe slander: *diabolas endekesthai* (80.4)		3.62.2–4		7.237*#; 8.90.1; 9.116.1–2	
5 His behaviour promotes flattery and lies, and leads to treachery (80.5)		3.65.1*, 67.1	3.72.4–5*; 4.134.3* & 135.2		1.136.2, 138.1#
6 He inhibits speech and thought (80.5)	1.88.2	3.35–6	4.97.5	7.10 (init.), 101.3–102.1*, 104.5*, 209.2*; 8.68α1*	

I	Cyrus	Cambyses	Darius	Xerxes	Persians in General
7 He errs seriously in his isolation (80.6)				7.103.1, 105, 209.1; 8.86(fin), 88.3, 90.4, 97.1	
He becomes wise only after a great loss	1.86.6#	3.64.3	4.134.2*	7.234.1*; 8.101.1	7.135.3*
8 He considers his subjects to be slaves and promotes servility (80.5)		2.1.2	3.88.1, 119.1, 155.5 & 157.2–4	7.39.1	
His rule is based on his own and his subjects' fears		3.35.4	3.86.2	9.111.3–5	
9 He disturbs ancestral law & custom: *nomaia kineei patria* (80.5)		3.3.3, 16.1, 30.1, 31.2–4, 38.1		7.238.1–2; 8.109.3*	
10 Power depends on one untried man, not on self-correcting institutions	1.107–30	2.1#	3.86.2, 88.3; 7.10γ2*	7.3.4, 10γ2*; 8.102.3*	

THE CHARACTERISTICS OF AUTOCRATS ... (Continued)

II	Lydian Kings	Median Kings	Egyptian Kings	Corinthian Tyrants	Other Greek Tyrants	Institutional Governments
A THE PERSONALITY OF THE AUTOCRAT						
1 He is ruled by arrogant pride:- hybris & megalophrosyne (3.80.2–3)	1.30.3, 38.2	1.99.1–2	2.136.4, 169.2		6.127.3	7.136.1#
2 He equates his will or fancy with the law (80.3)		1.100.1#,		5.92η1*	1.59.6#	3.142.1#; 7.102.1*#, 104.4*#
His acts are impulsive, unpredictable (80.3)	1.54.1	1.73.4				
3 He exhibits rapacious greed, and unchecked aggression (80.4)	1.73.1, 1.76.2	1.108.4, 119.3, 1.99.1		5.92ε2*, η1*	3.39.3–4, 3.122.2, 123.1; 5.92ζ3*	
4 He fears for his own life (80.4–5) and shows jealousy of others'		1.108.2, 98.2	2.161.2(bis), 173.1#	5.92ζ2*	1.64.1;	
His delicate honour always seems threatened (need for revenge)	1.73.1				3.44.2, 143.1 1.64.1	

II	Lydian Kings	Median Kings	Egyptian Kings	Corinthian Tyrants	Other Greek Tyrants	Institutional Governments
B THE UNJUST AND VIOLENT ACTS OF THE AUTOCRAT						
1 He commits atrocities: *atasthala* & *anarsia* (80.4: thematic words)			2.111.2	3.49.2		5.89.3; 9.37.1, 79.1*#
2 And he perpetrates other outrages	1.76.1–2	1.119.3–5, 128.2	2.129#, 162.5	3.48.2	3.44.2, 45.4; 4.202; 6.23.6	6.23.6#, 79; 7.133.1, 9.120
3 He forces his will on women (80.5)	1.11.2		2.131.1, 172.3	3.48.2, 5.92η1* & 3*	1.16.1	
He confuses sex and politics	1.8–12		2.121ε2, 126.1	3.48.2	1.61.2; 6.126	
4 He executes subjects without trial (80.5)	1.92.4	1.108.4, 119.3	2.129.1–2#	3.50.1; 5.92.η1*, ε2*, ζ1*	3.39.2, 143.2; 5.92α1*	5.87.2, 87.3#; 9.5.2

THE CHARACTERISTICS OF AUTOCRATS ... (*Concluded*)

	Lydian Kings	Median Kings	Egyptian Kings	Corinthian Tyrants	Other Greek Tyrants	Institutional Governments
II						
C THE AUTOCRAT SUFFERS SERIOUS LIABILITIES IN POLITICAL DECISIONS						
1 He is not accountable: *aneuthynos* (80.3)						5.92α1*#; 6.104.2#
2 He is hard to suit: *anarmostos* (80.5)	1.30–2*	1.117–18				
3 He shows hostility to virtue, and pleasure in wicked subjects: *phthonos & charis* (80.3–4)	1.30.3, 33	1.108.2			3.146.1	7.237.2*
4 He is gullible and prone to believe slander: *diabolas endekesthai* (80.4)						5.97.2
5 His behaviour promotes flattery and lies, and leads to treachery (80.5)		1.116.4–5, 118.1, 123.1				5.97.2
6 He inhibits speech and thought (80.5)	1.30.3	1.99.1, 100.2		3.52.6		5.78#
7 He errs seriously in his isolation (80.6)	1.56.1					5.51#, 97.2; 7.143.3#, 144.1#
He becomes wise only after a great loss	1.86.3	1.129	3.15.4#	3.124.2		

II	Lydian Kings	Median Kings	Egyptian Kings	Corinthian Tyrants	Other Greek Tyrants	Institutional Governments
8 He considers his subjects to be slaves and promotes servility (80.5)	1.34.3	1.98.2, 98.3, 100.2	2.124.1–2, 172.5		5.92α1*, 96.1; 7.156.3	3.142.4*; 5.62.1, 65.5, 66.1, 78, 91.1, 92α1*; 7.104.4*, 135.3*, 136.1; 8.143.1*; (all #)
His rule is based on his own and his subjects' fears		1.107.2		3.52.2; 5.92ε2*	1.64.1	6.12.4#
9 He disturbs ancestral law & custom: *nomaia kineei patria* (80.5)	1.8.4, 10.3, 11.2–4	1.108.4, 99.1, 119.3	2.124.1 & 1#, 127.1, 128, 129.1#, 177.1; 3.10.2, 43.1#		1.59.6#; 5.67.1–5, 68.1	7.102.1#
10 Power depends on one untried man, not on self-correcting institutions	1.8–13, 34.3	1.99.2, 108.2, 120.6	2.147.2#	3.53.4*	3.142.3*	3.142.3*#; 5.78#; 6.109.1–2#

equivalent to unlimited authority and power. He appreciated the paradox that the law for the king of Persia was that he could do whatever he wished (3.31.4).[33] Artabanus refers to Xerxes' rule as a despotism (7.51.2*), because he regards the king's subjects as slaves (3.88.1; 7.7). So does Xerxes himself (7.39.1*).[34] The despot's generosity is always untrustworthy (3.130.4; 4.84; 7.39; 8.140α* with 142.4–5*). The two Herodotean portraits – the efficient and energetic Xerxes and the Xerxes who is an imprudent aggressor against a poor people – are not entirely integrated, and yet the latter is emphasized, not because of ethnic prejudice, but because of the dominant theme of the self-destructive tendencies of autocracies.

The atrocities 'incidental to unbridled power' and 'to the failure of nerve after defeat' are 'normally described without censure,'[35] only because further judgment is not needed. Bodily mutilation and perverted sexual acts, 'harem intrigues,' and the confusion of sex and power illustrate the *hybris* of autocrats.[36] Their pre-emptive, inhuman actions (often in response to prophecies and omens) backfire, for instance for Astyages, Cambyses, and Periander (1.108.4; 3.29–35; 3.50–2). Apries' *hybris* met quick punishment (2.169.2–3); Cambyses' reversal was not long delayed (3.66.2); Cyrus' and Xerxes' recompensive punishment is both explicit and implicit (1.214.3–5; 8.109.3*, 9.110.3).

Having declared autocracy to be self-contradictory (ἀναρμοστότατον, 3.80.5*) by nature, Herodotus focuses on the descents rather than the ascents of despots,[37] because their collapse confirms his opinion. Various strategies reinforce the dogma. The 'wise adviser motif' offers a 'fictional ... poetic and philosophic dimension' which serves to illustrate despots' lack of common sense. The good advice is rarely followed. The verbs 'maltreat' and 'whip' (λυμαίνομαι, μαστίγω) belong to autocracy: Gigante calls 'the μάστιξ the inglorious symbol of Persian *nomos*.'[38] Ἀτασθαλίη, reckless wickedness, ascribed to tyrants as typical by Otanes, repeatedly characterizes Xerxes (3.80.4*; 7.35.2, 8.109.3*, 9.78.2*). The Persian kings abuse the dead and brutalize the living *pour encourager les autres*, but frequently without trial and sometimes on whim alone. Humiliation, disfigurement of defeated opponents, public punishment, and vengeful retribution are symbolic demonstrations of unfettered power in Herodotus, and the old Persian inscription of Darius at Behistun boasts of his gruesome mutilations of his challengers. Apries' mutilation of Patarbemis' face provides an egregious Egyptian parallel (2.162.5). Cambyses exemplifies every fault that Otanes mentions.

Persian rulers are portrayed as grasping, tyrannical, and aggressive. They embody greed and selfishness. The Ethiopian king says to Cambyses' spies: 'If he were just, he would not desire a land other than his own, nor would he lead into slavery men from whom he suffered no wrong' (3.21.4*). The scheme to march 'to the end of the world' is called 'mad and insane' (3.25.2–3, words reserved to and lavished upon Cambyses). Similarly Darius expresses the same systematic urge to conquer European territory, and Cyrus does also, when trying to subjugate the Massagetans (1.201, 205.1; 3.134). The Persian general Aryandes attacks North Africa with an excuse (πρόσχημα, 4.167.3) of wrong suffered, but in reality to subject more nations to Darius; he imitates his masters (5.105.2*, 6.94.1; 6.44.1). Mardonius too speaks the language of revenge (7.5.3), but concludes with the argument that a country as beautiful and fruitful as Greece deserved no less a master than the Persian king. He boasts of the conquest of races who have done the Persians no wrong (7.9.2*).[39] Herodotus presents Xerxes' real freedom of choice as somehow limited metaphysically by fate and his tragic destiny, but most importantly by his status and Persian νόμοι, from which any concept of international justice is absent. *Nomos* requires no explanation, because for Xerxes it is one. Xerxes justifies the proposed invasion to his council (7.8α1–2*):

The following *nomos* I do not introduce as new to you, but I received it and will use it. I hear from our elders that never yet have we Persians kept still, ever since we snatched power from the Medes ... But god leads us on and when we obey, it turns out for the better. What nations Cyrus, Cambyses, and my father subdued and acquired in addition, no one need tell to you who know it well. Now when I ascended this throne, I considered how I might not be left behind by earlier men who held it, and how I could acquire additional empire for the Persians ...[40]

The speech then chooses Greece as the obvious object of the further expansion mandated by the logic of empire. The conclusion reached is that *not* to attack Greece would be un-Persian, in fact passive (cf 7.50.3*, Xerxes again). The campaign will enslave guilty and innocent alike (7.8γ3*). Although Herodotus nowhere states that it is 'wrong to seek to rule others,' 'the ethics of the historian are incompatible with oppression.'[41] This latter proposition has now been buttressed by the preceding analysis of the conspirators' political theories.

Autocrats in the *Histories*

In Herodotus' view democracy is not a perfect system of government or even obviously preferable to other, more limited forms of national autonomy. He sympathizes with Megabyzus' and Darius' objections to the thoughtless haste of the people. À propos of the absence of Peloponnesian vessels and the presence of twenty Athenian ships bound for Miletus at the beginning of the Persian Wars, Herodotus remarks that 'one may reasonably conclude that it is easier to deceive many than one, since Aristagoras failed to deceive one Lacedaemonian, Cleomenes, but did deceive thirty thousand Athenians' (5.97.2). Darius' criticism of democracy and Otanes' praise for self-government obviously apply to the government of Athens itself. Herodotus does not proselytize for unlimited participation in political decision-making; but despotism, because it cannot help but violate law and custom, is self-limiting as well as undependable. Nor is he a chauvinist for any one city;[42] Hellas would have perished without Athens, Sparta would have fought Xerxes even if Athens had surrendered to Persia,[43] Corinth's good deeds at Salamis survive Athenian defamation (7.139.2–3; 7.102.2; 7.209; 8.94.4).[44] All have some form of institutional self-government and equal access to justice which make liberty and valour effective. Proponents of ἰσονομίη do not always succeed, as Otanes himself, Maeandrius of Samos, and Aristagoras demonstrate (3.80.6*, 3.142.3*, 5.37.2), but Herodotus praises their intentions: individual freedom, self-government, and justice for their communities (3.83.3, 142.4*, 143.2).

The narrative of Clisthenes' political reformation of Athens, moreover, illustrates the 'Seminar on Government.' Herodotus declares of Athens that 'although it was great before, once rid of the tyrants it became even greater' (5.66.1). Freedom of speech, 'a desirable thing,' brought Athens new increase in wealth and military power that Herodotus explicitly connects with the new form of government. He argues that a despot's soldiers have too little stake in battle to confront with success free men who fight to preserve self-government and to advance their state's power (5.78; cf 6.109.3, 6). The Spartans calculate that Athens ruled by a tyrant would be weak and obedient, but a free Athens would grow to threaten their own authority and power (5.91.1). Herodotus has Histiaeus state as an obvious fact that the cities of Ionia would prefer democracy to tyranny (4.137.2*). Freedom once inspired the Medes to liberate themselves from the Assyrians and to show themselves to be brave men (1.95.2), and freedom would inspire Hydarnes if only he experienced it: 'You know how to be a slave, but you have not yet tried freedom (ἐλευθερίη), nor do you know whether it is sweet or not. If you could try it, you would advise us to fight you for it not with spears only but even with axes' (7.135.3*).

Herodotus considers Greek governments other than tyrannies superior to oriental autocracies because of their relative moderation and humanity: they recognize human dignity and respect persons and ancestral institutions,[45] they require accountability to law and custom, and they are able to profit from criticism and select policies wisely. Unlike the autocrats who are tendered sound analyses but ignore them, in Herodotus Greek states can and often do benefit from open expression and from competition among proposals (eg, 5.66.1 with 78; 5.93.2; 6.109–10; 7.142–4; 8.79.3*). Of course, public debate does not insure success (eg, 5.97.2). All nations – except the Androphagoi, 'most brutish of all men' (4.106) – have *nomoi* and some system of justice, but these *nomoi* are not all equally valid or equally secured by geography and military preparedness. In the great war itself, it is not merely courage and tactical skill that win Herodotus' praise for the Greeks, but – above all – moral purpose, the cause of self-determination for which they fought.[46]

On occasion, a combination of patriotic local sources and his own preferences lead Herodotus to suppress or minimize unattractive truths. The Athenians' offering to Darius of earth and water in the last decade of the sixth century (5.73) in order 'to make an alliance with the Persians against the threat of certain war with Sparta,' is improbably presented as the independent and unsupported decision of the 'messenger-envoys' (ἄγγελοι). Herodotus maintains a discreet silence on Athenian politics after Clisthenes' reforms; on Clisthenes' possible participation in the deal; on the now eminent Alcmaeonids' past dealings with the tyrants and with the Persian Empire. These lacunae minimize the implication of the reported fact: the new democracy and perhaps its champion, just freed from a tyrant, had immediately (and wisely) appealed to the most powerful autocracy for aid against another Greek government. The power of the threatening barbarian autocrat, they must have reasoned, was further removed than the threatening Spartans. Herodotus' careful account does not strictly rule out the historical possibility that the Athenians temporary observed the treaty and later disavowed it at a convenient moment.[47] Not only autocrats break faith.

A similar obfuscation surrounds the truth about Polycrates' alliance with Egypt. Local 'revisionists' in Samos blamed Amasis for what certainly seems to have been Polycrates' decision to abandon their mutual alliance, once Persian power extended to his frontiers. Here a tyrant benefits from the suppression of the historical truth, because a more weighty historiographical theme, the danger of excessive prosperity, shapes the main narrative.[48] The principle to recognize, in such cases, is that from the many-sided facts of history, the historian presents the facet immediately useful or relevant to his present concern. Although autocrats in Herodotus are characterized by their irregular and ferocious acts, and Greek institutional governments are portrayed by their most admirable accomplishments, it is not hard to find, in an honest historian's text, good acts of bad men and bad acts of praised régimes.

Hohti has demonstrated the significance of the difference between Greek governments which did not restrict *isegorie* and the tyrannies and other autocracies that did.[49] Inhibition of candid views is 'characteristic of tyranny.' Herodotus often depicts scenes where even important viziers must like slaves request permission to speak (eg, 1.88.2*, 4.97.2);[50] or where subjects express a fear of speaking frankly (3.31.5; 4.97.5*; 7.10α1*; 7.101.3*; 8.68α1*); or where nervous subjects believe or opine to one another that honest advice cannot be proffered at all (7.10.1; 8.65.4–5*, to Dicaeus; 9.16.4–5*, to Thersander). When sound advice is tendered, the autocrat frequently rejects or rashly disbelieves it (7.11, 103–104.1*, 237.1*; 8.69.1–2). To speak one's mind is to act 'in a free manner' (7.46.1); those who behave thus with a despot often regret it (3.36, 7.11.1, 9.111.3–5).[51] Freedom, for Herodotus, promotes good counsel and effective government (as Otanes argued in 3.80.6*); despotisms may prosper but they carry the seed of self-destruction.

The paradoxical advantage of non-autocratic governments is, Herodotus believes, that envy, strife, and disunity – among men and nations – promote human freedom and perpetuate a fruitful diversity for the human race.[52] From the varied *nomoi* of the contumacious Greeks come growth and independence, whereas from oriental despotism and tyranny come conformity, irrationality, brutality, and fear of individual enterprise. Local autonomy encourages a sense of community identity, increased strife and envy on the parochial level (7.236.1*, 237.2*), but such competition sustains freedom, itself a necessary condition for *arete*.[53] Otanes says: 'Envy (φθόνος) is fundamental in human nature' (3.80.3*). The agonistic character of Greek institutions harnesses this energy. Hellenic strength results from disunity and strife, even war. Competitive units survive better 'because they are closer to the historical process.' Even local injustice sometimes promotes the good of Greece.[54] Dynamic cities extract energy from political conflict. Strenuous liberty, Demaratus implies, has unique advantages over autocracy.[55] Greek adaptability, flexibility, and contentiousness, promoted by a variable climate, poor land, institutional government, local autarchy and national near-anarchy, produces a peculiar *arete* and promotes survival in a threatening world (cf 5.66.1, 78; 7.10α3*, β1*, 102*, 104*, 135, 139).

When the unrestricted *nomos* of despotism contends with the restrictive *nomoi* of the little Greek states, the heterogeneous Greeks are victorious. Herodotus asks why. He seems to have found his answer in the way different political systems respond to the demands of *nomos* understood both as custom and as law. When the despot constitutes *nomos*, it is unstable and self-interested; when *nomos* is despot, the limitations provide an arena of freedom. Self-discipline and valour are encouraged by self-governing institutions; the 'Constitutional Debate' points to the outcome of the wars between the Greeks and the barbarians.

Isonomia

We conclude, first, that Herodotus' 'shares' Otanes' views, not because he endorses the ideology of democracy, but because Otanes' propositions most clearly favour the preservation of political and social *nomoi*, government by institutions, not undependable or absurd individuals. Otanes' proposal best promotes individual autonomy within a political context.[56] This position yields equal admiration for Sparta and Athens. Herodotus profoundly admires the unique and inimitable society of Sparta ruled by *nomos* and traditional institutions, not men.[57] The Spartans govern themselves and are free within clear and stable limits, within *nomoi*, despots more fear-provoking than Xerxes (7.104.4*). This praise of the despotic power of law and custom at Sparta varies the theme of the undependable and destructive despot. Because Spartan *nomoi* were suitable only for Sparta's uniquely demanding but self-governing system, Athens appears as the type of a community which prospered and became great quickly, specifically because of freedom and constitutional government (5.66.1, 78). The freedom of the Athenians is consonant with *nomos*; it recognizes limit; it enforces obligations, for instance, to help fellow Ionians and even all like-minded Hellenes.

Secondly, the Persian's criticism of all monarchs, in form quite theoretical, is borne out by the earlier and the subsequent narrative. The Constitutional Debate is a benchmark, for it shapes an expectation of the three forms of government in actual practice that is not disappointed in the narrative. This seminar in political theory presented as a dramatic confrontation does not however turn history into fiction. Reasoned inductions are based on wide observation reported in the narratives. The Persian despots and Greek tyrants are 'not mere representatives of a [well-known] type.'[58] They are historical personages who shape Herodotus' generalizing profile of unlimited power.

'Absolutism was bound to fail.' Herodotus' accumulation of evidence leads him to believe that absolute power and unlimited unification of diverse peoples and *nomoi* engender moral and social decay.[59] The Persians fail to conquer Greece because of inadequately conceived strategy (7.10η*, 49*), but also because of contradictions built into their system and empire. Their rulers mock even their own *nomoi* and break them; the Persians abandon the habits and life-style that had made them strong (3.31; 5.18–21; 1.126*, 7.8α2*, 9.122.3, etc).[60] Whereas despotism crushes initiative, *isonomie* and freedom encourage individual effort by holding out rewards to individuals and their nations (eg, 5.78 and 6.109.3*). Self-imposed constraints or *nomos* can promote national achievement. Greeks exert themselves for recognition of excellence (ἀρετή), for 'worthless' laurels, and for freedom, not for money, a tyrant's benediction, or from fear (7.102.2*, 103.3*, 8.26.3). There is a kind of explanation latent in this view, namely that social structure determines a nation's political fate, although Herodotus has not yet found the theoretical and abstract terminology to express it so concisely.

Thirdly, Herodotus' selection and arrangement of material produced clear and not unhistorical patterns of despotic behaviour. The positive accomplishments of tyrants and other despots gain less attention than their errors, sins, and failures. Herodotus argues by examples, he shows (*apodexis*), and the cumulative weight establishes an expectation, a pattern. In Toynbee's biological metaphor, which has demonstrable Herodotean antecedents (3.108–9), challenge promotes productive responses; certain groups are better adapted to respond to external and internal stimuli and challenges, namely the ones that promote their citizens' self-determination and individual development. The 'time of troubles,' 522–425 BCE (6.98.1–2) was also an acme of Hellenic accomplishment. 'The virtues of adversity' provides a fitting title to Toynbee's transcription of the conversation of Cyrus and Artembares that concludes the *Histories*.[61]

Selection and arrangement always govern historical emphasis. Herodotus calls Xerxes' expedition the largest ever (7.20.2–21), and its repulse the greatest Greek accomplishment to date (9.78.2*). The latter judgment reflects not quantity, but significance: free men defeat their would-be enslaver (cf 9.90.2*). The *Histories'* narratives, dialogues, and statistics provide the basis for these judgments; the patterns of behaviour displayed by autocrats and institutional governments entitle the historian's judgments to serious respect.

PART FOUR

Meaning and Method: How Herodotus Makes Particulars Resonate

9

Event and Explanation: Herodotean Interpretations

The Nature of Causal Argument in Herodotus

Any historical study is simpler and more coherent, in order to be more intelligible, than the reality it describes. A mere assemblage of random facts or an annalistic chronicle of events has neither a directing argument nor a clear meaning. The limited richness of the historian with an event to explain produces clearer meaning than a heap of unsifted facts.[1] Herodotus' inspired borrowings from various literary genres – tragic, comic, epigrammatic, epic, and novelistic moments – take the reader beyond the bare report of unrelated happenings, yet Herodotus still falls short of modern concepts of causation, in part because he stops short of hypostatized categories of cause and effect. But such causal reasoning does exist in the *Histories*.

Is there an argument unifying Herodotus' *Histories*? Not if by this we mean a universal lesson for the future, the revelation of pre-determined outcomes. One meets a non-mythic, essentially non-divine ἀπόδεξις or demonstration of how things happen. One finds historical speeches, protreptic in intent, which are also functional, *apodeictic* in Herodotus' historical representation. Herodotus, like Homer, looks at action from the actor's as well as the observer's point of view. His poetic, rhetorical, and historical skill produces a 'dramatic' narrative. Perhaps this is one reason why Herodotus was considered 'the most Homeric of authors' (*De sublimitate* 13.3). By radically expanding the subject-matter of the chronicler and geographer and by becoming 'an *imaginative* historian as well as the reporter of tradition,'[2] Herodotus redefines the meaning and use of the past.

Herodotus explains the world he knows through a logic for explicating recent human events and their causes. What is this logic? What are the causal arguments in Herodotus? That 'certain antecedents normally [lead] to certain consequents' is, according to R.G. Collingwood, 'no theory of causation,' at least no theory acceptable to 'the axiom of cause and effect' of modern inductive science. The untold riches of Croesus and Polycrates' good fortune are not really the *causes* of their disasters, but, at most, frequent signs of the precariousness of human fortunes. History among the Greeks claims to offer only 'prognostic judgments, not demonstrable but probable.'[3] One set of facts running parallel to another earlier set suggests likely consequences. Herodotus is fond of *analogizing* in this manner, a principal mode of reasoning in the Archaic age.[4] Even if, however, one grants that the subject of 'cause and effect' is more complex than mere consequence, it seems clear that Herodotus wishes to explain and indeed does explain the causes of the major events that he records. The present chapter will justify this statement.

The Greeks had terms for causal explanation: αἰτίη and αἴτιον, the 'reason why' and 'cause.' These two alone appear in more than 30 contexts.[5] For example, Herodotus wonders why Elis breeds no mules although it has a moderate climate 'and nothing else is obviously the cause of this aberration' (4.30.1–2). He searches for natural causes. He is sceptical of the Eleians' explanation that there has been a religious curse. Likewise, he has a natural explanation for feathers in the Scythian sky (4.31), and the long discussion of why the Nile floods (2.20–4) presents logical arguments and criticizes others' theories. No divine cause is even mentioned. Herodotus employs few abstract terms of causal analysis; from the proem onwards, however, he recognizes that events 'don't just happen' and need to be accounted for. Here alone he speaks of φύσις, δύναμις, ἱστορίη, ὁδοί, ἀνεπιστήμων, λογίζεσθαι, οἰκός, μαρτύριον, ἔλεγχος (nature, force, study, theory, unscientific, rational critique, probability, evidence, test or proof). He also offers a variety of logical arguments and thought-experiments in this discussion of a natural phenomenon.

Herodotus like Heraclitus is most comfortable when his own sense-perceptions concerning cause and effect can be recorded: ὅσων ὄψις ἀκοὴ μάθησις ταῦτα ἐγὼ προτιμέω, 'what can be seen, heard, or otherwise experienced, these things I trust more' (*Vors* B 55, but cf 107). And of these senses he prefers, again with Heraclitus, the eyes: ὀφθαλμοὶ τῶν ὤτων ἀκριβέστεροι μάρτυρες, 'eyes are more precise witnesses than ears' (*Vors* B 101a = Polybius 12.27.1; cf Candaules at Herodotus 1.8.2*: ὦτα γὰρ τυγχάνει ἀνθρώποισι ἐόντα ἀπιστότερα ὀφθαλμῶν, 'men in fact trust their ears less than their eyes.') When Herodotus moves from the visible monuments of Egypt to its past history, from ὄψις, γνώμη, and ἱστορίη (sight, rational judgment, and personal research) to the reports that he has only heard, he is obviously nervous and glad to add that he has had first-hand experience of some matters (2.99.1; cf 2.148.6). Hearsay, ἀκοή – threatened by the danger of leading questions – is indeed sometimes subject to confirmation by inquiry. A glance at 2.29.1 proves that: 'as far as Elephantine I went and looked myself; from there on I carried on my investigation by listening [to others] (ἀκοῇ ἤδη ἱστορέων).' Akoe, aural report, also submits to judgment, γνώμη. When Herodotus says, 'I write what I hear said by others ... let him believe these Egyptian stories, whoever can believe (πιθανά) such [silly] tales' (2.123.1), he means his judgment rejects them.

Herodotus never uses the word πιθανός, 'credible,' without qualification or denial. Four times with the word he emphatically rejects a tale; three times he uncomfortably selects the least objectionable version. [6] Different epochs demand different modes of inquiry and caution because inquiry into the past does not permit first-hand experience. The inaccessibility of the past is a constant frustration for the researcher. Herodotus leaps where he must. The word akoe does not appear after book 4, because it is henceforth the rule rather than the exception, since the inquiry examines unseeable, past events rather than observable objects.

While Herodotus keeps close to his principles, which include sticking to the observable whenever possible and reporting what is said often without endorsing it, he betrays a need to explain in an objective fashion how and why certain things happened as they did, or happen as they do. For this one needs to go beyond the evidence of the senses. His vehicle of analysis, unlike the modern historian's, will often be dramatic speech or frankly personal comment. His means of analytic explanation are limited by a *restricted abstract explanatory vocabulary*; for instance, particular causes are rarely distinguished from general. He did not create a new terminology, as Parmenides and Empedocles did. He was saving the past as it had been observed (δόξα), not questioning the ultimate nature of reality (τὸ ἐόν). The result, however, is not so much a paucity of explanation and causation as a richness and diversity of suggestive comparisons, analogues, parables, and parallels, along with historical analysis as the modern world defines it. Let us first consider the role of analogy in his explanations, and then, more systematically, look at several different but overlapping approaches to cause and effect.

Analogies in Herodotus and the Concept of Equalization

Analogy is our principal tool for illuminating the nature of things. It is simpler than cause and explains much less than it illustrates. For Herodotus there is an 'analogical structure of the world, by which the same laws are seen to govern its three main branches: animal kingdom, world geography, and peoples.' History is a diachronic 'analogue (as well as a part) of nature, or *physis*, as a whole.'[7] This analogical mode of thought explains the omnivorous, even cannibalistic instincts of Herodotean historiography: nothing is taboo, nothing undigestible. His curiosity finds interest and meaning in nearly everything because meaningful connections will render the world intelligible. What Lévi-Strauss says of anthropology is true of Herodotean historiography: it 'is an original mode of knowing rather than a source of particular types of knowledge.'[8] Comparison of prominent features – analogies and polarities – leads to curiosity about cause and the nature of the process that led to the known result.

Impelled to understand and compelled to experiment with genres, styles, and orders of presentation, Herodotus investigates, records, and commemorates the past for the appreciation of the future. This is his purpose in writing (proem with 1.5.3). Analogy assists him, both as a formal device for ordering the narrative and as a tool for categorizing his disparate data.[9] His frankness and clarity about his reasoning mark a noteworthy advance on the *obiter dicta* of the Presocratic philosophers.

Herodotus analogizes in space and in time. For example he extrapolates by analogy when he compares the silting of the Maeander's plain to that of the Nile's, 'if one may compare small things with great,' (ὥς γε εἶναι σμικρὰ ταῦτα μεγάλοισι συμβαλεῖν, 2.10; see the similar reasoning at 4.99.5). He believes (correctly, as it happens) that lower Egypt has been created from Nile silt, and the same has happened near Troy and Ephesus and at the mouth of the Acheloüs in Acarnania. This geographical analogy leads to a remarkable supposition on the future, a hypothesis bolder than Thucydides' parallel projection about Athens and Sparta (1.10.1–2). Herodotus predicts that the Nile in 20,000 years – perhaps even in 10,000 – could entirely silt up the Red Sea (ie, the Arabian gulf; 2.11.4). Here the analogies reinforce the instability of everything, even the earth itself.

Herodotus certainly knows about the traps of extrapolation by analogy. When he explains the summer spate of the Nile (due to the seasonal path of the sun and the evaporation of waters, 2.24.1) he says, rather diffidently: 'But if one must produce (ἀποδέξασθαι) one's own opinion about matters beyond investigation (ἀφάνεα), once having criticized other's stated opinions, I shall state [mine].' His economical and rational solution has an acknowledged basis in analogical situations that can be observed. The danger of analogy appears in his specious and improbable arguments that the Nile is equal in length to (or, rises at the same longitude as) the Ister (Danube), and mirrors its direction, as well as debouching directly south of it (2.31, 34.2). He expressly acknowledges that his method here is 'to argue by analogy from the known to the unknown' (συμβάλλομαι τοῖσι ἐμφανέσι τὰ μὴ γινωσκόμενα τεκμαιρόμενος, 2.33.2, trans de Sélincourt). Here the Hellenic impulse towards symmetry has captured the usually wary historian. Generally, however, he seems aware that there are limits to analogical extrapolation. Analogical explanations dominate the research of many of his contemporaries, especially the Ionian philosophers and the Hippocratic doctors (see eg, *Ancient Medicine* 22, 24). Herodotus wisely refrains, when he can, from relying on analogy to determine facts. As a tool of explanation, though, he and even his characters (eg, Artabanus) use it to some effect.[10] In his explicit reserve when speaking for himself we see a remarkable, perhaps unprecedented, reluctance to explain data by entirely untestable schemata.

Probability, when it is an argument based on analogy, is at best only provisional, a responsible alternative to complete agnosticism. Arguments from probability occasionally appear as an ancillary tool of history,[11] but Herodotus has an historian's distrust of them. His earnest defence of the Alcmaeonids as innocent of collusion with the Persians at Marathon rests principally on a *factual* record of hostility to the tyrants. In addition, however, he presents the negative argument that no *probable* gain for them from a Persian conquest could be imagined. This approach is based on political logic, a weak reed, and he seems ignorant of difficult facts like Clisthenes' archonship under the tyrants (6.121-4, especially 124.2: οὕτω οὐδὲ λόγος αἱρέει, 'it is unreasonable to hold that'; similar phrases appear only at 2.33.2 and 3.45.3, also in supplementary arguments). Xerxes scoffs at the idea of the Spartans' standing at Thermopylae because of its improbability (οὕτω μὲν ὀρθοῖτ' ἄν ὁ λόγος ... ἴδω παντὶ τῷ οἰκότι, 7.103*). His numerical logic is sound, but his understanding of probabilities based on historical *nomos* is faulty. Demaratus' reply stresses reasonable and likely behaviour (οὐκ ὦν οἰκός, 7.104.2*), but also the unexpected power of cultural constraints. The strange disappearance of Hamilcar receives a *probable* explanation in the absence of alternatives (οἰκότι χρεωμένων, 7.167). Herodotus' explanation for Demaratus' flight is buttressed by *probabilities* (ὡς μὲν ἐγὼ δοκέω, καὶ τὸ οἰκὸς ἐμοὶ συμμάχεται ... πάρεστι δὲ εἰκάζειν, 7.239.2; similar arguments appear at, eg, 1.137.2, 2.22.2). Although Herodotus can fall victim to the probable or the neatly schematic (Danube and Nile, 2.33-4; the Egyptian Labyrinth, 148.4),[12] he prefers what can be seen or heard. He laughs at constructs that depend primarily on logical consistency (4.36.1-2).[13]

Analogies expand the range of relevant historical information. They provide Herodotus with a mode of expressing causal relationships. They also furnish prognostic and cautionary paradigms.

The principle of 'evening out' or retribution (τίσις) furnishes the most important type of analogy. *Tisis* operates in nature, among men, and on a cosmic level to maintain τὸ ἴσον, balance or equipoise.[14] Analogical symmetry begins with the physical world, for instance, the equalities of the Danube and Nile noted above or the volume of the Danube (4.50.4): however much more water the sun draws up from the Danube by evaporation in summer, that much more is then fed in by its tributaries, so that a balance, ἀντισήκωσις, is produced by this offset of water lost, and the flow seems always to be the same (*ison*). This dynamic balance, a conservation of energy and matter, finds analogues in all of Herodotus' explanations of things.[15]

Herodotus finds a balance of advantages in nature between exotic and valuable products in remote lands against desirable temperate climates in poor nearby lands (3.106.1, 116.3); he sets the many progeny of timid and useful animals against the few offspring of savage and harmful predators (3.108.2); rabbits and birds are fecund and fertile, whereas lions produce one cub per lioness (3.108).[16] Biological limits to reproduction maintain the world's balance. The flying snakes of Arabia would make the world unliveable for men, were it not that the female, once the male has ejaculated his sperm, eats through her mate's neck. The offspring, as *tisis* for the father,[17] eat through the mother's belly and kill her (3.109).

Such *tisis* is also common on the human level. 'Every man will pay a payment equal to every wrong,' Hipparchus hears from an oracle.[18] Those who recognize man's circumscribed powers die in peace or 'off-stage': Amasis, Artabanus, and Solon. Those who ignore human limitations receive painful instruction: Croesus, Polycrates, and Xerxes, for example. Solon's advice to Croesus was ignored and the result was disaster. Polycrates, it is true, agreed to reduce his blessings, but his attempt at greater humility was superficial; he remained too fortunate and aggressive and so wound up killed and crucified. Xerxes accepts Artabanus' advice and seems to understand fortune's mutability and the weighty perils attendant on success, yet for him disaster is unavoidable; his nation's past progress drew him on to further expansion and, eventually, to failure. Human power, by its very increase, if not by an internal necessity, tends to destroy itself.[19] Individuals cannot realize appropriate limits.

Throughout the *Histories* there are many 'equalizing' actions of political powers: Greeks and Persians go to war to right perceived wrongs (1.1–5.2); Darius invades Scythia and Greece to extract retribution (τείσασθαι, 4.1.1; 5.105.2*; 6.101.3); diplomatic issues depend on balancing national offences (7.133, 134.2, 136.2); Xerxes' invades Greece because the doctrine of *tisis* justifies revenge (7.8α2*, β2*, 7.11.4*, etc).

'Evening things out,' equalizing, is thus the leading form of Herodotean analogy, whether the mode of expression is divine forethought, human 'revenge,' or 'judicial penalty' (5.106.1*; 6.87; 8.100.2*; 9.94.1). Ἰσηγορίη, ἰσοκρατίη and ἰσονομίη (equal freedom of speech, equality of political power, and equality before the law) all embody a dynamic counterbalance of forces, and all gain his commendation (5.78; 5.92α1*; 3.80.6*, 83.1, 142.3*; 5.37.2).[20] Socles of Corinth connects physics, zoology, and human politics (all realms of *nomoi*) by the traditional image of balance, of equal but separate dispensations: 'I must say, the sky will sink beneath the earth and the earth will float above the sky, and men will dwell in the sea and fish inhabit men's homes, if and when you, Lacedaemonians, once having smashed *isokratiai* [constitutional governments], prepare to establish in our cities tyrants, the most unjust and bloody of human inventions' (5.92α1*). To disturb established *nomoi* is to confuse the natural order, to turn the world upside down. Such interference invites trouble. Animals and physical objects cannot learn from the past or choose to adapt to circumstances, but men can direct their own lives to some degree so as to find a limited security. To this degree, history is an optimistic occupation, yet men always pursue boundless happiness and hope for continued good fortune (εὐδαιμονίη, εὐτυχίη) without realizing that the individual always is the plaything – from his own limited point of view – of accident: πᾶν ἔστι ἄνθρωπος συμφορή, (1.32.4*).

Particular events find their meaning in the *Histories* largely through the ideas of retribution and equalization, through *tisis* and *to ison*. These (often morally neutral) concepts are fundamental to Herodotus' relatively even-handed and generous presentation of the two sides in the Greco-Persian conflict. National mores affect eventual success. Neither party to the conflict monopolizes military or moral excellence or perspicacity. Description of political processes requires explanation of how national structures or *nomoi* came into being; evaluation is then needed to assess the meaning of the past for the present. *A causality is thus created by anecdote, inventories of customs, and narrative rather than through separate analysis.* There is 'cause and effect,' even though there is no articulated 'theory of causation.'

To ison, or *tisis*, the most common historical principle voiced by the author, applies as much to the historical realm (1.5.4) as to nature. Historical and biological ecology run parallel. There is a metaphysical balance: *tisis* preserves a healthy world, an equal justice (6.72.1, 8.105.1, etc). On the suprahuman level, *tisis* promotes equipoise through divine envy or the more abstract cosmic cycle (φθόνος, κύκλος: 1.32.1, 207.2*). Sometimes the gods are identified by one of his speakers as the custodians of this transcendent equality (2.120.5; 6.11.3* and 109.5* express pious hopes; 8.13*; 7.10ε*, 9.109.3*, 120.2*; 2.52.1). The correspondence among the sub-human,

human, and supra-human world is a coherent 'demonstration' of how things happen, of the processes that we witness.

We speak of 'explanation,' but analogy is both more and less. The success and failure of Croesus do not explain those of Xerxes at all, but Croesus prefigures Xerxes in many respects, and the resemblances in both words and deeds allow the reader certain expectations. Strife in nature, as in man, reveals the competitive and natural symbiosis which nourishes and controls earthly activities. History does not precisely repeat itself and one should not therefore over-emphasize the predictive value of patterns and historiographical patterning.[21] Yet the successive Eastern monarchies offer typological similarities that present comparable historical consequences. Thus the repetitive and recursive can be glimpsed, and Croesus, better known to the Greeks than his predecessors, serves as a potent paradigm. Such reasoning is descriptive, not predictive; prescientific, but post-gnomic. It probes more deeply into causation than pious or platitudinous *obiter dicta*, but it does not claim to offer laws open to the principle of falsification. But no historiography could conceivably offer repeatable outcomes, 'demonstrability' by some sort of verifiable experiment.

Every historical event has its unique causes, which Herodotus conscientiously tries to present, but certain habits of men in power and certain patterns of character permit an economy of multiple expression. That is to say, patterns of history need not be spelled out constantly or isolated each time in detail from their manifestations. The historian discovers the essential factors in a mass of observations, identifies what he regards as the syndrome, and selects the telling narratives that conform to a comprehensible pattern. Anywhere in the *Histories* one finds a range of analogical associations. These associations do not adequately explain events in the way that modern science may try to, but they supply contexts and patterns by which the events can be read. This, perhaps, is the most that history can do. Analogy is ubiquitous in Herodotus. He used it in a way that successors scorned or envied but could not duplicate.

Five Systems of Explanation

Herodotus uses at least five often overlapping, sometimes inconsistent systems for the explanation of historical events.[22] The most studied, although least frequently encountered, is an *immoral and divine jealousy*.[23] Solon, Amasis, Artabanus, and Themistocles, four individuals who are credited with perspicacity, endorse some such concept, and therefore it is unlikely that Herodotus rejects it,[24] yet there are no other references to it in the *Histories* whereas there are hundreds of other 'explanations.'[25] It does not provide Herodotus' preferred variety of historical cause. Divine envy represents 'more piety than theology, more curiosity than determined faith.'[26] Its early and privileged first appearance in the Solon episode establishes an important precedent, but every time that it is explicitly applied, there also appear human motives and causes sufficient for the action.

A determined destiny, *Fate*, sometimes appears as a second form of Herodotean causality. Delphi declared that neither Apollo nor the other gods could alter this fate, called μοῖρα (1.91.1* and 2*).[27] Croesus, Polycrates, Cambyses, and Arcesilaus meet their destined end (1.91, 3.142.3*, 3.64.5*, 4.164.4). Such destiny is often amoral and incomprehensible to man, and when Herodotus invokes it, he is trying to account for an unexpected occurrence, a terrifying reversal of expectations. From it there is no escape; this much wise men can know. A chastened Cambyses near death says: 'It was not possible for a human being to turn aside what was going to happen' (3.65.3*; cf 3.43.1). What must happen to Candaules, to Apries, to Scyles, or to Miltiades (χρή / δεῖ γενέσθαι, 1.8.2, 2.161.3, 4.79.1, 6.135.3) can only be known when it has happened, and therefore later generations can say 'it had to happen; look, it did happen,' without requiring any theology. Such a limited determinism will be divine, if a man believes in divinity, as Herodotus did. It is neither predictive nor even an historical theory since it offers no explanation.[28] It is invoked rarely, only when natural expectation has been confounded. Herodotus certainly did believe in moral choices, not in external determinism or fatalism.[29] When someone topples, the reader is told that he had to, not because he was fated to fall because of the stars or divine malice, but because being who he was, when and where he was, he had to err as he did.[30] There is an internal logic to political events.

Herodotus' alleged determinism seems supported by a few references to irrepressible cyclical movements in history. The 'cycle of history,' κύκλος, implies a circular or pendulum-like view, a history without progress or regress (the noun only appears at 1.207.2*, cf 1.5.4, 32*, 86.5–6). It is not a history without moral values, because this cycle reduces or destroys the great men and powers which seek aggrandizement. Morality based on Presocratic metaphors of statics ties in nicely with other metaphoric systems such as retribution and 'boundary transgression.' Asia and Europe are in counterpoise; they are separate but not unrelated, and no one should attempt to alter nature's arrangements (cf 1.174.5*, 7.22.3). The *kyklos* represents the active principle of equipoise, *to ison*, functioning through time, which will appear again in the fourth type of explanation.

References to divinity form the third group, a parallel but different set of explanations. They require extended comment to defend the historian from being dismissed as a cracker-barrel apologist for popular religion. Herodotus does not produce a theological explanation of the Persian Wars. He believes that supernatural powers exist, that they sometimes know events are about to occur (6.27.1, 98.1), and that humans obtain oracles and dreams that may be announcements from the gods (although these are very often comprehensible only after the event). Unlike Thucydides who generally suppresses the supernatural, except insofar as men's beliefs cause them to act in certain ways, Herodotus sprinkles his pages with tales of the supernatural, most of them reported as local or national tradition, and very few are recognized as due to divine causation. Croesus was a victim of god's *nemesis*, Troy was destroyed by the gods to show men that great crimes are punished, Pheretime died from a dreadful disease because her inhuman personal revenge was abominated by the gods (1.34.1; 2.120.5; 4.205). Other supposed cases, where, for instance, *tisis* is mentioned or oracles and dreams are cited or characters attribute events to divine interference, do not carry with them or establish the historian's belief. Herodotean *tisis* does not require gods; furthermore, oracles and dreams – as humans experience them – can be right without a god's say-so (as Thucydides notes, 5.26.3–4); finally, we know that Herodotus reports many statements that he does not endorse. Miracles are eschewed, not on the level of incidental events but as sufficient and necessary explanations. If we consider a difficult but unrepresentative passage in which the supernatural is extremely prominent, such as the passage from the priests at Delphi's temple (8.36–9: oracle, weapons moving themselves, thunderbolts, rocks breaking off, giant hero warriors), we find Herodotus to be very wary and he repeatedly distances himself from what he reports ('the Delphians say,' 'so I have been told,' 'the prophet reported the marvel to the Delphians who were present'). As so often, the bias of his sources appears to derail his rationalism but really calls forth his reserve. Herodotus believed in the divine, yet he gives non-divine explanations for all historical events. Aside from rumours of divine interference, he informs us that Croesus was an imperialist, that the Trojans could not make the demanded reparations, and that Pheretime contracted a fatal case of worms. Herodotus more often reports battles and the actual campaigns without recourse to any divine causality.

References to gods personalize nature and the tendency to balance and stability. The Delos earthquake was a τέρας, a portent of extraordinary disaster (6.98.3*). The oracle, divinity's mouthpiece, stated: 'I shall move Delos though it be unmoved and unmoveable.'[31] The god acts similarly to (and foreshadows) the Persian king: he shakes the order of the world. Herodotus avers: 'Somehow a sign is wont to appear beforehand, whenever great disaster approaches city or people' (6.27.1). In this passage only two of one hundred Chiote boys in a chorus sent to Delphi escape plague, and one of

120 Chiote schoolchildren survives the collapse of a school's roof just before the island suffers severe losses at Lade and subsequent conquest. The god gave advance notice of this catastrophe (6.27.3); indeed, the gods (θεοί) are those who arrange (θέντες) the universe, ordering all affairs in all their detail (2.52.1; cf 2.120.5), sometimes in a helpful way (3.108.2). Their will is done: 'Stranger-friend,' a Persian says at an Orchomenian banquet, 'whatever by the god's will must happen, there is no way for man to turn it aside' (9.16.4*; cf 3.65.3*). In a mere one hundred years the unprecedented might of the Persian empire developed, reached its greatest extent, and then was stopped and reduced on its western fringe. Cyrus created it, Darius led it to its height of power,[32] Xerxes mismanaged it more seriously than they had and caused the deaths of thousands. The period of expansion approaches term through divine will (7.10ε*). Solon's words to Croesus on the fickleness of prosperity are of the highest generality (1.86.3–5), yet their dogmatic philosophy does not supplant the novel and difficult business of explaining the recent past.

Herodotus prefers to limit his explanations of phenomena to subjects, times, and places that allow direct observation (ὄψις, 1.8.2*, 3.157, etc) and opportunities for verification.[33] When observation is not possible, he still prefers to limit his narrative to what could once have been observed and to events that his various informants as a group would vouch for, even if they disagreed on details, motives, and interpretation.

Herodotus generally suppresses the fantastic, as in his account of Gyges (no ring as in later versions, 1.8–13) and Croesus' salvation (no Apolline journey, 1.86–7), or disbelieves the absurd, such as the impossible accounts of Scyllias' ten-mile underwater swim (8.8) and of Sophanes' having held his hoplite's position by means of a real anchor at Plataea (9.74, cf 7.167.1). On occasion his loyalty to *opsis* prevents him from passing over the incredible, as in his report of Arion's miraculous rescue, where his personal observation of the statue (supposedly) of Arion on a dolphin leads him to report the tradition of the miraculous rescue (1.24.8). Even here the narrative abounds in prudential *caveats* (such as the distancing words λέγουσι, τῶν ἡμεῖς ἴδμεν, and the use of *oratio obliqua*) that permit various gradations of credence and allow him to preserve the fact (the existence of the man Arion), discount the probably fictitious tale (a dolphin saves him), and nevertheless present themes (bravery, disciplined skill, adherence to *nomos*) that are fundamental to the entire work.[34] Human agency and human actions keep their centrality; supposed incidents with specific divinities or supernatural events are more often 'explained,' doubted, or denied than admitted. For example, consider the talking birds of Zeus at Dodona and Poseidon's handiwork at Tempe (2.57.2; 7.129.4; further, 7.133.2, 189.1 and 3, 191.2; 8.41.2; cf 2.131.3).

Herodotus sometimes (although rarely and reluctantly) includes descriptions of gods (2.3.2–4.1, 2.45, 9.65.2), but hedges most statements about particular divinities by reporting them only on others' testimony. He recognizes only belief (δόξα), not knowledge, in these matters. He detects a pattern of divine action, but he suggests that it is distinct from historical causation, his particular concern. He doubts direct divine intervention (7.189.3, 191.2, cf 7.129.4), and he scoffs at Homer's and Hesiod's manufacture of Greek religion (2.53) and at Egyptian doctrines of metempsychosis (2.123.2–3). He prefers to speak vaguely of 'some god' or 'the divine.'[35]

'Coincidences' are sometimes understood to suggest Herodotus' endorsement of divine interference in history. That is, the specified events somehow appear more than accidentally synchronic. Examples include Aristagoras' and Histiaeus' plans for revolt (5.35.2 and 36.1), the oracle of disaster for both Miletus and Argos (6.18), and the fighting on the same day and at sanctuaries of the same goddess (Demeter) at Plataea and Mycale (9.100.2–101.1). This last pair of 'coincidences' is characterized by Herodotus as θεῖα, normally meaning 'divine,' but here only 'beyond human explication, remarkable'; there is no empirical basis for doubting the synchronism. The phrase 'divine fortune' (1.126.6*, 3.139.3, 4.8.3, 5.92γ3*) suggests that Herodotus' speakers see a certain few occurrences as manifestations of some non-human force, but it appears either in the speeches of others or in accounts of legends. No theology becomes evident or necessary. As with all the examples of coincidence noted earlier in this paragraph where the verb συμπίπτειν, 'to coincide,' occurs, the phrase θείη τύχη seems to mark something humanly remarkable rather than the divine and miraculous. Compare the current use of the word 'incredible.' Synchronisms are curious, but explain nothing. They are noted not to exhibit any world-view,[36] but to display the effect of religious belief on men and policy.

David Hume remarked in his essay 'Of Miracles' that men enjoy surprises, reputed miracles, and violations of the laws of nature. He denies however that these laws are violated and he avers that 'Experience only ... gives authority to human testimony.' 'No species of reasoning is more common, more useful, and even necessary to human life, than that ... derived from the testimony of man.' Degrees of assurance, he remarks, vary as interest, distance, time, and type of event separate an informant from the act reported. Herodotus' method, however, leads him to include even suspicious traditions that have only minimally historical origins or minuscule contemporary repercussions. External and internal criteria for testing or verifying data were by later standards rather elementary, and Herodotus would rather preserve a traditional error than discard a potential fact. Further, group belief as well as factuality was a criterion for inclusion in his search for why people had acted as they did. The historian of the unexpected victory had to be suspicious and cautious with information but also open to accounts that contradicted normal expectations or common opinions. Otherwise he would fall into the trap of Hecataean hyper-criticism and hyper-rationalism. Right or wrong, the method is empirical.[37] When he includes stories of miracles and divine interference, he searches for visible proof or at least some evidence. The mute boulders that broke off Mount Parnassus at Delphi and which Herodotus was taken to see, were an inadequate proof, of course, that gods were meddling in human affairs, and Herodotus does not here endorse that interpretation. The unlikely victory of the Greeks over powerful invaders requires acknowledgment of the possibility of extra-terrestrial aid (7.137.2; 8.36–9, 129.3), but Herodotus' search for explanation went much further.

Herodotus considers oracles of the gods to be unlikely sources for human knowledge of earthly phenomena. Even when they were 'right', they were generally misunderstood and too obscure to be useful (8.20.1, 96; 9.43). According to an oracle, for instance, the land of Attica had to fall to the Persians (ἔδεε, 8.53.1), but for Herodotus the oracle is only something that men spoke of, not the historical cause. It was a fifth-century game for intellectuals (including Herodotus) to show that oracles were sometimes right. Yet even if prophecies were a source of real knowledge, they never explain events or supply the most important causes. Herodotus works on explanations in human terms of the Greeks' military victory. He analyses the military and political issues: what would have happened to Greece had the Athenians joined the enemy Persians (7.139). The analysis of chaper 139 concentrates on the Athenians' freedom of political choice and praises them for their dangerous choice of freedom. The intrusions of the gods are brief because they are known only by inference and hearsay, not by investigation. The realm of the divine is clearly demarcated and largely dismissed.

An inventory of the passages where divine interference might have been expected would be less helpful than the observation that even in the mythic past, Herodotus prefers to rationalize and humanize divine tales rather than theologize earthly events. In the *Histories*, whether we count examples or examine the emphasis of the author, man is largely free to decide his own actions. Foolish or deliberate human choice, not external, divine compulsion, accounts for the 'rapes' which open his work, for the rape of Helen, and for Gyges' decision (1.1, 11; 2.120). The women choose to elope with their lovers and Gyges chooses to survive (1.4.2, 11.2). Gods are conspicuous by their absence. Homer's version of Helen's whereabouts is not fully disproved, but Herodotus dismisses it from rational historical discussion.

Herodotus, like the author of the Hippocratic treatise *On the Sacred Disease* will not assert that divinity cannot be found in nature (*De morbo sacro* 1.10–12), but claims that 'the divine is in no sense supernatural' (21.7–8); natural effects are the result of natural causes (2.41–6, 5.1–5). Herodotus and the medical writers desire to describe events accurately, explain adequately, and record without recourse to the supernatural (10.7–8; 13.24–5, 14.10–20; 16.42–6). Nevertheless a scientific, empirical approach need not rule out belief in divinity and divine activity on earth, if that belief does no violence to observable phenomena. An empiric may say: 'all things are both divine and human,' πάντα θεῖα καὶ πάντα ἀνθρώπινα (21.7–8).[38] Human responsibility for historical events is not decreased, even if some supernatural element affects the weather.

Miracles, marvels, and divine interference are not accepted so frequently as the believers in a naive Herodotus suggest. Exceptions to the laws of nature are often denied, doubted, rationalized, offered on the authority of others, or distanced by indirect discourse or by wholly historical alternative theories.[39]

The gods appear most frequently in the *Histories* not as the Pelasgians' organizers (2.52.1), but as a mysterious force disturbing human plans and expectations, as Solon says, ταραχῶδες (1.32.1*, 'baffling,' *hapax* in Herodotus; perhaps originally Hippocratic in the passive sense of 'disordered' or Herodotus' neologism). Herodotus need not choose between 'opposed conceptions of Destiny and all-powerful gods, between human liberty and divine providence,' not because 'il n'avait pas la tête philosophique,'[40] but because, from the common-sense and the historical point of view, these conceptions are not mutually exclusive, they do not conflict. A Christian historian, for example, can give an account of the deeds of Adolf Hitler without jettisoning his eschatology and his god.[41] On the rare occasion when Herodotus directly connects divinity with human punishment, he diffidently inserts a proviso acknowledging the unusual nature of the event and his personal astonishment before it: the punishment of the Mermnads, Alyattes' disease and cure, the fruits of Glaucus' impiety (according to Leotychides), the anger of Talthybius (μοὶ ... θειότατον φαίνεται γενέσθαι), the flood at Potidaea (εὖ λέγειν ἔμοιγε δοκέουσι), the absence of corpses in a Plataean sanctuary (εἴ τι περὶ θείων πρηγμάτων δοκέειν δεῖ), or the calendrical coincidence of the battles of Plataea and Mycale.[42] Choice opportunities to connect wickedness and divine wrath are ignored (eg, the Chians at 1.160 and 6.27). The Ethiopian Sabacus appears to outwit an allegedly divine dream by refusing to follow its advice (2.139). Explicit recognition of divinity meddling in human events is rare; Herodotus does not employ god to account fully for major historical events. Local or national legendary aetiologies do not lead Herodotus to abandon the hard work of history for the security of easy belief.

The fourth kind of explanation briefly acknowledges the gods, but this causality discovers a natural, dynamic equilibrium in historical events, not daily interference by supra-terrestrial beings. *Tisis* will be examined now as a type of explanation rather than as the structuring narrative principle of chapter six.

This explanation offers a cosmic ecology, the equalizing code of *tisis* in action, act for act, retribution for offence. Divinity reduces those with 'excessive' power or fortune, through *nemesis*, or *tisis*, the principal expression of *dike*, justice (1.32.5*; 7.10ε*; 8.13, 109.3*).[43] Divinity is thus posited as the guardian, but often the balance manages to restore itself. Occasionally a merely 'poetic justice' appears, as when Gyges sets out to slay Candaules 'from the same spot,' even 'at the same door' at which he has been posted by Candaules to view the naked queen (1.11.5, 12.1). Similarly Croesus dismisses his visitor Solon, thinking him a fool, specifically for giving him the very advice that eventually saves his own life (1.33). When humans seek *tisis* by executing their own vengeance (τιμωρίη), they risk offending the gods (4.205, 7.8α2*, 8.105–6), even if the justice of the wish is justified. An apparent exception proves the rule: Oroetes' capture of Polycrates is 'unholy' because 'he had not suffered any damage or been maligned by Polycrates – he had not even laid eyes on him' (3.120.1); that is, he had no reason to seek *tisis*. The nature of things – whether called 'the divine' or inner necessity - encourages the restoration of balance (1.34, 4.119.3; cf 6.11.3*, 6.109.5*, 8.13, 8.129.3) and ensures penalties matching the crime (2.120.5, 5.56.1*, 6.72.1, 6.84.3). Violating acknowledged laws of all mankind engenders some communal calamity for Athens (7.133.2). Europa was taken as compensation for Io, ἴσα πρὸς ἴσα (1.2.1), nature maintains a balance of species (3.108–9), Solon and Artabanus aver that misfortune balances good fortune (1.32.4*, 7.49.4*).

Explanations based on 'divine vengeance' have symbolic value for any god-fearing audience, but they always allow and often coexist with other, non-theological causes (1.167; 4.205; 6.84). When Cleomenes went mad and committed suicide, Herodotus comments that most Greeks explained it as punishment for corrupting Apollo's Pythian priestess, but the Athenians explained it as revenge for devastating the fields of the gods at Eleusis, and the Argives as revenge for the sacrilegious slaughter of Argive suppliants and the burning of the holy grove (6.75). Each people chooses the offence nearest and dearest to its heart and gives it the name of a god. The Spartans, however, explicitly deny any divine agency and ascribe his madness to a mundane cause, excessive drinking. Herodotus positions himself somewhere in between, endorsing the concept that Cleomenes 'got what he deserved' for abusing Demaratus (τίσιν ἐκτεῖσαι, 6.84.3), but not endorsing the hypothesis of divine interference.

Anaximander had said (*Vors* 12 B1): '[Every thing] pays a penalty (δίκη) and retribution (τίσις) to each other for injustice (ἀδικία) as time assesses it.' Here the physical universe is expressed in moral or judicial terms by an Ionian 'scientist'; history is conceived similarly by the Ionian historian. *Tisis* can effect its purposes without recourse to any *deus ex machina*.[44] Herodotus rejects the Hellenic search for simple and single – mythical or theological – root causes.

Herodotus' main concern is not religion and the supernatural, but the phenomena of terrestrial experience.[45] His analysis of historical action requires a fifth form of explanation: historicist, down-to-earth, political analysis, the sort of explanation expected from a modern historian.[46] For this he has no one term, but it is his invention, and often a first-person verb or pronoun indicates the presence of a novel, rational, and entirely human explanation. He is not the theoretician of this type of analysis, but no previous extant author had ever employed it. Human action reveals character, and individual and ethnic character appeared decisive to him for comprehending the historical process. From book 7 on, historical means of explication predominate, and the importance of vengeance and the other modes of explanation decline. Xerxes' expedition, for instance, is *both* voluntary and necessary, but the necessity grew out of the *nomoi* – habits, laws, and customs – of the Persians, Xerxes' own insecurity and need to prove himself, and his megalomania. Xerxes' Grand Council and the Dream represent two versions of the 'causes' of Xerxes' decision, either of which might have sufficed. If, however, Xerxes had been no more than the gods' joke, a victim, would Herodotus have written his history at all? A secular and a theological version of Xerxes' decision to attack the Hellenes may be juxtaposed in 7.1–19, but Herodotus did not suspend judgment.[47] The text presents a perfectly adequate set of human motives, both psychological and strategic analysis; it distances itself from the report of the dream. The ghoulish antics of the dream are entirely absent from Xerxes' sober reflections at 7.44–52, where he takes full responsibility as man and king for his expedition.[48] This secular interpretation represents Herodotus' own and final judgment.[49] Rational analysis is harder to remember in the *Histories*, because it does not lend itself to dramatic scenes; it never becomes a structural motif or acquires a set of striking images, and it is not clearly expounded as a theory of explanation. Nevertheless it is embedded in the text of each *logos* with historical content.[50]

Xerxes' failure may indicate to the faithful that the gods smash the over-weening and to the philosophical that vast power will corrupt a mere human, because the *Histories* provide different meanings on several levels. For the historically minded, it is enough to read of the acts of Xerxes' predecessors to see Xerxes as their successor following their policies, and to discover the immediate causes and the more systemic differences between Hellas and Persia. Xerxes' infamous but unique 'dream' inspired by Homer appears between two presentations of prosaic and historical motives (7.12–18). Its inclusion further dramatizes the *Histories'* most fully realized narrative. Nevertheless, it is redundant as explanation for an event destined to happen (7.17.2*) for other, more verifiable, historical reasons. Herodotus' world is as ruthless and harsh as Thucydides' in its aggression and imperialism. One might review, for instance, the Machiavellian arguments put in the mouth of Histiaeus when he opposed one Ionian revolt (4.137). At the very outset Herodotus shifts the ground quickly from mythical *aitie* to historical responsibility, human choices and action; not Io, Europa, Medea, and Helen, but the recent Oriental aggressor Croesus begins the greatest and decisive series of East-West conflicts (1.5.3, 6.2, 26.1–3, 28).

The student of Herodotus' thinking, faced with these disparate causes (really different levels of explanation) notes that it is futile 'to assess the relative importance of each of these motivations [of Xerxes' invasion] ... after we have realized that Herodotus resorts even to different styles for motives that have no common denominator.'[51] The table that follows summarizes the five systems for some major narratives. Divine vengeance or annoyance sometimes supplement but they never prevent human motives and political causes from appearing (eg, the story of Croesus, Polycrates' death, the fate of Pheretime's enemies). Herodotus' interpretation of events on individual, political, and metaphysical levels permits the audience to see events in more dimensions than most historical writers allow. The other inherited systems of explanation should not detract from Herodotus' accomplishment, the first extant presentation of recent events with their ascertainable causes, the invention of historical thinking. The αἰτίη or explanation of the war promised by the proem comprises all the kinds of αἴτια (causes) which Herodotus can assemble. His work constitutes a comprehensive and patient clarification of the elements that contributed to that fateful nexus, the Persian Wars. Perhaps Herodotus began his *Histories* to answer a limited question such as 'Why did the Greeks win the battle of Salamis?' Yet the work grew into a study and explanation of the clash of polities and their cultures.

Fact and Explanation in Herodotus

Herodotus' views on the world, the gods, and man are 'not always consistent.' This is not because he 'combined beliefs in an immutable order of

EXPLANATION IN HERODOTUS: SOME IMPORTANT NARRATIVES

Narrative Unit	1 Divine Jealousy (phthonos)	2a Fate (moira)	b The Cycle (kyklos)	3 Divinities (theos, theoi, to theion)	4 Act & Retribution (tisis)	5 Historical Analysis (logos; first person verbs and pronouns)
Croesus attacks the Persians	1.32.9*	1.91.1–2*	(1.5.4)	1.34.1, 91.3	1.73.1, 86.6	1.46.1, 73.1
Fall of Polycrates	3.40.2–3*	3.43.1–2*, 142.3; 4.164.4	3.40.2*	3.42.4	3.106–9 (general exposition), 126.1, 128.5	3.39, 44–5, 122.2, 131
Cyrus attacks the Massagetae	1.210.1, 212.3*	no evidence	1.204.2, 207.2*	1.210.1	1.214.5	1.204.2–205.1
Darius attack the Scythians	no evidence	no evidence	4.132.3*?, 134.2*?	no evidence	4.1.1, 118.4*, 119.3–4*; 7.20.2	3.134.2, 4*; 4.118.2*; 7.8 α1–γ1*
Darius attacks the Greeks	no evidence	no evidence	no evidence	6.27.1, 98.3, 106	3.137.3*; 5.102.1; 6.94.1, 101.3, 109.5*; 7.1.1, 4	6.44.1, 94.1
Xerxes attacks the Greeks	7.10ε*, 14*, 15.3*, 16α2* (the dream: 3 speakers), 46.4*	6.98.1–2	(1.5.4)	7.10ε, 134.1, 137	6.94.1; 7.8 α2, β1*, 11.4*	7.8 α2*, 11.2*, 50.3*, 138.1; 8.76.2
The successful repulse of Xerxes by the Greeks	8.109.3*	no evidence	(1.5.4) 9.120.4	8.129.3; 9.65.2, 100.2?	7.139.5	7.102*, 104.4–5* (Demaratus), 139.5, 144.2

nature and human fate, and in human initiative and responsibility ...'[52] The necessity of fate and the existence of human choice are two different, not incompatible, ways of looking at the same event: 'all human actions are both free and determined, and in addition cause and moral responsibility are different categories.'[53] Thus, the same man is both doomed before birth and personally guilty (1.13.2, 34.1), and the Persian Wars are both metaphysically destined and politically explicable (7.8*; 7.11.2*). Herodotus rejects one miracle and accepts another (2.54–7, 7.57), condemns and endorses topographical schematism (4.36.2, 2.33.2), but even when religious influence is the overriding consideration,[54] he will never rest content in telling us that an event was god's will or fate or the result of chance. Divine action stories 'are always "on information received," never given as historical "causes" (αἰτίαι).'[55] Chance, furthermore, plays a smaller role in Herodotean aetiology than in any subsequent ancient historian.[56]

It seems prejudicial to state that 'although [Herodotus] knew all the factors responsible for Xerxes' invasion of Greece, he preferred to believe that Xerxes was convinced against his better judgement by a vision of divine origin.'[57] The apparition in Xerxes' dream told him the truth: it is a realistic observation about political power and psychology that imperial states do not remain quiet for long. A monarch who inherits a kingdom must prove his worth in deeds, as Atossa also knew (3.134.2*). A prudent young king cannot always remain inactive; he must prove himself.[58] This is political and historical as well as psychological necessity.[59] Xerxes is firmly placed in the line of oriental despots. Human *hybris* is emphasized in his Hellespont crossing, in his treatment of Leonidas' corpse, and in many other anecdotes revelatory of character. Yet Xerxes, as he himself is made to say, must extend his race's glorious conquests. His world forces the invasion on him, as Darius was forced to invade Scythia (3.134*; 7.8α1–2*).[60] Herodotus does not have to choose between complementary types of explanation. His multiplicity of explanations creates a reservoir of meaning which makes the *logos* of Croesus, for instance, so rich in causal complexity.[61] Croesus plans to attack Cyrus both for personal and political reasons (vengeance for his brother-in-law, Astyages, and fear of Persia's growing power, 1.46.1, 71.1) and for metaphysical reasons beyond his control but still triggered by his foolish misunderstanding of the oracles from Delphi (doomed generation, divine *ate* and *nemesis*; 13.2, 32.6*, 34.1, 54.1, 75.2).[62]

Herodotus' inconsistencies are sometimes more apparent than real. Croesus' war against Cyrus is in one passage defensive, elsewhere aggressive (1.46.2; 1.71.1, 73.1), but no less contradictory in this respect than Rome's actions in the Second Punic War or Sparta's in the great Peloponnesian War. And the wealth of causes used to explain Croesus' invasion across the Halys river partly results from the different concerns of the Delphic priests and Herodotus. For the priestly establishment at Delphi, Croesus had to end his family's reign badly; for Herodotus, he began a long chain of misfortunes for the Greeks.[63] The apologists for the Delphic oracle were interested in establishing responsibility for Croesus' fall, not in Croesus as an instigator of later events. The 'confused theology' of 1.91 extricates Apollo's oracle at Delphi, but also argues clumsily for two distinctions, first between determinism and foreknowledge that allows for free will, and then between cause and guilt – both αἰτίη in Greek. The priests at Delphi forecast, but did not cause, Croesus' fall. For that, Croesus was αἴτιος, guilty. Croesus acknowledges his errors of policy and lack of strategic wisdom, something entirely different from his ancestor's crimes – regicide and wrongful seizure of the Lydian throne.[64]

The problem of developing a non-judgmental theory of causation arose partly from the extension of the morally neutral ἁμαρτ- root meaning 'miss the mark' to a definition of negative moral value, 'err, sin,' and the simultaneous but opposite process of extension from moral 'guilt' to the neutral 'cause' in a scientific sense which the αἰτι- root experienced.[65] Croesus' fatal attack was an error of military judgment as much as a manifestation of wicked and unseemly pride or an offence against divine wisdom. Croesus was the descendant fated to lose the kingdom. He is also shown in minor dramas as arrogant, hot-tempered, and aggressive.[66] Croesus' desire to strangle quickly the rival Persian power and to avenge his dethroned brother-in-law was sensible enough, but his military preparation and campaign strategy turned out to be inadequate. The main cause for Croesus' fall, then, was strategic error and military miscalculation, and Herodotus states this conclusion several times. Multiple aetiology is supplementary rather than contradictory.

Herodotus' inconclusiveness as to cause is a virtue; his paratactic style permits him to avoid reductive syllogisms and to hover between the general and the particular. His multiplicity of causal connections precludes logical rigour but includes much of the uncertainty of human existence that historians can ignore or minimize but cannot transcend.[67] Linear chains of actions and reactions are seen in perspective as historical cycles of success, overextension, and failure. Croesus' doom may have been clear to the Delphic priests in advance, but even his unseating finds sufficient historical explanation in his foolish decision to attack a poor, yet strong and brave foe. Since political 'expansionism is more basic (because it is more persistent) than vengeance,' and since expansion is described in terms of national policy and personal psychology, it seems untrue to state that, in the Croesus *logos*, 'the failure of expansionism is not explained by real historical factors but only by metaphysical ones.'[68] The *Histories* grope towards historical explanation in an epoch when causation was still a developing concept. Personal, political, and metaphysical motives and forces are active in and on everyone. The different forms of explanation found in the *Histories* may seem incongruous to us, but each one fits into both its own pattern and the structure of the whole. To tell as correctly as the evidence permits the story of events and to relate the main story to other stories may be the best that any historian can ever do.

For Herodotus, a nation's desire for power is a major motive force in human affairs. At 4.167.3 and 7.5.3 he explicitly distinguishes imperialism from pretences about Persian motives for aggression. The few accounts of past events that go no further than revenge – Phoenicians and Argives, Greeks and Trojans, Hellenes and Asiatics (1.1–4) – are ultimately trivial, ie, unhistorical. The preface announces something more useful than pretty stories and more difficult to construct: 'la mise en évidence de la cause profonde du conflit.' This search for the most satisfactory explanation requires a globular, not a linear approach, a *Gestalt*. The most comprehensive explanation does not exclude various secondary explanations. The Persians' insatiable appetite for conquest manifested in the attempts of Cyrus, Cambyses, and Darius against the Medes, Lydians, Babylonians, Massagetae, Egyptians, Ethiopians, Ionians, and Scythians, appears as the true and fundamental explanation (αἰτίη) of the war between the Greeks and the Persians. Failure and success both proceed from internal causes as well as from external pressures. Custom, the distribution of power, and social structure determine a nation's fate.

If the Greeks' victory was owed first to the gods (7.139.5; cf 8.109.3*) and then to the Athenians (ibid), Herodotus' parenthetical piety should not obscure[69] his thorough account of the mundane and complex efforts of all the independent Greeks to repel Xerxes' venture. The weight of the narrative overwhelms the pietistic aside.

Mention of the gods does not lessen the human historical accomplishment, for the gods are beyond history. 'The war between Athens and Aegina saved Hellas' (7.144.2). Here Herodotus asserts that not the gods but a parochial quarrel between two minor powers rescued the Greeks. He produces a secular and somewhat cynical explanation for the later Hellenic victory. Internecine war prepared both Hellenic combatants for a more serious foe, the Persians. Conflict can be productive (cf the good ἔρις of Hesiod *Works and Days* 11–26). The Greeks are shown rationally weighing submission to the Great King and choose to resist him in full knowledge of the consequences attendant on failure. The metaphysical dimension does not obscure the political, and the political dimension offers Herodotus' historical understanding. 'It gives access to a causality underneath the surface of events.'[70] In other words, *however deficient Herodotus' political history may be, he invented it, and he explains major events with it.* Xerxes' invasion of Greece was a politically necessary result of the continuous growth of Persian power through wars, a growth which constituted for the Great King 'a tradition, an obligation, and hence a powerful impulse.' This was Herodotus' original historical insight.

The epic trappings of private dialogues, council speeches, potentates' dreams, and of the popular motif of τίσις with its philosophic elaboration by Anaximander (*Vors* 12 B 1) were inherited from the literary conventions of the archaic epoch. The *Histories'* original applications of these conventions should not obscure the unprecedented contribution (in the previously undeveloped medium of artistic prose) which Herodotus has made to historical thinking. This contribution includes the central observation that governments of all types make policy on the basis of past political history, present political pressures internal and external, and often ruthless self-interest. Further, he recognized that national character often (and occasionally individuals) can determine a nation's survival. Through Herodotus, Greek thought surpassed mere sterile moralizing,[71] and freed itself, at least partially, from the strong grip that myth and the epic had exercised on the conception of the past, and from naiveté about the dynamics of history. Herodotus invented political history as the modern world knows it. No branch of modern research is closer than history to the best investigative achievement of fifth-century Greece, the histories of Thucydides and Herodotus.

10

The Failure and Success
of Herodotus

The conversion of legend-writing into the science of history was not native to the
Greek mind, it was a fifth-century invention, and Herodotus was the man who
invented it.

R.G. Collingwood *The Idea of History*

Introduction

The *Histories*, twice as extensive as the *Iliad*, were widely known and read at
least by the educated élite, but no one pursued Herodotus' method. It seemed
inadequate to many critics in antiquity and later. 'The father of history was
never, or almost never, recognized as a model historian, because he was not
considered trustworthy, even by his admirers.'[1] The innovation, in the form
that Herodotus gave it, did not survive its creator. Reasons of style played a
greater role than ideology or credibility in the devaluation of Herodotus, as a
cursory reading of Aristotle, Dionysius, or Cicero on historiography will
confirm. But 'the reputation of Herodotus in antiquity depends fundamentally on the direction that Thucydides imposed on historiography.'[2]
Thucydides was most influential just where he had rejected earlier historians' practice, but reading the *Histories* by his principles is anachronistic and
reductive.

Thucydides nowhere systematically criticizes Herodotus' method, never
even names the man. In fact, Thucydides' demonstrable criticisms of his
predecessors are sometimes aimed at other writers (eg, Hellanicus; see
1.97.3) who deserved them more.[3] It is even unclear when he read his
'predecessor.' Subsequent historians (eg, Ctesias, Megasthenes, Manetho)
quote the *Histories* generally in order to condemn particular reports, not to

debate historical method. The 'born story-teller,' to float a still too common phrase,[4] had no imitators. Following Collingwood's brief comments, I suggest three reasons for this peculiar isolation.

The Isolation of Herodotus

Literary Technique

Herodotus' manner and style puzzle readers of history. The lucid but apparently disconnected stories require a reminder that 'he writes not ... as a simple child of Nature; his style is the product of an energetic practice of his art ... The acme of his art can be found in the graceful but seemingly artless combination of literary styles.'[5]

He helped himself to the techniques of fiction and poetry more blatantly than his successors. Private motivation, family chats, secret deliberation, a brief gesture, as well as public deed, can seem as accessible to this historian as to the all-knowing poet. 'It is characteristic of his style that he likes to hide the formal character of his work behind the fiction of informal reporting.'[6] He presents many of his stories in a manner that conveys essential meanings without being hobbled by any strict rule of evidence, a procedure often misinterpreted as a lack of any principle or discernment. It is necessary and possible to distinguish explanatory anecdotes from the more factual narrative.[7]

Although he has seemed unbearably gullible to some readers, his structural and narrative techniques and syntactical subtlety reveal an unappreciated sophistication. He dissevers popular and prejudiced accounts from his own judgment without jettisoning that recalcitrant information entirely. He can be suspicious where even Thucydides is gullible, as in the instructive case of Pausanias. Herodotus doubts the story of that Spartan regent's betrothal to a Persian princess and of his tyrannical ambition to rule Greece as a Satrap. He does not allow later gossip and partisan rumors to mar the reputation of the victor of Plataea (5.32; 9.64.1, 76, 78–9, 82). His rhetorical strategies, when understood, do not require constant contradiction of reports. Thucydides, by contrast, wishes to suppress or explicitly deny what he does not trust. Nevertheless, even he promulgates Athenian propaganda, and publishes fanciful letters as history (cf Thucydides 1.95.1, 95.5, 128–9, 131, 134).[8]

Herodotus' habitual technique of inserting tales, or ring-composition, the structural device for framing stories by other stories, although found in the first book of Thucydides,[9] was soon discarded by historiography. His sequence of presentation seemed unplanned to readers expecting chronological linearity, although it has been excused or defended as the most efficient method of writing a lengthy account before the modern era of notecards, numbered pages, erasers, and footnotes.[10]

Aristotle cites Herodotus as an example of the 'old' prose style (*Rhetoric* 3.9.1–2 = 1409a–b), a 'running' style which 'has no end in itself, except insofar as the matter related reaches a conclusion. Its lack of limit (ἄπειρον) is disagreeable, for all men wish to discern the end.' Aristotle prefers a periodic style that is easily grasped, because the hearer continually thinks that he has secured something for himself, that a new conclusion has been reached. This approach may suit the poetics of Lysianic oratory and Sophoclean drama more comfortably than the radiating web of connections among historical events, where starting- and stopping-points present knotty problems.

The linearity of the new prose medium proved suitably mimetic of the successive empires of the East. Although the necessity of linear order caused problems in the presentation of events in the last three books, where parallel and simultaneous actions must be recorded consecutively, Herodotus had founded a method of ordering experience to account for the past to the present that his successors have yet to render obsolete. The educated traveller who lived in Athens and southern Italy in the age of Pericles may be presumed to have known of the artistic revolution in prose associated with those areas. Furthermore some parts of the *Histories* were penned up to five years after Thucydides started gathering notes and composing.[11] Herodotus can mark closure, when he wishes, as neatly as anyone by means of periodic sentences or a summary framing sentence.[12] His usual style, however, better reflects his idea that the larger forces at work in Aegean history had not yet reached term. The reader should not be deceived into believing that Persia and Hellas are yet quit of each other, or that they can ever wholly sunder their relations. The historian begins and ends somewhere, and Herodotus has at least his countryman Dionysius' praise for his choices,[13] but he would have falsified the facts, had he indicated that his end was truly *the* end of Greco-Persian conflict. Herodotus asserted the continuity of the years 522–424 BCE (6.98.2), three generations of unparalleled mischief, harm, and suffering for the Greeks. He did not insist that his chosen scope and subject were the only ones deserving of attention, as other historians were to do.

His *Histories*, therefore, are open-ended, and the debate about the last paragraph, 9.122, results from his literary methods. That this was the author's intended conclusion 'is no more than a belief ...; but the burden of proof lies on those who would leave the work incomplete, and they have proved nothing.'[14] Returning the reader to the beginning of Cyrus' Persian empire and aggression against the Greeks, the epilogue suggests structural similarities between the Persians then and the Greeks now (479 BCE). The literary method was immediately rejected, but the intellectual endeavour – history – inspired others to try to rethink the new discipline.[15]

Scope and Inclusiveness

Homer informs the conceptual frame and world-view of Herodotus. The internal and external disputes and warfare of the *Iliad* as well as the tightly co-ordinated plot and subordinated travel tales of the *Odyssey* shape and inspirit the work more than the item-by-item geography, ethnography, and empty rationalizing of Hecataeus' books.[16]

Thucydides, however, established certain canons of historiography concerning presuppositions, structure, and scope, that excluded Herodotus' epic comprehensiveness. Because no like-minded historian supervened, Herodotus was forever isolated. Thucydidean historiography laboriously cleanses muddy testimony, and removes irrelevant accretions and all 'wrong' versions of the facts from a severely limited series of events (generally, a war), whereas Herodotus has built an elaborate set of portraits of civilizations from a rich variety of their great and remarkable actions. Cultural history, Herodotus' invention, has been a by-product of imperial expansion in ancient and modern times. The age of Greek colonization, the growth of the Persian and Athenian empires, Alexander's conquests and Rome's, all strongly affected the nature and content of historical research.[17] With the Peloponnesian War, the Greek world began a nearly century-long period of contraction that turned the focus of many historians temporarily back to old Greece. Herodotus' concerns were not those of the next generation.

Herodotus had transcended myth but not god.[18] Thucydides tried to minimize or eliminate many metaphysical notions, especially cruder concepts of God and Destiny, from the historian's purview.[19] Thucydides' quest for the eternally exemplary event, however, introduced a new reductive metaphysic into history: the study of past events is said to provide valid inferences for understanding future events.

Thucydides also excluded earlier history from history that can be known in detail. He excised citations of sources, quotations of poetry, biographical essays, myths, anecdotes, and nearly everything else that was not obviously germane to his subject, the immediate war. Although exceptions can be cited, his approach is consistent enough to appear to be a rejection of the method of Herodotus. Thucydides' most striking contributions were an annalistic chronological framework, speeches packed with philosophical reflections, and a convoluted rhetoric that has always puzzled students. Again, the techniques of Herodotus seem consciously rejected. With the possible exception of the chronological scheme, however, these modifications were not imitated in antiquity.[20] When Thucydides treats ethical questions, he avoids drawing explicit conclusions from the data. This reticence, along with his habit of speaking of himself in the third-person, makes his text seem more neutral and distant from the events than is the case. Indeed, comparisons between the two historians' presentations of the great invasions that they record show more similarities than differences.

The approach of Herodotus makes equally strenuous, but different demands on the reader. Above all, he finds verbal and situational echoes and oblique cross-references to events past and future. These implicit analogies give coherence to the multitude of otherwise apparently unrelated happenings.

Like Odysseus, Herodotus had wandered far (μάλα πολλὰ πλάγχθη), seen many cities (ἀνθρώπων ἴδεν ἄστεα), and also learned and reported the thoughts of men (νόον ἔγνω). Herodotus sometimes accepted, often rejected the reports that his *Histories* transmit, but what men have believed – true or not – is as important to him as what they have done. The Muses told Hesiod that they knew both truth and falsehoods like to truth;[21] Herodotus also knew both, and he realized that both contribute to the historian's understanding of other men and other times, both deserve preservation, as long as the historian sifts them to the best of his ability and offers judgment. In presenting alternative versions or events of questionable reality, Herodotus preserved national traditions and sometimes a truth that he himself only dimly, if at all, perceived.

The poem of Aristeas, the prose authors of *Periodoi*, and Hecataeus are mentioned as sources of ethnological information (4.13.1, 16.1; 4.36.2; 6.55, 137.1). Wonderful tales of remote peoples, such as the gold of the Arimaspi, the virtue of the Ethiopians and of the Hyperboreans, the goat-footed men, and the community of wives of the Agathyrsi and others, probably reflect folk as well as literary sources, sometimes improving tales of Utopias and fictional travel narratives.[22] This material was not mere adornment or irrelevant divagation, but a mirror held up to Greek culture that gave secular, historical meaning to the Persian Wars. Ethnology – both true and merely reported – provided a necessary background and depth for the Persian attack. Many of his successors first rejected this material from history, then they confected it wholesale. Cultural history was largely excised from their subject for at least a century, because History proper had been redefined as political and military history, and annalistic, local, or even single-event histories became the rule.

Herodotus underlines the mutability of human affairs at the end of his proem when he promises 'to give equal consideration to small and great communities of mankind (ὁμοίως σμικρὰ καὶ μεγάλα ἄστεα ἀνθρώπων ἐπεξιών). For most cities which were formerly great have become small, and those which in my time were great, formerly were small. Therefore knowing that human prosperity and happiness never remain in the same place, I will mention both [large and small] equally.'[23]

Here appears some explanation of the *Histories'* idiosyncratic canons of inclusiveness. Mutability affects everything. Phenomenal instability is a Hellenic commonplace, of course. Xenophanes, for example, contrasts an immovable and effortless god with toiling, unstable man: αἰεὶ δ' ἐν τ' αὐτῷ μίμνει κινούμενον οὐδέν (*Vors* 21 B 23–6; cf Parmenides 28 B 8.29; Sophocles *Trachiniae* 132ff). Herodotus, however, here explains the relevance of incidents in his *Histories* which might *seem* trivial in themselves. His justification rests on the potential significance of any action for his theme of human instability. For this, Solon's supposed brief but dramatic audience with Croesus and the long chronicle of the rebellion of Ionia are equally important.

Herodotus, Thucydides, and Xenophon pondered the question of what matters for history. They noted the folly of dismissing events that befell insignificant places. Xenophon, old-fashioned as well as Socratic, derived ethical illumination from political events regardless of their magnitude. A polemical passage concerning little Phlius, a polis he knew well, states: 'If any large city achieves something noble, all the historians record it; but I think that if a city, although it is small, has accomplished many noble deeds (καλὰ ἔργα), it even more particularly deserves mention' (*Hellenica* 7.2.1; cf 2.3.56; 4.8.1; 5.1.4, 4.1). History seems to subserve the needs of philosophy for improving examples. For Thucydides, historical dynamics require a magnitude of men and monies, but significance can be found in even the severe misfortune of the hamlet Mycalessus, and the poor village of Mycenae presented an object lesson for historical research (7.29–30; 1.10; cf 1.1.3, 9.4, 21.1). Because mutability itself is one of Herodotus' themes, change on any scale and in any domain of human activity captured his attention and provided parallels to events of wholly different magnitudes. So the text echoes Croesus' 'circle of human events,' κύκλος τῶν ἀνθρωπηίων ... πρηγμάτων, itself an echo of Solon's pessimism about human prosperity (1.207.2*; 1.32*; cf 7.203.2*).

Herodotus had neither an optimistic evolutionary view of history nor the pessimistic one that Croesus' *kyklos* of human affairs might imply. The former is precluded by the proem's statement on the transitory nature of prosperity and power; the latter takes too literally the deterministic, cyclic image that implies the absence of constancy, but not the mechanical and necessarily immediate fall of any community that flourishes. Before the battle of Plataea, the Athenians similarly stress unpredictability to the

Spartans: 'But there is no point in mentioning these [past Athenian benefactions]. In fact the very men who once were brave and helpful could today be cowards, and yesterday's cowards might be today's heroes. So let us leave aside ancient history' (9.27.4*). Such a view of lability, shocking to one traditional, Hellenic moral notion of an unchanging nature (*physis*), is consistent with Herodotus' delicately cynical world-view, which holds that certain behaviours ought to be carefully avoided, but nothing stops men from misperceiving old errors or making new mistakes. Herodotus and Thucydides sought to emancipate their inquiries from a comfortable and parochial moralism. Exile showed them that historical magnitude and moral significance are distinct categories.

The fourth-century writers of *Hellenica* and *Universal Histories* acknowledge the example of Herodotus: Xenophon, especially when his entire corpus of history, romance, and philosophical reflection is considered; Theopompus, who abridged Herodotus and included sections on local wonders, ethnic customs (eg, the Etruscans), and biography in the *Philippica* (115 FGrHist T 1, FF 1–4, 64–76); and Ephorus (70 FGrHist T 1; FF 1–5, 7–92, especially 58–63; 173–88), who depended heavily on Herodotus for his comprehensive *Histories* that included geography, myth, and ethnography, and who produced other essays on discoveries and local history, topics often treated by Herodotus. The professional division of history into periods and sub-genres made Herodotus' comprehensive approach impracticable.

Furthermore, the example of Thucydides' 'psychological history' made the *Histories* look obsolete in their motivation of actions. Whether we agree that Thucydides was 'the man in whom the historical thought of Herodotus was overlaid and smothered beneath anti-historical motives,'[24] there is no doubt that he decisively altered the direction of Greek historiography. Herodotus had transformed Ionian investigation from quaint mythography and annotated description of exotic lands by unifying geography, local history, and ethnography into one narrative and by focusing, as Jacoby and von Fritz have shown, on a single diachronic theme, the growth of the Persian empire and its first defeat by the Hellenic coalition. Thucydides concentrated on a single decisive event in contemporary history to the exclusion of the past, distant peoples and places, and nearly all myth. He successfully polemicized against all previous approaches to the past. His 'redirection' implies an awareness of a further development, 'the recognition that even the portrayal of the immediate present from the best of information is hopelessly and inevitably saturated with that same "mythical" quality.'[25] Such self-reflection did not emerge so explicitly in antiquity, however, so we may return to Herodotus' peculiar but enduring work.

The first historian's self-appointed task in remembering, evaluating, and organizing so many oral traditions on so vast a scale defies explanation. 'The complexity, the sheer size of the work of Herodotus, is prodigious compared with that of all predecessors except Homer ...' Beginning with prehistoric intercontinental migrations and offences, then proceeding to the growth and Hellenic repulse of Persia, and ending with the Greeks' vengeance of 479, 'he has chosen numerous and entirely unrelated subjects and has made a single harmonious (σύμφονον) body of them.'[26] He and Gibbon may stand alone in the pleasure that they afford their readers, 'thanks to [their] great erudition and to a native capacity for choosing what is picturesque.'[27]

The Creative Vision of Herodotus

Finally, later historians avoided their predecessor's example because they did not perceive his intellectual depth. In some respects, Herodotus conforms to modern notions. He allows a very small role to chance and none to a deified Fortune (Τύχη), whereas later ancient historians regarded the former, at least, as central.[28] As for aitie, explanation, Herodotus generated both dramatic and efficient, 'short-range' 'causes' of a war and deeper 'causes.'[29] Refusing to simplify the Hellenic achievement sufficiently for later purposes of local politics and partisanship, Herodotus' account did not furnish useful applied knowledge for the next century's political problems.

The fraudulent Ctesias and the romancer Xenophon met the desire for accounts of the Orient and the Persian court.[30] Ctesias pathologically contradicted Herodotus everywhere, rarely or never for the better, as even the stolid Photius suspected (Bibliotheca 72, p 35b). The popularity of Ctesias suggests that many Greeks were not interested in accurate history. Simplification, distortion, omission, and deformation of the record better served the purposes of orators, adventurers, and patriotic historians. Past history provided a field of battle for present issues, while the names of past generals and battles became live ammunition and topical political catch-words.[31] Herodotus' unpartisan message was unwelcome.

Atthides, the Agesilaus and various Philippica, the sections about myth in Ephorus' Histories, imaginative novels produced by Ctesias, Xenophon, and the Alexander romancers provided novelty in form and content.[32] Serious students of human behaviour such as Aristotle and Plato never mention Thucydides;[33] they refer to Herodotus as a butt to ridicule or quarry him for anecdote and example.

This book may seem to some to overestimate the first historian's profundity and originality. Herodotus, like later ancient historians, had nothing very systematic to say about the causes of war, and did not discover unilinear, evolutionary development in constitutional, economic, or political history.[34] He sometimes inflated a unique event into a national custom, driven by a theme or pattern to overextend the meaning of an isolated fact.[35] Macan summarizes our quandary: 'Concerning the historic quality, credibility, or truth of the matters in these books [4–6], it is harder to frame any general proposition that can be of use. The truth (as distinct from the honesty) of the *Histories* of Herodotus cannot be adequately measured from volume to volume, nor even from Book to Book; every story, every sentence must be separately weighed ... A critical observer ... will [never] relax his vigilance over any page of this author without disaster, for there is no page on which fact and fiction – if so crude a distinction may be admitted for the sake of argument – are not to be found lying side by side, or indissolubly penetrated, mutually affected ...'[36]

The only historian before historiography had no theorists to refute or fall victim to, but the emergence of a new method is less noticeable and decisive for fellow historians than the refutation of an old one. Herodotus cannot now furnish a satisfactory model for historians, but his logic deserves a careful attention rarely afforded it. Some modern scholars express surprise that Herodotus in the preface did not mention the war itself (that is, other than its cause), but this theme was evident to his first audiences from the moment that 'great Greek and barbarian deeds' have been mentioned. How could an historian in the infancy of historiography have discussed how 'they came to war upon each other' without describing the war itself?

By current standards it is odd that Herodotus concentrated on Croesus' dramatic encounters with Solon, Delphi, and Cyrus, the death of his son, and the war with Cyrus, leaving less than three pages for the other events of a fourteen-year reign. We cannot disprove the recent and unlikely hypothesis that he could not obtain more information; we do not dispute the helpful observation that he never intended to write a survey of Greco-Lydian relations;[37] but we add a point about his rhetoric, namely that such a survey would have directed attention away from his real concern. If Lydia was to be the originator of Greco-barbarian warfare in historical times,[38] then Herodotus had to substantiate the important claim, but Croesus' privileged role in the structure of the *Histories* has been justified in three other distinct ways.

Croesus was the first barbarian to subdue and tax systematically the Greeks; he was the victim of the Persians who first drew that people into the Greek world;[39] and, most important for the *Histories*, his story offered a microcosmic view of the problems of autocracy. He provided a prototype that simultaneously organized and interpreted later historical events. If Croesus had not existed, Herodotus would have had to invent him. Indeed, in the extensive, dramatic narratives and conversations with Solon, Adrastus,

Atys, and Cyrus, Herodotus *did* invent a Croesus, understanding his 'invention' in the sense of a 'necessary, historical reconstruction.'

The *Histories* consist of much more than the simple recording of dinner-stories mentioned by Xenophanes (*Vors* B 22):

> By the winter-season's fire one converses
> Lying on a soft couch, full of food,
> Drinking sweet wine, munching chickpeas:
> Who are you and whence among men come you?
> How many years are yours, my good man?
> How old were you, when the Mede came?

Herodotus and Thucydides shared a hard-won and briefly sustained confidence in the empirical discovery of facts and the intelligibility of human affairs.[40] They recognized the uniqueness of historical events and thus did not analyse how every event relates to general truths, but they sought to comprehend this relation by selecting paradigmatic incidents. Gomme noted how this noteworthy achievement of two writers straddles the modern, absolute barrier between the composition of poetry and history, creative efforts that are two kinds of synthesizing, intellectual activity, *poiesis*: 'If a man writes history well enough, as Thucydides did, his narrative has all the power of poetry to compel our interest because it is written "generically" without ceasing to be an exact record of particular events, of what Greece, all Greece, "did and suffered" in the Peloponnesian War; that is, the generality, as in poetry, is embodied in particular instances.'[41]

Herodotus' and Subsequent Greek Notions of Historiography

Past events can now exist only as mumbling stones and timbers, the feeble memories of the living participants, and the partial records of contemporary and later recorders. Assertion does not require evidence, and motives for falsifying the existing evidence were known to Herodotus. For instance, he states with evident suspicion, perhaps on malicious Athenian authority, that after the battle at Plataea many grave-mounds, including the Aeginetans', were heaped up without bodies in them. The cities that did not join the battle were concerned to deceive future generations (χῶσαι κεινὰ τῶν ἐπιγενομένων εἵνεκεν ἀνθρώπων, 9.85.3).

'Men have no memory,' Pindar asserts (*Isthmians* 7.17), and Herodotus had reason to agree. The Egyptians are praised for their unique concern with preserving knowledge of past particulars (λογιώτατοι, 2.77.1). Calculation and uniquely dependable written inventories (2.145.3) enabled them to know details of national chronology. Such knowledge can provide a more trustworthy basis for reputation, κλέος,[42] but *kleos* itself requires more than names and dates, namely some permanent form such as monuments or literature. Men and deeds sometimes find (accurate or deceptive) concrete memorials such as pyramids, statues, barrows, and serpent columns, but the Persian Wars demanded something yet more eloquent and thorough, better able to explain and supply reasons and causes, than stones. *Logoi*, unwritten words and conversation among men, save the ephemeral facts only privately and for the moment. The phrase ἀπόδεξις ἱστορίης recognizes the double necessity of research into, and a permanent, public commemoration of, a past that is otherwise without stability, doomed to oblivion.

The past does not provide Herodotus with a scientific model for the future, 'prophecy in reverse,' or a field for free speculation. His investigations produced traditions, eye-witness reports, and empirical data, physical facts, an altogether untidy mélange, but, their limitations being understood, information better ascertained and more conducive to productive reflection than the harmonious world-systems of the early Greek philosophers.[43] The instability of the human condition permits at best a modest knowledge of probabilities, and 'man's narrow learning capacity' renders history less a useful technique for planning than a curious record of attempts and failures among communities.[44]

Herodotus might quote Aeschylus on the future (*Agamemnon* 251–2): 'When it happens you can hear of it. Before that, let it go.' He did not claim the didactic, future-oriented usefulness that Polybius asserted and Thucydides hoped for (eg, Polybius 1.1.1–2; 3.31; 9.2, 20.6; 36.1.7; Thucydides 1.22.4; 2.48.3; 3.31, 82.2).[45] For him, it sufficed to discover, transmit, and interpret what could be ascertained about significant past actions in the emergence of Persia and Hellas as Mediterranean powers.[46]

Herodotus was less sanguine than later historians about men's capacity to understand the future or manage contemporary events. The wise Cyrus and the headstrong Cambyses equally misinterpret divine foreshowing (1.209.4*– 210.1; 3.65.4). Sabacus' departure from power in Egypt appears to be based on the misinterpretation of a dream (2.139.2). The Magi's understanding of an eclipse to mean that the Greeks would leave their cities (7.37.3), while not entirely wrong, only encouraged Xerxes in his self-destructive overconfidence. Even the historian's alleged philosophical mouthpiece, Croesus, continues to err after 'learning' wisdom (1.53.3; 1.207–14 [bad advice]; 3.36); he furnishes a paradigm of the inability of humans to profit permanently from 'learning through suffering.' In fact, Croesus and later Artabanus eventually give up giving good advice. So the successful, the chastened, and even the wise fall victim to phantoms of desire and to disaster.[47] God may give advance warning, may be a *prodektor* (7.37.3; 6.27.1, 3), but the reader learns that men generally do not learn, or at least do not adequately digest past events, and have little chance of planning against future contingencies. Herodotus consequently attempted to recover an outline of great past accomplishments for future generations, but promised no usefulness in forecasting desirable policies.

The rare comment about the future generalizes about morality and vulnerability, not about political or military policy (eg, a reported message of a rhetorical cast at 7.203.2). Herodotus produced a version of the past so that subsequent men could know its vitality, achievements, and failures, not so that they could predict the course of future events or learn how to succeed in war or observe the unacceptability of imperialism.[48] Thus his κτῆμα ἐς αἰεί serves a different purpose than Thucydides'. Although 'the future did not loom large in the works of Greek historians,'[49] they display an awareness of posterity and a concern that the near past or present be appreciated in the future. Herodotus' purpose is 'distinctly "future-oriented,"' although he is aware of the modest, limited, and impermanent power of historical examples.

It is, I think, the opinion of Aristotle ... 'that it is no excuse for a poet who relates what is incredible, that the thing related is really a matter of fact' [cf *Poetics* 24.19 = 1460a; 25.27 = 1461b]. This may perhaps be allowed true with regard to poetry, but ... the historian ... is obliged to record matters as he finds them, though they may be of so extraordinary a nature as will require no small degree of historical faith to swallow them. Such was the successful armament of Xerxes described by Herodotus ... Such [astonishing] facts, however, as they occur in the thread of the story, nay, indeed, as they constitute the essential parts of it, the historian is not only justifiable in recording as they really happened, but indeed would be unpardonable should he omit or alter them.

Henry Fielding *Tom Jones* Book VIII, Chapter 1

The just critic seeks Herodotus' notion of history within the work. Aristotle (*Poetics* 23.1–3 = 1459a) denied 'poetic' unity to works of history. Since such a work must treat all events of a given period, in which relationships will often be casual or unrelated, he argued that only an anarchy of facts rather than the coherent unity of a 'poetic' action would emerge. Aristotle considered history to be a defective art of narration (ibid), because its only unity is a period of time, and his historian should report all that happened in that time, related or not: ὅσα ἐν τούτῳ συνέβη περὶ ἕνα ἢ πλείους, ὧν ἕκαστον ὡς ἔτυχεν ἔχει πρὸς ἄλληλα. It is consequently not εὐσύνοπτος like tragedy, not 'easily surveyable' or 'easily taken in by the mind,' concentrating on a single *praxis* – whole and complete with beginning, middle and end – and therefore satisfying to the aesthetic sense. On this view, 'to tell what happened ... fact by fact' is naturally less 'philosophical and serious' than poetry (*Poetics* 9 = 1451a; in 1451b, Herodotus is mentioned). 'What Alcibiades did or suffered' offered one-by-one events, contingent and often unintelligible.[50] There is no inevitable logic (τὸ ἐφεξῆς) to it, not even probability, just chance events and accidents, exactly like a badly constructed play (1451b–2a). Aristotle had not forgotten Herodotus' literary achievement or the unity of the later books of his account, but his reductive 'positivism' could not admit the imaginative dimension of history-writing. Presumably, where Herodotus was artistic, he was untruthful; and where he was truthful, he was necessarily disorganized.

Few historians have tackled as diverse a body of data and stamped their interpretation of the facts so completely on posterity as Herodotus. Aside from opening up new territory for investigation, he discovered a way to incorporate historical meaning in past actions, constants of human behaviour and patterns inherent in events that make the past instructive as well as pleasurable. How? Reconstructing the past demands not only a lucid picture of what happened and why, but also concessions to an audience's intellectual capacities and preconceptions, and these concessions to human frailty must also be considered part of the author's historiographical art. Herodotus, for instance, limited his main fields of inquiry, developed concepts of action that organize his historical data and sociological details, and moulded his *logoi* into a coherent whole. That moulding required invention, such as the words of his speeches and the gestures of his personalities.[51] Such invention seems legitimate and necessary, since memory, documents, topography, and monuments cannot in and of themselves explain the facts that need explanation. Aeschylus' neat and synoptic version of the Persian Wars oversimplified the historical facts, which are unpredictable, ἀμαθῶς (Thucydides 1.140.1*), because events rule men rather than the other way around in a world where powerful forces within and outside persons are erratically destructive and disturbing (Herodotus 7.49.3*, 1.32.1*). In fact, although Aristotle censures history in the *Poetics*, elsewhere he necessarily assumes or states that political behaviour falls into intelligible patterns: 'One must also study other peoples' wars as well as one's own, and how they turned out, because like results naturally arise from like causes' (*Rhetoric*, eg, 1.4.9 = 1360a; cf *Politics*).

Others, like Fielding above, have attempted to explain or refute Aristotle's unsystematic comments on historiography.[52] In the *Rhetoric* and *Poetics*, history serves as an adjunct, a treasure-house, for other subjects, the arts of poetry and persuasion. His observations require mention, however, just because Herodotus faced and in part solved these literary problems of arranging and explaining the seemingly meaningless and undifferentiated events of life as it is lived. Many facts were eliminated, some facts were privileged. If we find logic and unity in his *Histories*, the artist put them there.[53]

Herodotus' Achievement

Mais nous parlons comme si l'on avait un jour imposé définitivement une certaine forme, une certaine notion de l'histoire; en fait on peut toujours discuter de ce que doit être l'histoire et la cause historique.

J. de Romilly

Herodotus' original inquiry was not the culmination of a mature tradition, such as Homer's epic represents, but the invention of the first complex prose work in European literature. He discovered historical and historiographical problems that no one before had perceived. He tried to produce an account that conformed to certain rules of evidence. An analysis of causes, *aitiai*, structured the progression of his non-fictional and rational *apodexis* of the movements of history, especially the conflict between the Greeks and the barbarians. *Apodexis histories* as a genre has no inherent masterplan or *Tendenz*,[54] but each example will be shaped by some ideological beliefs. Herodotus can refer to the 'compulsion' of his *logos*, or the *logos* 'inquires or needs' something (2.65.2; 7.96.1, 139.1; 1.95.1; 4.30.1). These phrases are a convenience of the author's, but they also point to constraints that he thinks are imposed by the nature of the task at hand. Enough flexibility remains to allow him to borrow from other genres: before Croesus falls, *apodexis* already subsumes parody, comedy or melodrama, and tragedy (1–5, 9–14, 34–46).[55]

Every *apodexis histories* connects and structures some events, and ignores or fails to see others and other modes of linking them. It gains coherence as the reader becomes acquainted with the themes and the main frame of the structure, hinted at repeatedly at the beginning, here by Gyges, Solon, Croesus, and Tomyris. The order of presentation is deliberate and habitual.

Herodotus made Persia's skein of victories provide a thematic and historical principle. To this chain he attached the discontinuous, memorable actions and non-historical aspects of other peoples, Greek and barbarian.[56] The historical *logos* of the Persian empire subsumed every ethnographic *logos* that ends each time the Persians conquer a nation.

For example, the Egyptian *logos*, despite a pretence of chronological organization, has no consistent historical direction but is content to instruct and entertain by exotic descriptions, paradox, polemic, and *Märchen*. It is connected, however, to the great design by two structural elements, the principle of polarity throughout and the historical event of Persian conquest which rings the *logos* at 2.1 and 3.1. At 1.95.1, the historian states his principle: 'Henceforth our *logos* inquires as to who was this Cyrus who destroyed Croesus' empire and how did the Persians come to rule Asia.'[57]

Within the major units, the great Persian *logos*, the ethnographic *logoi*, and the history of Xerxes' invasion,[58] many associative digressions are tied to the *Histories*, sometimes weakly motivated by their immediate context but always strongly fastened by analogical resemblances. Every so-called digression contributes to the whole in two ways: it fleshes out a larger, immediate story either temporally or geographically, and offers information by analogy on later and earlier events. Individuals and communities mentioned parenthetically in the earlier books often recur as events move towards the crisis. These parallels become ever more noticeable as the work progresses, until the decisive events of 480–479 permit less interference.

To employ Persian expansion as an organizing and unifying concept for thousands of historical facts revolutionized – rather, founded – historiography: the subordination of nations to Persia co-ordinated the *logoi* of book 1 through chapter 27 of book 5, and then Herodotus transformed this theme from a link and a motive to *the* subject of the remainder. He found visible monuments and curious customs and tales but little past history for most of the subject, barbarian peoples. For even the Persians, the monuments of Persepolis and Susa are conspicuous by their absence. When Persians and Greeks had become neighbours, the political-historical thread became the subject, because the Persian Wars could only be understood from their constituent processes, historical acts and institutional facts, not from stone monuments. *Opsis*, sense perception of mute objects left from the past, largely yielded to *historie*, inquiry into past actions by investigation of written and living, oral sources.[59] The historian preserved the strange patina on the surface of events because he dealt first-hand with informants for the Persian Wars who often knew the *what*, but rarely knew the *why*; who joined in the sweating, the rowing, and the bloodying, without sharing in the hard thinking and arguments of the previous night's strategic discussions.

Explanatory strategies, ranging from the repeated single word to patterns of action and systems of cause and effect, make these reported actions intelligible and meaningful for his own and later generations. Herodotus managed to hover between the particular and the general. Facts, not speaking for themselves, required the author to 'put things next to one another' (συμβάλλεσθαι). The result has a unity and meaning easier to sense than to state, because Herodotus saw connections and dynamic counterbalancing everywhere. Nevertheless, his chief concern was to commemorate events and not to theorize about their deepest causes. His philosophical assumptions and his theological beliefs about the world's workings are the least important cement to the work and are not its subject.[60]

The theme of conflict between a centralized, expanding empire and autonomous and quarrelsome weaker neighbours rises repeatedly to a climax, each time with Persia victorious, or largely so, until we reach the independent Greek cities' decision to fight at Marathon, Thermopylae, Salamis, and Plataea. A charming folktale, a close political debate, or a variously reported narrative of a battle can convey Herodotus' interpretation, but his admiration of liberty remains central, almost never presented analytically or systematically but hammered home by repeated key-words and phrases, arresting analogies, dramatic dialogues, and narratives that share certain profiles. Advancing his inquiry beyond the vatic religious vision of Aeschylus and the unreflective piety of the ordinary Hellene who considered the Greek victories to be simply the gods' punishment of Persian *hybris*, Herodotus showed the power of self-determination and documented the victory of those who used, however grudgingly and cantankerously, their wit, will, and combined strength.

Relativist and empiricist that he was, however, Herodotus first laid out for comparison most of the cultures that came under the Persian aegis and were mobilized to conquer Hellas, and then summarized the actual clash, so his audience could judge matters for itself.

A plurality of meanings constituted another remarkable achievement. Thoughtful students are invited to ponder ambivalent outcomes. In presenting 'might have been's,' not only what happened but what might have happened, he engaged in a necessary part of the historian's task, 'the retrospective calculation of probabilities.'[61] 'There are even those who will argue that history took a step backwards after Herodotus.'[62]

Some histories must be gotten right and argued (the shield at Marathon, for instance), some histories can be left suspended in an anecdotal, essentially timeless and placeless limbo (Atys, Glaucus, Evenius). Stories of vice and virtue to please a crowd abound.[63] The dichotomy of fact and fiction provides but a crude distinction for understanding the past, as Macan noted. Furthermore, some fictions, properly understood, may tell more about the important facts than other facts. That is why Herodotus offers, for instance, the preposterous story about the Persian courtiers who lighten the escaping Xerxes' ship by jumping overboard. In the *Histories* facts and fictions reported to Herodotus became significant insofar as they clarified the wonderful success of Persia and the more wonderful victory of the Hellenes over the Oriental juggernaut.

Proper commemoration required Herodotus to establish the meaning of the acts recorded. His *apodexis histories* conceptualized a problem, collected information that addressed the question, and produced a careful account and explanation whose meaning reflects on events before and after the Persian Wars, near and remote connections that would explain how and why the Greeks had arrived where they were. The world's first coherent narrative of notable events 'easily taken in by the mind' is an adroit manipulation of organizing ideas: commemoration of notable achievements, boundary transgression, the Hellenic-Barbarian polarity, the schemata supplied by the 'constitutional debate,' and so forth.

Modern expectations of a narrow subject, 'cause and effect' reasoning, a rigorous canon of relevance, and subordination to one governing idea are disappointed by the *Histories*. Dionysius considered this a conscious literary excellence, variety in Homer's style,[64] but the modern critic observes, among other things, a historiographically desirable absence of a single 'systematic interpretation of universal history in accordance with a principle by which historical events and successions are unified and directed toward an ultimate meaning.' Such a teleological 'philosophy of history' requires some sense of a 'transcendent purpose that comprehends the whole course of events,' such as Christianity.[65] No transcendent eschatology of this sort pollutes the *Histories*; Herodotus was no theologian nor did he want to be one.

Herodotus' prose saved the events of the previous generation so that no one would ever again need to inquire fruitlessly: 'What happened and what did it all mean for us?' The proem asserts this intent for a new intellectual and literary genre, and the *Histories* fulfil it. Historiography as we know it was then created at one time and by one man, Herodotus.

NOTES

1 All citations of Herodotus refer to Carolus Hude's Oxford Classical Text, 3rd
  edition (Oxford 1927) 2 vols. An asterisk after a citation marks the passage as
  presented in *oratio recta*, following Powell's (1938) useful and important convention. A list of modern works on Herodotus noted more than once will be
  found in the Bibliography.
2 Jacoby (1913) passim, especially 281–352; von Fritz (1967) discusses Jacoby's
  work: I 121, 131, 443, 490. At I 154–7, 451–2, von Fritz infers from present
  'knowledge' of Herodotus' travels a theory of the historian's development from
  something else: ethnographer, geographer, even entertaining lecturer. Cf
  Fornara (1971) 4–9; Solmsen (1974) 3 note 3. Legrande (1932) offered 175 pages
  'sur la vie et la personnalité d'Hérodote.' Herodotus says remarkably little
  about himself, so this portrait depends very heavily on inferences from an
  impersonal text. The 'genetic mirage' continues to haunt classical erudition.
  For useful summaries of the question of composition, see the surveys of Paul
  MacKendrick, CW 47 (1954) 145–52, 56 (1963) 269–75, 63 (1969) 37–44,
  and the lengthier discussions of von Fritz (1967) I 104–27, 442–75, and Cobet
  (1971). Drews (1973) 36–47 summarizes a century's scholarship on how
  Herodotus came to write history.
3 Eg, Jacoby (1913) 341, 353; von Fritz (1936)
4 Preceded: Macan (1908) xlvii; Gomme (1954) 78. Followed: Jacoby (1913)
  352–72, esp 365–9. Hignett (1963) 37 describes the futility of trying to prove
  any statement about the order of composition of *logoi* or the hypothesis of a
  continuous draft.
5 Lattimore (1958) 9 may represent this approach: 'I believe that the text of
  Herodotus as we have it is a continuous piece of writing which Herodotus set

down from beginning to end in the *order* in which we now have it.' That the opening sentence was the first sentence written, and that 'the first draft was always meant to be the final draft' may stand as the extreme statement of the 'unitarian' credo. Even Pohlenz (1937) 212 admitted later insertions (eg, 6.98; 7.137, 233; 9.73 *fin*).

6 Regenbogen (1930) and then Pohlenz (1937) redirected criticism of Herodotus in a literary direction after the analytical excesses of Jacoby's masterful *RE* article (1913), although Focke (1927) had already drawn attention to Herodotus' historiographical unity. The two 'unitarian' approaches: Immerwahr (1966) 315 and Drews (1973) 36, 84–96; see his index, sv 'Great Event.' 'Unitarianism' has at least one other schism: those who believe in a unity of time of composition, 'one session of writing,' eg, A. Kirchhoff, *Über die Entstehungszeit des herodotischen Geschichtswerkes* (Berlin 1878[2]), Powell (1939), and Lattimore (1958); and the other group, recently more influential, which believes in a unity of conception and is not concerned with when the various *logoi* were composed, eg, Pohlenz (1937), Myres (1953), and Immerwahr (1966). Fornara (1971) 5–13 summarizes well the conceptual problems of the 'unitarians.'

7 Fornara (1971) 5

8 The 'analyst' Fornara exhibits some of the inadequacies of that school: insufficient awareness of the subjectivism inherent in the separatist approach (eg, on the question of the date of Herodotus' trip to Egypt). It seems a common but naive 'analytic' belief that Herodotus could only have realized that Persian conquest intercepted and joined together all of the ethnographic *logoi after* he had done his fieldwork (cf p 33). Also unfortunate in his perceptive essay is an unprovable and heavily criticized anachronistic emphasis on the role of the Archidamian War in the the historian's development. He believes that the *Histories* present an anti-imperialist message addressed to the Greeks immersed in Thucydides' war, 'a tract for the times,' a view that forgets the proem. Momigliano (1972) 28 found no evidence that ancient historians expected their histories to explain immediate, present-day problems. Thucydides 1.22.4 speaks of the past and future but studiously ignores the historian's present.

9 Several recent essays assume a different sort of unity and come up with extreme views of a Herodotus who was not any sort of historian. See, eg, Fehling (1971), esp 8–10, 180–2, and Drexler (1972) esp 11, 186; cf Verdin's review (1975) of recent scholarship.

10 I do not claim to purvey a new interpretation for the meaning of the whole work, there being perhaps already too many examples of such macrocosmic criticism. Problems of imperial strategy, internal political history, military logistics, and ancient religion are also rarely touched on. Our concern is not to determine whether Herodotus was right on any historical point, but how he arrived at his conception and exposition, and why he thought that was the right one.

11 W.C. Sellar and R.J. Yeatman *1066 and All That* (London 1930; repr 1961) 5
12 E. Auerbach, *Mimesis* (1946; English trans W. Trask, Princeton 1953) 20.
Auerbach's bold claim ought to be extended to include *all* historians.
13 Consider Herodotus 9.27*, esp section 4; Thucydides 1.73.2–75.2; 2.36.1–4,
41.2–4; 7.69.2, etc. Cf A. Momigliano 'History between Medicine and
Rhetoric' *ASNP* 15 (1985) 767–80.
14 Cf Drews (1973) 44. Myres (1953) 67 expresses pictorially this view of the first
sentence.
15 Momigliano (1958) 1 = *Studies* 127
16 Flory (1980) 27–8; J. Goody, *The Interface between the Written and the Oral*
(Cambridge 1987)
17 See Powell *Lexicon*, sv ἀποδείκνυμι; Erbse (1956) 210; G. Nagy 'Herodotus the
logios' *Arethusa* 20 (1987) 175–84, analyses the word differently.
18 Similarly Pohlenz (1937) 2; Erbse (1956) 211
19 Herodotus rarely employed the noun and the Thucydidean verb for the writing
of history, ξυγγράφειν, 'write up' or 'compose,' except to refer to matters
not worth recording (1.93.1; 3.103; 6.14.1). The other appearances of the word
denote the mechanical transcription of verbal prophecy (1.47.1, 48.1; 7.142.1;
8.135.3).
20 As adjective (9), noun (3), and adverb (42), the word appears 54 times in the
Histories. Thucydides never uses it, nor any other Attic prose author. It is a
legacy from Homer and a favourite of the Hippocratic writers. Hesiod preferred
ἀλήθεια, another ἀ- privative formation; cf *Theogony* 26–8. The notion of
the root *τρεκ- is that of the Latin *torq- and Sanskrit *tarkus*: turn, twist,
deform. ἀτρεκέως λέγειν, πυθέσθαι, κτλ, then, mean to tell or learn something 'straight.' See the distinction between ἀλήθεια and ἀτρεκείη drawn by
W. Schadewaldt 'Die Anfänge der Geschichtsschreibung bei den Griechen'
Die Antike 10 (1934) 411–12 = Marg 115; also Krischer (1965b).

CHAPTER 1

1 Eg, Edward Gibbon *Decline and Fall* ch 24, n 54 (c 1780; = II 495 in Bury's
edition [London 1935¹⁰] and quoted by Bury [1908] 57): 'Herodotus sometimes writes for children and sometimes for philosophers'; Thomas Macaulay
(1828) 72–89: 'a delightful child' (73); Sayce (1883) xiii–xxxiii. For an
assessment of ancient and modern opinion, see Momigliano (1958) passim; for
recent views, see Verdin (1975), Hampl (1975), or Dewald and Marincola (1987).
2 Collingwood (1946) 28; Gomme (1954) 106–8 praises his understanding both of
the main strategic problems of the war and of the historical meaning of the
decades of conflict. For a survey of opinion on the structure of the *Histories*,
consult Cobet (1971) esp 4–42, 188–98.

3 See, for example, Macan (1895) x–xxvii, three groups of three books; Jacoby (1913) 283–326; Myres (1953) 118–34, pedimental composition of the whole and of parts, esp 62, 64, 85 (sketch); Immerwahr (1966) 329–62, and 75–8, 261–5 on concentric framing; S. Cagnazzi 'Notizia di 28 logoi di Erodoto' *AFLB* 16 (1973) 89–96; idem 'Tavola dei 28 logoi di Erodoto' *Hermes* 103 (1975) 385–423, esp 421–3, schema.

4 Immerwahr (1966) 6

5 So Jacoby (1913) 292 and 381 terms the Egyptian *logos* an excursus; cf von Fritz (1967) 158–208, developing his earlier theory of the geographer transformed into an historian: (1936) 315–40. Further, Fornara (1971) 18–21, 24, 'an antiquarian showpiece'; Drews (1973) 66–77. Drexler (1972) 187–227 provides a critical doxography of twenty-one recent authors; cf Myres (1953) ch. 2: 'Herodotus and his critics.'

6 Gomme (1956) 25–9; earlier, eg, Pohlenz (1937) 8, and Dionysius. Thucydides seems readier to accept the historicity of Minos (1.4), a figure whom Herodotus would prefer to discard as prior to retrievable history (3.122, but cf 1.171, 173; 7.169–71).

7 Myres (1953) 67, 117, 300 points out how the first sentence creates expectations that are answered throughout the *Histories*.

8 On θωμαστά, see Barth (1968) 93 ff. ἐξ ἀνθρώπων is best taken as 'agency' with τὰ γενόμενα (so Powell, *Lexicon*, sv ἐκ [c, 3]), but it has also been understood with ἐξίτηλα, emphasizing the degree of obliteration. Krischer (1965) 159–60 offers an intelligent three-part schema for the sentence. The stylistic *Schlüssel* offered by Hommel (1981) 282–7 seems unlikely to me and unprovable in any case.

9 Stein (1901) *ad loc*, Aly (1921) 59, Immerwahr (1966) 18. Jacoby (1913) 335 *contra* with false parallels, because τε ἄλλα καί is different from the rhetorical and emphatically anticipatory τε ἄλλα καὶ δὴ καί. See Denniston (1954) 255–6 and, for instances, 1.1.1, 2.131.3, 3.155.6. Erbse (1956) 212 and Krischer (1965) 161–2 also dispute Jacoby. τε ἄλλα καί is not a merely decorative transition; it announces books 1 through 5.27. See Drexler (1972) for a similar interpretation of the movement, but not the meaning, of the proem. For a review of interpretations of this *Satzungetüm*, see Hommel (1981) 277–82.

10 Erbse (1956) 213–18 discusses difficulties in the last clause of the proem. The principal effect of τά τε ἄλλα is clearly to throw the chief weight on αἰτίην ἐπολέμησαν, on the desire to supply circumstances (*all* great and wonderful deeds) from which one (*the* cause for which they went to war) is to receive concentrated attention, as in the adverbial phrase τά τε ἄλλα καί (Powell *Lexicon* sv, в II 6a, eg, 2.129.2). Here τά τε ἄλλα compactly suggests a comprehensive account of Greek and barbarian actions. Calling the phrase only 'anticipatory' destroys half its meaning, here and elsewhere (cf 1.174.4, 180.3;

6.147.3*; 8.88.3). Herodotus assumed the new responsibility of preserving for posterity historical deeds. Just as αἰτίη refers to more than the immediate cause of the war (Erbse 221), so τὰ ἄλλα should not be unduly restricted. Dionysius *De Thucydide* 5 criticized Herodotus' predecessors for having no literary organizing principle at all.

11 Pagel (1927) 3, Pohlenz (1937) 3 with note 1, et al, try to limit ἔργα to actions, πρἀξεις. It refers to any isolable event or object of significant quantity and quality. H.R. Immerwahr 'Ergon: History as monument in Herodotus and Thucydides' *AJP* 81 (1960) 264 and 270 explains why ἔργον cannot be limited to either deeds or monuments.

12 Therefore Jacoby (1913) 335 was wrong to claim that the proem 'shoved in' a theme different from the actual one, the war itself. It is circular reasoning to deduce Herodotus' subject from a reading of his text and then, misreading the proem, to argue that he has not provided what he promised to do. Why should he misstate, much less misunderstand, his chosen subject? The war itself was only the greatest discrete manifestation of the cultural and institutional differences that made up the 'real subject.' This explanation of τά τε ἄλλα καί may answer Drexler's question (1972) 7–8: Why *cause* rather than *the war* in the proem? Immerwahr (1966) 63 observes that ancient proems offer 'never a complete survey of what is to come, but merely initiate in some way a sequence.' Lang (1984) 3 analyses the first sentence as a directional marker and not a table of contents.

13 Fränkel (1960²) = Marg 737–47 (excerpt only) elaborates on Herodotus' reluctance to rend the complex fabric of human events. He follows a path that often turns but never ends, or even pauses (740). Not at all naive, this technique cleaves closer to reality than a modern historian's frequent divisions, posited cause, and narrower drama of background, focused action, and catastrophe followed by a curtain, perhaps an epilogue (742). For Fränkel, framing-composition is a triumph of the artist who draws the reader insensibly ever further. Similarly Immerwahr (1966) 15: 'He likes to hide the formal character of his work behind the fiction of informal reporting.'

14 Ephorus and other universal historians destroyed their one good idea, the connectedness of events, by lack of any other. Most of them were chroniclers or epitomators (eg, Diodorus, Justin). They did not recognize or articulate the superior coherence of certain selected series of events or of epochs that deserved prolonged investigation.

15 Fornara (1971 b) 25–34 argues that Herodotus gave his text to the public after 421 BCE, but the apparent imitation of the first part of Herodotus' preface in Aristophanes' *Acharnians* (425 BCE; vv 523–9) seems to confirm the view that the *Histories* were already well known by that date (Drews [1973] 155 n 18). Fornara, speculating that Aristophanes and Herodotus offer *parallel* parodies,

has again argued for a date *after* the Archidamian War (*Hermes* 109 [1981] 149–56). *Non constat*, and given the probability of partial publication(s) and revisions, and the possibility of readings to small or large audiences, 'publication' is probably a crude and anachronistic concept. Cf J.A.S. Evans 'Herodotus' publication date' *Athenaeum* 57 (1979) 145–9, esp 148.

16 Strasburger (1966) 54–62

17 Immerwahr (1966) 187, 188; Plescia (1972) passim; Herodotus 3.38.4; 5.78; 5.91.1. The value of variety in the natural world is stressed at 3.108.2; 4.30. Hannah Arendt eloquently articulated the positive value of diversity in *Eichmann in Jerusalem* (New York 1963, 1965^2) 268–9, 275–6.

18 Men squatted and women stood for micturation in pre-Western Japan, in ancient Ireland, in primitive Australia, New Zealand, Angola, Nicaragua, and commonly among North American Indians, eg, the Apache: Havelock Ellis *Man and Woman* (London 1930^6) 78–9. Cf Hesiod *Erga* 727ff: 'avoid exposing the penis while passing water,' a magical belief.

19 Passages concerned with gods are descriptive of human belief and non-committal as to agency, for the most part. The 'equalization' of 8.13 is an exceptional attempt to explain a heavenly phenomenon, the storm off the coast of Euboea, since human agents were obviously not responsible. 7.189.1 and 3 convey the author's more usual scepticism. Recent historians, who are not deemed 'theological,' also employ personifying phrases, such as 'the weather aided the British campaign.'

20 Lang (1984) 167–72 indexes all speeches in the *Histories*.

21 Norden (1909) 27–8, 35–41, and Kennedy (1963) 44–51 provide little help for historiography, since their interests lie elsewhere, in prose-style and rhetoric proper. On philosophical issues, see P. Gardiner ed *Theories of History* (Glencoe, Ill. 1959); Ligota (1982) 7–9, 13. G. Gennette 'Time and narrative' in *A la recherche du temps perdu, Aspects of Narrative* ed J.H. Miller (New York 1971) 93–118 supplies some useful literary categories. Suggestive avenues for literary approaches to Herodotus can be found in Deborah Boedeker ed *Herodotus and the Invention of History* in *Arethusa* 20.1–2 (1987), especially the articles of Konstan, Marincola, and Dewald.

22 4.30.1; 7.171.1 on the previous digression about Tarentum; cf Lattimore (1958) 9–11 on footnotes and pages; Erbse (1961) 239–57, modified by Cobet (1971), esp 41–2. Herodotus points out with care (2.99.1) the moment when his sources change from autopsy and personal judgment to hearsay, because he is alert to the audience's possible misconceptions. Parenthetical statements provide another avenue for briefly interrupting the main line of an argument (eg, 2.4.1: ἐμοὶ δοκέειν).

23 See D. Fehling *Die Wiederholungsfiguren und ihr Gebrauch bei den Griechen vor Gorgias* (Berlin 1969), a study that makes good use of Herodotus.

24 Norden (1909) 28, 36–7, 39, 41, and *Nachträge* 36 quoting a letter from Jacoby. See also H. Diels 'Herodot und Hekataios' *Hermes* 22 (1887) 424. Nestle (1908) and Aly (1921) 286–96 discuss Sophistic influence on Herodotus' prose; Meyer I (1892) 202 surprisingly and alone denies Sophistic influence on Herodotus or even Pericles. Herodotus' debt to Homer is detailed by G. Steinger *Epische Elemente im Redenstil des Herodot* (diss Kiel 1957; *non vidi*), Huber (1965b), and Lateiner (1987). Chiasson (1982) 156–61 identifies words seemingly borrowed from tragedy, and observes that they cluster about Xerxes. They thus colour our evaluation of one protagonist's choices and actions.

25 Hignett (1963) 34; cf Stein 'Einleitung' I (1901⁶) xxxviii–xxxix; Meyer IV/1 (1939) 229; Myres (1953) 71; Waters (1966), esp 167, or Pearson (1941) 349. Thucydides' procedure turns out to be much the same, even though 1.22.1 probably intends to reject his predecessor's manner.

26 Solmsen (1974) 14 note 37, 23 note 67; even Hauvette (1894) 506 granted this much.

27 A paraphrase of Stein 'Einleitung' I (1901⁶) xxxviii–xxxix; Cooper (1974) 28 note 8 and 41 note 19 develops the point. This estrangement from responsibility holds for speeches in anecdotes and folktales but not for the major dialogues of the recent past. Large-scale legendary narratives can also be denied belief: Darius' method of winning the throne, the account of the arrest of Intaphrenes, and the calculation of the wealth of Pythius the Lydian (3.85.1, 3.118.1, 7.27.1) are marked off from the main narrative by other types of strong transitions, although such transitions do not consistently dissociate the author from a story.

28 Gomme (1954) 112 tried to defend Herodotus against charges of invention and dramatization, but at least the latter effort contradicted his own statements about Herodotus' 'poetic' manner (see pp v, 76, etc). The attempt probably originated from his positivist prejudices.

29 A.W. Verrall, in 'Two unpublished inscriptions from Herodotus' *CR* 17 (1903) 98–102, attempted to reconstruct the original hexameter memorials on which Herodotus supposedly based his anecdotes at 8.3.1, 9.16.4, and 9.76. Verrall praises Herodotus' 'taste and memory which prompted him to verbal fidelity' towards epigraphical evidence. *Contra*, West (1986) esp 285–7.

30 Solmsen (1974) 32 and note 95, on 7.8–18; Ligota (1982) 10 on 'bare facts' (below).

31 Gigante (1956) 115–16 = Marg 259

32 One may never equate automatically the words of any person in the *Histories* with Herodotus' own opinion; eg, Xerxes' intelligent comments (7.50*) on the need for a continuation of Persian expansion are not likely to represent the author's judgment. Not even Solon or the reformed Croesus appears solely to serve as a mouthpiece. There is no uniform rule for this delicate question.

33 Jacoby (1949) 216; Verdin (1970) 194

34 Cf Benardete (1969) 21, note 25. λέγεται may refer to written as well as oral sources.

35 Cooper (1974) 23–76, esp 24, referring to his *Zur syntaktischen Theorie und Textkritik der attischen Autoren* (diss Zurich 1971) 65–83. The theory has promising consequences for certain textual problems. See below, chapter 3 with note 10 for another of Cooper's suggestions: Herodotus distances himself from accounts by the use of optative verb forms in constructions where they are not to be expected.

36 Cooper (1974) 37–9, note 17 *fin*; 42 note 20: examples in variant versions: 3.87, 4.8.3, 5.86.3, 6.84.1, 7.150.3; also 33–4, note 14; 55. R.N. Frye 'The institutions' *Beiträge zur Achaemenidgeschichte* ed G. Walser (*Historia Einzelschriften* 18; Wiesbaden 1972) 83–93, esp 91–3, discusses Persian respect for 'the law which altereth not' (Daniel 6.8), and our inability to evaluate Greek accounts of the Persian administration of justice.

37 Cooper (1974) 68, 70–6. Some indication of a source (4 times): 3.102.2–105.2, 5.9.1–10, 6.54, 6.105.1–3. Examples 2 and 4 employ explicit provisos. No preparation (5 times): 1.59.1–3, 1.86.1–6, 2.162.4–5, 3.14.10–1, 3.23.2–3.

38 Carolyn Dewald does this in her study in progress: *The Voice of the Histor: Narrator and Narrative in Herodotus' Histories*. Cf John Marincola 'Herodotean narrative and the narrator's presence' *Arethusa* (1987) 121–37.

39 Pohlenz (1937) 208–11, Pearce (1981) 87–90, and Lang (1984) discuss oral elements in Herodotus' work, such as transitions, epic regression (event, then the events that lead up to it in reverse order), and ring composition. Although certain aspects of his style are oral *in origin*, this proves little or nothing about what he did with the earlier or final version of the huge written text that he left for posterity. See my reviews of Hunter (1982) and Lang: *CP* 80 (1985) esp 74 and *CW* 79 (1986) 290.

40 See Munson (1983) for a general study and thorough attention to books 1 and 5.

41 Aristotle *Poetics* 17.3 = 1455a approves the technique for poets. Desmond Morris et al *Gestures, Their Origins and Distribution* (New York 1979) offers a popular account with extensive bibliography; Lateiner (1987) offers bibliography for Herodotus and ancient studies, including a brief survey of nonverbal communication in Greek epic.

42 F. Cornford *Thucydides Mythistoricus* (London 1907; 1965) 134–5 says that τὸ μυθῶδες means inventive embellishment (fable, superstition, magnification), but not 'dramatic construction,' because Cornford believes that Thucydides unconsciously shared this 'poetic' way of comprehending the world. But the dramas of Herodotus are of a different ilk, and Thucydides certainly criticized his predecessor for it. On the later historian, see Kitto (1966) 272; H.-P. Stahl *Thukydides: Die Stellung der Menschen im geschichtlichen Prozess* (Munich

1966) 133–40; J.R. Grant 'Toward knowing Thucydides' *Phoenix* 28 (1974) 81–94, esp 81–3, 87–8; D. Lateiner 'Pathos in Thucydides' *Antichthon* 11 (1977) 42–51.

43 Ritualized gestures, those which are customary rather than spontaneous, are mentioned in all the ethnographies. For instance, the documentary mode includes Egyptian, Thracian, and Spartan mourning procedures; elsewhere, personal greetings and farewells, wedding customs, festival behaviours, and other religious usages of a nonverbal nature are common. See the five categorized inventories at the end of Lateiner (1987): ritualized social conventions; informal, voluntary acts; psychophysical reactions; subconscious gesticulation and sounds; and objects and tokens.

44 Cf R. Firth 'Verbal and bodily rituals of greeting and parting' *The Interpretation of Ritual* ed J.S. La Fontaine (London 1972) 1–38.

45 1.86.3, 116.4; 3.64.1; cf Marg (1953) 1106 = Marg 294 with note 1.

46 Shrieks: 1.8.3, Gyges; 3.155.1, Darius; 7.18.1 Artabanus; 3.38.4, Callatiae. Weeping: eg, 1.109.1, 3; 1.111.2*, 4*; 3.14 (ten words for weepy sorrow); 3.66.1; 7.159*; 8.99.2; 9.24

47 1.86.3, Croesus on the pyre; 2.175.5, Amasis' architect; 6.80, Cleomenes for his Argive setback; 6.107.4, Hippias' dental omen. In a monograph in progress I explore nonverbal behaviours in ancient epic.

48 Lateiner (1977) and S.G. Flory 'Laughter, tears, and wisdom in Herodotus' *AJP* 99 (1978) 145–53, discover pattern in Herodotus' presentation of individual psychology. C. De Heer ΜΑΚΑΡ-ΕΥΔΑΙΜΩΝ-ΟΛΒΙΟΣ-ΕΥΤΥΧΗΣ (The Hague 1969) provides a semantic analysis of words for 'prosperous happiness' in Herodotus and contemporaries.

49 The only exceptions: the infant Cypselus burbles innocently; the Ethiopian king, Cleisthenes of Sicyon, and Herodotus himself each enjoy one metaphorical laugh: 5.92γ3; 3. 22.2; 5.68.1; 4.36.2.

50 Amasis attracted other earthy tales such as stories about another class of meaningful wordless messages, significant objects, eg, the golden piss-pot (2.172.3–5).

51 Κλαίειν λέγω, variously translated because of its expletival (nonverbal) force: 'Go howl' (Rawlinson), 'You shall repent it' (How and Wells), 'Be damned to you' (de Sélincourt). Informal but voluntary (intentional) nonverbal communication is discussed at greater length in Lateiner (1987) 86, 93–4, 95–100, 114.

52 See Cook (1976) 29; Ph. Thompson and P. Davenport *The Dictionary of Visual Language* (London 1980). For the monuments (mentioned below) including inscriptions, see the cautionary remarks of Raubitschek (1961) and West (1985).

53 Denniston (1934) 491 note 1

54 Pohlenz (1937) 208–11 attributes these peculiarities to the 'Einfluss des mündlichen Vortrags.' He cites 3.6.2, 3.37.2, 4.81.5, 4.99.5, passages that enlist the reader's commitment, one way or the other. At 4.76.6, with the command ἴστω, Herodotus sounds professorial. Translators often ignore this personal note.

55 *De sublimitate* 26.2 quotes Herodotus 2.29, and approves the vivid effect of change in person.

56 Denniston (1934) 58 discusses this mental habit; Lattimore (1958) 18 regards such devices as characteristic of this author's style and mode of composition.

57 Powell *Lexicon* sv; Denniston (1952) 491

58 Immerwahr (1966) 7

59 Fornara (1971) 22–3 for the two quotations

60 Denniston (1952) 6; cf idem (1934) 491, less satisfactory.

61 *Contra*, Fehling (1971) passim, esp 11–66

62 In direct speech, see Thucydides 2.87.2*, 5.99* *bis*, 7.68.1*.

63 Also 7.22.1, 7.223.1, 9.102.1, and Powell *Lexicon*, sv, 2c. Thucydides often approximated figures or qualified his statistical accuracy for troop and warship numbers, but Herodotus hesitated less here than on inconsequential personal matters, a fact which reveals their very different methods and concerns. See C.R. Rubincam 'Qualification of numerals in Thucydides' *AJAH* 4 (1979) 77–95; eadem 'Thucydides 1.74.1 ...' *CP* 74 (1979) 327–37.

64 These two paragraphs summarize C.R. Rubincam 'Numbers and numeral qualification in Herodotus' (1985, unpublished). I thank the author for letting me refer to her work in progress. She argues against Fehling's (1971) criticisms of numbers in the *Histories*: they are formulaic, or the result of 'freie Erfindung,' and they include wholly fraudulent acknowledgments of sources. Rubincam's paper will show that the higher frequency of certain figures can be explained by the universal human tendencies – of sources as well as of historians – to round off numbers and to remember certain ones more commonly. Furthermore, certain round numbers are the result of reported calculations (eg, the dimensions of the Black Sea), and thus less likely to be wholly concocted. Herodotus is not to be faulted when conventional numbers were reported to him; he could not be more precise than his sources, and he could not pretend to accuracy in, eg, distances, when he had to report the rough estimates of others. P. Keyser 'Errors of calculation in Herodotus' *CJ* 81 (1986) 230–42 reports that such errors are very few (seven in all; 234) and can usually be explained by the problems encountered in Greek arithmetical manipulations. The textual transmission of numbers in the *Histories* thus appears to be trustworthy.

65 See for example 6.11.1, 6.128.2, 7.12.1, 9.113.1. Κου sometimes appears with καὶ δὲ καί, both phrases sketching in background to highlight a particular

person or thing. Πού can be used 'ironically with assumed diffidence by a speaker who is quite sure of his ground' (Denniston [1934] 491; cf my next section). This rhetorical use, often with ironic δή, occurs only in direct speech, as when Otanes says of Atossa (3.68.4*): 'Indeed she really must (πάντως γὰρ δή κου) know her own brother!' The word fluctuates in colloquial contexts so much that Powell (*Lexicon*, sv 2) must offer the ungainly pair: 'surely, perhaps.' See also, eg, 3.72.1*, 73.2*; 1.68.2*. Cf 1.87.4*, where Croesus felt bound to acknowledge supernatural forces at work.

66 Bury (1909) 47 reacting to 8.41.2, the snake on the Athenian acropolis

67 For a particular case of irony, at the expense of a much admired group, he presents the Spartans as late (1.83, 6.120) or disorganized (1.65.2; 6.66; 9.53–7, 106); cf Meyer IV/1 (1939) 227. Spartan customs were bizarre as well as unique (1.65–8; 6.51–60; 7.102.2–3*, 208.3, 231), and they expressed themselves in strange ways (3.46; 7.226, 228.2). Herodotus was sceptical of their announced policies (9.54.1). Perhaps Athenian prejudice in his informants can be detected here, but they too receive their share of criticism (eg, 1.60.3, 5.97.2–3, and various atrocities).

68 Cooper (1974) 34 note 14. For parodies of women, consider also, besides the opening incidents of alleged rapes and consequent continental hatreds, the inquisitive mother-in-law of Pisistratus, the endless nagging of Atossa for Spartan serving-girls, and the foolish insistence of Artaÿnte for a special robe (1.61.2; 3.134; 9.109; cf the wisdom of the babe Gorgo, 5.51). Dewald (1981) believes that the actions of women in the *Histories* are generally found praiseworthy. For a demonstration of the parodic tone of Plato's Athenian 'history' in the *Menexenus*, see Ch. Kahn 'Plato's funeral oration' *CP* 57 (1962) 220–34.

69 Cf. Fränkel (1960²) 83–4 = Marg 741; on asyndeton, see reff. in Cooper (1974) 34 note 14. For chiasmus and 'epic regression' see Pearce (1981); for other, more complex forms of transition and connection, esp in books 1 and 5, see Munson (1983).

70 He also included the 'who, how, and where?' of many major inventions and discoveries, a facet of his interest in cultural change. Schmid-Stählin I/2 (1934) 567 note 9 list firsts and other examples of τί μάλιστα in Herodotus, and note important parallels in earlier Greek literature. Kleingünther (1933) develops the topic.

71 Wikarjak (1959) 272–5, 281, offers more examples of commencements in the text. I thank Dr Joseph Patwell for translating this Polish article.

72 Immerwahr allows these tales only the ludicrous, parodic element: (1956) 253, 260; cf chapter 6 below.

73 Herodotus also noted that the Scyths first attacked the Persians (1.103.3, 4.1.1), and that the Aeginetans and the Athenians still dispute the origin of their

enmity (5.82–89.1). On the special problems posed by Herodotus' treatment of
the Ionian rebellion, such as sources, chronology, partiality of the author, see
P. Tozzi *La rivolta ionica* (Pisa 1978); Lateiner (1982); and H.T. Wallinga 'The
Ionian revolt' *Mnemosyne* 37 (1984) 401–37.

74 The parody, formally distinguished from the rest of the *Histories* by mention of
the Persians at beginning and end, criticizes this particular form of simplistic
and insufficient *cherchez la femme* causation. Cf Lang (1972) 410–14, who
notes that Herodotus mentions only prehistoric rapes (1.1–4; 2.113.1; 7.169.2,
191.2; 6.138.1) as (alleged) causes for war. The parody also mocks all popular
views that imagine neat origins for any great historical process. Livy's
preface apologizes for just such an unsatisfactory performance soon to come.
Herodotus' achievement suggests that, in comparison to Livy at least, the desire
to commemorate perhaps promotes veracity more than the desire to edify.
See also Momigliano (1954) 200 = (1966) 114; Drews (1973) 89. Immerwahr
(1956) 249 incorrectly asserted that Herodotus ridiculed this 'Persian' view
because he wished to assign war-guilt to the Asiatics. Macan (1927) 407 notes
that more than once in Herodotus a woman is exhibited as the cause, or at
least a cause, of major historical events. He also mentions the accession of
Gyges, the fate of Cyrus, the invasion of Egypt, the Scythian expedition, and
the exploration of the West, none of them a part of recent history.

75 Cf A.B. Lloyd (1975) 175–6, 185–94. Hecateus also had his chronology
destroyed by Egyptian demonstration (δεικνύντες, 2.143) 2.142.2 presents
Herodotus' only explicit statement on the generational approach to chronological
method (three generations equal one hundred years; cf 6.98.2, where the same
equation can be inferred). Cf Mitchel (1956) 48–69, Strasburger (1956), and
Mosshammer (1979) on issues of time-reckoning in Herodotus.

76 Atossa's pillow-talk with Darius and the Persian diplomats' threat at Croton
(3.134, 137.4) are in the style of the 'rape debate' and inconsequential for the
question of the true causes of the East-West conflict.

77 Fränkel's term (1960²) 65–7 = Marg 738–40 for a purposeful style rather than a
mere hodge-podge

78 ἐγὼ δὲ περὶ μὲν τούτων οὐχ ἔρχομαι ἐρέων ὡς οὕτως ἢ ἄλλως κως ταῦτα
ἐγένετο, τὸν δὲ οἶδα αὐτὸς πρῶτον ὑπάρξαντα ἀδίκων ἔργων ... The
second underlined phrase is rare, found only in expressions of the gravest
scepticism (3.24.2; 7.191.2). The first and third underlined phrases polemicize
assertively and show confidence in his own explanation.

79 Wardman (1961) 136, modified by Shimron (1973) 45–51. See below, chapter 5.

80 Hellman (1934) 23–9, 69–98. The Lydian *logos* has two beginnings and ends
arranged in rings, or chiastically: a complexive beginning (1.5.3) that marks
the connection to, while it abstracts the Lydian *logos* from, the larger story; a
formal beginning for Croesus' ancestors (1.7); a formal end to that Mermnad

dynasty (1.86.1); and a complexive end (1.94.7–95.1) that returns the narrative to the larger story.

81 Exactly how is Croesus first in time for the historian? Myres (1953) 61: first in injustice, not because he was first to attack, but because he conquered and then failed to protect. Immerwahr (1966) 30: the Lydian was first to achieve permanent conquest, not a mere raider. Shimron (1973) 46, 48–50: the first conqueror in the historical period, the period that we know, the epoch of Croesus and the generation of Herodotus' grandfather. Information, but no trustworthy knowledge, exists for Gyges, the Medes, etc.

82 Fornara (1971) 17–23 regards it as the last *logos* to have been written. Arguments over the order of composition of the various books can be no more than reasonable: no hypothesis can be proved. Drews (1973) 50–7, and 169 note 8, shrewdly noted that the *Histories* devote little attention to Croesus' actions against the Greeks, reasonably assumed from 1.5.3 to be the justification of the Lydian *logos*. Thirteen of approximately seven hundred lines describe his Greek conquests. Drews' insufficient explanation, that Herodotus offers only 'an account of those [Lydian] kings who had most fascinated the Greeks,' trivializes the issue. The importance of the themes developed in the Lydian narrative explains its position. The leading stories therein – the deed of Gyges, Solon's visit abroad, the demise of Adrastus, Gyges' and Croesus' dealings with Delphi – furnish patterns of historical action. Persia's conquest of Lydia, an achievement that made a subsequent attack on the Hellenes inevitable, provided a window in two directions for the history of the Persians.

83 Chronological linearity would place the story of Lydia after 1.140, in the due course of Persian imperialism. As the story of Gyges sets the tone for the Lydian *logos*, so the story of Psammetichus' linguistic experiment (2.2), which belongs later, at 2.152–4, enjoys a privileged position at the beginning of its *logos*. We need a separate study of all the narratives 'displaced' from chronological order.

84 *Pace* Fränkel (1960²) 85 = Marg 743. The proem itself speaks of cause and consequences, and of human events becoming τῷ χρόνῳ ἐξίτηλα, thus both recognizing time as an historical factor and an organizing principle of human reflection and also admitting time as a destructive agency and source of interference for that process. Systems for measuring time appear only much later in the *Histories*. See, further, A.B. Lloyd (1975) 'Chronology' 171–94, esp 171–2, 193–4, and below, chapter 5.

85 Similarly, battle descriptions (eg, Marathon and Salamis) are brief, except when they convey moral or psychological truths of interest to Herodotus (Immerwahr [1966] 241). The emphasis on cultural milieux and political decisions reveals interests beyond the annalist's.

86 So too Erbse (1956) 220, but for different reasons. See Dionysius *De Thucydide*

5, 7 for comparison to earlier, less selective writers. Also Myres (1953) 91; Immerwahr (1966) 28.

87 Cf Ch. Starr 'The awakening of the Greek historical spirit and early Greek coinage' *NC* 7 (1966) 1–7, esp 1–2, 7. R.G. Osborne 'The viewing and obscuring of the Parthenon frieze' *JHS* 107 (1987) 98–105, argues that the idealizing tendency of classical art has been unduly emphasized.

88 The more distant the place and time of reported narratives, the less validity Herodotus claims for the accounts; see chapter 5 below and Helm (1981) 85–90, who shows that the defects of this rationalized, pseudo-historicized, 'fictional' narrative of a far-away and long defunct kingdom have been produced by the available sources: popular saga, Achaemenid royal propaganda, oral histories, and Greek chronographers.

89 *Epistula ad Pompeium* § 3 (767 U-R = Roberts 106), 'For this same proem is the beginning and end of history.' W.R. Roberts *The Three Literary Letters* (Cambridge 1901) 107 incomprehensibly translates: 'the end of his *Histories*.' Fornara (1971) surprisingly does not consider the proem in his account of Herodotus' themes.

90 On the typology of ancient proems, see Earl (1972) 842–56; also M. Pohlenz 'Thukydides-Studien II–III' *NAWG* (1920) 58; Bizer (1937) 4–7; Krischer (1965); Immerwahr (1966) 63–7; Drews (1973) 70–1; only Wikarjak (1961) finds it sufficiently lucid.

91 Krischer (1965) 159, 162, 165–7. The text of the *Histories* that follows his concise proem allows us to read this program back into the proem.

92 Jacoby (1913) 335 called it the 'first excursus'; Legrande considered it part of the proem. Macan (1927) 407 and Myres (1953) 135–6, discuss Herodotus' rejection of both the personal and romantic *cherchez la femme* theory and the regional and racial theory of East against West.

93 Drews (1973) 89 on 1.1.3 and chapter 5 below

94 Jacoby (1913) 334–5; Immerwahr (1966) 17. Thucydides also presents the treatment of women as a subject of fable or as merely a *pretext* for war, a useful allegation which he then contrasts to better reasons for war: cf 1.126.1 with 1.9.2, 127; 2.101.5, etc; see T. Wiedemann 'Thucydides, women, and the limits of rational analysis' *GR* 30 (1983) 163–70.

95 Pohlenz (1937) 8 and Immerwahr (1956) 247 believe that the proem extends to the end of 1.6. This reasonable view does not recognize the strictly limited number of formal elements that constitute an ancient proem.

96 The Lydian *logos* alone appears before the history of Persia, and it alone was ripped from the chronological sequence of Persian conquests, as Jacoby (1913) 337 noted. This uniqueness further justifies the view of this section as paradigmatic of the author's method and more than just another Persian advance. The Lydian *logos* demonstrated a new kind of truth, sharply contrasted to the

folderol of the Persian *logioi*, and a history of great significance to the Great War between the Greeks and the barbarians.

97 Fornara (1971) 17–19 believes that book 1 was the last written, an equivalent to a modern author's exposition of his 'philosophy of history.' His argument does not consider the shift in pace and purpose that occurs when Herodotus reaches the history of the Persians at 1.95, if not earlier at 1.75 or even 1.46.

98 R. Lisle 'Thucydides 1.22.4' *CJ* 72 (1977) 342–7, analyses the similar use of σκοπεῖν in Thucydides. The word connotes both a selective and a synoptic view.

99 In book 1 alone, see 68.6, 130.3, 174.1, 191.6, 214.5. Also, eg, 3.15.4, 3.26.1, 3.97.1, 3.159.1, 7.234.1, 8.126.1, 9.88, and Rosaria Munson (1983) esp 25–120.

100 2.117, Homer and the *Cypria*; 4.96.2, the divinity of Salmoxis. The researcher sometimes grew impatient.

101 1.140.3, a foul Persian custom. Once Herodotus halts *in medias res* seemingly because he has strayed too far: 'About Rhodopis, I'll stop here' (2.135.6).

102 Nine occurrences: 1.92.4, Croesus' dedications; 2.34.2, the Nile; 2.76.3, Egyptian zoology; 3.113.1, Arabian perfumes; 4.15.4, Aristeas; 4.36.1, the Hyperboreans; 4.45.5, Europa's travels; 4.199.2, Cyrenaic fertility; 6.55, Perseus' descendants. The author seems to think that he has strayed long enough from his immediate topic.

103 The Athenian also reduced his presence to distant third-person *formulae*, almost as if another person were the author (eg, 2.70.4, 'These things happened in the winter, and the second year of the war ended which Thucydides recorded').

104 Pohlenz (1937) 164–7, on 6.42–3, 9.41, etc, following Jacoby (1913) 372–9; Immerwahr (1966) 145 and note 188 discusses the problem.

105 On the so-called 'epitaphs' for individuals such as Themistocles, Pericles, Brasidas, and Nicias, 'explicit judgements on ability and character,' see H.D. Westlake *Individuals in Thucydides* (Cambridge 1968) 5–19, esp 16–17, where he compares the practice of Herodotus and Thucydides, and D. Lateiner 'Nicias' inadequate encouragement' *CP* 80 (1985) esp 208–13.

106 There are many other brief summarizing accounts when man or state is evaluated in retrospect: eg, after Melos fell and after the Delians were displaced (5.116.3–4; 8.108.4); further, D. Lateiner '*Pathos* in Thucydides' *Antichthon* 11 (1977) 42–51.

107 Other favourable aspects of Pausanias' character: 9.80.1, 88, 76; cf 8.3.2. See Ch. Fornara 'Some aspects of the career of Pausanias of Sparta' *Historia* 15 (1966) 257–71. Another quiet ending: Xerxes' subdued conversation with Demaratus after the battle of Thermopylae (7.234–5).

108 Cf Wolff (1964) 55–6 = Marg 673–5; Erbse (1956) 220. Wolff (58 = Marg

678) calls the story of Masistes the *Schlussstein* of the work, positioned to illustrate central concerns; Waters (1971) 82–5 argues less persuasively that the story is too unclear, too unedifying, and in fact too late to be the 'keystone.' Just before his demise in the text, Prince Masistes' high standing in his brother's estimation had been carefully confirmed in the text by an incident in which the Halicarnassian Xenagoras was richly rewarded after he saved Masistes from an angry assailant.

109 Bischoff (1932) 82–3 = Marg 686

110 U. von Wilamowitz-Moellendorf *Aristoteles und Athen* I (Berlin 1893) 26; Meyer II (1899) 217 = Marg 679–80 with note 2; cf Meyer IV/1 (1939) 227 note 1; Jacoby (1913) 376. Schmid-Stählin I/2 (1934) 595–7 provide earlier bibliography.

111 Pohlenz (1937) 175–6. Fornara (1971) 82 (with note 10) has a similar attitude towards periodization in this historian.

112 Pohlenz (1937) 177; Immerwahr (1966) 145 (with note 188), 8–9, 52. Others who are satisfied with the present conclusion: Bischoff (1932) 78 = Marg 681; Myres (1953) 299–300; Fornara (1971) 37 (with note 1), 81. Not all scholars properly distinguish the end of the historical events narrated (9.121) from the epilogue in the next chapter.

113 9.122.1: τούτου δὲ τοῦ Ἀρταΰκτεω τοῦ ἀνακρεμασθέντος προπάτωρ Ἀρϐ τεμβάρης ἐστί ...

114 Sinko (1959/60) 18–20; Bischoff (1932) 78–82 = Marg 681–6

115 The folktales sometimes contradict each other: the Persians actively chose a life of wealth and ease under Cyrus the Pretender (1.126), not the hardship that the wiser King Cyrus recommends (9.122.3–4). See the end of chapter 7 below. Gibbon, without explaining their inclusion, remarked in his copy of Herodotus at 1.110, 'We sometimes detect a Romance by the easy, though wonderful annihilation of space and time.'

116 See R. Meiggs *The Athenian Empire* (Oxford 1972) 4–5, 375–6: Herodotus cynically chastises the Athenian form of government; he condemns the expedition to Ionia; he suggests that the hegemony was seized in 479 under false pretences (5.97.2–3; 8.3.2). See also Fornara (1971) 44–53, 79–80.

117 No textual evidence suggests that the *Histories* have been mutilated at the end or that this paragraph is otherwise irregular. Furthermore, extended epilogues are an infrequent part of the epic and archaic Greek literature: cf Immerwahr (1966) 9, 43, 52–3 (with note 27), 145 (with note 189).

118 See Cook (1976), esp 45; Redfield (1985) 117–18. Herodotus never explicitly claims to have transcended his own values and society (Halicarnassian, Dorian and Ionian, and Greek). Some belief in Hellenic superiority and a desire to prove it by past events may well have supplied the strongest motive for his intellectual enterprise – if I may briefly enter the inconclusive genetic

controversies. His frequent comparative judgments, however, suggest that he judged without ethnocentric bias.

119 Erbse (1956) 211; Drews (1973) 19, 137. Phrynichus' *Sack of Miletus* drew outrage, censorship, and a monetary penalty. His *Phoenissae* and Aeschylus' *Persae*, despite their success, attracted few imitators. An expensive and dangerous form of political propaganda was abandoned soon after its invention.

INTRODUCTION TO PART TWO

1 Herodotus clearly was no formal epistemologist, nor was he interested in metaphysical theory. The only early philosophical thinkers that he mentions by name are Thales and Pythagoras, and they appear for their effect on history, not their philosophy. Certain ideas of Anaximander, Anaxagoras, and others are mentioned anonymously, but the attempts of W. Nestle, *Vom Mythos zum Logos* (Stuttgart 1942²) 505–13 and others to locate traces of specific philosophers and Sophists (Protagoras and Hippias have respectable cases) suggest more about the range of fifth-century intellectual interests and the lack of compartmentalization than demonstrable borrowings. For Anaximander, see Diels *Vors* 12 B 1 with 3.109.2: τίσιν ἀποτίνειν, and cf 6.72.1, 84.3; 8.76.2.

2 For instance, Verdin (1977) 75; also Hunter (1982) 18, 93, and chapter 6, although in a sense different from that proposed here

3 H. Barth 'Einwirkung der vorsokratischen Philosophie auf die Herausbildung der historiographischen Methoden Herodots' *Neue Beiträge zur Geschichte der alten Welt* (Berlin 1964) 173–6, notes the use of the participial construction for trustworthy reports (eg, 1.214.1; 5.9.1) and the infinitive for accounts that Herodotus will not vouch for (1.170.1; 6.117.3); cf her note 17 and the articles of Cooper.

4 Schepens (1975) 81–93. Principal ancient statements about 'seeing for oneself': Herodotus 2.29.1, 34.1; 3.115.2; 4.116.1; cf 8.79.4*, 80.1*; Thucydides 1.22.1–2; 5.26.5; Polybius 3.4.13; 12.25 h4; 20.12.8. Homer himself has Odysseus rank autopsy before hearsay: *Odyssey* 8.491.

CHAPTER 2

1 Jacoby (1913) 379–92; Pohlenz (1937) 59–73; Myres (1953) 73, chart of ethnographic topics; Immerwahr (1966) 17–46; Drews (1973) 47–69, 77–84, 134–5; Cobet (1971) 42–82

2 How and Wells (1912) I 35 regard this claim as showing a consciousness that 'his criteria of truth were deficient.' It was meant to forestall accusations of credulity. See, more recently, Verdin (1971) 1–53.

3 See Glover (1924) 68 and 3 (he knows 'what to leave in the ink-pot'); Myres (1953) 178; Solmsen (1974) 17 note 48. Cf Dionysus *Epistula ad Pompeium* 3, U-R 771.

4 See Barth (1968) 93–110 on θῶμα and related words. Drexler (1972) 28–57 with useful, if incomplete, lists. References to ἄξιος λόγου: 1.133.2, 2.138.2, 4.28.2, 8.35.2, 8.91. References to ἀξιοπήγητος: 5.57.2 (only negative); 2.70.1

5 Sayce (1883) xv; Drews (1973) 71 points out that no dramatic action was required for the annexation of the Phoenicians. Very little is known about their capitulation.

6 Tacit omission, an artistic method which leads 'the hearer by what [Herodotus] does not say as much as by what he does,' offers 'irony, pathos, paradox, and tragedy,' but the topic of omissions does not allow convenient limits or strictly verifiable instances. See Fornara (1971) 61 ff.

7 The divisions refer to the lists at the end of this chapter.

8 On epistemological reticence, cf the brief remarks of Meyer (1899) II 253 (= Marg 13). Herodotus' modesty compares well with the cosmological utterances of the Presocratic philosophers and some of the writers in the Hippocratic corpus: eg, *De vetera medicina* 1, *De natura hominis* 1 (*contra*), *De flatibus* 5, *De victu* 1.2, 4–5 (*pro*), and cf Lateiner (1986), Glover (1924) 3, 67–8.

9 At 4.152.3, qualified by 'of all the Hellenes of whom we know the truth.' 7.152.2 asserts certain knowledge of human nature rather than of historical fact. Fornara (1971) 21–2, note 34, remarks a progression in sophistication from the systematic 'hedge' in books 2 and 4 to an awareness of tendentious falsification of *certain* statements in books 6 and 7.

10 The treasurer may not have asserted that the Nile commenced in the region of the first cataract, just south of Elephantine. Rather, Herodotus may have misunderstood the Egyptian custom of giving each section of the river a different name. For this, Myres (1953) 153, Wainwright (1953) 104–7.

11 See the similar passages, 1.182.1; 2.121 ε1; 3.116.2; 4.42.4; 5.86.3; 7.214.2; 8.119; 8.120; cf Powell, *Lexicon, sv* πιστός.

12 Glover (1924) 67. See also above, pp 22–3.

13 Only two in Thucydides: 7.46.1; 8.96.2. See Lang (1984) 37–41 for a comparison of rhetorical questions in Herodotus and Homer.

14 Myres (1953) 51. Herodotus 8.13, the story of the storm off the Hollows of Euboea, may pose an exception. Even there, however, Herodotus reports a consequence (the fleets made more equal) rather than explains the storm, and he proposes no causal connection between the storm and the prayers of men (Linforth [1928] 214). See, further, chapter 9 below, on Herodotean causality.

15 So Sourdille (1925) 289ff, attempting to modify the conclusions of Linforth (1924) 269–92; cf Linforth (1928) 201–43, esp 202, 240.

16 Sourdille (1910) chapter 1, (1925) 301–4. Seven times Herodotus explicitly

omits a 'holy tale' (2.46, 47, 48, 51, 62, 65, 81). Osiris appears by name: 2.42.2, 144.2 (bis), 156.4. This additional defect in the hypothesis of Sourdille (1910; 1925) leads me to prefer the argument of Linforth (1924) 280–2, (1928) 240–3, that 'personal preference rather than religious scruple' – the nature of the evidence rather than piety – determines Herodotus' decision to include an item; cf οὐκ εἰμὶ πρόθυμος ... and τὰ θεῖα πρήγματα, τὰ ἐγὼ φεύγω μάλιστα ἀπηγέεσθαι. Mythology is everywhere equally fanciful and uncertain. Lachenaud (1976) also argues for Herodotus' commitment to rationality, human autonomy, and prudent reserve on unobservable matters such as the gods.

17 Evident in the two chief exceptions to his silence: 2.43–5, 4.8–10 (Heracles), and 2.142–6 (the time that has elapsed since Egyptian gods 'appeared' on earth); Linforth (1928) 207, developing his earlier argument, (1924) 288–92. Stories of the gods appear when required in negative arguments for path-breaking chronological research – Herodotus reclaimed 16,000 years for Greek consciousness (Linforth [1924] 292); or when a ritual or popular story of divine intervention in human time was to be recorded (cf Linforth [1926] 13–15).

18 Sayce (1883) xxvi. His preface asserts that Herodotus constantly affected knowledge which he did not have, purveyed 'deliberate falsehoods,' was guilty of 'flagrant' prevarication, and offered merely Märchen 'current among the Greek loungers and half-caste dragomen' of the Persian empire (xxvi–xxviii; xii, xxxi). This severe but not baseless approach is far from dead; cf Fehling (1971) passim, Armayor (1978) 59–73 and (1978b) 45–62, or the more moderate West (1985) 285, 294–5, 302–3.

19 Linforth (1924) 273. For lists of explicit silences on religious subjects, see How and Wells I 158; also Linforth (1924) 281 and (1928) 240, who offers fourteen passages where a religious silence obtains. 2.45.3 is included for questionable reasons.

20 Cf Cooper (1974) 71–2

21 At 7.137.2 Herodotus contrasts though he does not oppose τὸ δίκαιον and τὸ θεῖον, what was only right with what the divinity desired.

22 Linforth (1928) esp 218–37, a monograph on τὸ θεῖον

23 See Drexler (1972) 62–4 for a shorter list and discussion. After listing Herodotus' interests, Drexler (73) concludes that he is interested 'an Dingen, die zum guten Teil mit "Geschichte" gar nichts zu tun haben.' This puts the cart before the horse, or Drexler before Herodotus, in determining what is history and worthy of historical inquiry. The present study prefers to accept as history what Herodotus offers. See Gibbon, Decline and Fall, chapter 48 fin: of sixty emperors only the good Comnenus and a few bad emperors deserve mention; 'the remainder of the Imperial crowd could only desire and expect to be forgotten by posterity.'

24 This is a probable interpretation of his notorious unfulfilled promise to compose Assyrian *logoi* (1.106.2; 1.184); so G. Rawlinson's edition (1860; New York 1893) 192, note 1, on 1.106; Stein, I (1901⁶) xlvii; Huxley (1965) 207–12; Drews (1970) 183, note 7; *idem* (1973) 92–5, 191–2, note 194, with good discussion of the problem. The author fulfilled his promise in the cross-reference to the Didyma dedications (6.19.3 with 1.92.2 and 5.36.3).

25 If Herodotus had not travelled east to Babylon, the statement would be at best disingenuous. See, however, Drews (1973) 79–80 on Herodotus' travels.

26 3.125.3. How and Wells (1928) *ad loc* think the barbarity was unbecoming to literature, but they point out that 4.202.1 betrays no reticence. 1.119 and 9.112 are also painful reading. More likely there was nothing remarkable to report about the demeaning execution and impalement.

27 Myres (1953) 176 ff. lists the other passages relevant to Athenian government. Note how this limiting phrase (ὅσα ... ἀξιόχρεα ἀπηγήσιος ... φράσω) proves that Herodotus often reports less than he has heard.

28 How and Wells (1928) *ad loc*, following Macan, IV–VI (1908) lxxxiii note, regard this reticence to repeat the work of others as untrue for other parts of the *Histories*. No real evidence supports their suggestion.

29 See Pohlenz (1937) 92 note 4. Pausanias (3.14.1) recorded a *stele* with their names. How here recognized that Herodotus 'had [unused] reserves of knowledge.' Carolyn Dewald has suggested in a letter to me that the implicit *praeteritio* follows from the unsuitability of a lengthy roll-call.

30 No other battle so emphatically pits Greek courage against oriental despotism and material advantage. The moral significance of the deed apears in Leonidas, a Homeric hero, 'an extreme of courage,' 'the prime representative of absolute standards of value' (Immerwahr [1966] 262–3).

31 1.95.1; 2.3.2, 65.2; 9.65.2, etc. Or the *logos* explicitly does not compel: ἡγεμόνες, τῶν ἐγώ, οὐ γὰρ ἀναγκαίη ἐξέργομαι ἐς ἱστορίης λόγον, οὐ παραμέμνημαι (7.96.1). They were slaves rather than soldiers, less noteworthy therefore (7.96.2). Furthermore, reporting their names serves no purpose of the author's, as certain information on the Egyptian gods and on the Athenians' service to Greece does. In the latter cases there is even a 'necessity' constraining the historian.

32 2.22.4, 24.1; 5.62.1, 67.3; 7.96.1, 99.1, 139.1. See Pohlenz (1937) 56–8, explaining how Herodotus, but not earlier Hecataeus, found his theme exercising some dominion over his work in progress.

33 4.30.1; 7.171.1; cf 6.18.2 where Herodotus asserts his control

CHAPTER 3

1 The salient exception, 8.87, in which Thucydides inquired why the Phoenician

fleet never passed west of Aspendus, has aroused considerable controversy. See D. Lateiner, 'Tissaphernes and the Phoenician fleet' *TAPA* 106 (1976) 267–90: Thucydides' unresolved and unresolvable perplexity concerning Tissaphernes' Hellenic strategy accounts for the many conjectures.

2 See Verdin (1970) 183; Fornara (1983) 47–8. Darbo-Peschanski (1985) 109 and 125 note 11 contrasts Thucydides' 'monophonie' with Herodotus' 'polyphonie' with regard to willingness to cite and quote sources.

3 Verdin (1970) 194. Cf Benardete (1969) 4–5.

4 Pearson (1941) 344. Herodotus does not exhibit Tacitus' malicious use of variant versions; Schmid-Stählin 1/2 (1934) 630 note 5. In 8.118–19, the use of *logos legomenos* and intrusive oblique infinitives implies, from the beginning, Herodotus' scepticism.

5 See Solmsen (1974) 7–24, and Lang (1984) 18–21, 52–8, 155 note 3, for recent discussions.

6 1.1.3; 3.42.1; 1.30.1; 5.51.1; 2.121.1; 1.126.1; 2.13.1; 2.89.1. See also Fehling (1971) 155–67, 'Typische Zahlen ...'

7 1.5.3; 3.24.2; 2.23; 2.120.3; 7.184.3. For other examples of 'otherwise,' see also 3.33, 7.191.2.

8 Groten (1963) 79–87, esp 87 (last paragraph). Cf Jacoby (1913) 399–401; Schmid-Stählin 1/2 (1934) 629–31. A partial list of variants: Drexler (1972) 58–9; Myres (1953) 18

9 This study excludes narratives that are vouched for by two or more sources in agreement, eg, 1.23; 2.75.4, 147.1; 2.99.1 (?); 4.12.3 (ξυνὸς ... λόγος), 105.2, 150.1, 154.1; 5.54.1 (Aristagoras and reality), 87.1; 7.151; 8.94.4. One sees that Herodotus appreciated the historiographical principle that concord among sources that are hostile to each other, improves the chances of that account being veracious. In addition, such passages attest efforts to obtain more than one version.

10 Indicative ἀπέδοντο contrasted to optative λέγουσι ὡς ... ἀπελοίατο ... ἀπαιρεθείησαν. See also 3.87; 9.82, and the elegant demonstration of Cooper (1975) 29–34. See also chapter 1 above, where Cooper's work on intrusive oblique infinitives (1974) is discussed.

11 See, eg, 1.172.1; 2.103.2; 3.116.1; 5.86.2; 6.14.1 (seemingly insoluble because of partisanship); 8.8.2–3, 87.1 (insoluble); 9.18.2, 84.1–2. Herodotus rarely offers sheer conjectures like his estimate (ἐπεικάσαι) of a force of 50,000 Greek allies for Mardonius at Plataea (9.32.2), but here the absence of any contemporary report, itself a result of an original absence of information, begs for some estimate. Herodotus also uses *eikazo* for historical conjecture at 1.34.1; 2.104.2; 7.239.2 (if genuine).

12 2.103.2; 2.181.1–2; 4.164.4, 7.239.2

13 Cambyses: 3.1.5 and 21.2; Darius: 4.1.1 and 118.1; 6.94.1; Xerxes: 7.8*, 138.1

14 Similarly, de Romilly (1971); *contra*, Wardman (1961)

15 1.191.5; 3.15.2; 7.168.3; 8.136.3; 9.113.2; cf 8.119, a diatribe on a story's irrationality. In the third and fifth passages the author stresses his use of reconstructive imagination with a first-person pronoun or verb.

16 5.3.1; 7.229.2; 7.120.2

17 7.139 passim. The following presents a paraphrase of Herodotus' text. See also Solmsen (1974) 24–7.

18 Lloyd (1975) 146, among others, but he offers good comments on paradoxography. Immerwahr (1966) 325 protests eloquently against the 'conglomeration view.' Lang (1984) 1–17 discusses story-telling techniques and the logic of Herodotean narrative.

19 *Contra* Jacoby (1913) 350; see also (rightly) Hignett (1963) 32.

20 Wolff (1964) 58 = Marg 678. 1.5.3 also presents Herodotus' original standards of relevance and historicity. This chronological boundary is momentarily violated.

21 Hignett (1963) 32, following Jacoby (1913) 473ff, who cites Thucydides 2.5.6 and 1.20.2 as examples of the two types of motives in an historian reluctant to cite variants.

22 Stories of divine matters merit different degrees of respect (eg, 1.182.1; 2.145.1, 146.1), although Herodotus eschews theology as such, since he does not regard it as suitable for his *historie* (2.3.2). Hypotheses of his own from this realm are hesitantly presented (eg, 2.56.1, 120.3: *nb* εἰ χρή τι τοῖσι ἐποποιοῖσι χρεώμενον λέγειν). Cf Darbo-Peschanski (1985) 118.

23 Heraclitus recognized the dangers of scepticism in *divine* matters: ἀλλὰ τῶν μὲν θείων τὰ πολλά ... ἀπιστίῃ διαφυγγάνει μὴ γιγνώσκεσθαι (*Vors* 22 B 86).

24 Cf Jacoby (1913) 398–9 for a list; Lloyd (1975) 83, 140, chapter 3 passim; Darbo-Peschanski (1985) 110.

25 See Myres (1953) 9, and Evans (1968) 16, quoting *Iliad* 18.501; 23.486.

26 See Darbo-Peschanski (1985) 121–4.

CHAPTER 4

1 Momigliano (1961/2) 186–97 = *Studies* 212

2 Starr (1968) 348–59 = (1979) 163–74. Cf idem (1968b) 107ff; Dewald (1983).

3 Pearson (1941) 348

4 Heidel (1935) 134, note 3 for the quotation; Parke (1946) 80–4. Thucydides has one reference by name to a predecessor, Hellanicus, 1.97.2. He never mentions the names of Herodotus or, eg, Hecataeus or Antiochus of Syracuse. On Herodotus' written sources, see Jacoby (1913) 392–419 and Drews (1973) 166, notes 91–2.

5 He takes the Egyptian temple accountant's story (2.28) of Krophi and Mophi to be a bad joke (ἔμοιγε παίζειν ἐδόκεε, φάμενος εἰδέναι ἀτρεκέως), knowing as he did by observation that the Nile extends south far beyond the first cataract, which is just south of Elephantine. Wainwright (1953) 105 understands the passage as an innocent misunderstanding between speakers of different languages.

6 4.36.2 and 42.1; 3.80.1 and 6.43.3; 4.52.5; 4.77.2; 4.109.1; 7.214.2

7 Jacoby (1912) 2679. How and Wells at 2.145; G. Lloyd (1975) 86; see F.W. Walbank (1962) 1–12, esp 1–3, for a brief consideration of polemic in Greek historiography.

8 *Pace* How and Wells, at 4.29, who strangely assert that 'Herodotus uses Homer ... as our ancestors used the Bible, to prove everything.' Prophetic and epigraphic verse (eg, 8.77, 7.228) as well as legends perhaps known in poetical versions (eg, 7.189.1, 191.2, 197, 198.2) are excluded here, the first two because their character as verse is incidental to their significance, and the third because their fifth-century form is unknown and they are presented as non-historical *logoi*.

9 See Powell *Lexicon* (1937) sv οἶδα[1], for further examples. Also Wardman (1961) 140–1.

10 Sayce (1883) xxii; Parke (1946) 80, 84; Appfel (1957) 87–9

11 See, eg, Parke (1946) 80–92; for a list of possibilities compare Dionysius *de Thucydide* 5. Scylax' writings are never mentioned, although his achievements are (4.44.1); cf *FGrHist* 709 T 3. On Hecataeus, see also Walbank (1962) 1–2 referring to Jacoby commenting on *FGrHist* 1 F 302. Poets are frequently named; cf How and Wells I 21 note 2.

12 Such ethnics may often conceal a reference to a single writer; cf Jacoby (1913) 402–3.

13 Cf Josephus *Contra Apionem* 1.15–18 (3); D.H. Fischer *Historians' Fallacies* (New York 1970) 299–300; von Fritz (1967) I 178.

14 Parke (1946) 82–4

15 The older view, clearly stated by Sayce (1883) xxix and Heidel (1935) esp 116–17, that Herodotus borrowed and copied without respite from his predecessor, is now generally abandoned. Heidel (117) refers to Herodotus' criticism of his predecessor as 'the carping criticism of the hack-reviewer, who knows little of the subject in hand.' See also von Fritz (Hardt 1958) 22; idem (1936) 322. The hypothesis that Hecataeus stands behind much of Herodotus' ethography is now revived by O.K. Armayor, eg, (1978c) 7; (1978b) 45–62.

16 Drews (1973) 17–18; Lloyd (1975) 135–7

17 Von Fritz (1936) 315–40; idem (1952–4) 200–23

18 T. Krischer 'ΕΤΥΜΟΣ und ΑΛΗΘΗΣ' *Philologus* 109 (1965) 173; Laserre (1976) 116–18 carefully notes that Hecataeus' advance in the *Genealogies* was

entirely of a negative sort, but that in his *Geographical Researches*, he produced the germ of a positive method.

19 However, he can fail to live up to his own method (eg, on the course of the Ister/Danube: 2.33. 2–3; cf 4.36.1, his objection to the Hypernotians) or reach the wrong conclusion by the right empirical method (eg, 3.115, the Eridanus; 4.42.4, the sun below the equator; 4.8.2, the peripheral Ocean, *nb*: ἔργῳ δέ οὐκ ἀποδείκνυσι).

20 Finley (1965) 288; Drews (1973) 10, 17, 19, 137; cf Meyer (1899) II 252 (= Marg 12). He too, nevertheless, was overly systematizing and rational, rather than empirical, on some geographical questions, esp in books 2 and 4 (cf von Fritz [1936] 326–7). His Egyptian research led to a reaction against Hecataean hyper-rationalization and, afterwards, to a cautious and sometimes defensive attitude towards the inclusion of his strangest tales, those that refer to unnatural beings (eg, 3.116.2, 4.36.1) and supernatural interference (eg, 8.37.2, 77).

21 Momigliano (1961/2) 186–97 = *Studies* 212. Herodotus praises Hecataeus as statesman, despite a lack of respect for his predecessor's logographical theories and history; Fränkel (1962/1975) 343; Benardete (1969) 152.

22 Walbank (1962) 4, though he underestimates the frequency of criticism of literary manner and historical method to be found before Duris and Timaeus

23 See How and Wells I 24–7, with lists of references on 24–5; Lloyd (1975) 84–139; Jacoby (1912) 2678, for argument that 'Ionian' often means simply 'Hekataios.' Fränkel (1962/1975) 344 remarks of Hecataeus' style: 'His list registers each detail in its own right, just as one would repeat the same symbol close together on a map.'

24 Did Herodotus learn of Hecataeus' discomfiture from the latter's books? Perhaps Hecataeus reported it in illustration of the thesis of the preface to his *Genealogies*; less likely it came from the *Periegesis* (Drews [1973] 13; 149 note 40 *contra* Jacoby, Heidel, Pearson, etc; 171 note 33). This malicious swipe at the inadequate time-span of Hecataeus does not prevent Herodotus elsewhere from giving the hero Heracles to Leonidas as an ancestor a mere nine hundred years (2.145.4) or twenty generations previously (7.204). In this case, due honour and the heroic genealogical catalogue outweigh 'mere' chronology.

25 See the detailed discussion of this problem, with references to the earlier literature, in Pearson (1934) 328–37. Wardman (1961) 141 somehow believes autopsy allowed Herodotus to *deny* the existence of Ocean and the Tin Islands. Lloyd (1975) 138–9 offers a list of Herodotean passages indebted to Hecataeus.

26 2.178.3; 6.124.2; 7.139.1, 5; 8.73.3; 3.80.1 and 6.43.3. Nancy Demand 'Herodotus' encomium of Athens: science or rhetoric?' *AJPh* 108 (1987) 746–58, argues the logical insufficiency of the historian's use of counter-factual arguments. She sees them as a kind of rhetorical embellishment.

27 One sign of the urgency of these passages is that each repeats a key word: μεταποιεῦνται, ἀναδεχθῆναι (*ter*), ἀληθές, κάτημαι, ἐλέχθησαν etc.

28 Pearson (1941) 335–55 emphasizes the former. He does not consider syntactical techniques for casting doubt on accounts (see chapters 1 and 3) but notes that Herodotus is more explicitly sceptical in historical accounts than in his geography (348). von Fritz (1936) attempted to explain this discrepancy by the analytic or genetic approach, an inheritance from Jacoby (1913) 352–60. See note 29 below.

29 Fornara (1971) 15–21 argues that book 2 was written first, others argue that it came last. von Fritz (1967) I 177–81, 455–60, regards it as crucial in Herodotus' development from a revisionist geographer in Hecataeus' footsteps to a sceptical and original historian. A.R. Burn, in his introduction to de Sélincourt's translation (1972²) 19–21, judges the issue of priority unresolvable.

30 Müller (1981) 307–10

31 The word μῦθος appears only here, where it is 'silly' (εὐήθης), and in chapter 23 where it is used for an account of Ocean which 'has no proof or disproof' (ἔλεγχος).

32 2.5.1: 'It is clear to anyone with eyes and common sense even if he has no prior information.' This passage on Egyptian geography perhaps includes a quotation from Hecataeus (cf FGrHist 1 F 301). 17.2: 'If we follow age-old Hellenic opinion.' 118.1: 'I asked whether the Greek version was baseless.' 134.1–2: 'Those Greeks are wrong who say Rhodopis was a hetaira; they seem to me not to know who she was.'

33 2.154.4; 6.53; 6.55

34 Pearson (1941) 342–8; see Jacoby (1913) 398–9, a list of ethnic and individual sources.

35 2.53.2; 2.23; 2.118.1. See Verdin (1977) 53–76.

36 2.82.1; 2.156.1; 3.115.2; 4.13.1

37 2.116.1; 2.120.3. Herodotus as Homer's remorseless critic on historical matters: Neville (1977) 4–7. The Lyric poets receive better treatment; despite their subjectivity, they speak of their own experiences and their communities. See Verdin (1977) 65.

38 Cf Gomme (1956) at 1.9.4; Pohlenz (1937) 7, in his translation of 1.5.3 adds 'die mythische Zeit,' and thereby cuts the knot by assuming what must be proved. Herodotus puts Minos in the Heroic, not the historical epoch (1.171–3 [τὸ παλαιόν], 3.122.2, and 7.171.1), but believes he once existed.

39 2.28.2; 2.73.1, 3; 2.156.2. Cf Dandamayev (1985) 92.

40 Jacoby (1913) 416. Sayce (1883), Armayor passim, Fehling (1971) share the view that Herodotus fabricates wholesale.

41 Verdin (1977) 62

42 See, eg, Cameron (1955) 77–97, esp 82, 85; Drews (1973) 31, 158–9, notes 43–4; R.T. Hallock The Evidence of the Persepolis Tablets (Cambridge 1971) 1–3, 8–9; Lewis (1985) 102–4, 108–11; West (1986) considers all the epigraphical evidence in Herodotus and at 298–302 discusses the eleven Oriental

inscriptions mentioned in his text. Dandamayev (1985) 92 confirms by reference to the Elamite tablets the essential accuracy of innumerable Near-Eastern names, institutions, and events in the *Histories*.

43 See Jacoby (1913) 414–15, 423–4; at 419–67 he analyses the sources for each *logos* in the *Histories*. Sayce (1883) xx, Meyer (1899) 231, and Bury (1908/1958) 66–8 are confident that there were written sources; J. Wells 'The Persian friends of Herodotus' *JHS* 27 (1907) 37ff = (1923) 95–111; Drews (1973) 28–31 with notes, 82–3; an excellent survey in Lewis (1985) 102–6. Helm (1981) 85–90; H. Tolman 'The historical and the legendary in Herodotus' account of the accession of Darius ...' *TAPA* 38 (1907) xxiv–xxvi; A. Kuhrt 'A brief guide to some recent work on the Achaemenid Empire' *LCM* 8 (1983) 146–53: only 100 old Persian inscriptions are known, none private; Dandamayev (1985) 93.

44 The case is argued in detail by Wells (1907).

45 Cf, eg, Burn (1962) 6, 94, 109–12; Raubitschek (1961) 59–61 does not discuss barbarian items; Lewis (1985) 113–17; Dandamayev (1985) 94–6

46 Summarized adequately by Burn (1962) 395–6; Hignett (1965) 379–85

47 2.77.1, 2.5, 3.1 (λογιώτατοι). He reports an Egyptian inscription, 2.106.1.

48 2.49.2–3. Kleingünther (1933) 53 asserts that, in Herodotus, the Greeks are always borrowers and never lenders. Wikarjak (1959) dissents but does not refute, since his examples are of the first Greeks to do something, not the first men. Herodotus thus ignores Greek inventiveness.

49 Powell (1939), omitting examples in direct speech (although not all the rest are spoken *in propria persona*), produces the following lexical statistics. Herodotus employs ἀληθ- stems 54 times, ἀτρεκ- stems 49 times, ἀπατα- stems 10 times, σαφε- stems 8 times, and ψευδ- stems 17 times. The distribution of these words requires another study, but the numbers indicate that Herodotus' concern for verity and verification is not occasional or accidental.

50 Redfield (1985) 117–18

51 In this generosity, Herodotus differs from Polybius; see Walbank (1972) 11–12; Fornara (1983) 100, 112–15. The erratically ungenerous treatment in the *Histories* of a few persons such as Cleomenes and Themistocles was a result of Herodotus' failure to recognize hostile sources.

INTRODUCTION TO PART THREE

1 Kitto (1966) 259–61, 290–2, 320–1. The following *inter alios* address Herodotean 'poetics': Gomme (1954) 73–115 = Marg 202–48; Fornara (1971) 35, 72–3; Lang (1984); and Timothy Long *Repetition and Variation in the Short Stories of Herodotus* (Frankfurt 1987), who at 176–92 compares Herodotus' technique to that of the Attic tragedians.

CHAPTER 5

1 Jacoby (1949) 397 note 45. See further, note 8 below.
2 Thucydides emphasizes how quickly men come to misconceive the past (1.20.3: πολλὰ δὲ καὶ ἄλλα ἔτι καὶ νῦν ὄντα καὶ οὐ χρόνῳ ἀμνηστούμενα), and his own account of 479–431 is scrappy, imprecise in chronology, and full of surprising omissions (so Gomme [1956] 365–89). Like the so-called 'Archaeology,' its purpose is severely subordinated to the narrative of the contemporary war.
3 Momigliano (1966) 2 = (1969) 14 thought it necessary to argue this.
4 The knowledge of a contemporary is here differentiated from *kleos*, the subsequent rumour, fame, or reputation of past events that reaches the poet.
5 Jacoby (1913) 333–4; cf Drews (1973) 137. See Pindar *Nemeans* 4.6; 7.13–16.
6 Finley (1965) 292
7 Mosshammer (1979) 108, 110 notes the many temporal contradictions that Herodotus' inquiries must have uncovered.
8 Jacoby (1913) 405; idem (1949) 171, 360 note 49; 397 note 45; White (1969) 42; E. Posner *Archives in the Ancient World* (Cambridge 1972) 102–7, with earlier bibliography; Alan Boegehold 'The establishment of a central archive at Athens' *AJA* 76 (1972) 23–30; Finley (1965) 292; cf Josephus *Contra Apionem* 1.19–22 (4). Hammond (1955) 382, 390–1 and R. Stroud 'State documents in archaic Athens' *Athens Comes of Age* (Princeton 1978) 20–42, esp 34ff, believe that the first two historians had access to extensive lists of officials and dated events, but do not adequately explain why they made so little use of them. Hammond sees the chronological methods and concerns of the two early historians as basically the same. Mosshammer (1979) 17, 86, 88, 326 note 6, 92–7 clearly expounds the problem.
9 *Vors* 21 B 22. cf Simonides F 77 (Diehl). Xenophanes also composed poems on the foundings of Colophon and Elea. Such *ktiseis* or foundation stories, a minor branch of 'horography,' mixed legend, family glorification, invention, and fact without concern for verification. Such antiquarian work, although including *historie*, inquiry, was not history in Herodotus' sense or ours (Drews [1973] 10–11, 40–2, 49, 148 note 28).
10 Strasburger (1956) 137–8 = Marg 700–1
11 For the fragments, see *FGrHist* IIIC 687, 765, IIIA 262, and IIIC 709. Drews (1973) chapter 2 seems to stretch the evidence about these writers to fit his hypothesis about the impetus that the Persian *Wars* (31, his italics) gave to Greek historiography, when he argues that Hellanicus (!), Charon, Dionysius, and Scylax all preceded Herodotus in publication and all featured the Persian Wars, not merely a description of Persia's empire or the *res gestae* of her kings. Cf Fornara (1971) 25–7.

12 Cf Jacoby (1913) 468; Pearson (1939) 27, 128–34, 145–7; Drews (1973) 23–36, 100. Pohlenz (1937) 21 and von Fritz (1967) 78 delete Dionysius.

13 Herodotus and Thucydides (2.2.1) both give only one fixed date from which they count forwards and backwards. 8.51.1 mentions Calliades, the Athenian archon of 480, and dates to an Athenian year Xerxes' arrival in Attica (as well as – relative to this – his crossing of the Hellespont three months earlier). At 2.53.2, Herodotus appears to compute on his own a date for Homer and Hesiod, four hundred years before his own time. Chronological indications of season and relative times multiply in the account of the Ionian rebellion: 6.42, 43, 46. On this subject, consult Jacoby (1913) 404–5; How and Wells (1928) 1 app 14; von Leyden (1949); Strasburger (1956) = (revised) Marg 688–736; White (1969); Shimron (1973); and Sacks (1976) who focuses on the account of Xerxes' invasion. An event that furnishes an exact date, the eclipse of 2 October 480 (9.10.2–3), is not presented as a temporal indication to his Greek audience. The eclipses of 1.74–5 and 7.37.2 are misdated by Herodotus; see How and Wells, ad loc; Mosshammer (1979) 263–5.

14 So Jacoby (1949) 360 note 49; cf Gomme (1956) 3 note 1.

15 Mosshammer (1979) 108, 111

16 White (1969) 42–3 sees 5.28 as the dividing passage. Hammond (1955) 386–7, Strasburger (1956) 152–4 = Marg 723–5, and R. van Compernolle 'La date de la bataille navale de Lade ...' AC 27 (1958) 383–9, discuss this revolt's chronological cruces.

17 Herodotus scants *precise* dates before Croesus for important events in order to avoid misleading the reader. The chronological consequences frustrate the modern historian. See, eg, on the Ionian revolt, Burn (1962) 198; on the dates for the Corinthian tyranny, see, eg, Sealey (1976b) 53–5; Mosshammer (1979) Part II.

18 Jacoby (1913) 472; Hignett (1963) 33; Mosshammer (1979) 92.

19 Cf Fränkel (1960²) 2; see 3.125.4–126.1: Oroetes falls χρόνου δὲ οὐ πολλῷ ὕστερον, 'soon after' Polycrates' death. In fact, the latter died under Cambyses, the former under the next king, Darius, but neither the precise date nor the interval nor even the ruler at the time is important to Herodotus' momentary purpose.

20 Powell *Lexicon* sv οἶδα 1. Three other times the phrase occurs in reported speech. In Herodotus' rhetoric, sometimes the phrase merely underscores or limits the superlative. See further Macan (1895) civ and note 9, Shimron (1973), and Munson (1983) 86–96 who discusses this and related 'celebratory' transitions.

21 It also satisfied the ubiquitous Greek desire to trace everything to a single originator: πρῶτος εὑρετής; Kleingünther (1933) esp 46–65 for Herodotus.

22 De Sélincourt's translation, slightly modified. Thucydides does not express such

strong doubts about the historicity of Minos (1.4, 8.2); Gomme (1956) 110; Legrande (1932) 39.

23 Mitchel (1956) 58, 52, 68. Mitchel argues that all Thucydides' dates in the 'Archaeology' are adopted from this work and are not independently calculated (53). Hammond (1955) 382, 396 believes that both Herodotus and Thucydides drew on one literary chronology for the period before the Persian Wars, and that all their calculations agree.

24 Mosshammer (1979) 108–9

25 Mitchel (1956) 61, 64, 66–7 for quotation, 53, with the examples of reckoning by generations. Mitchel rightly rejects suggestions that Herodotus used any generation of fixed extent (33 1/3 years or 40 years); see, ibid 64–6 against, eg, D.W. Prakken 'Herodotus and the Spartan king lists' *TAPA* 71 (1940) 460–72. Mosshammer (1979) 105–7, 328 note 25 demolishes remaining theories that hold that Herodotus' chronologies are consistent or based on genealogy.

26 Herodotus also dates by seasons (6.43.1, 7.37.1, etc) and offers exact numbers and intervals of years (6.18, 31.1, 46.1; 7.1.2, 4.1., 7, 20.1, 22.1, etc) and even days: eg, forty-five days for Xerxes' journey from Salamis back to the Hellespont (8.115.1). Pohlenz (1937) 198–9 claims that Herodotus was Thucydides' instructor in chronology.

27 Gomme (1956) 2–3, and note 2; cf Strasburger (1956) 131 = Marg 692; Mosshammer (1979) 88

28 Strasburger (1956) 130–1 (= Marg 691), 160–1 (= Marg 735–6)

29 Lattimore (1958) 18

30 Condemned as spurious by Macan (1908) 828; Powell (1939) 79–80; Hignett (1963) 457. The annalistic statement has parallels (6.42.1; 9.41.1, 107.3) and is defended by Immerwahr (1966) 145 with note 188.

31 Mosshammer (1979) 111

32 Carolyn Dewald *Taxis: The Organization of Thucydides' History, Books ii–viii* (Diss Berkeley 1975) presents a useful corrective to overly simple interpretations of the divisions of Thucydides' text. His thoughtful systems of causality and relationships in time escape Dionysius' purely literary criticism.

33 Thucydides' paragraphs of evaluation of a man or state include Pericles, 2.65.5–9; Athens, 2.65.10–13; Brasidas, 4.81; Nicias, 7.86; Pleistoanax, 5.16; Alcibiades, 6.15; the effect on Athens of the fortification of Deceleia, 7.28. See D. Lateiner 'Nicias' inadequate encouragement (Thuc. 7.69.2)' *CP* 80 (1985) 208–13.

34 In terms of the text, chapters 50–53 of book 3 nestle within 44–56, a unit on the attack which itself comprises an incident within the larger story of Polycrates' harsh treatment of his fellow citizens (44–59), itself the focus of the 'Samian *logos*' (39–60).

35 Lang (1984) 1–17 analyses forward and backward movements in the narrative;

Powell *Lexicon* sv *logos* 4eβ for Herodotus' references to parts of the
Histories; for references to events after 478, see Jacoby (1913) 230–2; Schmid-
Stählin 1/2 (1934) 590 note 9; Fornara (1981).

36 Drews (1973) 51 with 169 note 17 so suggests, but an Asiatic Greek must have
known more than this. Cf Lydian Xanthus 765 *FGrHist* IIIC FF 1–30 esp 8, 12,
14, 19; and Pearson (1939) chapter 3.

37 Fornara (1971) 34–5 for the quotation. This was a matter of Herodotus' choice.
The materials could not force the method on him, *pace* Fornara who
employed as epigraph (vi) the apposite passage from Fielding quoted above.

38 A significant constitutional development, such as the choosing of archons by
sortition (*Athenaion politeia* 22.5), was not germane to Herodotus' subject. Cf
How and Wells at 5.69.1, 6.51, and esp 6.109.2; also P. Karavites 'Realities
and appearances, 490–480 B.C.' *Historia* 26 (1977) 129–47.

39 Herodotus was not unappreciative of Themistocles; Fornara (1971) 69–74;
contra, eg, Burn (1962) 283; Hignett (1963) 37; A.J. Podlecki *The Life of
Themistocles* (Montreal 1975) 71 and 230 sv Herodotus; R.J. Lenardon *The
Saga of Themistocles* (London 1978).

40 On these heralds, consult Sealey (1976). Herodotus postponed one half of the
epicene Delphic oracle at 6.19 to 6.77. He postponed but never provided
accounts of Assyria and Ephialtes (1.106.2, 184; 7.213.3). See also 5.22.1 with
8.137 on Perdiccas' descendants; 1.75.1 with 107ff on Astyages; 2.38.2 with
3.29 on clean Egyptian sacrifices; 6.39.1 with 103 on the death of Cimon;
2.161.3 with 4.159.5ff on Apries' Libyan expedition. For cross-references to
earlier books, see How and Wells II *ad* 5.36.4.

41 Herodotus' difficult account of Cleomenes is not so much brief as minimizing
and disconnected (he appears in four books). The abundant information is
distorted by hostile informants who tried to downplay the great Spartan king's
role in preparing Sparta and Greece for the coming war, while favouring the
failure Dorieus and the renegade Demaratus. The latter's family was settled on
royal territory in the Troad (Xenophon *Hellenica* 3.1.6) and may have
supplied Herodotus with material; cf Lewis (1985) 105. A forceful and successful
ruler of nearly thirty years ought not to be characterized as lacking in manly
merit and 'ruling for no long time' (5.39.1, 48). Cf How and Wells II app
XVII, 'Sparta under King Cleomenes' 347–53; Burn (1962) 283; P. Cartledge
Sparta and Lakonia (London 1979) 143–54.

42 On whom see How and Wells II 276–7 at 8.126; on Persian sources in general,
Lewis (1985) passim.

43 Immerwahr (1956) 227. Until Herodotus' time, there was no such thing as an
absolute date or chronography: Mosshammer (1979) 17, 92.

44 On Polycrates and the Samian *logoi*, see Immerwahr (1957); Mosshammer
(1979) 290–304.

45 Fornara (1971) 18 finds book 1 expounding a 'philosophy of history.' Such phrasing seems a considerable overstatement to those who regard it as 'a muddled amalgam of traditional wisdom.' See, eg, J.R. Grant, review of Fornara in *Phoenix* 26 (1972) 92–5 at 93. The truth lies in between. Book 1 implies and demonstrates so many attitudes towards past events that find subsequent parallels that the assumption of a paradigmatic function for it seems reasonable, perhaps necessary. Those attitudes towards the more distant past are often unoriginal (except for Herodotus' frequency of historical *caveat*), but the establishment of literary patterns for past events and the pointing of intellectual issues of a historical nature created a new, historical way of thinking. Therefore, the 'philosophy' of book 1 is less significant than the premise of inquiry, and less revolutionary than the marshalling of the evidence in Herodotus' practice for the remainder, especially for books 7–9 where political analysis predominates (see chapter 9).

46 See Dionysius *Epistula ad Pompeium* 3 (= 773–4 U-R); also Gomme (1954) 75–6, discussing the odd placement of the battle of Himera (7.166–7), long before the battle of Salamis (8.83–96), which is alleged to have occurred on the same day.

47 Sometimes a pseudo-precision signals the presence of legend. We hear, for example, that long before the Trojan War the daughter of the king of Argos was taken away 'on the fifth or the sixth day after the Phoenicians arrived' (1.1.3; cf the ring of Polycrates' story, 3.42.1). Similarly Solon tours Croesus' treasury 'on the third or fourth day' after his arrival in Sardis (1.30.1). Such precision belongs to legend, not history, and Herodotus colours his stories with such details precisely and only when he does not want his audience to think that the subsidiary facts are historically accurate (cf 3.14.1, 52.3). Thomas Macaulay 'History' *Edinburgh Review* (1828) repr in Fr. Stern ed *The Varieties of History* (New York 1956, 1973) 74, noted this over-great minuteness, but did not draw the right inferences from it. Such fictional omniscience resembles quickly recognized fabulous time ('for seven days and seven nights Darius suffered from insomnia' [3.129.3]), and has nothing in common with the chronological data of Xerxes' campaign (eg, 7.31, 192.1, 8.15.1). Fehling (l971) 155–67, a chapter on 'Typische Zahlen,' recognizes the fictional nature of many of these numbers, in accord with his principle of interpretation: 'Detail macht glaubwürdig' (91, in a section on 'Die Tricks der Lügenliteratur'). He thinks that Herodotus consciously created an illusion of accuracy from materials which Herodotus well knew were merely the products of his own imagination (180–1). Protestation of truthfulness by an ancient author constitutes merely another tool of fictive *Erzählkunst* (92–4). The presentation of alternative versions is another persuasive trick (10–16, 180–1). Fehling's literary study, a corrective to Herodotolatric excesses, seems a perverse contribution to

historiography. His and Armayor's view of Herodotus, now regarded as eccentric, is in essence that of antiquity and the nineteenth-century critics (1–3, 10), for example, the hypercritical Sayce (1883) and H. Panofsky *De historiae Herodoteae fontibus* (diss Berlin 1885) [*non vidi*]. A thorough refutation of their historiographical assumptions is wanted; a good start may be found in W.K. Pritchett's work cited below, note 57, and see Lewis (1985) 104–6.

48 Starr (1966) 24–35, esp 27. There is an Ionian awareness of historical perspective in his views on the Nile's silt, the antiquity of Dionysus and other Greek gods, and the Veneti (2.15.2, 49.2, 53.1; 5.9.3). Frequent use of phrases such as 'until my day' or 'even still to this moment' suggests that Herodotus was aware of continuity and change within the historical period. *Contra*, eg, Wilamowitz *Reden und Vorträge* II (1926⁴) 220ff = *Greek Historical Writing* (Oxford 1908) 6; How and Wells I 437ff

49 Herodotus' scepticism about knowledge of the past is overshadowed by Thucydides', but the proper comparison is with Hecataeus. The proto-historian began by criticizing the stories of the Greeks and their contradictions (F 1; cf Fornara [1983] 5–6), but he confidently, if inconsistently (FF 15–17), reconstructed all past ages by rationalizing the miraculous and assuming continuity between mythic and historical time. Herodotus reacted strongly against his predecessor's credulity including the wild tales of Heracles (FF 25–7) and divine presences (F 305). The still frequent divine and heroic stories in the *Histories* probably form part of his sustained polemic against his most eminent predecessor (cf Gomme [1956] 110).

50 Shimron (1973) 45–51, by this distinction among three periods, seeks to obviate the *aporia* stated by Jacoby (1913) 338, and inadequately handled by Wardman (1961) 136. Thucydides also employs a triple division of time (1.1.1,3), but he draws the divisions differently and has little confidence in specific facts (as opposed to plausible hypotheses about patterns of historical processes) in the two earlier periods (τὰ πρὸ αὐτῶν καὶ τὰ ἔτι παλαίτερα) for which he has no direct information. All the details are doubtful; all the facts deserve suspicion (1.21.1).

51 Herodotus' devotion to the visible, to monuments that justify credence in long-past people and events, appears here and elsewhere: the statue of Arion (1.24.8) or the fallen boulders at Delphi (8.37.3, 39.2). His loyalty to *opsis* here prevents him from passing over the incredible, cf Müller (1981) passim; Raubitschek (1939) 222.

52 How and Wells at 1.14.4

53 Von Leyden (1949/50) 89–104 passim (92–7 = Marg 169–81). He, however, grants 200 years to the historical period for the Greeks, much too long (95). See also White (1969) 47–8 for the three-generation extent of historical knowledge. The historical epoch began earlier for the record-keeping Egyptians, later for the illiterate Thracians.

54 De Romilly (1971) 336–7

55 Burn (1962) 339; Hignett (1963) 34, 456, and app v and xiv; von Fritz i/1 (1967), 205. Perhaps the deserter Zopyrus, son of the general Megabyzos, brought such a 'log'; Burn (ibid) 109. Xenophanes (*Vors* b 8) knew when the conquest of Ionia by Harpagus occurred, but knew the year of his own birth only approximately. See Lewis (1985) 105–6.

56 Hignett (1963) 449, 455–6. On the temporal cross-references of the Persian invasion from Themopylae to Salamis, see Sacks (1976) passim.

57 Topographers now grant Herodotus more credit for his labours – in an age without maps – than previous generations did. See, eg, Hammond's many studies; Burn (1962) 380: 'careful notes, but lacking the time or inclination to leave the road' [at Thermopylae]; 414; 535; 'how clearly Herodotus, for the men of his own time, defined positions on the battlefield' [at Plataea]; or the historian Hignett (1963) 129: 'detailed description' of Thermopylae. Of course he made errors, such as the shape of Euboea or the compass orientation of Thermopylae (Burn 390; Hignett 129). See also W.K. Pritchett *Studies in Ancient Greek Topography* (Berkeley and Los Angeles 1965–82) i–iv, esp i 83–121 on Marathon, Salamis, and Plataea, with references to his earlier studies, and iv 176–285 on Thermopylae and Herodotus' veracity. The general conclusion of this severe critic is that Herodotus enables us to identify most features in the region of Thermopylae (177), suggesting personal autopsy (210); he makes *geographical* errors but not with intent to deceive (178 note 7, 238–42); and he needs correction much less than modern writers believe, being neither careless nor a liar (281). Topography and archaeology confirm what they can of Herodotus's account, even in Scythia (253). Similarly the account of the satrapies now finds increased respect among scholars. See, eg, Burn (1969) 109, 120ff; D.M. Lewis *Sparta and Persia* (Leiden 1977) chapter 1, and 52–3; idem (1985) 116.

58 Finley (1965) 282–302 esp 283–6, 294–5, for this paragraph. See also Collingwood (1946) 20–1; 26–9; Starr (1968) 57–77 esp 57–60.

CHAPTER 6

1 P. Brown *The World of Late Antiquity* (London 1971) 38. On Gibbon's 'controlling metaphor,' see L. Braudy *Narrative Form in History and Fiction* (Princeton 1970) 215–16. 'Periodization' can have the same distorting and beneficial consequences.

2 *Poetics* 4 = 1449a14–15; Polybius 6.9.10–14: cf K. von Fritz *Aristotle's Contribution to the Practice and Theory of Historiography* (Howison Lecture 1957), *University of California Publications in Philosophy* 28/3 (Berkeley and Los Angeles 1958) 128.

3 See Barth (1968) 93–110. In addition to the zoology and botany of 3.106–14, other discussions of animals, most dense in book 2, include cats, dogs, crocodiles, hippopotamuses, otters, the phoenix (2.65–73), fish, gnats (2.93, 95), ants, mules, the fauna of Africa (3.102–5; 4.30, 192); other discussions of plants include the lily, castor-oil plant, acacia-trees, and hemp (2.92, 94, 96; 4.74). Limit also affects the number of offspring that noxious species produce (3.108–9).

4 Immerwahr (1956) 250; idem (1966) 43

5 Herodotus mentions Aeschylus (2.156.6) as a borrower of Egyptian 'Artemis' myth; his debt to Aeschylus: Hauvette (1894) 125–6; Aly (1921) 146 note 1, 168ff, 173 note 1; Pohlenz (1937) 121; on Aeschylus' version of Salamis, H.D. Broadhead *The Persae of Aeschylus* (Cambridge 1960) 322–39; also Kitto (1966) 74–101 in his chapter 'How intelligent were the Athenians?' defends the historical accuracy of the tragedian's account.

6 G. Devereux *Dreams in Greek Tragedy* (Berkeley 1976), 'Atossa's dream' 3–20, esp 10–11. See also Schmid-Stählin I/2 (1934) 569–72, esp 569, note 7, and Chiasson (1982) for echoes of tragic diction and their occurrence in clusters that render Xerxes, eg, a figure of tragic stature. Schmid-Stählin overrate the influence of tragedy, finding, eg, the colloquy of 7.46–52 to be the equivalent of 'ein tragische Chorlied' (570 note 12).

7 Cf Cameron (1955) 83 quoting the Cyrus-cylinder (line 22) on which Cyrus is 'ruler of all the world ... king of totality, great king, mighty king ... king of the four world quarters.' The inscription, if genuine, provides a documentary basis for Xerxes' claim in the *Histories* that he was only following his nation's *nomos*.

8 Solmsen (1974) 5, note 10, referring to Immerwahr (1966) 84, note 17, and 293, who refers to von Scheliha (1931). See p 11 of von Scheliha's monograph.

9 Immerwahr (1966) 293. This is excessively schematic. See, eg, 1.191; 2.124.2; 5.11.1; 5.23.1; 8.25.1 (the last four are straits rather than rivers); 5.52.2, 77.2, 83.1; 6.2.2, 5.2, 70.2 (*bis*); 9.6 (*bis*), etc.

10 Von Scheliha (1931) 99–100. Xerxes' offence in maltreating nature is also foreshadowed by Sesostris' ἀτασθαλίη, when he speared the Nile (2.112.2; 7.35.2).

11 See Immerwahr (1966) 84, 293; also Aeschylus *Persae* 65.

12 Fornara's publications examine these problems. See, most recently, J.A.S. Evans 'Herodotus 9.73.3 ...' *CP* 82 (1987) 226–8, who argues again for Jacoby's 424 BCE as the *terminus ante quem*.

13 Most of the recorded atrocious punishments (judged by our standards, anyway) are meted out by Persians – though not by Cyrus: Cambyses (several in 3.29–35); Darius (4.84, 6.32, 7.194.2, but cf 3.130.4, 155.2*); Xerxes (7.39.3, 238; 8.140α*). Note also *inter alia*, nasty deeds of the Mede Astyages and the Egyptian Apries (1.118–19, 2.162.5). These autocrats can sometimes show

surprising generosity, eg, Darius with Metiochus, and Xerxes with the Spartan sacrificial victims (6.41.4; 7.136.2). Cf Nylander (1980); chapter 8 below, esp note 38.

14 Although the capture of Sestos freed Europe of all but a token Persian presence at Eion and Drabescus (7.106–7, Thucydides 1.98), scores of Greek cities in Ionia remained unliberated. The account of the victory at Sestos is more important for the structure and intentions of the *Histories* than for Greek history itself.

15 As well as the chronological narrative, the entire work ceases with a 'Janus' scene (9.122) that echoes other parts of the *Histories*, not least the proem (eg, echoes of θωμαστά). See Krischer (1974) 93–100 and the last section of chapter 1, above.

16 See G. de Ste Croix *The Origins of the Peloponnesian War* (London 1972) 34ff with bibliography; R. Meiggs *The Athenian Empire* (Oxford 1972) 411–12. Herodotus' few indirect comments on the Athenians' acquisition of a league are not enthusiastic: 8.3.2 (πρόφασις), 5.32 (Pausanias' Medism); see also H. Rawlings 'Thucydides on the purpose of the Delian league' *Phoenix* 31 (1977) 1–8, esp 8; *contra* Rawlings on Thucydides' attitude, A. French 'Athenian ambitions and the Delian alliance' *Phoenix* 33 (1979) 134–41, esp 134. J.A.S. Evans' proposal in 'The evidence of the encomium' *AC* 48 (1979) 112–18, that 7.139 proves that Herodotus was sympathetic to Athenian behaviour in the 430s, should be rejected.

17 So Legrande (1932) 104 argues without sufficient warrant against Jacoby (1913) 357–60. A survey of the relevant literature would produce a chapter in itself. Strasburger (1955) 1–25 (= Marg 574–608) questions whether Herodotus admired imperial Athens at all, but Harvey (1966) 254–5 argues that Herodotus sympathized with the historical achievement of the city and the necessary consequences. The political credo of 5.78 is not seriously challenged by 3.81*, 5.97, 6.131, 8.3, 8.111, and the point where the narrative stops; cf Fornara (1971) 37–58. Dan Gillis *Collaboration with the Persians*, Historia Einzelschriften 34 (Wiesbaden 1979) esp 1–13 and 45–58 argues that Herodotus was the Alcmaeonid 'house historian' (58), a charge even less defensible.

18 Macan at 7.102.2, 209; Jacoby (1913) 357; Fornara (1971) 49–50; Forrest (1984) 6–8. Sparta's prominence in the *Histories* was inevitable, as the most powerful and the most peculiar of non-tyrannical Greek states. Sparta was a magnificent anomaly that no Greek chose to imitate. Prominence in the narrative and the historian's admiration are not the same thing, but the subject of Sparta in the *Histories* requires a separate study.

19 Wardman (1961) 148–9. See eg, 1.83; 1.152.2; 6.106.3; 8.144.4–5* with 9.7β1*; 9.7 *init* with 9.8.1; 9.102.2–3 (?); 9.106.2–3 (with Meyer [1899] 2, 217, note 1 [= Marg 679]).

20 Fornara (1971) 77, 79–88, a strong case marred by some overstatement; *contra*, see Drews' review of Cobet (1971) in *Gnomon* 47 (1975) 330; Waters (1971) 69; Forrest (1984) 7–10.

21 5.97.3; 1.87.4*; 6.98.2; 7.104.3*; 8.3.1. Cf Pindar's equally disapproving attitude towards war: fragment 99 (Bowra).

22 Jacoby (1913) 482, followed by Hignett (1963) 36, mistakenly asserts that Herodotus prefers theological to historical explanations. Their favourite example, Xerxes' decision to attack Hellas, has been argued to prove just the opposite, even by historians who also stress his religiosity (eg, Ste Croix [1977] 141–4 and note 20).

23 Redfield (1975) 43, on Homer. J. Cobet ' Herodotus and Thucydides on war' *Past Perspectives* ed I.D. Moxon et al (Cambridge 1986) 1–18, esp 12–14, discounts as exceptional the passages that detail the calamities of war.

24 Nitocris of Babylon (1.185.1), Tomyris of the Massagetae (1.205.1, 214), and Artemisia of Halicarnassus (7.99.1, 3) are admired for their mental and strategic abilities, the last also for her ἀνδρηίη, 'manly courage,' a marvellous paradox to Herodotus. Dewald (1981) 123–4 provides a list of women in Herodotus who exercise public power. R. Munson, 'Artemisia in Herodotus' *CA* 7 (1988) 91–106 discusses Artemisia as a rule-proving exception, a woman to other women as Athens is to other states and its polity to other forms of polity. Pheretime of Cyrene (4.165.1), Nitocris of Egypt (2.100.2–3), and Queen Amestris of Persia (7.114.2) are notable chiefly for their monstrous deeds.

25 The recent and welcome interest in women covers all periods and aspects of history, eg, Elise Boulding *The Underside of History* (Boulder, Colorado 1976); N. Broude and M. Garrard *Feminism and Art History* (New York 1982); P.H. Labalme ed *Beyond their Sex* (New York 1984). For antiquity, eg, the sober study of Sarah Pomeroy *Goddesses, Whores, Wives, and Slaves* (New York 1975); P. Grimal ed *Histoire mondiale de la femme* I (Paris 1965); recently, the art historical survey of women in certain classes of Attic cups, Eva Keuls *The Reign of the Phallus* (New York 1984), esp chapter 13 'Sex among the barbarians,' discussing polarities similar to chapter 7 below; the mythological study of Wm. Tyrrell *Amazons* (Baltimore 1984) 41–3, 61–2 considers women with power in Herodotus. Pembroke (1967) 1–35 criticizes certain anthropological observations about women in Herodotus, and corrects some of Herodotus' ethnographic assertions, especially on matriarchy; see also M. Rosellini and S. Saïd 'Usages de femmes et autres nomoi chez les "sauvages" d' Hérodote' *ASNP* 8 (1978) 949–1005. For a survey with a thorough inventory of women in the *Histories*, see Dewald (1981) 93–127 esp 122–5. Dewald at 105–6 observes Herodotus' un-Greek openness to the idea of women performing all the important tasks in one barbarian society or another. Sancisi-Weerdenburg (1983) discusses the portrayal of Persian women in particular.

26 Sancisi-Weerdenburg (1983) 20–33 explains the origins of the distortions. See chapters 4, 7, and notes 12–14 in chapter 8, for further discussion of the appropriation and comprehension of non-Greek sources.

27 See on women, eg, as property, Helen (2.114.2*, 115.4*, 118.3, 119.1); the lady of Cos (9.76.2*). As machines, the view of the Ethiopian deserters, which Herodotus seems to disapprove of (2.30.4; also 5.39.2*). As victims (2.89.2; 5.92η3* [necrophilia]; 2.131.1 [Mycerinus accused of raping his daughter]; 7.33 [Artaÿctes raped women in sacred precincts]; 5.18.5 [Persians at a Macedonian party]). Cf Xenophon Hiero 1.26.

28 In addition to the quotation of Pindar in 3.38.4 (= F 169), see Oxyrhynchus Papyri 2448 verses 2–3, and 2450, the latter providing some context for the much used and probably abused quotation. In these passages, Pindar, like Herodotus, finds an acceptable place for violence in human experience without jettisoning a normative concept of right behaviour. A separate study of nomos in Herodotus is desirable; S. Humphreys 'Law, custom, and culture in Herodotus' Arethusa 20 (1987) 211–20 discusses the Pindar papyrus and the explanatory power of the term for Herodotus. Ostwald (1969) attempts to determine original and root meanings of the political and legal term.

29 Women: 1.110, 185, 205–14; 9.108–10; 8.68–9, 87–8, 93, 101–3; 3.32, 119, 68–9, 124; 6.68–9. Children: 1.85.4; 5.51, 92γ2–4*. See the third section of this chapter for analysis of the role of children in the Histories.

30 M. Lefkowitz 'Women's heroism' Heroines and Hysterics (New York 1981) 1–11; 'Influential women' Images of Women in Antiquity ed A. Cameron and A. Kuhrt (Detroit and London 1983) 49–64

31 See Dewald (1981) 95, 115.

32 2.64.1–2: ἔμοιγε οὐκ ἀρεστά; cf 4.180.5. Herodotus' accounts show no comprehension of 'sacred prostitution:' Pembroke (1967) 4–5. Disapproval of prostitution implied at 1.94.1, 181.5–82; of seigneurial defloration at 4.168.2

33 Candaules' wife: ἀναγκαίη ἐνδέειν; Xerxes: παντοῖος ἐγίνετο οὐ βουλόμενος δοῦναι ...

34 Chrysis of Argos and her successor as priestess, Phaeinis (2.2.1 and 4.133.2–3, both occasions used for chronological purposes); Hippias' daughter and wife, Archedice and Myrrhine (6.59.3, 55.1); the mythical Procne (2.29.3); and the savage Thracian Brauro, who helped kill her husband, the Edonian king (4.107.3). Cf D. Schaps 'The woman least mentioned ...' CQ 27 (1977) 323–30; D. Harvey 'Women in Thucydides' Arethusa 18 (1985) 67–90.

35 2.4.2, 4; 6.4, 78.3; Corcyra, 3.74.1; cf Argos, 5.82.6.

36 See also Thucydides 1.103.3 (Ithome); 2.27 (Aegina); 3.36.2; 4.123.4; 5.32 (Scione), 116.4 (Melos); 7.29.4 (Mycalessus), 68.2*. On Thucydides' attitude towards the rules of war, see the author's 'Heralds and corpses in Thucydides' CW 71 (1977) 97–106; D. Schaps 'Women in Greece in wartime' CP 77 (1982) 193–213.

37 How and Wells I 43 complain in bold-face letters that 'his history is too theological,' but they hedge their complaint in the next sentence. De Romilly (1971) 314–15 corrects Hellman (1934) on the same point.

38 Gigante (1956) 115–28; Benardete (1969) 191–3; Cook (1976) 39–43; Redfield (1985) 117–18

39 Erbse (1956) 220: Herodotus begins and ends his work with despotic arbitrariness. Wolff (1964) 51–8 = Marg 668–78 has an excellent analysis of the episode and its structural function. Immerwahr (1966) 43: 'The work begins and ends at points that are not at all arbitrary.' In history, all divisions, especially beginnings, are in some sense arbitrarily chosen, but Herodotus' are certainly not without point or purpose. See chapter 1 above.

40 1.8.1,4*; χρῆν γὰρ Κανδαύλῃ γενέσθαι κακῶς, 1.8.2; 1.12.2. For the aphorism, see A.E. Raubitschek 'Ein neues Pittakeion' WS 71 (1958) 170–2; cf idem (1957) 139–40.

41 9.108.1–2; 9.111.4

42 The brief accounts of Croesus' and Miltiades' outrages against morality (1.92.4, 6.134), by being saved until the end of their logoi, are not fully integrated into the major multi-dimensional theme of boundary violation. Their violations of nomos are not tied into the main narrative as elsewhere, because these men function in the Histories not primarily as examples of impiety, but of the dangers of success and the folly of overextending dominion.

43 1.109.3*, 130.3. His punishment of Harpagus inflicts on that disobedient servant the extirpation of heirs, that precious blessing he had sought for himself. Harpagus' revenge in effect serves to put the vizier in Astyages' position as Cyrus' creator (saviour).

44 Herodotus notes both that his younger sister had the same two parents, and that incestuous unions were not a Persian custom (3.31.1–2). Next-of-kin marriage was, in fact, a common feature of Zoroastrianism.

45 3.31.1–2, 38.1, 66.2. The mythical fathers without sons: 5. 67.4; 7.61.3. Contrast the polyprogenitive bliss of Solon's Tellus (1.30.4*), and the man who is εὔπαις, blessed with children (1.32.6*).

46 5.48; 7.205.1; cf How and Wells (1928) II app xvii 347–53, esp 347–8. We might add Periander perhaps, Polycrates (cf Amasis' use of πρόρριζος, 3.40.3*), and Pericles, inter alios, but Herodotus did not.

47 ἀθέμιστα (7.33), ἀτάσθαλος (9.116.1). He had sexually violated women on sacred ground and lied to his king. His son was stoned to death before his eyes prior to his own crucifixion. Pindar celebrates good deeds by a congruent confidence in generational kleos and survival: Nemeans 7.100–1: παίδων δὲ παῖδες ἔχοιεν αἰεί/ γέρας; Olympians 8.70–1: πατρὶ δὲ πατρὸς ἐνέπνευσεν μένος γήραος ἀντίπαλον. On τίσις as Herodotus' less than most profound explanation of major events, see de Romilly (1971) 318.

48 Croesus had threatened Lampsacus thus (6.37, esp 37.2); πρόρριζος is applied
once to a man, once to this *polis*, and once to human fortune in general
(1.32.9*).
49 8.106.2–3, τὰ τέκνα καὶ τὴν γυναῖκα ... πανοικίῃ. Note the use of direct speech.
50 Cf 5.99.1, ὀφειλόμενά σφι ἀποδιδόντες, Athenians succour Milesians;
Xerxes' wrathful comment to Masistes: μάθῃς τὰ διδόμενα δέκεσθαι
(9.111.5*); and cf 1.158–60 on surrendering lawful suppliants.
51 This speech with its embedded drama clarifies significant issues and suggests
patterns of human experience. See, for parallels, L. Solmsen (1943) 194–5;
eadem (1944) 242, 253; Fornara (1971) 22; thus already Sayce (1883) xxv.
52 1.32.9*; 3.40.3*. Croesus' line ended with himself since Atys died, and he did
not consider his other son suitable to command (1.34.2*; cf Periander's
dim-witted son, 3.53.1). On this Homeric word, cf Aly (1921) 91 note 1.
53 παῖς παρὰ πατρός: 1.7.4; 2.65.3; 2.166.2
54 I would like to thank Professor Ronald Stroud for useful suggestions in revising
this chapter.

CHAPTER 7

1 Immerwahr (1966) 315; Grant (1969) 266–7; also Cook (1976) 48. Herodotus
himself is more diffident when he relies on reports alone; cf eg, 2.99.1. Yet
autopsy itself requires other equally historical modes of inquiry before the
historian can complete his work.
2 See Benardete (1969) 154. All references in the first half of this chapter are to
book 2 unless otherwise noted.
3 1.193.4–5; 2.11.2, 14.2, 77.4; 77.3, 84; 4.17.2, 28.1, 48.1, 63, 108.1–2; 2.36.3,
37.2, 104.2, 104.3–4. Castration: see Powell's *Lexicon* sv ἐκτομή, εὐνοῦχος.
Circumcision was an incomprehensible *nomos*, voluntarily endured, while
castration was a mutilation endured only under duress.
4 J. Vogt 'Herodot in Ägypten' *Genethliakon W. Schmid* (Stuttgart 1929), repr
Orbis (Freiburg 1960) 11–46 passim (selections in Marg 412–33)
5 See H. Fränkel (1951¹) 657–8 = (1962²) 603–5 (index) for an exposition of the
importance of this principle in various areas of early Greek thought. G.E.R.
Lloyd (1966) passim.
6 35.1, trans de Sélincourt; cf A.B. Lloyd (1975) 141–3; How and Wells I 179 at
2.35 for the similar views of other ancient authors.
7 See Raubitschek (1939) 217–22. The monuments exacted a credence that unseen
wonders and untestable explanations could not command. Herodotus
suspended belief before many 'tall' Egyptian stories, among them the tales of
the Nile's sources, the phoenix, and the identity of the female Colossi (28.1–2,
73, 131).

8 3.3.3*: τὰ μὲν ἄνω κάτω θήσω, τὰ δὲ κάτω ἄνω

9 Wells in How and Wells (1928) I 180 at 2.35.2. Furthermore, Herodotus was only too ready to swallow Egyptian heuristic claims: 'No Babylonians were present to controvert these preposterous claims ...' (Olmstead [1948] 320). He was perhaps too credulous for Egyptian self-restraint (ibid, 319). Certain of his errors follow from the probably brief duration of his Egyptian sojourn. Consequently, limited observation led to over-generalization. See C. Sourdille *La Durée et l'étendue du voyage d'Hérodote en Egypte* (Paris 1910) 5ff and Spiegelberg (1926) 14ff. Lloyd (1975) 61ff has fairly criticized some of Sourdille's results. For the historian's generally respectable record on Egypt and a forgivable lapse concerning the Ethiopians, see S.M. Burstein 'Herodotus and the emergence of Meroë' *JSSEA* 11 (1981) 1–5. Cf note 27 below.

10 So, eg, Fornara (1971) 18–21, who also argues for 'the *utter absence* in II of the moral or philosophical element' (18, his italics). As we shall see below, no book is more 'philosophical.'

11 Immerwahr (1966) 317; Pembroke (1967) 29–30

12 2.35.2–4, 36.3, 48.2. For female bestiality, noted as unique, 46.4. Herodotus was surprised that he encountered no Egyptian priestesses (35.4), and recorded this fact, as well as others that he did not and could not explain. Women, who appear 375 times in the *Histories*, occur twice as frequently in 1–4 as in 6–9: Dewald (1981) 92; Benardete (1969) 148. In the ethnologies and dramatic stories, where customs and symbols rather than unique political acts are central, women regain some of their real importance for social realities and individual psychology.

13 2.4.1, 4.180.4, 2.4.2 and 52.2–3. 2.167.3 suggests that Greek disdain for manual labour may have been learned from the Egyptians – or may just be human nature.

14 2.156.6, 49.2–3, 123.2. See Redfield (1985).

15 43.2, 49.2, 50.1, 51.1 (Heracles, Dionysus, Hermes), 82.1; 64.1. In respect for elders, only the Lacedaemonians can match the Egyptians (80.1).

16 This analysis of book 2 owes much to James Redfield: (1976) unpublished; (1985) 97–118.

17 142; 35.1; cf 148.2, 3.60

18 Benardete's (1969) provocative speculations on Herodotus' account of Egypt have been unduly neglected. See also Redfield (1985). The frequency of polemic in book 2 results from his logographic predecessors' energetic researches in that country of marvels – here he had books to argue with – as well as from the mirror image of Greek custom that that country offered for his aetiology of Greek success in maintaining local autonomy.

19 Cook (1976) 45

20 See Kleingünther (1933) 52–64. For instance, Solon and the Athenians decided

to borrow an Egyptian law and continue to use it since it was a helpful
innovation (2.177.2).

21 These barbarian laws are discussed by Benardete (1969) 11; less perceptively by
Schmid-Stählin I/2 (1934) 565–6.

22 Plutarch, *De malignitate Herodoti* 11–19 in *Moralia* 856E–858F, is wrong not in
calling him *philobarbaros*, but in condemning him for any statement that
does not glorify the Greeks. Plutarch as polemicist never cares to ask the source
or motive for Herodotus' inquiries into Near Eastern history and ethnography.
He bludgeons Herodotus for his doubts on Helen's role in the Trojan War, for
defending Busiris against a charge of human sacrifice (2.45), for criticizing
Menelaus for butchery, for blaming Persian pederasty on the Greeks, for
crediting the Egyptians as the source of much in Greek religion, for discrediting
Greek myths, for attacking the ancestry of Heracles, Dorian Kings, and the
Seven Sages, for abusing the Alcmaeonids, the Spartans at Thermopylae (!),
the Corinthians, the Athenians, the Ionians, and so on. In his enthusiastic
defamation, he also condemns Herodotus illogically for blackening the
memory of non-Greeks such as Croesus, Deioces, and Cyrus. A Greek writer
might be so chauvinistic and parochial, but Herodotus never was. This
puzzling essay by Plutarch has never received a thorough commentary dealing
with tone and intention as well as sources. See now G.B. Philipp ῎Αλλος
οὗτος ῾Ηρακλῆς, zu Plutarchus, *De malignitate Herodoti 13/14, 857*C–E
Gymnasium 89 (1982) 67ff.

23 Consult Cobet (1971) 158–68, with the review of R. Drews *Gnomon* 47 (1975)
329–34; also Immerwahr (1966) 31 note 48.

24 Apparent exceptions emphasize the absolute power of master over slave (4.3.4*)
and Zopyrus' devotion that equalled his master's power (3.154.2, 157.1 with
155.2*).

25 Benardete (1969) 4–6, 78–9, and chapter 3 passim, explores the paradoxical
qualities of royal, barbarian 'justice.'

26 4.28, 5.1, 59.1, 46.2–3, 59.1–2, 46.1, 82. Schmid-Stählin I/2 (1934) 566
overrate Herodotus' respect for the Scyths.

27 Their lack of noteworthy visible monuments and any literature and their failure
to pose a real threat to others kept them mysterious to the Greeks and
Romans. The Soviet excavations of Scythian burial mounds are now revealing
their material culture, but race, character, and language remain obscure. See,
for Herodotus, K. Meuli 'Scythica' *Hermes* 70 (1935) 121–76 (121–31 = Marg
455–70) with earlier bibliography; *From the Lands of the Scythians* (New
York 1975?), a catalogue of an exhibit at the New York Metropolitan Museum
of Art; Armayor (1978) 45–62, to be read with the refutation and
bibliography of Pritchett (1982) 234–85; also above, chapter 5 note 57.
Armayor's arguments about Herodotus' journeys return to the hypercriticism

of Sayce and Heidel (in modern times), an attempt to reject a sound account based on honest inquiry in favour of charges of fraud and mendacity. Schmid-Stählin I/2 (1934) 632 notes 1–2 provide a useful list of supposed blunders.

Armayor concludes (here and in a similar inquiry into whether Herdodotus ever went to Egypt [1978b 59–73]) that the author never visited the regions that he described, and that his only 'evidence' was fabulous literary, artistic, and oral tradition. Armayor and Fehling (1971) sceptically regard Herodotus' repeated assertions of autopsy as baseless claims, worthless guarantees, logographic lies suitable to the fictional genre.

28 Libya, likewise, has no monuments, no political consciousness (4.167.3, 197.1), and is subject more to the whims of harsh nature than to any human contrivance. Here too Persian aggression reached its limit without achieving the success it desired. As in Europe, the furthest Western limit of Persian arms is formulaically marked (4.204; 9.14). On the relation of the rivers Ister and Nile to Herodotus' development as an historian, cf von Fritz (1967) I.60–5, 143ff. On the Scyths, see Hartog (1979) 135–48, expanded in his *Le Miroir d'Hérodote: Essai sur la représentation de l'autre* (Paris 1980) part 1, an exploration of inversion, analogy, and polarity in the historian's presentation of non-Greeks.

29 Balcer (1972) 242–58; Pritchett (1982) 239–54 defends Herodotus' account of the geography of the Black Sea as well as his honest intentions and genuine efforts, throughout his researches, to determine the facts and the truth. Hartog (1979) 145–6 develops the Scyth-Athenian analogies. See also Hunter (1982) 207, 214.

30 Aeschylus employs the word neutrally to indicate alien or unintelligible speech (eg, *Persae* 635, *Agamemnon* 1051). Ten of fourteen occurrences appear in the *Persae* where dramatic logic demands that Persians use the term positively or neutrally. *Agamemnon* 919 furnishes the only clear case of pejorative connotation.

31 Hignett (1963) 33 so believed. Cf Legrande (1932) 93 who is more cautious. Herodotus notes that the Persians and Egyptians think themselves superior to all others (1.134.2, 2.121ζ2). Pisistratus' ruse at 1.60.3 provokes Herodotus' own sarcastic assertion concerning the lack of Greek and Athenian sophistication. At 1.58 *fin*, the Pelasgians are dismissed for lack of notable achievements, a fault that, for once, seems a result of their simply being barbarians.

32 Immerwahr (1966) 15; idem (1956) 279 (his italics)

33 1.142.1–2, 3.106.1; 4.46; 9.122.3–4; Hippocrates *De aere* 12, 23–4; Aristotle * *Politics* 7.7 = 1327b23–33. See Lateiner (1986) for discussion of similarities between the thought of the historian and the medical writers.

34 When Herodotus (1.93.2) describes the tomb of Alyattes, King of Lydia, as 'the greatest *ergon* by far except for those of the Egyptians and Babylonians,' it becomes evident that the Greeks are not even in competition.

35 An example of a statement that has been extended to a rule from a few isolated moments of observation.

36 7.9β2*, 138.1–2; *De aere* 23–4; Aristotle *Politics* 7.7 = 1327b23–6

37 Consult L. Camerer *Praktische Klugheit bei Herodot* (diss Tübingen 1965); *non vidi*. Grant (1983) 287–8.

38 7.102.1*, 8.111.3*. Curiously, both Mardonius and Xerxes seem to contradict the author by praising Greece for its agricultural wealth and productivity (7.5.3, 8α2*). Rather than contradiction, two points of view emerge. For the Greeks, the relative poverty, compared to more powerful neighbours, required stress; for the Persians, the relative profitability, compared to other subjected states, eg, the deserts of Bactria or Arabia, aroused interest.

39 7.102.1*, 5.92α1*, 5.78, 3.142.3*

40 Eg, 8.79.3*. See chapter 8.

41 For instance, he recognizes that Hellenes will show fear in the face of a foe (eg, 7.102.2*, 138.2, 139.2, 207), and some will bow to irresistible pressure (7.138.2, 152.3 [doubted], 8.73.3). Examples of faults could easily be multiplied, eg, 5.28, 97.3; 6.67.3, 98.2 on Hellenic responsibility for the Persian invasions.

42 Greek respect for the gods plays less of an explanatory role than royal Persian impiety (7.8γ1*, 35, 238.2; 8.53.2; 9.79*). Herodotus in his own voice gives minimal attention to divine causes (contrast 8.66 with the oft quoted 8.13, 65.2*, 109.3*). See chapter 9 for the gods as explanatory factors.

43 Krischer (1974) 93–100, based on Stein's references to Homer. Plescia (1972) 302–4

44 Cf Immerwahr (1966) 176–83 on Xerxes; 177 note 86 on 7.24; Drews (1973) 5.

CHAPTER 8

1 Kitto (1966) 320–1, 348–54; Redfield (1976) 2; idem (1985) 118

2 Redfield (1975) 58–66, 133

3 Cook (1976) 35; Drews (1973) 77. Critics rightly doubt whether accounts free from any interpretation are possible.

4 Redfield (1985) 102 for the quotation; Cook (1976) and idem 'Particular and general in Thucydides' *ICS* 10 (1985) 23–51

5 Immerwahr (1966) 176–7, 184. See A. Mantel *Herodotus Historien, Patronen en historische Werklijkeid bij Herodot* (Amsterdam 1976) for a reconsideration of patterning in Herodotus.

6 K.H. Waters (1971) 7, 85, 15, 99, 41, 90. See Diesner (1959) 212 on Herodotus' attitude towards autocrats; also Ferrill (1978). Gammie (1986) most soundly and thoroughly re-evaluates the treatment of kings and tyrants. See his conclusions (195).

7 Waters (1966) 169 on invented speeches as 'more genuinely historical'

8 Eg, K.H. Kinzl's review in *Gymnasium* 81 (1974) 104–5 complains of Waters'

hair-splitting, circular arguments, his reduction of the narrative to one dimension, and his lack of a coherent terminology for his critical approach. Gammie (1986) 187–90 generously comments on Waters' monograph.

9 Kitto (1966) 368

10 Cook (1976) 31, 35, 42. Thus the account of the Mermnads and Polycrates serve as cautionary tales, paradigms of historical action and relevant antecedents to the Great War, much as the Corcyrean and Plataean narratives do in Thucydides. Despite the former's inclusive and the latter's exclusive tendencies, the two historians share a dislike of facile schematization, though they do find recursive patterns in historical actions.

11 Immerwahr (1966) 87 notes a similarity between 3.80 and Pisistratus' career; Waters (1971) 58–9 briefly mentions this debate. John Gammie a decade ago suggested to me the value of comparing Otanes' speech and the career of Xerxes; cf his article (1986).

12 Wüst (1935) 47–52; H. Ryffel *Metabole Politeion* (1949; repr New York 1973) 64–73; Apffel (1957) argues for a Persian source and, on 9–23, offers an *Überblick* of scholarly opinion. Ostwald (1969) 178–9 presents a sane statement of the problems. See also Bringmann (1976) 266–79. An 'unofficial' Persian source seems most likely for the bare fact of a council-meeting. Herodotus' unique insistence on the reality of the conspirators' meeting and discussion suggests a Persian substrate for the story, and even more, a Persian informant for Herodotus. Perhaps Otanes' descendants preserved the outline, for he is presented as instigator of the conspiracy and ancestor of Persia's only free family (3.83.3).

13 Eg, K.F. Stroheker 'Zu den Anfängen der monarchischen Theorie in der Sophistik' *Historia* 2 (1953/4) 381ff, argues for Protagoras; Pohlenz (1937) 107, 123 note 1, 185–6 emphasizes Sophistic influence of some sort. Persian sources: Meyer (1892) 202; Apffel (1957) 96; Ostwald (1969) 178–9. Laserre (1976) 69 believes that Herodotus had a Persian source for the historical context but presents essentially Protagoras' arguments for different forms of government.

14 The philosophical vocabulary (cf Apffel [1957] 59–70) and form of the reflections probably cannot antedate the middle of the fifth century or originate from non-Greek sources, but the discoveries of G. Kirk and others on Greek myth, G. Anderson on the Greek novel, etc, encourage prudence in denying oriental influence on any branch of Greek thought. A.E. Raubitschek has challenged my own confidence in a purely Greek origin of the 'Debate,' pointing to 1 Samuel 8:10–18, an example of oriental reflections on kingship.

15 3.80.5: τὰ δὲ δὴ μέγιστα ἔρχομαι ἐρέων· νόμαιά τε κινέει πάτρια καὶ βιᾶται γυναῖκας κτείνει τε ἀκρίτους. Gammie (1986) 174 summarizes the autocrat's defects. Irresponsible power, 'unconstitutional' violence, and an

unaccountable administration of justice contribute to Prometheus' portrait of
the tyrant Zeus in Aeschylus (*Prometheus Vinctus* 149–50, 189–90, 324–6,
671–2, 735–7); G. Thomson *The Prometheus Bound* (Cambridge 1932) 6–9;
B.H. Fowler 'The imagery of the *Prometheus Bound' AJP* 78 (1957) 177–8.
On Aeschylus' politics, see A.J. Podlecki *The Political Background of
Aeschylean Tragedy* (Ann Arbor 1966) 103–18.

16 3.80.6: πάλῳ μὲν ἀρχὰς ἄρχει, ὑπεύθυνον δὲ ἀρχὴν ἔχει, βουλεύματα δὲ
πάντα ἐς τὸ κοινὸν ἀναφέρει. Although Otanes does not expressly mention
δημοκρατίη, his proposal embodies several essential elements found in
democracy (πλῆθος δὲ ἄρχον). I believe that Herodotus approves of all
governments that promote political equality, but here suggests that 'isonomie
and the institutions which manifest it in the Debate are perhaps found most
consistently in ... democracies' (so Ostwald [1969] 111–13). Vlastos (1964)
2–3, arguing that the noun 'democracy' had not yet been coined, states that
'Isonomia is identified with democracy in the most positive and unmistakable
way.' The collocation of 3.83.1 and 6.43.3 supports his view, because when the
latter refers to the Debate about *isonomia*, Otanes' proposal is identified by
the term δημοκρατέεσθαι. The historian emphasized political rights, not
merely equality before the law, in Otanes' analysis of *isonomie* (Vlastos 15–17).
The term, then, refers to self-government, or access to self-government, here
democracy. The term's links with democracy can be illustrated from Thucydides
and Plato (13–17, 22–33, esp 33). Mere equality before the law does not
preclude despotic regimes, as Deioces' career demonstrates (1.100.1).

17 81.1–2: ἀξύνετος, ὠθέει τε ἐμπεσών, ἀχρήϊος. These criticisms are also
exemplified by the narrative. The political gullibility of the reputedly sophisticated Athenians provokes Herodotus' scorn (1.60.3; 5.97.2). Reasonable men
regard 'the people' as unreliable in judgment (3.81.1–2*, 82.4*); tyrants regard
the *demos* as 'the most unpleasant housemate' (συνοίκημα ἀχαριτώτατον,
7.156.3).

18 Most Greek governments were *de facto* oligarchies, but that is not the present
concern. Wüst (1935) 54, 62, discusses the short shrift oligarchy receives.
Vlastos (1964) 5 note 2 believes that the brevity of Megabyzus' speech results
chiefly from Otanes' having already stated the case against monarchy, but he
does not explain why Otanes has left oligarchy for Darius to discuss. The brief
Persian oligarchy's few reported actions undercut Megabyzus' endorsement.
The conspirators assassinate one ruler, fail to agree on a suitable regime, and
allow one of their number to secede from politics. The hasty manner in
which they dissolve their junta and select a monarch, however unhistorical,
suggests the author's doubts about the stability of oligarchies. Darius'
fraudulent success confirms that negative judgment, a view that Darius has
already presented in his speech. The *Histories'* preceding and subsequent narra-

tive never explicitly praises any oligarchical régime. When Sparta or Corinth is praised, it is not for the form of government (as defined in this debate).

19 Benardete (1969) 84, 86 and note 35, 87, recognizes that Darius mocks and destroys the Persian traditions of truth and thereby trust. See also Apffel (1957) 28 who observes that his sophistic half-argument – he 'proves' the inevitability of monarchy, not its preferability – ignores all moral values (29). Other statements hostile to democratic government, most of which fall by their own weight, are put in the mouths of Xerxes (7.103*, 237*) and of Gelon (7.156.3, 162.1*).

20 Cf Aristotle *Politics* 3.7.5 = 1279b5ff. In fact, Otanes' criticisms apply better to Greek tyrannies than to Persia's theocratic kingship; Bringmann (1976) 270.

21 Cambyses states as much in his death-bed prayer: 3.65.7; cf 1.210.2*.

22 See Waters' appendix (1971) 42–4 for a tabulation.

23 See, eg, How and Wells II app xvi 338–47; A. Andrewes *The Greek Tyrants* (London 1956); H. Berve *Die Tyrannis bei den Griechen* (Munich 1967). There are several incidental remarks in favour of autocrats: Cyrus (3.82.5*, 7.2.3*; cf 1.210.2*), Gelon (7.154.2, 156.2; cf 3.125.2), Hamilcar (7.166), Polycrates (3.125.2). Tyrants, however, are assumed to be brutal, selfish, and violent (eg, 3.48.2, 7.156.2) unless proven otherwise, when good behaviour elicits Herodotus' surprised praise (eg, 1.59.6).

24 Cf Aristotle *Politics* 5.11 = 1313b24; Diesner (1959) 217–28 cannot reconcile the favourable judgment of 3.125.2 with this silence. One cannot safely generalize about the extent to which Herodotus' various *logoi* were influenced by popular legends and his informants' prejudices. The Corinthians utterly condemned their former tyrants, but in Samos the sentiments of the historian's aristocratic (?) friends (?) were more ambivalent. Polycrates' thalassocracy and public works were applauded, while his Medism and tyrannical form of government were not. Direct praise of the tyrant (for the honourable burial of a Spartan or for his engineering feats: 3.55.2 and 60) was 'bad form,' yet Samian patriots exonerated his expedient desertion of the Egyptian alliance and nostalgically admired the pre-eminent position which the tyranny had won for the island (3.39.3–4, 122.2). Herodotus' unfavourable judgments on Aristagoras and the Ionian revolt, his accounts of the battle of Lade and the Samian colony at Zancle, and his emphasis on the Samian role in bringing about the Greek campaign of 479 that led to the battle of Mycale suggest strong Samian influence, especially in books 5–6. Equivocal sentiments in both informant and author may explain inconsistencies of judgment in the Samian *logos*; see B.M. Mitchell 'Herodotus and Samos' *JHS* 95 (1975) 75–91. On Lade and Herodotus' alleged Samian bias, see Lateiner (1982) 151–7.

25 Pearson (1954) 141. The Polycrates *logos* is similarly dominated by popular legend; Diesner (1959) 218–19 and note 22. J.-P. Vernant 'From Oedipus to

275 Notes to page 171

Periander: Lameness, tyranny, incest in legend and history' *Arethusa* 15 (1982) 19–38 discusses legendary models for Herodotus' tyrants and their social isolation.

26 Pearson (1954) 141–2; Wüst (1935) 59–60. Deioces presents a partial exception; see below.

27 See Benardete (1969) 136 with his note 5 for the concentration on tyrannies in book 5. Clisthenes of Sicyon is impressive as a person but maliciously subverts traditions (5.67); the tyrants of Corinth are paradigms of inversion (92*, Socles' account); and Aristagoras destroys peace for personal gain, drawing in Naxos, Ionia, and the rest of Greece (30.5*, 35.2, 37.1, 124). Histiaeus' reported motives appear to have been no better (35.4).

28 Pharaoh Amasis receives a flattering portrait, probably because of his personal popularity in Egypt and his position as the last monarch during Egypt's final period of national independence. Herodotus' informants had no complaints of him, and Herodotus, since no control was here available, repeats what he had been told.

29 This presentation follows from the national prejudices of his Egyptian sources, especially the self-serving accounts of the Egyptian priests. Cambyses, for instance, probably respected local cults in all the provinces and probably did not kill the Apis calf.

30 This refutes Waters (1971) 56, 70, part II in general. See Olmstead (1948) chapters 6, 10, 16, 20 for the positive aspects of these kings. Even Darius meets more blame than praise in the *Histories*. Not charismatic, divinely chosen, or even honest in word, deed, or principle, his single-minded pursuit of power among the Persians is related in a detached, semi-amused manner. Compared to Cambyses and Xerxes, nevertheless, his rule seemed rational and successful.

31 Darius, for instance, advises others to 'lie when you must,' a sentiment at variance with reported Persian custom (3.72.4–5* and 1.136.2). The discrepancy reveals the autocrat's perversion of his nation's *nomoi* and ought not to be explained merely as a result of different sources (*sic* W. Aly *Formprobleme der frühen griechischen Prosa, Philologus* Supplementband 21/3 [1929] 139). While no evidence proves that Herodotus had seen or had reported to him the Behistun inscription, Darius' own composition, which is filled with condemnations of his opponents as personified 'lies' and liars, and which asserts that when Smerdis was murdered, 'the lie became great in the land,' the two versions of events and the names are remarkably close. Whatever his sources, the words that Herodotus puts in Darius' mouth are a delicious irony, because of the strong Persian condemnation of lying in all circumstances (1.136.2, 138.1).

For the Behistun inscription, text and translation, see R.H. Kent *Old Persian: Grammar, Texts and Lexicon* (New Haven 1950), Olmstead (1948) 108–18, and

Burn (1962) 96–105. This official propaganda, intended to impress, remade history as Darius wished. Its general effectiveness in becoming the Authorized Version is evident in Herodotus' 'account [which] differs only in details' (Cameron [1955] 91; Burn [1962] 120). These Herodotean details, however, are important for the historian's characterization of Darius as one whose bluffing, moral relativism, and Machiavellian power-seeking gained him an empire. Darius, the unscrupulous huckster (3.89.3), could not function in Herodotus, as he does in Aeschylus, as the voice of wisdom. Few wise advisers are functioning autocrats, although Cyrus serves this purpose at the end. The portrait of Darius, in contrast to the narrative of dynastic succession, differs sharply from the god-chosen, charismatic, dynastically legitimate figure of the Behistun inscription. See Bringmann (1976) 266–79, esp 276–9; I. Gershevitch 'The false Smerdis' *AAHung* 27 (1979) 337-51; Lewis (1985) 102–3.

32 The twelve words with δίκη in their stem in 1.96.2–97.1, twenty-two lines of text, emphasize how a legitimate concern for access to justice can lead to an illegitimate and repressive form of government. Deioces illustrates both Darius' theory of the inevitability of autocracy and Otanes' severe criticisms of the autocrat's disruption of politics and misuse of power. Deioces' continued regard for justice among his subjects comfortably coexists with his own despotic elevation: he makes himself invisible to his people, punishes laughter in his presence, and sets spies all over his dominion (1.99–100). Deception is thematic in Herodotus when Greek and oriental despots pursue power. See the previous note. Pisistratus, Gelon, the Magus, and especially Darius gain power by deceiving their fellows.

33 'The justice of kings is understood by themselves, and even by their subjects, with an ample indulgence for the gratification of passion and interest'; Gibbon *Decline and Fall* chapter 42.

34 In a consideration of Herodotus' use of the words *tyrannos, basileus, monarchos*, and their cognates, Ferrill (1978) 385–98 demolishes the view that *tyrannos* is a neutral term merely meaning 'ruler.' 'Tyrant' always denotes an arbitrary and despotic ruler, even when, like oriental kings, they come to power legitimately. *Monarchos* is a carefully employed neutral term. Herodotus distinguishes the terms even in *oratio recta* to colour a situation or to characterize the dangers of speaking truth to power. See J.L. O'Neil 'The semantic usage of *tyrannos* and related words' *Antichthon* 20 (1986) 26–40 for a wider study that reaches similar conclusions for Herodotus' idiom.

35 Myres (1953) 150; 150 note 1 lists the principal physical outrages commanded by despots.

36 Sancisi-Weerdenburg (1983) analyses the role of Persian women in the *Histories*. She credits Herodotus with the least steriotyped Persian women and

the most generous portraits among Greek historiographers, but he, like later Greek writers, had no better sources than Persian oral tradition and legend, not personal experience. Certain principal points, however, are confirmed by inscriptions (25) or other accounts, and if modern knowledge of Persian history and custom is thin, Persian values do penetrate the Greek literary accounts.

37 Immerwahr (1966) 195, 87, 77. Yet royal accession is a frequent narrative motif and magnet for illustrative anecdotes. Note that all the accessions of Persian kings require palace intrigues.

38 Fornara (171) 22; Gigante (1956) 116 (= Marg 260). The Achaemenids systematically disfigured their enemies and their images: Nylander (1980) 329–33. Torture of defeated leaders and damage to their conquered images allowed the Achaemenids real and symbolic revenge and furnished a warning to neighbours and potential rebels. Herodotus used their technique of propaganda to bolster his presentation of the savage, inhuman violence of the oriental despot (3.80.4*).

39 The more sympathetically portrayed tyrant Croesus had treated his victims no better: 'He displaced and scattered the Syrians although they were guilty of no wrong' (1.26.3, 76.2).

40 Evans (1961) 109–11 shows the importance of this speech for the *Histories*; also von Fritz (1967) I, 252ff; Solmsen (1974) 7–9. Orlin (1976) 255–66 tries to reconstruct the authentic Persian view of the war of 480 BCE. If the historicity of the treaty between Athens and Persia, c 507 BCE be accepted (eg, Raubitschek [1964] 151–4), Xerxes' campaign was a Zoroastrian crusade against rebel vassals to restore 'truth' and order, a war incumbent on the Persian monarch for reasons other than those of Herodotus, but incidentally part of the effort that Herodotus mentions to make the earthly empire resemble that of the cosmos (Orlin 263; cf Herodotus 7.8γ2).

41 Waters (1971) 69 for the first formulation; for the more accurate second, Fornara (1971) 90. The latter, however, overstates 'the cancerous nature of imperialism' in Herodotus' work (88). Even the epilogue at 9.122 argues not against imperialism, but against growing weak through self-indulgence and losing control of one's subjects. Cf G. de Ste Croix, review of Fornara *EHR* 88 (1973) 158.

42 See Strasburger (1955) 25 (= Marg 608) and Erbse (1955) 109 note 34; *contra* the 'Athenian fanatic partisan' of Meyer (1899) II 97 and Jacoby (1913) 356–9.

43 This statement of Spartan heroism at 7.139.3 is modified by section 4 where Spartan Medism is envisioned as a possibility.

44 Fornara (1971) 50, and note 25, referring to Macan (1908) at 7.209 on Sparta; on Corinth, Legrande (1932) 106–9

45 See Legrande (1932) 94; Gigante (1956) 124–5; Ostwald (1969) 108–9 on ἐλευθερίη.

46 Cf Solmsen (1974) 25. Drexler (1972) 144–61 oddly denies that Herodotus

praises the Greeks for their love of freedom (esp 160, criticizing K. von Fritz 'Die griechische ἐλευθερίη bei Herodot' *WS* 78 [1965] 5–31).

47 See How and Wells II 40 and 359–60 on Alcmaeonid Medizing; *contra* R.D. Cromey 'Kleisthenes' Fate' *Historia* 28 (1979) 132–3; Raubitschek (1964) 151–4, on the reality of the treaty; Fr. Schachermeyr 'Athen als Stadt der Grosskoenigs' *GB* 1 (1973) 211–20, on its consequences; Orlin (1976) 255–7, on the tendentious nature of this section of Herodotus' narrative. Herodotus does not report Clisthenes' archonship under the tyrants when defending the Alcmaeonids against charges of Medism and co-operation with the tyrants (6.121, 123; see R. Meiggs and D. Lewis *A Selection of Greek Historical Inscriptions* [Oxford 1969] 11–12 for the archonship). The historian records nothing of Clisthenes after the reforms. His disappearance from the political record may well be fortuitous, or a conscientious choice on his part to retire in order that his isonomic government might stand on its own. On this last point, Cromey 139–46, who compares Solon, Demonax, and Cadmus. Herodotus' reticence about this period seems intentional.

48 Van Ooteghem (1940) 311–14; Mitchell (1975) 79–82

49 Hohti (1974) 19–28. The fine for Phrynichus' *Capture of Miletus* (6.21.2) was an exceptional restriction on Athenian free speech, but the circumstances involved state religious ritual, not political debate.

50 Artabanus, however, when he awakened from his frightening vision, was too excited for court etiquette and blurted out his vision to nephew Xerxes (7.18.1).

51 Cf Aeschylus *Persae* 591–4, fear of speaking freely to a monarch; Euripides *Supplices* 435–41, the freedom that democracy affords.

52 Immerwahr (1966) 307, 313–14; Plescia (1972) 310–11. Note how verbal contention concerning the Greek combatant who most advanced the Hellenic cause best illuminates Themistocles' services (8.123–4).

53 Plescia (1972) 302–4

54 Immerwahr (1966) 199, 213

55 Cf Plescia (1972) passim.

56 Strasburger (1955) and Waters (1972), eg, deny any partisan attitude towards the Athenian government. Even if Otto Regenbogen was right in finding no ideological consistency in the *Histories*, 'eine einheitliche politische Haltung Herodots zu konstruieren ist unmöglich' ('Herodot und sein Werk' *Die Antike* 6 [1930] 202–48, this quotation also on Marg 84), it is wrong to deny him any political inclinations, as Wüst (1935) 38 does. See W.G. Forrest 'Herodotos and Athens' *Phoenix* 38 (1984) 1–11 who attributes to the historian 'superhuman open-mindedness' without denying sympathy for Cimon and the Alcmaeonids in Athens, and for the dual hegemony in international politics.

57 See Gigante (1956) 115–17 (= Marg 259–61); the author of *De aere* 16 expresses similar ideas.

58 Waters (1971) 85. Gammie (1986) 174, 195 presents a more measured view, although he inclines to the other extreme, regarding Herodotus' portraits of kings and tyrants as less objective history than illustrations of a conventional model or norm (185).

59 Immerwahr (1966) 45, 199, 307

60 Political ineffectiveness can have other causes. The Scyths, and the Medes before Deioces, had no cities, no central government, and consequently no power with which to expand or to confront enemies (4.46.2–3; 1.96.2 and 98.3, Ecbatana founded). See Ostwald (1972) 283–6; Wood (1972) 39 note 30.

61 A. Toynbee *A Study of History* (Oxford 1946, abridgment) I 85–8, 199, 202, 190–1. Gibbon on 'immoderate greatness' argues similarly; *Decline and Fall*, chapter 38 end, 'General Observations.'

CHAPTER 9

1 Redfield (1975) chapter 1, esp 54

2 Drews (1973) 77; Fornara (1971) 35, his italics

3 Collingwood (1946) 23

4 Fränkel (1951^1) 438–52; G.E. Lloyd (1966) 341–4; A.B. Lloyd (1975) 164

5 Immerwahr (1956) 243–7 provides the fundamental account of Herodotean causation. Some passages do not support his argument that '*Aitie* is used only in a human (ethical) context, and nearly always ... blame is attached' (244 and note 7). 2.91.6; 3.139.1; 4.167.3; and 6.3, have αἰτίη as explanation, cause, or political charge. See also 3.108.4; 4.30.1–2; 7.125, αἴτιον as biological cause.

6 2.123.1; 3.3.1; 4.5.1, a variant reading; 4.95.5; 1.214.5, 3.9.2 (*bis*)

7 Pagel (1927) first applied systematically the principles of *tisis* and analogy to Herodotus. On the latter, see G.E. Lloyd (1966) 341–4; Immerwahr (1966) 315, 15, for the two quotations. Fish can reverse gender roles (2.93.2), men can choose to do everything in a way opposite to others (2.35.2), rivers can go into reverse (2.19.3), and – in a speaker's strong trope – even heaven and earth can switch roles (5.92α*).

8 Lévi-Strauss (1967b) 42

9 Wood (1972) 19–20 notes this point.

10 Artabanus analogizes Xerxes' Greek expedition to Darius' Scythian (7.10γ*); Scyth messengers compare Darius' pretences to his actions and arrive at the truth by analogy (4.118.2–5). See also G.E. Lloyd (1966) 344; A.B. Lloyd (1976) at 2.19–34; Lateiner (1987) 99–100.

11 See Kennedy (1963) 44–7, who is interested only in the rhetoric; G.E. Lloyd (1966) 424 on the probably interpolated chapter 7.239. On εἰκός in fifth-century thought, consult J. Finley *Three Essays on Thucydides* (Cambridge,

Mass. 1967) and Fr. Solmsen *Intellectual Experiments of the Greek Enlightenment* (Princeton 1975) 123ff, 222ff, 230.

12 See A.B. Lloyd (1975) 149–53 for additional examples.

13 Chapters 2–4 above consider stories and explanations that Herodotus dismisses as unworthy of credence for various reasons.

14 Pagel (1927) develops these hypotheses in chapter 3, pp. 29–40. On revenge, de Romilly (1971); on analogical symmetry, consult von Fritz (1967) I 138–9. Or as the obscure Heraclitus said (*Vors* B 51): 'They do not realize how coming apart it fits together with itself. There is a harmony of counter-stretched tension just as with the bow or lyre.'

15 Persian *hybris* disturbs the land and water of the natural world (Athos, the Hellespont, and Trojan and Thracian rivers: 7.22.3, 34–6, 43, 108), troubles the human world (war, human sacrifice, and movements of population; 3.93.2, 159.2; 5.15.3; 6.119, 7.114), and even would affront the divine realm ('equality with Zeus,' 7.8γ2*).

16 So too Protagoras may have argued (Plato *Protagoras* 320e–21a, with a vocabulary unusual for Platonic discussion). Cf Pagel (1927) 32–3.

17 ἡ δὲ θήλεα τίσιν ἀποτίνει τῷ ἔρσενι.

18 οὐδεὶς ἀνθρώπων ἀδικῶν τίσιν οὐκ ἀποτίσει (5.56.1*, oracle); cf *Iliad* 3.351–4*, *Odyssey* 20.392–4.

19 Gomme (1954) 81, a cautious student of of the prudence of Thucydides, terms Herodotus' views on prosperity, *hybris*, etc, not primitive belief but 'the result of *observation* of human affairs' (his italics).

20 See Ostwald (1969) 107–13, 135, 167. For *isokratie*, a political word of considerable interest (cf 4.26.2), see idem (1972) 277–91.

21 As Immerwahr (1966) occasionally does. See, eg, the review by R. Drews in *AJP* 90 (1969) 89–92; or Waters (1971) 5 note 9, 7, 41, 99–100.

22 See Pippidi (1960) 75–92 for one useful analysis; de Romilly (1971) 314–37 for another, as well as Immerwahr (1966) passim. De Ste Croix' (1977) three systems of causation (moral/Gods, immoral/Nemesis, and amoral/Fate or δεῖ γενέσθαι, κ.τ.λ.) deserve to be better known, especially by those who believe that Herodotus' gods play a large role in his history. We agree on the historian's emphasis of man's moral choice and (therefore) historical responsibility (141–3) but disagree on how religious a man the author was.

23 Hellman (1934) 9, 13, 117–19 = Marg 48ff; Pippidi (1960) 80–1, Waters (1971) 99, and de Ste Croix (1977) 139 deprecate it. See Immerwahr (1966) 313–14 for a brief exposition. H. Lloyd-Jones *The Justice of Zeus* (Berkeley and Los Angeles 1971) 68–70 argues that Herodotean φθόνος has been refined and made moral, representing not malice but just retribution on evil men. Versnel (1977) 36–9 detheologizes Polycrates' tale, placing it in the context of folktales of talisman, substitute sacrifice, and inescapable fate.

24 As Pippidi (1960) 87–9 suggests he does, despite Herodotus' endorsement, 1.34.1. Legrande (1932) 135–6 successfully reconciles Herodotus' coexisting conceptions of divinity, described in the text as systems one and four, namely divine jealousy and equipoise.

25 1.32.1, 9*; 3.40.2*; 7.10ϵ*, 46.4*; 8.109.3*. None of the 16 other occurrences of the words for jealousy, φθονερός, φθονέω, or φθόνος, refers to gods. Six refer to despots, ten refer to an individual or to mankind in general.

26 De Romilly (1971) 316. In fact, Herodotus and Hecataeus, on the basis of what they had learned in Egypt, pushed back the limit between divine and human history by approximately 10,000 years (2.142–5). The new boundary between the divine and the human epoch contradicted the usual ancient claims that found divine participation ubiquitous in human affairs; cf Linforth (1924) 292. In the *Histories*, specific divinities are invoked less than τὸ θεῖον, and τὸ θεῖον much less than human motive and act. Never does Herodotus allege or corroborate a god's visible interference in any human event.

27 In his copy of Herodotus, Gibbon wrote at 1.91, 'I should like to know, how much Herodotus received from the priests of Delphi.'

28 Pagel (1927) 39–40 lists relevant passages. Pippidi (1960) 82–3 discusses the absence of a moral dimension in these passages; de Romilly (1971) 317, and note 2, the effort to discover political causes.

29 Immerwahr (1954) 32–3 argues that the contrast between choice and necessity is unresolved in Herodotus. Insofar as Immerwahr here refers to *divine* necessity, Xerxes' puzzling dream should not be seen as decisive for the invasion of Greece. Xerxes does indeed choose to invade Hellas, and chooses rationally, as Solmsen (1974) 22 demonstrates; cf Gomme (1954) 109; de Ste Croix (1977) 141.

30 Only once (5.33.2) do we hear that something was fated *not* to happen; Naxos was fated not to meet destruction at the hands of *Megabates'* expedition. How did Herodotus know? The island then survived, although later (6.96) Datis' force easily captured and burnt the city. Given Naxos' situation, no other 'fate' was then possible.

31 Herodotus' interest in oracles and in their fulfilment in unexpected ways provides another group of popular traditions that he chose to report. His delight in the 'providence' of oracles presents an issue separate from the role of gods as historical cause. Once we excise the Salamis oracle and its context (8.77), the author's endorsement of – as opposed to willingness to report – such vaticination becomes less clear. Krüger and Powell expel the entire chapter for its abrupt transition, anomalous vocabulary, dislocated syntax, unique formulae, and 'delirious' (*sic*, Powell ad loc) expression. Whenever Delphic or Delian tradition appears in the *Histories*, so do divine explanations. Forrest (1979)

311–12 disposes of alleged divine explanation at 6.105; 8.13, 129; the tale of Polycrates (3.40–3) is unique in its implausible divine motivation, but Versnel (1977) has accounted for the folktale aspects of this unusual story with unusual vocabulary.

32 A point reinforced, as Immerwahr (1966) 22 and Solmsen (1974) 7 observe, by the catalogue of Darius' satrapies and revenues (3.89, 97).

33 Canfora (1972) 21–8, 49. For a reasonable qualification concerning Herodotus' reliability as a researcher, consult Jacoby (1913) 474, 478–9; for an accusation of pure fiction, see Fehling (1971) passim. Gabba (1981) 50–62 describes the truly pseudo-historical literature of antiquity. It remains unclear how much archaeological confirmation of Herodotus' statements of what he saw himself is needed to persuade the extreme sceptics of the historian's *bona fides*. Grant (1983) discusses Herodotus' critical method.

34 See Flory (1979) 411–21, esp 419; R. Munson 'The celebratory purpose of Herodotus: the story of Arion in *Histories* 1.23–24' *Ramus* 15 (1986) 93–104. Pearson (1941) 348 compares his limited scepticism in the areas of natural history and geography (*contra* Hecataeus) to his higher standards in recent political history. Von Fritz (1936) perceived a maturation from mere empiricism and rationalism to scepticism and the withholding of judgments. Müller (1981) 313.

35 Cf Linforth (1928) 218–23, 236. Some suspect the influence of Hecataeus here. The religious beliefs of Herodotus must be left for another discussion, but see Müller (1981) 316–17, who, exceptionally, finds agnosticism in his statements, scepticism towards reported divine interference, and an inclination to report but not seek enlightenment from oracles.

36 Cf further Hignett (1963) app xiv; Powell *Lexicon* (1938) *sv*, 3 and 4; also συμβαίνειν as at 7.166 (simultaneity of the battles of Himera and Salamis). Herodotus' belief in retribution does not lead to easy but ill-grounded connections or combinations of events. See 7.133.2 where Herodotus explicitly dissociates an Athenian diplomatic crime from Athens' subsequent devastation; see Hellman (1934) 9–10 (= Marg 48–50) esp note 9. The presence of these explicit synchronisms should not revive the corpse of the naive and awestruck churchgoing philosopher. All of them are historically trivial, and Herodotus does not dwell on them. 9.100.2 seems exceptional, until one notes that the subject is the army's superstition, and its effects, not Herodotus' explanation.

37 As Meyer (1899) noted, 252–4 (= Marg 11–14)

38 The author of *Regimen* 4.87 allows for prayer so long as it does not interfere with medical treatment.

39 Denied: the phoenix' burial of parents, goat-men, lycanthropy (2.73.3; 4.25, 105). Doubted: Salmoxis and Pythagoras; Boreas; Thetis (4.94–6; 7.189,

191). Rationalized: the 'sacred' disease, earthquake (3.33; 7.129). Others'
authority: the 'female' disease, offences against the sun, the diggers' injuries at
Cnidus' canal, Pan's surprise appearance (1.105, 138, 174.3–6; 6.106).
Distancing *oratio obliqua*: Pheros' blindness; transmigration of souls;
Hamilcar's disappearance (2.111, 123.2; 7.167.1). Historical alternatives: death
of Pheretime, Cleomenes (4.205; 6.84).

    G.E. Lloyd *Magic, Reason and Experience* (Cambridge 1979) 26–32; [Hipp.]
De morbo sacro 22. Lloyd employs Herodotus as an example of the persistence
of traditional beliefs, although recognizing his interest in explaining natural
phenomena as obeying natural laws.

40 Legrande (1932) 133–4. Dodds (1951) 30–1 and 42, also quickly dismisses
Herodotus' thinking as 'overdetermined,' 'doubly determined,' full of 'popular
fatalism,' and 'religious anxiety.'

41 Eg, Löwith (1949) 191–203, esp 198

42 1.13.2, 19–22; 6.86*; 7.137.1–2; 8.129.3; 9.65.2, 100.2. Such divine τίσις
is not to be confused with a solely human desire for revenge, eg, 2.152.3,
4.118.4, 5.79.1, 6.84.2. See further, on divine intervention, Legrande (1932)
135–6. The first person pronouns (ἐμοί) recognize the subjective element in
asserting supernatural incursions and suggest the limited epistemological
authority of such an opinion. Cf Ligota (1982) 9 with note 43.

43 Sinko (1959/60) 8–9; Legrande (1932) 134–5. Lateiner (1980) 30–2 analyses
Herodotus' precise use of this idiom to indicate not his own, but his
characters' confidence in a divine dispensation.

44 De Romilly (1971) 318, 334, denies that Herodotus believes in a system
of divine compensation. Rather, vengeance is 'plutôt ... une liaison commode
qu'une analyse sérieuse.' Immerwahr (1956) 253 had already noted that
'Vengeance ... is also the primary means of tying events together.'
De Romilly's examples of 'prétextes narratifs' (319–26) show that vengeance
is not a *sufficient* cause, that political causes also appear. The accounts
of storms at 7.188–91 and 8.13 mention divine causes, but such hypotheses
are irrelevant to Herodotus' inquiry into human responsibility for the Greek
victory.

45 Immerwahr (1954) 33–5. The reader, not Herodotus, must supply any
theological interpretation to Xerxes' dream. Thus, Herodotus notes a man's or a
nation's prosperity before a calamity to signal to the reader by the use of
certain words that someone's prosperity was soon to be terminated. See Lateiner
(1982) 97–101.

46 De Romilly (1971) 326–33 expresses the essentials. Cf de Ste Croix (1977)
141–4; Grant (1983) 292.

47 Solmsen (1974) 9; 12–19; Legrande (1932) 134 regards Herodotus as hostile to
the view that sees 'man as a passive plaything of destiny.'

48 Herodotus introduces the tale with the doubting καὶ δή κου and the distancing ὡς λέγεται ὑπὸ Περσέων. Solmsen (1974) 21–3 sees this and compares the phantom in Aeschylus' *Persians* who does not at all lessen man's responsibility. Hermogenes (*De ideis* II 421 Spengel) regards Xerxes' colloquies with Artabanus as the summit of literary sublimity.

49 Note that even Artabanus later minimized the vision's importance, and returned to his former negative judgment on Xerxes' expedition (7.47.2*; Solmsen [1974] 21). Cf 1.204.2: Cyrus' decision to attack Tomyris.

50 De Romilly (1971) 326; Forrest (1979) 312, 320–21: political explanations are presented but not developed. That Miltiades' expedition against the Parians is given a political explanation only as *pretext* and a personal motive as the real explanation, seems historiographically regressive, but here, and elsewhere in a subsidiary story with Cimonids and Themistocles, one encounters 'forensic evidence' (Wade-Gery's useful term), recollections of the subsequent political battle in court, rather than Herodotus' analysis.

51 Solmsen (1974) 23, de Ste Croix (1977) 144–5 on the dream. This demonstrated diversity answers the assertion of Diesner (1959) 216, that Herodotus is interested only in individual psychology, not in major political issues.

52 Myres (1953) 47

53 E.H. Carr *What is History?* (New York 1961) 124; de Romilly (1971) 335

54 Jacoby (1913) 482, followed by Hignett (1963) 35–6, overstates Herodotus' theological cast of mind.

55 Myres (1953) 51–2

56 The noun τύχη appears 14 times in Herodotus' text, but 40 times in Thucydides', which is of comparable length. On Polybius' notorious dependence on the noun, see Walbank (1957) 16–26. See chapter 10, notes 28–29, for further references.

57 Hignett (1963) 36

58 Von Fritz in Hardt (1958) 26; idem (1967) I 249; Solmsen (1974) 19 and note 52; Immerwahr (1954) 39–40, 43–4.

59 Nevertheless Solmsen (1974) 13 note 34 reasonably emphasizes that the dream-vision's reappearance for Artabanus precludes a wholly secular and political meaning. A clue is provided by the psychologist's concept of 'overdetermina-tion,' applied by Dodds (1951) 7, 30–1, to archaic Greek thought and to Herodotus specifically. He compares Homer's Patroclus who attributes his death to an immediate agent Euphorbus, a divine will (Apollo's), and subjectively to his own bad μοῖρα (*Iliad* 16.849–50). For Croesus, we have the political foe Cyrus, the divine φθόνος (= *nemesis*) of Apollo working contrarily, and Croesus' own imperialist actions committed under the influence of ἄτη. The parallel is not exact, but it suggests how reductive is the modern dichotomy of free-will/determinism. Daniel Tompkins has suggested to me that even

Thucydides presents 'over-determination' of events: eg, Athens fails at Syracuse because of (1) bad political judgment (6.31), (2) *hybris* in reaching
always for more (6.10.5*; cf F.M. Cornford *Thucydides Mythistoricus* [London
1908]), (3) the manifestations of τύχη such as an eclipse (7.50.4), and because
(4) 'everything by nature eventually declines' (2.64.3*). Linear and simple
sequences of cause and effect were not the aim of all ancient historians.

60 Legrande (1932) 229–30; Evans (1961) 190–1; cf Redfield (1975) 91: 'Error is
imposed on the actor by the limitations or contradictions of his culture; he is
more or less forced to go wrong.'

61 Immerwahr (1956) 255–7, 264; Solmsen (1974) 5

62 See above, p 197, for an examination of Fate as a subsequent historical judgment
rather than as a causal and metaphysical explanation.

63 Wardman (1961) 145–7; cf 5.28, 97.3; 6.67.3.

64 Linforth (1928) 231. At both 1.91.6 and 1 ἁμαρτάς appears, but Powell *sv*
marks the distinction, and Herodotus carefully defines Gyges' crime.

65 See LSJ⁹ *sv*. On the ἁμαρτα- stem, see M. Ostwald, 'Aristotle on 'AMAPTIA
and Sophocles' "Oedipus Tyrannus"' *Festschrift ... E. Kapp* (Hamburg 1958)
93–108. Aἴτιος and related words develop from 'culpability' to 'responsibility'
to 'cause,' and 'explanation' in general.

66 Legrande (1932) 136 argues that Herodotus is inconsistent in his assignment of
motives, when he implies that ὕβρις is a cause for divine interference in
human affairs.

67 Cook (1976) 63–4; Pippidi (1960) 75–80; Solmsen (1974) 23; Legrande (1932)
133. *Contra,* Burn (1969) 130 alleges that Herodotus shows a 'lack of any but
the most primitive ideas on historical causation.'

68 Immerwahr (1956) 253, 280. The richness of explanation in the Lydian *logos*
may result from Croesus' being too remote for Herodotus to have much
accurate information, as Wardman (1961) 149–50 suggests. Solmsen (1974) 5
note 11 underrates Herodotus' awareness of political motivation.

69 As it does for Jacoby (1913) 479–83; How at 7.139.5; Pohlenz (1937) 162;
Hignett (1963) 35–9 with earlier literature; Grant (1983) 292. Better:
Hauvette (1894) 502; Legrande (1932) 229–30; Kleinknecht (1940) 263–4 (=
Marg 572–3). In one of these passages Themistocles is trying to persuade the
stodgy and religious Spartans to act; in the other, by μετά γε θεούς, Herodotus
softens his still emphatic and potentially objectionable (ἐπίφθονος)
encomium of the saviours of Greece, (the Athenians): αὐτοὶ οὗτοι ἦσαν ...
βασιλέα ... ἀνωσάμενοι.

70 Solmsen (1974) 31–2 for this and the next quotation. Cf de Romilly (1971) 334:
'La causalité la plus profonde demeure latente et inavouée.'

71 Hellman (1934) 13 = Marg 116: 'Kein Prediger spricht hier mit dem erhobenen
fabula-docet-Finger ...'

CHAPTER 10

1 Momigliano (1961/2) = *Studies* 213. Cf the ancient remarks of Josephus *Contra Apionem* 1.16, 18, or the early modern comments of Macaulay (1828; repr 1972) 71–89, esp 73–5 on 'a delightful child.' Flory (1980) 12–28 discusses the size of Herodotus' ancient text and the likely nature of his readership.

2 Momigliano (1961/2) = *Studies* 214. Murray (1972) 200–13 surveys the debt that Alexandrian writers owed to Herodotus. Although he lists historians as well as geographers and epitomators (Nearchus, Hecataeus of Abdera, Megasthenes, Berossus, Manetho), none of them attempted Herodotean history. Polybius, the historian of comparable scope, never mentions Herodotus.

3 Cf Gomme (1956) 138, 142 with note 2.

4 Eg, Hignett (1963) 34

5 G. Kaibel *Stil und Text der Athenaion Politeia des Aristoteles* (Berlin 1893) 66; cf *De sublimitate* 22.1. At 31.2, the author refers to Herodotus' choice of vivid words that border on the vulgar (referring to 6.75.3, 7.181.1) and to his (and Thucydides') astonishing hyperboles (eg, Herodotus 7.225.3; Thucydides 7.84.3–5).

6 Immerwahr (1966) 15

7 Legrande (1932) 160–77, 'de l'effort littéraire chez Hérodote,' minimizes the conscious art. He believes that the *Histories* were composed without science or artifice by an author who 'abandons himself' to any association of ideas (163). His use of Homer is 'naive borrowing'; isocolon, alliteration, paronomasia, etc, occur only by accident (172–5, some examples discussed). His charming stories are no more than redactions of material dictated to him, the work of a likeable, friendly, sensible conversationalist who happened upon interesting material (176–7). Meyer (1899) 264 = Marg 23 warned against judging Herodotus' accomplishment by later standards – in vain.

8 Thucydides failed to question the self-serving Athenian ascription of motives and acts to Pausanias – even the tripod inscription reported in 1.132.2 probably misdescribes a private dedication as an act of public *hybris*; see A. Andrewes 'Spartan imperialism' in *Imperialism in the Ancient World* ed P. Garnsey and C.R. Whittaker (Cambridge 1978) 91–102, esp 91–5 and 303 note 9.

9 N.G.L. Hammond 'The arrangement of thought in the proem and in other parts of Thucydides 1' *CQ* ns 2 (1952) 127–41; R. Katičič 'Die Ringkomposition im ersten Buch des thukydideische Geschichtswerkes' *WS* 70 (1957) 179–96

10 Lattimore (1958) 10–15 discusses the unwieldy 'progressive style.' The logic of this theory precludes any architectonic structure at all in the *Histories*. Flory (1980) 17 note 20 accepts the theory of the 'unrevised first draft.' Gomme (1954) 102, by contrast, unduly minimizes the difficulties of writing and their consequences.

11 A comparison of Thucydides 1.1.1 and 5.26.5 to the positively post-431 references in the *Histories* (sometimes called 'insertions,' which begs the question of composition) requires this inference. For a list, see Fornara (1981) 149ff.

12 The former is well illustrated by 1.45.3, discussed by Denniston (1952) 5–8 = Marg 754–8; for the latter, see Immerwahr (1966) 12, referring to the 1948 Dutch edition of W. van Otterlo's study, better known in its German edition as *Untersuchungen über Begriff ... der griechische Ringkomposition*, *Mededelingen der koninklijke Nederlandse Akademie* 7/3 (Amsterdam 1944) 131–76.

13 Dionysius *Epistula ad Pompeium* 769 (= Roberts 108)

14 Lattimore (1958) 21 note 28; Meyer II (1899) 217–18 = Marg 679–80

15 The intended profile of Thucydides' truncated *History* is a speculative subject; cf H. Rawlings *The Structure of Thucydides' History* (Princeton 1981). Xenophon sidestepped artistic commencement and closure by selecting arbitrary moments in the midst of wars. He imitated crudely but not without intended effect a shapeless and endless series of depressing historical events, as his conclusion intimates (*Hellenica* 7.5.27).

16 Cf Drews (1973) 49, 77, 186 note 154, on Herodotus' enhancement of the scope of *historie*.

17 Cf Polybius 3.57–9, esp 58.5, 59.3–5. See Murray (1972) 200–4, and A. Momigliano *Alien Wisdom* (Cambridge 1975) 22–33, on the uses made by others of the works of Polybius and Posidonius. Herodotean ethnography remained the model in that field until Posidonius; this was his principal legacy to research (Murray 204).

18 Cook (1976) 26

19 The Herodotean *topos* of *arete* appears often enough in the speeches composed by Thucydides, but appeals to it fail. As an observable force it is non-functional, like the gods. Books 6 and 7 have been read as a 'mythical infiguration [by an art form] in a traditional mould,' that is, as a tragic drama concerned with power and success, but this idea of Cornford's is contrary to Thucydides' intent – as Cornford admits (*Thucydides Mythistoricus* [London 1907; 1965] ix, 135, 140).

20 See Parke (1946) 92.

21 *Theogony* 26–8; cf *Odyssey* 19.203; Herodotus 8.8.3 on Themistocles

22 The most complete survey of Herodotus' sources remains Jacoby (1913) 392–467. *Tendenzerzählungen*: Jacoby (1912) 2755; M. Hadas 'Utopian sources in Herodotus' *CP* 30 (1935) 113–21. Macan (1895) II 43 exclaimed: 'What standard of historical probability is exhibited by an author who commits himself to such a performance [Darius' Scythian campaign], in which satire and fun seem to run riot?'

23 *Homoios* is the emphatic first and last word of the passage quoted. This explana-

tion of his coverage does not anticipate Thucydides' profound realizations that present power tells nothing of past influence or that the present dispensation of wealth can easily mislead future investigators. Nor is Herodotus' promise a precursor of recent trends in historiography that see the events of ordinary life as equally informative as the extraordinary war.

24 Collingwood (1946; 1966⁹) 30, a polemical but influential passage; the proper balance between the two men's contributions has yet to be achieved. G. de Ste Croix *The Origins of the Peloponnesian War* (London 1972) 5–7 fairly criticizes the one-sidedness of the passage. Hunter (1982) narrows down the differences between the two, a useful attempt, but see my review in *CP* 80 (1985) 69–74.

25 Powell (1939) 44–5

26 Lattimore (1958) 16. Dionysius *Epistula ad Pompeium* 774 (= Roberts 112)

27 Momigliano (1954) 460 = *Studies* 51

28 See H. Herter 'Freiheit und Gebundenheit des Staatsmannes bei Thukydides' *RhM* 93 (1950) 133–53; H.P. Stahl *Thukydides, die Stellung der Menschen im geschichtlichen Prozess* (Munich 1966) 94ff and 107ff; L. Edmunds *Chance and Intelligence in Thucydides* (Cambridge, Mass. 1975) 174–204. On Herodotus, brief remarks in Wood (1972) 117 note 6 and Immerwahr (1956) 280 with note 80

29 Ibid 278, and consider 1.46.1; 2.161.3; 4.79.1, 145.1; 6.94.1; 7.1–18, esp 8; 9.106. Bounds and their violation provide a kind of formal cause that defines essential character, but rarely an efficient cause that precipitates events (cf chapter 6).

30 Jacoby 'Ktesias' *RE* (1922) 2032–73, esp 2051, 2066–8; Drews (1973) 103–19; J. Bigwood 'Ctesias as historian of the Persian Wars' *Phoenix* 32 (1978) 19–41. For recent work on Xenophon, consult S. Hirsch *The Friendship of the Barbarians. Xenophon and the Persian Empire* (Hanover, NH 1985).

31 Ligota (1982) 1; Ch. Starr 'Why did the Greeks defeat the Persians?' *PP* 86 (1962) 321–32 (= *Essays* 193–204), esp 321–2, 328, 332

32 Cf Josephus *Contra Apionem* 1.23–7 (5), 44–6 (8)

33 De Ste Croix (1975) 46 believes that *Poetics* 9.4 = 1451b, mentioning Alcibiades, must refer to Thucydides' account, but the renegade general was a popular subject for contemporary and subsequent writers: Plato, Xenophon, Theopompus, Ephorus, Duris, and Plutarch, for instance.

34 Cf Momigliano (1972) 290 = *Essays* 172; cf Burn (1969) 4; Legrande (1932) 158–60: not 'un savant' but a man characterized by 'une complaisante réceptivité.'

35 Hellmann (1934) 13 = Marg 115. One overgeneralized report: mummified cats (2.66.3–67), for which see New York *Times* 9 June 1981, 15, 'Science Watch.'

36 Macan (1895) I xxvii

37 Drews (1973) 188 note 162 and 50 with 169 note 8 raises these real problems.
   Jacoby (1949) 330, note 16, similarly explains Herodotus' silence about
   Athenian *gene* as the result of ignorance, but here the idea seems less likely.

38 Shimron (1973) faces the apparent contradiction between 1.5.3 and 14.1; cf
   chapter 5 above.

39 Drews (1973) 52–4 believes that the wars and gifts of Croesus to Delphi are
   detailed to document the magnitude and power of Persia's first Greek-world
   victim, but in the narrative, Croesus' forces are outnumbered (1.77.1) and
   completely outclassed on the battlefield. The Delphic episodes serve thematic
   philosophical purposes: paradigms of the uncertainty and incomprehensibility
   of human fortunes, and of the weakness of human understanding. Croesus
   learned that his fall was his and his ancestors' fault, not the god's (1.91.6).
   This interpretation, probably promulgated at Delphi, theologically justified his
   unexpected catastrophe.

40 Hunter (1982) 226–96 draws out many similarities.

41 Gomme (1954) 180. Also Thibaudet on Thucydides (quoted by de Romilly in
   REG 84 [1971] 208): 'la plus grande exactitude matérielle et la plus grande
   généralité.' Aristotle (*Poetics* 9.9 = 1451b) admitted a limited congruence:
   'even if the poet happens to portray real events, he is no less a poet, for
   nothing prevents *some* real events from being such as would probably or
   possibly occur.' Herodotus moulded the disparate details of the Persian Wars
   into a 'probable,' perhaps 'necessary,' story.

42 Herodotus granted epic *kleos*, a quality to deposit for future renown and benefit
   (καταθέσθαι, 7.220.4; 9.78.2*), only to the Spartans. It is attributed to
   Leonidas, Pausanias, and the Spartans in general by an enemy (ibid, 9.48.3*).
   The *kleos* that Herodotus will preserve for Greek and barbarian actions is of
   another order, because it rests on historical investigation, not the fancies of a
   poet or participants. Pindar once seems to believe optimistically that the
   future will by itself establish the truth (*Olympians* 1.33–4, but cf *Nemeans*
   4.6), but Herodotus dissented, and Thucydides developed the *topos* of the
   impossibility (*anexelengkta*, 1.21.1) of discovering the truth about events that
   time has obscured and made more 'mythic.'

43 Cf Starr (1968) 348–59.

44 Stahl (1975) 29

45 Sophistic influence probably impelled Thucydides to provide later generations
   with useful generalizations on political man (1.22.4, 3.82.2, etc). Cf Fornara
   (1971) 60 on his intended audience; or Löwith (1949) 6.

46 The mythographers 'reconstructed' a world beyond verification, and the
   ethnographers and geographers made little attempt to explore the past and its
   shaping influence (Drews [1973] 96).

47 Stahl (1975) 26–31. Amasis foresaw the bad end of Polycrates (3.43.1), but here

two literary forces confuse the narrative: the theme of human blindness and sources hostile to Polycrates that wished to paint the Samian tyrant in the darkest colours.

48 Fornara (1971) 61 believes that 'Herodotus directed himself exclusively to his own generation,' but this comment ignores the proem, as J.R. Grant's review pointed out (*Phoenix* 26 [1972] 95).

49 Momigliano (1966b) 17 = (1977) 193; idem (1972) 14–15, 28; cf Starr (1968b) 352

50 Pippidi (1948) 483–6

51 Immerwahr (1966) 4 averred that 'the historian reconstructs the past by using all the aspects of imagination except invention,' but this restriction is untenable.

52 See Pippidi (1948) 488–9, Gomme (1954) 72–181, Kitto (1966) 290–2. De Ste Croix (1975) 45–58 refutes Aristotle on his own principles: no science can be more precise than its subject admits. History offers knowledge of the generally true. Thucydides believes in, and implicitly presents, patterns, sequences of events likely to be repeated, more or less. Since the 'generally true' is closer to the 'necessarily true' than the merely probable or the 'fictional particular' of the poets, historical research is capable of producing genuine knowledge, *episteme*. Since Aristotle himself wrote historical works, he must have thought history a worthwhile study.

53 Von Fritz (Hardt 1958) 32, although to Meyer IV/1 (1939³) 230 = Marg 11, the unity was only formal: 'seine Darstellung behält, trotz alles dessen, was er aus eigenem Ermessen hinzugetan hat, den Charakter des Mosaiks.' Also A. Lesky *A History of Greek Literature* trans J. Willis and C. de Heer (London 1966²) 306: 'a patchwork quality ... not yet arrived at organic unity.' See Cobet (1972) passim on the question of unity.

54 Fränkel (1924) 87 = Marg 746 exaggerated, when he said that Herodotus aimed only 'leidlich wahrheitsgetreu und recht gut zu erzählen,' but the influence of this attitude has been considerable; cf Legrande (1932) 160–77; *contra*, Pohlenz (1937) 165.

55 Myres (1953) v; cf the Lydian *logos* as 'the prose scenario for a tragic "Capture of Sardis,"' an idea developed in his 'Herodotus the tragedian' in *A Miscellany Presented to J.M. Mackay* ed O. Elton (Liverpool 1914) 88–96. The bibliography on the so-called 'Gyges Drama' papyrus (*Oxyrhynchus Papyri* 2382) is large; for early bibliography, see A.E. Raubitschek 'Gyges in Herodotus' *CW* 48 (1955) 48–50; and for more recent literature, consult J.A. Evans 'Candaules whom the Greeks name Myrsilus' *GRBS* 26 (1985) 229–33.

56 Fornara (1971) 65, 73, 33; Drews (1973) 65–6, 70, 76–7. This image or concept tries to explain the present organization, not the genesis of the various *logoi* now found in the text.

57 Fornara (1971) 21, 32, 25, 27, following G. de Sanctis 'La composizione della

storia di Erodoto' *RFIC* 54 (1926) 289ff = *Studi di Storia della Storiografia Greca* (Firenze 1951) 25ff; Drews (1973) 65

58 Herodotus permanently abandoned the Persian focus at 7.138.

59 Drews (1973) 74–7, 82

60 Drews reviewing Cobet (1972) in *Gnomon* (1975) 333

61 Raymond Aron *Introduction à la philosophie de l'histoire* (Paris 1948) 165; S. Hook *The Hero in History* (1943; Boston 1969[7]) 119–36, '"If" in History'; earlier, Kleinknecht (1940) 246 = Marg 548 on Weber and Meyer's discussion of *Verursachung*; cf D. Lateiner 'Tissaphernes and the Phoenician fleet' *TAPA* 106 (1976) 267–73 for a rare Thucydidean example at 8.87.

62 N. Austin *The Greek Historians* (New York 1969) 44

63 Aristotle *Rhetoric* 3.16.5 = 1417a quotes Herodotus' tale about the soldiers who deserted Psammetichus (2.30).

64 *Epistula ad Pompeium* § 3 = 773–4 U-R; cf *De Thucydide* 23 = 360 U-R.

65 Löwith (1949) 1–6

SELECT BIBLIOGRAPHY

This selection of work on Herodotus contains primarily those books and articles cited above more than once and bibliographical surveys, marked with an asterisk (*). Literary studies are more fully represented than historical, but this is often a misleading distinction, especially in the case of Herodotus' *Histories*. Periodicals have the familiar English abbreviations or those found in *L'Année Philologique*. Publications excerpted or included whole in the useful anthology edited by Walter Marg (1965[2]) are noted

Aly, W. 1921 *Volksmärchen, Sage und Novelle bei Herodot und seinen Zeitgenossen* (Göttingen; repr 1969)
– 1929 *Formprobleme der frühen griechischen Prosa. Philologus* Supplementband 21/3 (Leipzig)
Apffel, H. 1957 *Die Verfassungsdebatte bei Herodot* (diss Erlangen)
Armayor, O.K. 1978 'Did Herodotus ever go to Egypt?' *JARCE* 15:59–73
– 1978b 'Did Herodotus ever go to the Black sea?' *HSCP* 82:45–62
– 1978c 'Herodotus' catalogues of the Persian empire in the light of the monuments and the Greek literary tradition' *TAPA* 108:1–9
Audiat, J. 1940 'Apologie pour Hérodote (1.32)' *REA* 42:3–8
Avery, H. 1972 'Herodotus 6.112.2' *TAPA* 103:15–22
Balcer, J.M. 1972 'The Persian occupation of Thrace' *Actes du IIe Congrès international des études du sud-est Europe* (Athens) 2:242–58
Baldwin, B. 1964 'How credulous was Herodotus?' *G&R* 11:167–77
Barnes, J. 1982[2] *The Presocratic Philosophers* (London)
Barth, H. 1968 'Zur Bewertung und Auswahl des Stoffes durch Herodot' *Klio* 50:93–110
Beck, I. 1971 *Die Ringkomposition bei Herodot* (Hildesheim)
Benardete, S. 1969 *Herodotean Inquiries* (The Hague)

Bergson, L. 1966* 'Herodotus 1937–1960' *Lustrum* 11:71–138

Bischoff, W. 1932 *Der Warner bei Herodot* (diss Marburg) = Marg 302–19, 681–7

Bizer, Fr. 1937 *Untersuchungen zur Archäologie des Thukydides* (repr Darmstadt 1968)

Brannan, P.T. 1963 'Herodotus and history: the constitutional debate preceeding Darius' accession' *Traditio* 19:427–38

Bringmann, K. 1976 'Die Verfassungsdebatte bei Herodot, 3.80–82, und Dareios' Aufstieg zur Königsherrschaft' *Hermes* 104:266–79

Brown, Truesdale 1965 'Herodotus speculates about Egypt' *AJP* 86:60–76

Burn, A.R. 1962 *Persia and the Greeks* (London)

Bury, J.B. 1908 *The Ancient Greek Historians* (repr New York 1958)

– et al, edd 1926 *The Cambridge Ancient History IV: The Persian Empire and the West* (Cambridge)

Cameron, G. 1955 'Ancient Persia' in *The Idea of History in the Ancient Near East*, ed R.C. Denton (New Haven and London, repr 1967) 77–97

Canfora, L. 1972 *Totalità e selezione nella storiografia classica* (Bari)

Chiasson, Ch. 1982 'Tragic diction in Herodotus: some possibilities' *Phoenix* 36:156–61

Cobet J. 1971 *Herodots Exkurse und die Frage der Einheit seines Werkes. Historia Einzelschrift* 17 (Wiesbaden)

Collingwood, R.G. 1946 *The Idea of History* (Oxford, repr 1966[9])

Cook, A. 1976 'Herodotus: the act of inquiry as a liberation from myth' *Helios* 3:23–66

Cooper, G.L. 1974 'Intrusive oblique infinitives in Herodotus' *TAPA* 104:23–76

– 1975 'The ironic force of the pure optative in ὅτι (ὡς) constructions of the primary sequence' *TAPA* 105:29–34

Dandamayev, M.A. 1985 'Herodotus' information on Persia and the latest discoveries of cuneiform texts' *StdSt* 7:92–100

Darbo-Peschanski, C. 1985 'Les logoi des autres dans les *Histoires* d'Hérodote' *QS* 22:105–28.

Denniston, J.D. 1934 *The Greek Particles* (Oxford, repr 1966[4])

– 1952 *Greek Prose Style* (Oxford 1965[2]) = Marg 754–8 (excerpt)

Dewald, Carolyn 1981 'Women and culture in Herodotus' *Histories*' *Women's Studies* 8:93–127

– 1985 'Practical knowledge and the historian's role in Herodotus and Thucydides' *The Greek Historians: Papers presented to A.E. Raubitschek* (Palo Alto, Ca.) 47–63

– and Marincola, J. 1987* 'A selective introduction to Herodotean Studies' *Arethusa* 20:9–40, 263–82

Diels, H., and Kranz, W. 1951/2 *Die Fragmente der Vorsokratiker* (Berlin[6])

Diesner, H. 1959 'Die Gestalt des Tyrannen Polykrates bei Herodot' *AAHung* 7:211–19

Dodds, E.R. 1951 *The Greeks and the Irrational* (Berkeley and Los Angeles)

Drews, R. 1970 'Herodotus' other *logoi*' *AJP* 91:181–91

– 1973 *The Greek Accounts of Eastern History* (Cambridge, Mass.)

Drexler, H. 1972 *Herodot-Studien* (Hildesheim)

Duchesne-Guillemin, J. 1967/8 'Religion et politique, de Cyrus à Xerxes' *Persica* 3:1–9

Earl, D. 1972 'Prologue-form in ancient historiography' *Aufstieg und Niedergang der römischen Welt* (Berlin) I/2 42–56

Erbse, H. 1955 'Vier Bemerkungen zu Herodot' *RhM* 98:99–120

– 1956 'Der erste Satz im Werke Herodots' *Festschrift Bruno Snell* (Munich) 209–22

– 1961 'Tradition und Form im Werke Herodots' *Gymnasium* 68:239–57

Evans, J.A. 1961 'The dream of Xerxes and the "nomoi" of the Persians' *CJ* 57:109–11

– 1964 'The "final problem" at Thermopylae' *GRBS* 5:231–7

– 1968 'Father of history or father of lies; the reputation of Herodotus' *CJ* 64:11–17

– 1976 'The settlement of Artaphrenes' *CP* 71:344–8

– 1976b 'Herodotus and the Ionian revolt' *Historia* 25:31–7

Fehling, D. 1971 *Die Quellenangaben bei Herodot: Studien zur Erzählkunst Herodots* (Berlin and New York)

Ferrill, A. 1966 'Herodotus and the strategy and tactics of the invasion of Xerxes' *AHR* 72:102–15

– 1978 'Herodotus on tyranny' *Historia* 27:385–98

Finley, M.I. 1965 'Myth, memory and history' *H&T* 4:281–302

Flory, S. 1978 'Arion's leap: brave gestures in Herodotus' *AJP* 99:411–21

– 1980 'Who read Herodotus' *Histories*?' *AJP* 101:12–28

Fornara, Ch. 1971 *Herodotus. An Interpretive Essay* (Oxford)

– 1971b 'Evidence for the date of Herodotus' publication' *JHS* 91:25–34

– 1981 'Herodotus' knowledge of the Archidamian war' *Hermes* 109:149–56

– 1983 *The Nature of History in Ancient Greece and Rome* (Berkeley and Los Angeles)

Forrest, W.G. 1984 'Herodotus and Athens' *Phoenix* 38:1–11

– 1979 'Motivation in Herodotus: the case of the Ionian revolt' *IHR* 1:311–22

Fränkel, H. 1924 'Eine Stileigenheit der frühgriechischen Literatur' *NAWG* 63–126 = *Wege und Formen der frühgriechischen Denkens* (Munich 1960²) 40–96 = Marg 737–47 (excerpt)

– 1951 *Dichtung und Philosophie des frühen Griechentums* (New York; Munich 1960²; English trans London 1973, New York 1975)

von Fritz, K. 1936 'Herodotus and the growth of Greek historiography' *TAPA* 67:315–40

– 1952/54 'Die gemeinsame Ursprung der Geschichtsschreibung und der exakten Wissenschaften bei den Griechen' *Philosophia Naturalis* 2:200–23

– 1967 *Die griechische Geschichtsschreibung* (Berlin) 2 vols

Frye, R. 1963 *The Heritage of Persia* (New York)

Gabba, E. 1981 'True history and false history in classical antiquity' *JRS* 71:50–62

Gammie, J. 1986 'Herodotus on kings and tyrants: objective historiography or conventional portraiture?' *JNES* 45:171–95

Gardiner, P. 1952 *The Nature of Historical Explanation* (Oxford, repr 1961)

Gay, P. 1974 *Style in History* (New York)

Gigante, M. 1956 *Nomos Basileus* (Naples) = Marg 259–81 (excerpt)

Glover, T.R. 1924 *Herodotus* (Berkeley)

Gomme, A.W. 1954 *The Greek Attitude to Poetry and History* (Berkeley and Los Angeles) esp 73–115 = Marg 202–48

– 1956 *A Historical Commentary on Thucydides* (Oxford) I

Grant, J.R. 1961 'Leonidas' last stand' *Phoenix* 15:14–27

– 1969 'ἐκ τοῦ παρατυχόντος πυνθανόμενος' *Phoenix* 23:264–8

– 1983 'Some thoughts on Herodotus' *Phoenix* 37:283–98

Grene, D. 1961 'Herodotus, the historian as dramatist' *JPh* 58:477–88

Groten, F.J. 1963 'Herodotus' use of variant versions' *Phoenix* 17:79–87

Hammond, N.G.L. 1955 'Studies in Greek chronology of the sixth and fifth centuries B.C.' *Historia* 4:371–412

Hampl, F. 1975* 'Herodot. Ein kritischer Forschungsbericht nach methodischen Gesichtspunkt' *GB* 4:97–136

Harder, R. 1953 'Herodot 1.8.3' *Studies presented to D.M. Robinson* (St Louis) II 446–9 = Marg 370–4

Hardt 1958 *Histoire et historiens dans l'antiquité* ([Fondation Hardt] Vandoeuvres-Geneva) IV. Papers and discussion by K. Latte, J. de Romilly, K von Fritz, A. Momigliano, and others

Hartog, Fr. 1979 'La question du nomadisme. Les Scythes d'Hérodote' *AAHung* 27:135–48

Harvey, F. 1966 'The political sympathies of Herodotus' *Historia* 15:254–5

Hauvette, A. 1894 *Hérodote, historien des guerres médiques* (Paris)

Heidel, W.A. 1935 *Hecataeus and the Egyptian Priests in Herodotus, Book II* (Boston)

Hellman, Fr. 1934 *Herodots Kroisos-Logos* (Berlin) = Marg 40–56 (excerpt)

Helm, P.R. 1981 'Herodotus' *Medikos Logos* and Median history' *Iran* 19:85–90

Hereward, D. 1958 'The flight of Demaratos' *RhM* 101:238–49

Hignett, Ch. 1963 *Xerxes' Invasion of Greece* (Oxford)

Hirst, G.M. 1938 'Herodotus on tyranny *versus* Athens and democracy (a study of book III of Herodotus' *History*)' *Collected Classical Papers* (Oxford) 97–110

Hohti, P. 1974 'Freedom of speech in the speech sections in the *Histories* of Herodotus' *Arctos* 8:19–27

– 1977 'Συμβάλλεσθαι. A note on conjectures in Herodotus' *Arctos* 11:5–14

Hommel, H. 1981 'Herodots Einleitungssatz: ein Schlüssel zur Analyse des Gesamtswerks?' *Gnomosyne. Festschrift Walter Marg* (Munich) 271–87

How, W.W., and Wells, J. 1928 *A Commentary on Herodotus* (Oxford, repr 1964) 2 vols

Huber, L. 1963 *Religiöse und politische Beweggründe des Handelns in der Geschichtschreibung des Herodot* (diss Tübingen)

– 1965 'Herodots Homerverständnis' *Synusia ... Festgabe W. Schadewaldt* (Pfullingen) 29–52

Hude, Carolus 1927³ *Herodoti Historiae* (Oxford)

Hunter, V. 1982 *Past and Process in Herodotus and Thucydides* (Princeton)

Huxley, G. 1965 'A fragment of the Ἀσσύριοι λόγοι of Herodotus' *GRBS* 6:207–12

Immerwahr, H. 1954 'Historical action in Herodotus' *TAPA* 85:16–45 = Marg 497–540 (revised)

– 1956 'Aspects of historical causation in Herodotus' *TAPA* 87:241–80

– 1957 'The Samian stories of Herodotus' *CJ* 52:312–22

– 1966 *Form and Thought in Herodotus* (Cleveland)

Jacoby, F. 1909 'Über die Entwicklung der griechischen Historiographie' *Klio* 9:80–123

– 1912 'Hekataios' in Pauly-Wissowa-Kroll, edd, *Realencyclopädie der classischen Altertumswissenschaft* (Stuttgart) vii 2666–769 = idem 1956 *Griechische Historiker* (Stuttgart) 185–237

– 1913 'Herodotos' in Pauly-Wissowa-Kroll, edd, *RE Supplement* 2:205–520 = idem 1956 *Griechische Historiker* 7–164 (with bibliography) = Marg 27–34 (excerpt)

– 1949 *Atthis* (Oxford, repr New York 1973)

– 1957 *Die Fragmente der Griechischen Historiker* i² (Leiden)

Jones, W.H. 1913 'A note on the vague use of θεός' *CR* 27:252–5

Kazazis, J.N. 1978 *Herodotus' Stories and History: A Proppian Analysis of his Narrative Techniques* (diss University of Illinois)

Kennedy, G. 1963 *The Art of Persuasion in Ancient Greece* (Princeton)

Kitto, H.D. 1966 *Poiesis. Structure and Thought* (Berkeley and Los Angeles)

Kleingünther, A. 1933 Πρῶτος Εὑρετής *Philologus* Suppl 26 (Leipzig) 43–65 for Herodotus

Kleinknecht, H. 1940 'Herodot und Athen, 7.139/8.140–44' *Hermes* 75:241–64 = Marg 541–73

Konstan, D. 1983 'The stories in Herodotus' *Histories*: Book I' *Helios* 10:1–22

Krischer, T. 1965 'Herodots Prooimion' *Hermes* 93:159–67

– 1965b 'Ἔτυμος und ἀληθής' *Philologus* 109:161–74

– 1974 'Herodots Schlusskapitel, seine Topik und seine Quellen' *Eranos* 72:93–100

Lachenaud, G. 1979 *Mythologies, religion et philosophie de l'histoire dans Hérodote* (Paris)

Lang, M. 1944 *Biographical Patterns of Folklore and Morality in Herodotus' History* (diss Bryn Mawr)

– 1972 'War and the rape-motif, or why did Cambyses invade Egypt?' *PAmPhS* 116:410–14

– 1984 *Herodotean Narrative and Discourse* (Cambridge, Mass.)

Lasserre, F. 1976 'L'historiographie grecque à l'époque archaïque' *QS* 4:113–42

– 1976b 'Hérodote et Protagoras: le débat sur les constitutions' *MH* 33:65–84

Lateiner, D. 1977 'No laughing matter: a literary tactic in Herodotus' *TAPA* 107:173–82

– 1980 'A note on ΔΙΚΑΣ ΔΙΔΟΝΑΙ in Herodotus' *CQ* 30:30–2

– 1982 'The failure of the Ionian revolt' *Historia* 31:129–60

– 1982b 'A note on the perils of prosperity in Herodotus' *RhM* 125:97–101

– 1984 'Herodotean historiographical patterning: the constitutional debate' *QS* 20:257–84

– 1985 'Polarità: il principio della differenza complementare' *QS* 22:79–103

– 1985b 'Limit, propriety, and transgression in the *Histories* of Herodotus' *The Greek Historians. Papers presented to A.E. Raubitschek* (Palo Alto, Ca.) 87–100

– 1986 'The empirical element in the methods of the early Greek medical writers and Herodotus: a shared epistemological response' *Antichthon* 20:1–20

– 1987 'Nonverbal communication in the *Histories* of Herodotus' *Arethusa* 20:83–119 and 143–5

Latte, K. 1958 'Die Anfänge der griechischen Geschichtsschreibung' *Histoire et historiens dans l'antiquité*, Fondation Hardt (Vandoeuvres-Geneva) IV 21–37 = Marg 122–36

Lattimore, R. 1939 'The wise advisor in Herodotus' *CP* 34:24–35

– 1958 'The composition of the *Histories* of Herodotus' *CP* 53:9–21

Legrande, Ph.-E. 1932 *Hérodote. Introduction* (Paris) = Marg 282–3 (excerpt)

– 1937 'Hérodote, croyait-il aux oracles?' *Mélanges P. Desroussaux* (Paris) 275–84

Lewis, D.M. 1985 'Persians in Herodotus' *The Greek Historians. Papers presented to A.E Raubitschek* (Palo Alto, Ca.) 101–17

Lévi-Strauss, Cl. 1967 *Tristes Tropiques* (Paris 1955; English trans J. Russell, 1961, 1967)

– 1967b *The Scope of Anthropology* (Paris, 1960; English trans S.O. and R.A. Paul)

von Leyden, W.M. 1949/50 'Spatium historicum' *DUJ* 11:89–104 = Marg 169–81

Ligota, C.R. 1982 '"This story is not true." Fact and fiction in antiquity' *JWI* 45:1–13

Lilja, S. 1967 'Indebtedness to Hecataeus in Herodotus II. 70–71' *Arctos* 5:85–96

Linforth, I. 1924 'Herodotus' avowal of silence in his account of Egypt' *UCPCPh*
7:269–92
– 1926 'Greek gods and foreign gods in Herodotus' *UCPCPh* 9:1–25
– 1928 'Named and unnamed gods in Herodotus' *UCPCPh* 9:201–43
Lloyd, A.B. 1975/76 *Herodotus. Book II, Introduction and Commentary 1–99*
(Leiden) 2 vols
Lloyd, G.E.R. 1966 *Polarity and Analogy in Early Greek Thought* (Cambridge)
Löwith, K. 1949 *Meaning in History* (Chicago)
Macan, R.W. 1895 *Herodotus. The Fourth, Fifth and Sixth Books* (London) 2 vols
– 1908 *Herodotus. The Seventh, Eighth and Ninth Books* (London) 2 vols
– 1927 'Herodotus and Thucydides' *The Cambridge Ancient History*, ed J.B. Bury
et al (Cambridge) v 398–419
Macaulay, Th. B. 1828 'History' *Edinburgh Review*; reprinted in *The Varieties of
History* ed Fr. Stern (New York 1973²) 72–89
MacKendrick, P. 1954*, 1963*, 1969* 'Herodotus' *CW* 47:145–52; 56:269–75;
63:37–44
Mallowan, M. 1972 'Cyrus the Great (558–529 B.C.)' *Iran* 10:1–17
Marg, W. 1953 'Selbstsicherheit bei Herodot' *Studies presented to D.M. Robinson*
(St Louis) II 1103–11 = Marg 290–301
– ed 1965² *Herodot. Eine Auswahl aus der neueren Forschung* (Munich 1962;
Darmstadt) with bibliography
Meyer, Ed. 1892/99 *Forschungen zur alten Geschichte* (Halle) I 151–210; II
196–268 = Marg 12–26 and 679–80 (excerpts)
– 1939 *Geschichte des Altertums* (Munich 1939³, repr Darmstadt 1975)
Mitchel, F. 1956 'Herodotus' use of genealogical chronology' *Phoenix* 10:48–69
Mitchell, B. 1975 'Herodotus and Samos' *JHS* 95:75–91
Momigliano, A. 1966 *Studies in Historiography* (New York)
– 1977 *Essays in Ancient and Modern Historiography* (Middletown, Conn.)
– 1954/58 'Some observations on causes of war in ancient historiography' *Acta
Congressus Madvigiani* I 199–211
– 1954 'Gibbon's contribution to historical method' *Historia* 2:450–63
– 1958* 'The place of Herodotus in the history of historiography' *History* 43:1–13
= Marg 137–56
– 1961/2 'Historiography on written tradition and historiography on oral tradition'
Atti ... Torino 96:1–12
– 1966b 'Time in ancient historiography' *H&T* 5 Beiheft 6:1–23
– 1972 'Tradition and the classical historian' *H&T* 11:279–93
Mosshammer, A.A. 1979 *The Chronicle of Eusebius and Greek Chronographic
Tradition* (Lewisburg, Pa.)
Müller, D. 1981 'Herodot – Vater des Empirismus? Mensch und Erkenntnis im
Denken Herodots' *Gnomosyne. Festschrift Walter Marg* (Munich) 299–318

Munson, Rosaria 1983 *Transitions in Herodotus* (diss University of Pennsylvania)

Murray, O. 1972 'Herodotus and Hellenistic culture' *CQ* 22:200–13

Myres, J. 1953 *Herodotus, Father of History* (repr Chicago 1971) = Marg 284–85 (excerpt)

Nestle, W. 1908 *Herodots Verhältnis zur Philosophie und Sophistik* (Schoental)

Neville, J. 1977 'Herodotus on the Trojan war' *G&R* 24:3–12

Norden, Ed. 1909[2] *Die antike Kunstprosa* (repr Stuttgart 1958) I

Nylander, C. 1980 'Earless in Nineveh: Who mutilated Sargon's head?' *AJA* 84:329–33

Olmstead, A.T. 1948 *History of the Persian Empire* (Chicago)

van Ooteghem, J. 1940 'L'anneau de Polycrate' *LEC* 9:311–14

Orlin, L. 1976 'Athens and Persia ca. 507 B.C.: a neglected perspective' *Studies [for] G.G. Cameron* (Ann Arbor) 255–66

Ostwald, M. 1969 *Nomos and the Beginnings of the Athenian Democracy* (Oxford)

– 1972 'Isokratia as a political concept (Herodotus 5. 92α 1)' *Islamic Philosophy and the Classical Tradition. Studies [for] R. Walzer* (Oxford) 277–91

Pagel, K.A. 1927 *Die Bedeutung des aitiologischen Momentes für Herodots Geschichtsschreibung* (diss Berlin)

Parke, H.W. 1946 'Citation and recitation, a convention in early Greek historians' *Hermathena* 67:80–92

Pearce, T.E.V. 1981 'Epic regression in Herodotus' *Eranos* 79:87–90

Pearson, L.I.C. 1934 'Herodotus on the sources of the Danube' *CP* 39:328–37

– 1939 *Early Ionian Historians* (Oxford)

– 1941 'Credulity and scepticism in Herodotus' *TAPA* 72:335–55

– 1954 'Real and conventional personalities in Greek history' *JHI* 15:136–45

– 1983 *Selected Papers* ed D. Lateiner and S.A. Stephens (Chico, Ca.)

Pembroke, S. 1967 'Women in charge ...' *JWI* 30:1–35

Pippidi, D.M. 1948 'Aristote et Thucydide; en marge du ch. ix de la *Poétique*' *Mélanges J. Marouzeau* (Paris) 483–90

Plescia, J. 1972 'Herodotus and the case for Eris (Strife)' *PP* 27:301–11

Pohlenz, M. 1937 *Herodot, der erste Geschichtsschreiber des Abendlandes* (Leipzig, repr Darmstadt 1973) = Marg 748–53 (excerpt)

Powell, J.E. 1938 *A Lexicon to Herodotus* (Cambridge, repr Hildesheim 1966)

– 1939 *The History of Herodotus* (Cambridge)

Pritchett, W.K. 1982 'Some recent critiques of the veracity of Herodotus' *Studies in Ancient Greek Topography* (Berkeley and Los Angeles) IV 234–85

Raubitschek, A.E. 1939 'Ἔργα μεγάλα τε καὶ θωμαστά' *REA* 41:217–22

– 1957 'Die schamlose Ehefrau (Herodot 1.8.3)' *RhM* 100:139–41

– 1961 'Herodotus and the inscriptions' *BICS* 8:59–61

– 1964 'The treaties between Persia and Athens' *GRBS* 5:151–9

Rawlinson, G. 1860 *The History of Herodotus* (New York; repr 1893) 4 vols

Redfield, J. 1975 *Nature and Culture in the Iliad* (Chicago)
- 1976 'Themes and boundaries in Herodotus' Unpublished typescript
- 1985 'Herodotus the tourist' *CP* 80:97–118
de Romilly, J. 1971 'La vengeance comme explication historique dans Hérodote' *REG* 84:314–37
Sacks, K.S. 1976 'Herodotus and the dating of the battle of Thermopylae' *CQ* 26:232–48
de Ste Croix, G.E.M. 1975 'Aristotle on history and poetry' *The Ancient Historian and his Materials. Studies [for] C.E. Stevens* ed B. Levick (Farnborough) 45–58
- 1977 'Herodotus' *G&R* 24:130–48
Sancisi-Weerdenburg, H. 1983 'Exit Atossa; images of women in Greek historiography on Persia' *Images of Women in Antiquity* ed A. Cameron and A. Kuhrt (London) 20–33
Sayce, A.H. 1883 *The Ancient Empires of the East* (London)
von Scheliha, R. 1931 *Die Wassergrenzung im Altertum* (diss Breslau)
Schepens, G. 1975 'L'idéal de l'information complète chez les historiens grecs' *REG* 88:81–93
Schmid, W., and Stählin, O. 1934 *Geschichte der griechischen Literatur* (Munich) 1/2 550–673
Schwartz, J. 1969 'Hérodote et Periclès' *Historia* 18:367–70
Sealey, R. 1957 'Thucydides, Herodotus and the causes of war' *CQ* 7:1–12
- 1976 'The pit and the well: the Persian heralds of 491 B.C.' *CJ* 72:13–20
- 1976b *A History of the Greek City States* (Berkeley and Los Angeles)
Sélincourt, Aubrey de 1972² *Herodotus. The Histories* (Harmondsworth and Baltimore)
Shimron, B. 1973 'Πρῶτος τῶν ἡμεῖς ἴδμεν' *Eranos* 71:45–51
Sinko, T. 1959/60 'L'historiosophie dans le prologue et l'épilogue de l'oeuvre d'Hérodote d'Halicarnasse' *Eos* 50:3–20
Solmsen, Fr. 1974 'Two crucial decisions in Herodotus' *Mededelingen der koninklijke Nederlandse Akademie*, AFD Letterkunde (Amsterdam) 37/6:139–70
Solmsen, L. 1943 'Speeches in Herodotus' account of the Ionian revolt' *AJP* 64:194–207 = Marg 629–44
- 1944 'Speeches in Herodotus' account of the battle of Plataea' *CP* 39:241–53 = Marg 645–67
Sourdille, C. 1910 *Hérodote et la religion d'Égypte* (Paris)
- 1925 'Sur une nouvelle explication de la discrétion d'Hérodote en matière de religion' *REG* 38:289–305
Spiegelberg, W. 1926 *Die Glaubwürdigkeit von Herodots Bericht über Ägypten* ... (Heidelberg; English trans A.M. Blackman, Oxford 1927)
Stahl, H.-P. 1975 'Learning through suffering?' *YCS* 24:1–36

Stannard, J. 1965 'The Presocratic origin of explanatory method' *PhQ* 15:193–206

Starr, C.G. 1966 'Historical and philosophical time' *H&T* 5 Beiheft 6:24–35

– 1968 *The Awakening of the Greek Historical Spirit* (New York)

– 1968b 'Ideas of truth in early Greece' *PP* 23:348–59

– 1979 *Essays on Ancient History* ed A. Ferrill and Th. Kelly (Leiden)

Stein, H. 1856–1908⁶ *Herodot* (Berlin)

Strasburger, H. 1955 'Herodot und das perikleische Athen' *Historia* 4:1–25 = Marg 574–608

– 1956 'Herodots Zeitrechnung' *Historia* 5:129–61 = Marg 688–736

– 1966 'Die Wesenbestimmung der Geschichte durch die Antike Geschichtsschreibung' *Sitzungberichte der Goethe-Universität, Frankfurt* 3:47–96

Stroud, R. 1978 'State documents in archaic Athens' *Athens Comes of Age* (Princeton) 20–42

Tarn, W.W. 1908 'The fleet of Xerxes' *JHS* 28:202–33

Tourraix, A. 1976 'La femme et le pouvoir chez Hérodote' *DHA* 2:369–90

Verdin, H. 1970 'Notes sur l'attitude des historiens grecs à l'égard de la tradition locale' *AS* 1:183–200

– 1971 *De Historisch-Kritische Methode van Herodotus* (Brussels) English summary: 223–34

– 1975 'Hérodote historien? Quelques interpretations recentes' *AC* 44:668–85

– 1977 'Les remarques critiques d'Hérodote et de Thucydide sur la poésie en tant que source historique' *Historiographia Antiqua. Commentationes in Honorem W. Peremans* (Louvain): 53–76

Versnel, H.S. 1977 'Polycrates and his ring' *Studi Storico-Religiosi* 1:17–46

Veyne, P. 1971 *Comment on écrit l'histoire. Essai d'épistémologie* (Paris)

Vlastos, G. 1953 'Isonomia' *AJP* 74:337–66

– 1964 'Ἰσονομία πολιτική' *Isonomia* ... ed J. Mau and E.G. Schmidt (Berlin) 1–35

Wainwright, G.A. 1953 'Herodotus II, 28 on the sources of the Nile' *JHS* 73:104–7

Walbank, F.W. 1957 *A Historical Commentary on Polybius* (Oxford) 1

– 1962 'Polemic in Polybius' *JRS* 52:1–12

Walser, G. 1976 'La notion de l'état chez les Grecs et les Achéménides' *Assimilation et résistance à la culture gréco-romaine dans le monde ancien. VIth International Congress of Classical Studies* [Madrid 1974] (Bucharest) 227–31

Wardman, A.E. 1959 'Tactics and the tradition of the Persian wars' *Historia* 8:49–60

– 1960 'Myth in Greek historiography' *Historia* 9:403–13

– 1961 'Herodotus on the cause of the Greco-Persian wars' *AJP* 82:133–50

Waters, K.H. 1966 'The purposes of dramatisation in Herodotus' *Historia* 15:157–71

- 1970 'Herodotus and the Ionian revolt' *Historia* 19:504–8
- 1971 *Herodotus on Tyrants and Despots. A Study in Objectivity. Historia Einzelschrift* 15 (Wiesbaden)
- 1972 'Herodotus and politics' *G&R* 19:136–50
- 1974 'The structure of Herodotus' narrative' *Antichthon* 8:1–10
Wells, J. 1907 'The Persian friends of Herodotus' *JHS* 27:37–47 = Wells (1923) 95–111
- 1923 *Studies in Herodotus* (Oxford)
West, S. 1985 'Herodotus' epigraphical interests' *CQ* 35:278–305
Whatley, N. 1964 'On the possibility of reconstructing Marathon and other ancient battles' *JHS* 84:119–39 (written before 1920)
White, Mary 1969 'Herodotus' starting point' *Phoenix* 23:39–48
Wikarjak, J. 1959 '"Αρχαι Herodota' *Meander* 14:271–82
Wolff, E. 1964 'Das Weib des Masistes' *Hermes* 92:51–8 = Marg 668–78
Wood, H. 1972 *The Histories of Herodotus* (The Hague)
Wüst, K. 1935 *Politisches Denken bei Herodot* (diss Munich)

INDEX LOCORUM

GENERAL INDEX

Phoenix Supplementary Volumes Series